EXPLORING WINE REGIONS

Bordeaux France

Written & Photographed by

Michael C. Higgins, PhD
Author, Photojournalist & Publisher

The Forward by

Dany Rolland, Oenologist
Partner and Manager of the Dany & Michel Rolland wine estates and Rolland Laboratories

Published by
International Exploration Society
United States of America

On The Cover: The magnificence of French landscape at Château de La Rivière in Fronsac
Above: In the air over Saint-Émilion, Château La Dominique (left) and Château Cheval Blanc (right)
Next Page: The vineyards of Château La Grace Dieu des Prieurs

ExploringWineRegions.com

Dany and Michel Rolland at their Château Fontenil winery in Fronsac (page 437)

THE FOREWORD
Introducing Our Special Bordeaux

By Dany Rolland, Oenologist
A gifted and highly regarded winemaker in Fronsac, Pomerol and Saint-Émilion
Partner and Manager of the Dany and Michel Rolland wine estates and Rolland Laboratories

Bordeaux is the center of our story. It is our place to live a life of love. Michel and I have our roots here, reaching back seven generations in viticulture. And if you really study the history of Bordeaux and its wine, it dates back thousands of years. Our history is rich and tells the story of how we launched the wine industry worldwide.

The author, Michael Higgins, has done a meticulous and thorough job articulating this long and beautiful history of the city, the wines, the ports and even reaches further back to the evolution of our landscape and topography. And as viticulture and winemaking have constantly evolved through the years, we continue to preserve the soul of Bordeaux wines. There must be a delicate balance of rigidity and open-mindedness to stay at the highest level of quality of each terroir.

There is much more to it than that of course. Understanding the qualities of a grape based on which appellation they are grown is not so simple. The notion of terroir adds to the complexity. To achieve excellence, we need soils, subsoils, climate, landscapes, work and know-how. And when this synergism occurs, the result is exceptional.

Bordeaux is a beautiful city with a splendid 18th century facade facing the Garonne River, the spinal cord of the region, with its two banks becoming their own proper nouns: Left Bank and Right Bank. There is much to see and experience in both the city and the wine regions.

Generations of families have enhanced the unique potential of their properties. Many of the vineyards are perfectly manicured. Their châteaux are welcoming. The food and wine experiences are everywhere. Gastronomy is on par with our splendid wines.

Today, châteaux make huge efforts to develop wine tourism which perhaps was historically a little neglected. Visits of the vineyards, history of the cru and wine tasting have become a standard for the appreciation of Bordeaux. In recent years, creative and even luxurious experiences are available for your enjoyment. Tourism has been cultivated to express our culture of life and work, architecture and its history. We want you to understand, taste, love and "spread the word" of Bordeaux and our wine.

The author brings his sensitivity, his vision, his knowledge and interpretation to everything that makes Bordeaux so special. Michael diligently breaks down each component and features the highlights of each region. This allows you to organize your travels based on your preferences. This book is a guide, an invitation, filled with beautiful pictures, exchanges with winegrowers, and numerous suggestions. Anyone who has any interest in wine needs this book to awaken their desire to discover more deeply a part of our great history of wines.

WORK SPACE. I sure love my work.

WHY BORDEAUX FRANCE?

Well, it all started because Bordeaux, for me, is the center of the universe for wine. I see this to be very real. The world grows Bordeaux grapes. Not Bordeaux grows other country's grapes. Not at all! Cabernet Sauvignon and Merlot, the two primary grapes of Bordeaux, are the two most planted grapes around the world. Wineries bottle and blend these grapes with huge success. Look at Napa Valley California. Their success is all about Bordeaux varietals. What is Napa without Cabernet Sauvignon? Australia, South Africa and Chile are also good examples. Look at the phenomenal success Argentina has had with Malbec, another one of the six Bordeaux red grape varietals. I could go on and on. All these grapes originally came from Bordeaux France. How can you love wine and not want to visit the mecca?

Outside of France, we see wines labeled "Bordeaux Blend" produced in other countries emulating this ever so famous and desired composition. Vintners grow Bordeaux grapes because consumers want Bordeaux grapes. And let's face it, Cabernet Sauvignon tastes so good!

The New World is different from France. Cabernet Sauvignon is sold as a single grape wine, versus Bordeaux wines are always blends. Bottles are labeled with the grape varieties, versus Bordeaux only identifies the location of the winery. Even if the wine is a New World blend, all the grapes are still identified on the label. New World wineries regularly make several different types of wines. In Bordeaux, their wine is made from the best of the property and then possibly a second wine is made from the leftover grapes of the primary bend. When you are used to New World wines, it is hard to understand wines labeled geographically. The New World has trained us to shop by the varietals on the bottle. Because this is not the case with Bordeaux wines, traveling to these places is necessary for understanding these wines.

This became my quest: to understand Bordeaux wines. To figure it out. To uncomplicate it all. To understand their terroir-driven winemaking. And to find excellent wines. We already know Château Latour has extraordinary wine; however, are we really going to spend a $1,000 a bottle every day? I am on a quest to find the good wines at good prices, and the extraordinary wines at better prices.

And to find the exceptional tourism experiences. Remember, I am in love with travel, in love with the whole food and wine experience, and in love with exploring wine regions. I am out to find the most interesting Bordeaux châteaux with the best activities in order to share them with you.

Everything in this book is from my personal experiences and interactions. The photos are authentic from my camera and my eye.

It's time to go explore and enjoy the journey.

Happy Tasting,

Michael C. Higgins, PhD

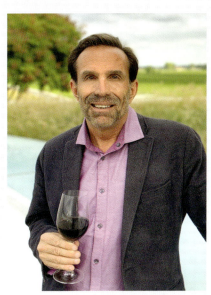

Michael C. Higgins, PhD
Author, Photojournalist & Publisher

For more than 20 years, author, photographer and wine expert Michael C. Higgins has been the publisher of *Flying Adventures*, a lifestyle travel magazine for food and wine lovers who own and travel on private airplanes. As a private pilot, travel enthusiast, and food and wine lover himself, Higgins continues to live the story he's been sharing for decades.

Between the magazine and this book series, Higgins has participated in some of the most extraordinary experiences. He has virtually done it all: from pruning vines, picking grapes, working alongside winemakers, to participating in blind tastings, food and wine pairings, judging Cru Bourgeois wines, and sharing many meals with world-renowned winemakers, over countless hours, discussing everything wine. His time in wine regions add up to thousands of days and counting. And as an accomplished photographer, he has captured even more spectacular images of the wine world.

Higgins has participated in many unique wine experiences, indulged in the most exclusive culinary affairs, been pampered in highly luxurious destinations and jumped into the wildest of adventures. His goal is to inspire his readers to join him in exploring the wine regions of the world and experiencing the unimaginable. Higgins has a BA in Commercial Art, an MBA and a PhD in Business Administration. He is a California native and lives in Pasadena, California.

EXPLORING WINE REGIONS™ • 2ND EDITION • BORDEAUX FRANCE

Text, Design and Photography Copyright © 2017-2020 by Michael C. Higgins. All rights reserved. No part of this book may be used or reproduced by any means, graphic, electronic, or mechanical, including photocopying, recording, taping, or by any information storage retrieval system without the written permission of Michael C. Higgins, except in the case of crediting quotations embodied in articles or reviews. Exploring Wine Regions is a trademark of Michael C. Higgins.

ISBN 978-0-9969660-2-3 - Printed Edition   •   ISBN 978-0-9969660-3-0 - eBook Travel Edition

Published by: **International Exploration Society**
Box 93613 • Pasadena, CA 91109-3613 • USA • 626-618-4000

CONTENTS

14	**OF BORDEAUX**
	Unraveling The Complexities 14
	History In The Making 16
	The Geography 20
	How To Best Read This Book 22
24	**BORDEAUX CITY CENTER**
	The Mini Paris 28
	UNESCO Landmark City 30
	Food & Wine Experiences 36
56	**MÉDOC WINE REGIONS**
	Haut-Médoc (South) 66
	Margaux 78
	Moulis and Listrac 116
	Haut-Médoc (Central) 130
	Saint-Julien 140
	Pauillac 160
	Saint-Estèphe 194
	Médoc 210
224	**THE MÉDOC ATLANTIQUE**
	Port-Médoc 226
	Northern Beaches 228
	Lacanau Ocean 233

240	**GRAVES WINE REGIONS**
	Pessac-Léognan 246
	Graves 266
	Sauternes and Barsac 274 & 298
310	**LIBOURNAIS WINE REGIONS**
	Saint-Émilion 316
	Saint-Émilion Village 400
	Fronsac 416
	Pomerol 442
462	**SPECIAL ADDITIONS**
	Entre-Deux-Mers 463
	Cognac & Cooperage 469
472	**CONCLUSION**
	The Index 474
	Collect Our Books 477
	Travel With Us 479
	Discover Our Website 482
	Get Extra Chapters - Free 483
	Glossary 484
	eBook Travel Edition 485
	Acknowledgements 486
	Professional Speaker 487

UNRAVELING THE COMPLEXITIES **OF BORDEAUX**

The Traditions, Terroir, Talents, Tragedies, Triumphs, Technology, & Timelessness

So you love Bordeaux wines? So do I.

This is Old World winemaking at its best. With numerous traditions mixed with innovations (sometimes), price and quality can be subjective and is debated. Plus labeling can be difficult to decipher and absent of important information. It is just the way the French produce wine. Complex. Intricate. Involved. Tricky.

If you are like me, you found a few great Bordeaux wines that you love. Or you discovered the appellation that appeals to your palate the most and you stick to wines coming from that region. Simple. Straightforward. Satisfying. Yet without exploration and further discovery.

How much do you really know and understand Bordeaux? Maybe you are like me and know a few things like Left Bank versus Right Bank, and yet not really know all the nuances of each terroir? And when you discovered there were 60 appellations on 120,000 hectares (297,000 acres) with over 7,000 wineries producing more than 10,000 different bottles annually in Bordeaux... you say to yourself, oh my gosh, now what? And then you add the reputation of the first-growths classifications of 1855. Why does the French Emperor Napoléon III still get to declare the best wines 150 years after his death?

Because Bordeaux's weather varies greatly each year, their vintages are significantly affected. How to keep track when drinking wines from all over the world, decades of vintages, trying to remember which were Bordeaux's best vintages? And not get that confused with Napa and Tuscany? Are there five Bordeaux varietals or more? What happened to Malbec? White Bordeaux? Why do some châteaux only makes one wine? A first label. And now a second wine? And how to actually read labels to know what everything means? Castles, why castles? And how to be able to stay in one? So much to learn!

It is complicated. Involved. Elaborate. Confusing. Even torturous. My goal is to uncomplicate Bordeaux so that you can enjoy everything about it... their wines, their wineries and the nuances that make them great. So you can visit in extraordinary ways and venture behind-the-scenes like an insider. And so you can stay on their beautiful properties, and even in castles!

Wine to me is a passion
A love affair with my senses

A seductive perfume
Drawing me closer

Wine is as luscious as a beautiful kiss
Lingering on my lips

It wets my appetite from foreplay on
Leaving me with utter satisfaction

Wine reaches deep into my soul
Finds my heart and my emotions

Wine is complicated yet simple
Heavenly and devilish

Wine is meant to be shared
It is romance and friendship

Wine is the art of living

– Michael C. Higgins

Château Margaux

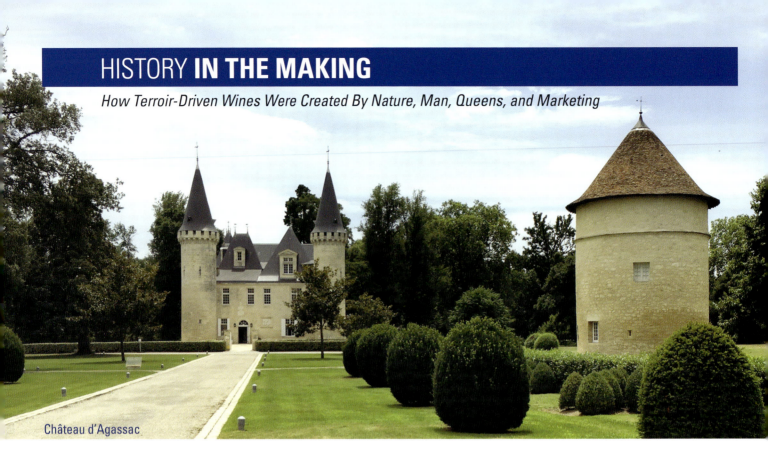

Château d'Agassac

HISTORY IN THE MAKING

How Terroir-Driven Wines Were Created By Nature, Man, Queens, and Marketing

The tale of Bordeaux's history should really begin with the development of their topography. After all, the landscape is a huge aspect of terroir. And terroir defines Bordeaux wines. It is really about knowing the sense of place. Châteaux grow their vines in particular locations, which define their wine. So where it all began means everything to this terroir-driven wine region.

Some 100 million years ago, give or take a few years, two ancient continents were on a collision course. The Eurasian and Iberian continents' plates were applying intense pressure to very large areas, uplifting the Earth. This didn't quite happen overnight. It took 50 to 75 million years, and voilà, the Pyrénées Mountains emerged, separating Spain and France and creating a funnel-shape valley extending out of the Bay of Biscay from the Atlantic Ocean; the perfect spot for Bordeaux to spawn.

Rivers began to flow into this valley from the Pyrénées, an extensive mountain range, spreading 267 miles from the coast of the Atlantic to the Mediterranean. With peaks rising over 11,000 feet in elevation, areas of glaciers were born, providing a year-round flow of water. The Garonne River carved its place through the middle of Bordeaux, creating the Left Bank and Right Bank we hear defined today. The city of Bordeaux was eventually built along the river, having access to the Atlantic Ocean as a major shipping port for exporting wine.

The Garonne River runs 374 miles from deep within the Pyrénées. A massive water flow (23,000 cu ft/s) carrying gravel and stones commonly found along the Left Bank. The name "Garonne" comes from the Latin word *garumna*, meaning stony river. And stony it was, creating the magical terroir of the Médoc and Graves (French for gravelly land).

Flowing from the east out of the Auvergne Mountains is the other major river of Bordeaux, the Dordogne River. This is another high flowing river (16,000 cu ft/s), bringing clay 310 miles to the Saint Émilion, Pomerol and Fronsac areas prior to meeting up with the Garonne River. It then merges into the Gironde Estuary and flows another 62 miles along the Médoc into the Atlantic Ocean. The map on page 21 shows all this very well.

Now think terroir as a result of these rivers. Gravel and stone, most conducive for Cabernet Sauvignon, are plentiful along the Left Bank of Bordeaux, in both the Médoc and Graves (photo below), where the wines are predominately Cabernet Sauvignon. And clay, loved by Merlot, is an intrinsically valuable part of the Right Bank areas of Saint-Émilion, Pomerol and Fronsac, where the wines are predominately Merlot.

Let's fast-forward to 500 BC when the Romans were moving throughout much of Western Europe. The Romans came to France planting vineyards and spreading Christianity. Grapevines can be traced back as far as the 6th century BC in France. Eventually, the Roman Empire licensed regions to produce wines. During the Middle Ages, the monks developed winemaking skills as the monasteries had the resources and security to produce wine for profit and Mass services. Their wine was considered to be the best. Then nobility became attracted to this success and developed their own vineyards, until the French Revolution when vineyards were confiscated and heads rolled. Literally.

My take on why certain grapes are found in certain regions around France is the element of survival. The Romans planted numerous varieties of vines all over the country. Not with any varietal specificity, as not much was known back then. Sophisticated irrigation systems did not exist either.

The survival of the vines was a matter of natural selection, and in my deduction, a matter of terroir. Certain vines survived in certain places, in the terroir which they could thrive. Pinot Noir vines flourish in the cool terroir of Burgundy. Other varieties died away. Then Bordeaux, with its hotter environment and rocky soils of the Left Bank, produced Cabernet Sauvignon grapes of extraordinary quality, which not just survived, thrived. And thus, the outstanding Bordeaux reputation was born.

It is all about terroir. Then and now. Even today, the French government prohibits any irrigation of vines in Bordeaux. None. Cabernet Sauvignon must survive in its terroir as it has for thousands of years.

Along the way, man has dramatically improved the terroir, especially in the Médoc. The British and the Dutch were the primary consumers of Bordeaux wines. The 17th century was considered the "Dutch Golden Age," as they had money and desire for the best Bordeaux wines. At the same time, the Dutch were building canals in Amsterdam and perfecting the techniques, then bringing this canal expertise to Bordeaux.

The Dutch were looking for ways to improve wine transportation in the Médoc which was primarily swampland. And further, they wanted to expand the land use, turning swamps into vineyard. So the Dutch built canals in the Médoc and drained the swamp. It worked! Up until the draining, vineyards were only on the higher hills. Now the Médoc could grow, and it did. Not just grapes in vineyards. Their growth included the ability to ship their wines. And to this today, the canal system is still in place providing drainage, critically needed for the vineyards against heavy rains. Terroir. Man has altered the soil here for the benefit of the grapes.

Another man-modification in the Médoc, as well as Graves and Sauternes, took place in the 1800s when massive forests were planted along the coast of Bordeaux. Known as the Landes Forest, it has become the largest man-made forest in Western Europe. It spans more than 100 miles from the northern tip of the Médoc, south almost all the way to Spain and the Pyrénées Mountains, covering over 5,000 square miles (photo below).

Originally, the forest was planted to hold in place the eroding sand dunes along the coastline of Bordeaux's Atlantic. And to cleanse the soil. This was marshland. People walked with tall stilts here to get from place to place. Now the trees have drunk the water and halted the erosion. The sand dunes are stabilized and the marshes have turned into farmland with a paper and timber industry.

While the Landes Forest accomplished its intended purpose, it resulted in a very unexpected and fortunate benefit to the wine industry. The Atlantic Ocean has always offered a moderate maritime climate that has been valuable to the wine regions here. However, the ocean also produces big storms that hit land and dumps massive amounts of water on vineyards. Not good, and even worse, the water is salty. Add to that, strong winds hurt the vines and you can see where the Atlantic Ocean is a double-edged sword. The forest put an end to all that. As it grew tall and dense, it created a barrier against the storms, halting the high winds and salty water, thus protecting the vineyards. This has been a huge benefit, as man further altered terroir here, thus improving Bordeaux's climate.

And there is more. The Landes Forest created the weather effect south of Bordeaux city, which made Sauternes wines possible. Sauternes is located in a magic triangle of the Garonne River to the east, the Ciron River to the north and the Landes Forest to the west and south. The forest shades the Ciron River making it much cooler than the Garonne River. When the cold Ciron flows into the warm Garonne, it produces fog and mist (held in place by the forest wall) in the autumn mornings, creating the perfect environment for botrytis, Noble Rot, (photo below) to grow. It sure is fascinating to me how man and the environment together created such a unique terroir found nowhere else in the world.

Continuing with the British and Dutch, they were both major purchasers of Bordeaux wines. The Dutch were interested in the value wines, while the British and the Royal families of Europe, sought the better wines. Between the two, the demand across all qualities of Bordeaux wines was creating a thriving international market for Bordeaux.

Let's step back a little and remember that the British ruled Bordeaux for 300 years. They sent ships from London with supplies for Bordeaux and filled the ships with wine for return to the United Kingdom. This made wine production in Bordeaux commercially feasible. Bordeaux boomed!

Let's step back even further and remember that it was the Romans who planted the grapes and licensed regions to produce wine. The Romans really started the wine regions of France and created commercial viability. And during the British rule, commerce expanded, with the visibility and demand for Bordeaux wines being promoted by the British wine merchants who then controlled the distribution of wine.

This all became possible because of Eleanor of Aquitaine. Eleanor inherited a massive 16,000 square mile region in Southwestern France, which included Bordeaux, its capital (in 2016, the regions became Nouvelle-Aquitaine). Eleanor was born in Bordeaux and inherited Aquitaine in 1137 at age 15, making her the Duchess of Aquitaine until her death in 1204. Eleanor was considered one of the most powerful and wealthiest women in all of Western Europe. She was a contrast of personalities: both a patron of the arts and a leader of armies.

Eleanor's story gets even more interesting. Eleanor of Aquitaine was the most eligible woman in Europe now. So what does she do? Just three months after inheriting Aquitaine and becoming Duchess, she marries King Louis IV of France at age 15, becoming the Queen of France. There was a problem though. They only produced daughters. She asked the Pope for an annulment; however, he refused.

After 15 years of marriage and a second daughter born, King Louis, who could do whatever he wanted, granted her the annulment. Now she is back to being the Duchess of Aquitaine and the most eligible woman again. She immediately gets engaged to the Duke of Normandy and is married eight weeks later. Two years later, he becomes King Henry II of England. Now she is the Queen of England. This is so interesting! Has anyone ever become Queen of two different countries? Let alone become a queen! During the next 13 years, they produced five sons, three of which became kings, and three daughters.

Here is the marvel. She is now both Queen Eleanor of England and Eleanor of Aquitaine France, with enormous power and wealth in both countries. This is how the British control of Bordeaux began. And it lived on for 300 years, surviving her and her children, and paving the way for British wine merchants to produce wine for export, international consumption and acclaim. This was a golden era for Bordeaux, as the English rule of Bordeaux created a thriving economy. King Henry II's love of Bordeaux wines helped create a demand from the people of his county. He even granted tax-free trade status to further stimulate the importation. This was a very important aspect of history in Bordeaux's success and worldwide demand.

Let's get to the next leader who made a lasting impact on Bordeaux wines. In front of the World Fair in 1855, French Emperior Napoléon III wanted to show the world who had the very best wines. The *Exposition Universelle de Paris* was the perfect opportunity for France to showcase the best it had to offer for the entire world to see. To do this, Napoléon wanted Bordeaux wines to be classified and ranked. He ordered an official classification through the Gironde Chamber of Commerce and the Wine Brokers Union of Bordeaux.

The Grand Cru Classé of 1855 was born (see page 61). They created rankings in five classes called "growths" with a total of 61 châteaux making the grade. The wines were all reds and all from the Médoc, except for Château Haut-Brion from Graves, which was included due to its worldwide fame. The sweet wines from Sauternes and Barsac were also included although with only three classes. Since 1855, the classification has only allowed one major modification: Château Mouton Rothschild was promoted from second to first-growth on June 21, 1973. First-growths, known as Premiers Crus, have just five châteaux: Lafite Rothschild, Margaux, Latour, Haut-Brion and Mouton Rothschild.

The Grand Cru Classés of 1855 remains the prominent classification today, 150 years later

Château du Taillan

promoting the best wines. And Napoléon does not even get royalties for implementing such long-lasting prestige. Then Cru Bourgeois (page 60) became a new classification in 1932 for ranking wines in the Médoc based on independent blind tastings and quality requirements of the châteaux. Other Grand Cru classifications were born in Saint-Émilion (page 316) and Pessac-Léognan (page 246 to further expose the higher quality wines.

In 1936, the government responded to winemakers wanting all wines identified by their place of origin. Terroir! Not just Bordeaux, France is a terroir-driven winemaking country, so it is natural that winemakers would demand such identification for all regions in France to name their wines by the place in which they are produced. Appellation d'Origine Protégée or AOP was established this year and later updated to Appellation d'Origine Contrôlée (AOC). Under French law, it is illegal to make wine under one of the AOC-controlled geographical indications if it does not comply with the strict criteria of the AOC.

All these classifications for wines in Bordeaux have proven to be important marketing successes. As a result, buyers can know the unique terroir of each bottle acquired and know they are purchasing an excellent wine, which allows their guests to know they are being treated to something special.

It began with nature creating an ideal terroir for wine growing, followed by man's unique intervention to enhance the terroir, followed by important events in history, which created the demand and distribution of Bordeaux wine to the world, and finally, the classifications to control and delineate quality. Today we have Bordeaux, while as complicated as it may seem, that is a land of terroir-driven wines that, as you discover your liking, will have you discovering magic for your palate.

THE GEOGRAPHY OF BORDEAUX
A Most Unique Place in the World

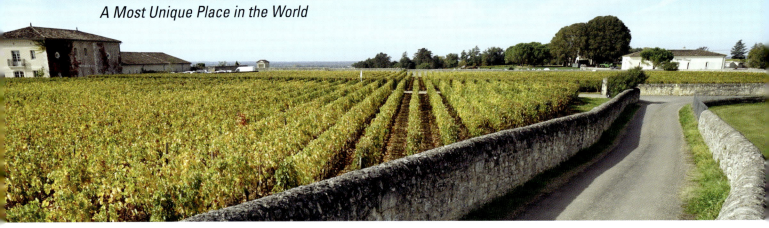

Vineyards on the famous limestone plateau immediately west of the village of Saint-Émilion

THE LAY OF THE LAND

France is the second largest wine producing country in the world, behind Italy and ahead of Spain, United States and Argentina. Within France, there are eight major wine producing regions, with Bordeaux, Champagne and Burgundy being the most well known. Bordeaux is located in southwest France along the Atlantic Ocean and is the second largest wine producing region in France.

Bordeaux is 90% red wines, primarily Cabernet Sauvignon and Merlot. Wines here are always blended. Think of the winemakers as chefs, using the ingredients of their properties to make the very best wine possible. The wineries will have a first label representing their château, and maybe a second wine to use up the leftover juice and sell it at a very good price. The six red wine grapes of Bordeaux are: Cabernet Sauvignon, Merlot, Cabernet Franc, Petit Verdot, Malbec, and Carménère.

Bordeaux does have a white wine, primarily Sauvignon Blanc, blended with smaller amounts of Semillon and Muscadelle. I have come to love white Bordeaux as they are clean, fresh, acidic wines ideal for food with lots of crisp citrus flavors.

Bordeaux is the birthplace of the world's wine regions with these six red grape varietals planted all over the world. California, Argentina, Chile, Australia, South Africa, to name a few, are extensively planted with these Bordeaux varietals.

LEFT BANK VERSUS RIGHT BANK

On the map you will see the Garonne River (that comes from the Pyrénées Mountains) merging with the Dordogne River from the east out of the Auvergne Mountains, both flowing into the Gironde Estuary, out to the Atlantic Ocean. The Left Bank is everything left or west of the Garonne River and Gironde Estuary. This is the Médoc and Graves. The Right Bank is then what is right or east of the Garonne River and Gironde Estuary, including the Saint-Émilion area along the Dordogne River.

The Left Bank is primarily stones and gravel and predominately Cabernet Sauvignon. The Right Bank has lots of clay and limestone conducive for Merlot. The Left Bank is known for the big powerful wines that can age for many decades. They also need a good ten years (or lots of decanting) to be ready for consumption. The Right Bank wines are much softer and ready to drink much earlier. This is a generality, as there are pockets of clay on the Left Bank with châteaux producing softer ready-to-drink-earlier wines. And the Right Bank has some beautifully big wines, some even pricier than the Left Bank.

Entre-Deux-Mers literally means between two seas, and in this case, between two rivers. Primarily, this region produces the volume value wines. I did find a couple extraordinary châteaux here with amazing wines that I share with you in this book.

LEFT BANK — The Médoc and Graves have sub-appellations which are distinct and noteworthy. The Médoc is known for the famous Grand Cru Classés of 1855 and the Cru Bourgeois châteaux. Famous sub-appellations include Margaux and Pauillac, for example. Graves includes Pessac-Léognan as a distinct sub-appellation with extraordinary wines. Also, at the very far south of Graves is Sauternes, the famous region for the sweet wines made from the Noble Rot.

RIGHT BANK — Saint-Émilion is a medieval village surrounded by many outstanding châteaux. Pomerol and Fronsac are neighbors. Pomerol is known for the blue clay and special wines. Fronsac is another appellation where you can find excellent wines; not as well known and the good prices reflect such.

MÉDOC ATLANTIQUE — This is a great escape from the wine regions to go to the lakes, forests and beach communities along the Atlantic Ocean, close to the Médoc wine regions. Farther south, west of Bordeaux city, is Arcachon Bay, another beautiful escape with oysters and massive sand dunes.

DOWNTOWN BORDEAUX — The city is the largest UNESCO World Heritage Site in the world, with many amazing food and wine experiences, super great hotels and interesting landmarks that will make you feel as I do: *This is Mini Paris!*

HOW TO BEST READ THIS BOOK

View from the backyard of Château Sigalas Rabaud looking across their vineyards to Château d'Yquem on top of the hill

NAVIGATING BORDEAUX

I like being methodically organized and geographically oriented, to make it simpler to navigate and easier to find places. This should help you tremendously as you make your way through this book and Bordeaux.

I begin this book in the center of the region. The city, Bordeaux, is a beautiful historical place, even medieval. It is a place I like to affectionately call *The Mini Paris*. While Paris has a large population of 2.1 million (metro is 12.5 million), Bordeaux has a 250,000 population (metro is 1.2 million).

From Bordeaux city, I take us northward, into the Médoc, traversing the Médoc sub-appellations from south to north. At the top, the north tip of the Médoc, I present to you the port and its beautiful yacht harbor. This is the mouth where the rivers flow into the sea.

Now, turning back south along the Atlantic Ocean, this is known as the Médoc Atlantique, with beautiful beaches, lakes and forests. Continuing farther south we arrive at the Arcachon Bay and back to the city of Bordeaux, directly east.

Heading south of the Bordeaux city, we move through the Graves appellation, from Pessac-Léognan through Graves all the way to Sauternes and Barsac to the farthest south.

Next, we travel east of the city, cross over Entre-Deux-Mers, where I later present a couple of not-to-be-missed châteaux, and arrive at Saint Émilion.

Saint-Émilion is a spectacular village, much smaller that Bordeaux, rich in its history, dating back to when the monasteries were making wine here. Worthy of your exploration. Out from the village of Saint-Émilion, we explore their wine regions and two of their neighbors, Pomerol and Fronsac, also producing excellent wines.

I do take us on a side trip to Cognac. Cognac is a cute little town in the middle of the Cognac region, just an hour north of Bordeaux, where we visit a historic Cognac factory. The original reason for this side trip was to visit a cooperage. Coopers are the people who make the oak wine barrels used to vinify and age wine. The process is fascinating, especially with the engineering talents at this large cooperage of top-level quality.

Another side trip to consider is Paris. From the United States, and many other countries, you cannot fly directly to Bordeaux. Paris is France's connection to Bordeaux. If you are stopping in Paris, why not spend a few days there and enjoy amazing food and wine experiences, and spectacular world-renowned monuments?

As you travel Bordeaux, I want you to be thinking terroir. More terroir than grape variety. This is the land of terroir and the wines here are all blended to express the terroir. Here, the relationship between soil, grape and climate is the magic inside Bordeaux wines. This is an important threesome that, if you are looking, thinking and asking, you can discover the tremendous differences and subtle nuances as you explore Bordeaux.

HOW THE BOOK IS LAID OUT

I have just explained the geographic order of the book. Within each region and appellation, I present the châteaux in their classification ranking order.

Maps. I love maps, which is why there are 29 in this book. They lead each wine region and their appellations and sub-appellations, followed by its characteristics and uniqueness.

The gray side-column provides the basics: wine region, appellation, classification, ranking, business type, name, address, phone, e-mail, website, languages spoken, visiting times and if reservations are needed. For wineries, I have added a photo of their bottle/label and their complete list of wines.

ARRIVING & TRAVERSING

Bordeaux-Mérignac Airport (BOD)
Located 12 km (7.5 mi) west of the city of Bordeaux in the town of Mérignac.

Bordeaux-Saint-Jean Railway Station (ZFQ)
Located in the city center, with an electric tram stop and car rentals at the station.

The Bordeaux airport has direct flights from numerous Western European and Northern African cities. If you are flying from the United States, for example, you will need a connecting flight. Paris is a popular connection, and if this is what you choose, you might also want to consider taking the train from Paris to Bordeaux for several reasons.

Time: By the time you wait for your next flight, the train could already have you in Bordeaux. It departs from inside Paris - Charles De Gaulle Airport and takes only 3.5 hours. If you choose the high-speed train from downtown Paris, the train is only a 2 hours ride to downtown Bordeaux!

Stop Over: If you do stop over in Paris, there is a train station in the city center (Montparnasse) that is just a 2 hour ride to Bordeaux. The Paris airport is located 34 km (21 miles) from the city center, so that could take you an hour (two hours with heavy city traffic) just to get to the airport.

Quality: Even if you are flying first-class, the train is nicer. First-class on a flight from Paris to Bordeaux is simply coach seating in the front of the airplane. The train however, is much more spacious and luxurious in coach. Plus, the train has first-class cars as well, for not much more money.

While in Bordeaux city, the tram system is all you need to get around. It connects with the train station and runs all over, as you can see on the map. Plus, so much of the city is simply walkable.

Exploring the wine regions, though, you will definitely need a car. Both the train station and the airport have numerous, both European and American, car rental companies.

GPS is a must! I experimented with both the GPS in the rental car and my iPhone. The iPhone was more reliable. You will absolutely positively need GPS to be able to find many of the wineries. Remember, this is spread-out agriculture.

WHO GOT IN?

Not everyone. With over 7,000 châteaux here, I had to make deliberate choices on who to include.

My first priority was that every winery must be open to the public for visits. Bordeaux has had a reputation for wineries not being open to the public. They make wine, leave them alone. This has changed significantly during the last decade.

I recognize two people for inspiring tourism in Bordeaux. Baron Philippe de Rothschild, who, back in 1922 at 20 years old I might add, had the vision to invite people to enjoy his estate. Beyond the tour, he created an art gallery which includes original works of Picasso, Dali and Warhol, for example, and Museum of Art & Wine. See Mouton Rothschild.

And Bernard Magrez, who owns five châteaux in multiple appellations, focuses on having luxury tourism experiences. You can stay overnight in his castles, enjoy gourmet meals, blend your own wine, take interesting workshops, and more. Plus, he has luxury hotels and a restaurant in the city. See Pape Clément, Fombrauge and La Grande Maison.

This tourism is what I look for to include in the book. They must provide wine experiences for their guests at their property. Some have become quite creative and innovative with truly unique experiences that you have never seen before. Read what I have written and find what appeals to you.

Every place I have written about in this book is from my own personal, hands-on experience. No one has paid me to write any of these reviews.

Networking has been key. I worked extensively with locals, wine lovers, winemakers, publishers, travel and tourism professionals, wine councils, chefs, restaurateurs, sommeliers, government officials, and other organizations at the forefront of food, wine and tourism in Bordeaux.

Who is out? If all they do is offer a tasting? Boring! If they do not even open the doors? No way! If the wine is not excellent? Why bother! Life is too short to drink bad wine. What you can count on from me is that I was actually there, I know the experiences, and I know the wines are excellent. And some will simply blow you away.

Petit Verdot

BORDEAUX · CITY CENTER
A Most Spectacular Mini Paris

Miroir d'Eau in front of Place de la Bourse

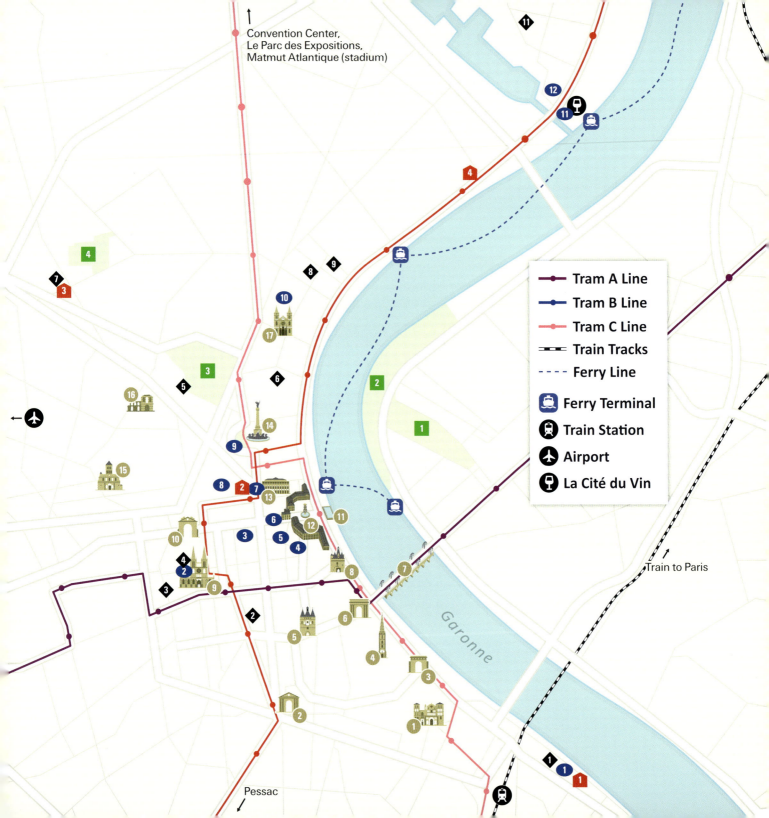

BORDEAUX · CITY CENTER MAP

Map is to scale. The locations are plotted numerically from south to north.

LANDMARKS

1. Sainte-Croix Church, p. 30
2. Place de la Victoire, p.30
3. Porte de la Monnaie, p.30
4. Saint-Michel Spire, p.30
5. Grosse Cloche, p.30
6. Porte de Bourgogne, p.30
7. Pont de Pierre, p.30
8. Porte Cailhau, p.31
9. Saint-André Cathedral, p.31
10. Porte Dijeaux, p.31
11. Miroir d'Eau, p.31
12. Place de la Bourse, p.32
13. Grand Théâtre de Bordeaux, p.32
14. Monument aux Girondins, p.32
15. Basilique Saint-Seurin, p.33
16. Palais Gallien, p.33
17. Saint-Louis Church, p.33

RESTAURANTS

1. La Boca Foodcourt, p.49
2. Le Café Français, p.39
3. Big Fernand, p.40
4. Osteria da Luigi, p.40
5. Bar du Boucher, p.40
6. La Brasserie Bordelaise, p.39 and Fufu Ramen, p.39
7. Le Quatrième Mur, p.37 and Comptoir Cuisine, p.36
8. Le Chapon Fin, p.41
9. Le 1925, p.37
10. El Nacional, p.51 and Sister, p.51
11. Le 7, p.52
12. Les Halles de Bacalan, p.51

MUSEUMS

1. La Méca, p.48-49
2. Musée d'Aquitaine
3. Musée des Beaux Arts
4. Musée des Arts Décoratifs
5. Musée de Bordeaux
6. CAPC - Museum of Contemporary Art
7. Institut Culturel Bernard Magrez, p.55
8. Musée du Vin et du Négoce
9. Musée de l'Histoire Maritime
10. 🍷 La Cité du Vin, p.53
11. Musée Mer Marine, p33

PARKS

1. Botanical Gardens
2. Parc aux Angéliques
3. Jardin Public
4. Parc Rivière

HOTELS

1. Hilton Garden Inn, p.49
2. Grand Hôtel de Bordeaux, p.34-35
3. La Grande Maison, p.54
4. Seeko'o Hôtel Design, p.50

3 Porte de la Monnaie, Landmark

Grand Théâtre de Bordea[ux]

BORDEAUX A MINI PARIS
A City Alive with Food, Wine, Culture, History, and Friendship

I ♥ BORDEAUX

This is one of my favorite cities in the world. I could live here very happily. The vibe is youthful and energetic. Almost everyone speaks English. The French accent is alluring. Bordeaux City Center is walkable and deeply historic with meandering cobblestone streets and interesting medieval buildings everywhere. There is an electric tram system that moves about the city with ease and frequency. The people are nice and friendly, not at all like the reputation Parisians alternatively get.

Bordeaux truly is a "Mini Paris." It is also a medieval city. The entire downtown area is a UNESCO World Heritage Site. There is an extensive array of historical landmarks all within the city. Bordeaux is not all spread out like Paris. Everything is within this beautiful historical city, a miniature and contained version of Paris.

The culinary scene in Bordeaux is second to none. This is not just my opinion. A survey conducted by Atabula, France's leading gastronomy website, revealed that French people ranked Bordeaux as the No. 1 city in France where they can most expect to find the best restaurant cuisine. And to this, Bordeaux's mayor Alain Juppé says, "Ouaaaah!"

There are so many restaurants around this city that it gets me excited every time I think about it. I have eaten at dozens and dozens of them, both fancy and local hole-in-the-walls, and they are all amazing in their own way. Plus, they have international cuisine, not just French food. Even Michelin has weighed in on the city's restaurant scene by awarding two 2-stars, three 1-stars, 21 Plates, five Bib Gourmands and 17 Mentions. Need I say more? This is a food and wine lovers' paradise. Just wait until you read my reviews and begin to taste.

I have heard and read (but I cannot find the data to show it) that Bordeaux has the greatest number of restaurants per capita in all of France, more than Paris and Lyon. What I can tell you is that restaurants are everywhere. And I have some gems to share with you in these pages.

Bordeaux is a college town with world-class universities, with the intelligent students in the community to go with it.

Hotels are excellent with both renovated historic properties with modern conveniences, as well as new modern hotels built in select places around Bordeaux. And most of them have restaurants of great quality too.

Shopping is really good and plentiful. The stores are conveniently centralized on some great shopping streets. There is a good mix of local and well-known brands. And affordable. Fashionable French brands cost much less here than in the USA.

Are you getting the picture of how cool it would be to live here? How amazing it would be to simply visit Bordeaux for even just a few days visit?

DOWN TO THE NITTY-GRITTY

Bordeaux is the name of this beautiful city that shares its name with, and is located within, one of the most important wine regions in the world. I consider it to be the center of the universe for wine. Bordeaux city is located in the heart of this exciting wine region and is the capital of the Nouvelle-Aquitaine region. As the wine capital, it brings in a whopping €14.5 billion in revenue each year.

Bordeaux is the sixth largest city in France, with a population of 250,000. The metropolitan area, including its two large adjoining suburbs of Pessac and Mérignac (airport location) and satellite towns, has 1.2 million people. Bordeaux City Center became a Unesco World Heritage Site in 1999.

Bordeaux is built on the Left Bank at a bend in the Garonne River and is a vital port city for the wine trade. North is the Médoc, south is Graves. Across the river to the east is the Right Bank of the Libournais wine regions.

Bordeaux is 500km (310mi) southwest of Paris, a one-hour flight or about a five-hours drive. The high-speed train is a non-stop ride of just two hours. There are an average of 24 trains per day from 6:00am to 10:00pm. Arriving at Gare de Bordeaux-Saint-Jean puts you in Bordeaux City Center at the tram station to take you where you need to go without a car. Rental cars are available at the train station when you are leaving the city for the wine regions. I have flown, driven and taken the train, and I would hands down always pick taking the train. It is faster, easier, cheaper and the seats are more comfortable and spacious.

Pack for diverse weather. It can be sunny and hot one day, then rain and cloudy the next, and very cold at night. More often than not, this can all happen on the same day. Layering is best. Seriously, it rains in every month of the year, and it would not be unusual to be wearing a jacket on a cold summer day. More so, it is difficult to predict.

Let me say this about Bordeaux: You must take in this city. It is a food and wine lovers' paradise. The historical architecture is captivating. The city is alive with energy with so much to do.

When I first arrive, I always stay one night to get a nice meal, sip Bordeaux wine and get in the Bordeaux mood for exploring the wine regions. At the end of my trips, I always plan a few extra days in Bordeaux to prepare for my journey home. There is a lot of wine available in the city to complete my wine luggage and get what might have been missed in the regions. More so, this city has so much to see and do that I can never get enough of it. And I have spent 21 weeks in Bordeaux!

SPECTACULAR LANDMARKS

Bordeaux is a land of historical significance. Meandering its quaint little cobblestone side streets, you'll find interesting architecture at every bend and landmarks of statuesque beauty. You will feel their pride here be seeing how they protect and enjoy their history. UNESCO just confirms it all. This capital city has 362 preserved buildings labeled as historic monuments, second only to Paris.

Bordeaux landmarks have a deeper and richer history. The Eiffel Tower and Arc de Triomphe may be renowned and awe-inspiring; however, they are really not that old. Bordeaux is medieval and it is all concentrated downtown, making for an easy walk, tram or bike ride to each of them. I highlight 17 of the more prominent landmarks here (also plotted on the map). My navigation is from south to north.

① Sainte-Croix Church
This is the Church of the Holy Cross, an active Roman Catholic church located in south part of Bordeaux. It was built in the 11th and early 12th centuries in a Romanesque architectural style.

② Place de la Victoire
A square of convergence of many streets including Rue Sainte-Catherine, the longest pedestrian street in France. It has a 17th century stone arch and a 16-meter high bronze and marble sculpture featuring two huge tortoises.

③ Porte de la Monnaie
Meaning "door of the mint," it is an arched doorway through the city walls that led from the port to where the money was minted. Built from 1758-1759. Photo on page 27.

④ Saint-Michel Spire
La Flèche ("The Arrow" in French), as the Bordelais refer with pride to this freestanding bell tower, is 114 meters high and soars toward the sky as the tallest in Southern France. It was built on solid ground (alongside its cathedral) versus on top of the church where most bell towers are constructed. There are 230 steps to the top. I know because I counted each and every one of them!

The bell tower was built in the 15th century on an ancient burial ground, so they put in steps downward into the crypt. It is dark down there where you can sit and watch a film about mummies. Creepy? Then turn towards the stairs and head up to find the amazing view as seen in the photo below.

⑤ Grosse Cloche
This is a "big bell" (literal meaning) with striking characteristics. Definitely worth your visit. Built in the 13th century, it is the oldest belfry in France, a gateway tower to the city and once functioned as a prison for children who misbehaved. It's so iconic it is featured on the city's coat of arms.

The bell weighs nearly 8,000 kilos and rings on the first Sunday of every month at noon, plus six celebration days, including New Year's Day.

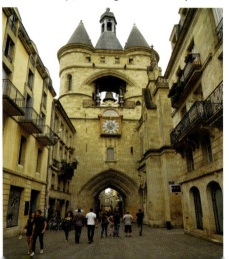

⑥ Porte de Bourgogne
Built in the 1757, the "Gate of Burgundy" is a Roman-style stone arch that was the official medieval entrance to Bordeaux when arriving on the old road from Paris. This is the largest arch I found in the city and it resembles the look and feel of the Arcs de Triomphe in Paris. Cours Victor Hugo is a major road that crosses the Garonne River over the historic **Pont de Pierre** stone bridge and into the city, passing under this massive arch.

⑦ Pont de Pierre
"Stone Bridge" is the first bridge connecting the Left Bank and Right Bank and was the only bridge for 150 years crossing over the Garonne River.

It was built as a result of Napoléon arriving at the river's right bank and not being able to cross into the city. He ordered the bridge to be built. And it was with 17 spans, one for each letter in his name (Napoléon Bonaparte). Interesting.

Cours Victor Hugo is a major road that crosses the bridge and arrives in Bordeaux entering the city under the **Porte de Bourgogne**.

8 Porte Cailhau

Built in 1495, this landmark has a castle-like exterior and was once the main gate-house to the city. It was also a part of the defensive walls of the city and gave entrance to the Palais de l'Ombrière, the residence of the Dukes of Guyenne and then to the seat of the Parliament of Bordeaux. It is a fascinating building to look at. While it is of Gothic architecture, its creative design resembles a Disney fairytale castle.

10 Porte Dijeaux

Built in the 18th century, this Neoclassical style historic city gate of Bordeaux is the gateway for the west side of the city. Its name comes from the road passing through it that leads into a popular shopping and restaurant area of the city. There is dining below the arch, as you can see in the photo below. A beautiful lively place at night.

11 Miroir d'Eau

This is the spectacular water mirror photo starting this chapter on page 24. It is the largest reflection pool in the world. It is 3,450 square meters of granite slabs covered by 2cm (3/4 inch) of water and creates fog every 15 minutes. It was built in 2006 and is located between the Garonne River and in front of the Place de la Bourse. It is a playful spot. As the water disappears, people walk on, the fog enters, the water sprays and people run!

9 Saint-André Cathedral

This is Bordeaux's main cathedral, a Roman Catholic church dedicated to Saint Andrew and located in the center of downtown Bordeaux. It is the seat of the Archbishop of Bordeaux.

The structure is massive and ornate with different sections being built and added from the 9th through the 15th centuries.

⑫ Place de la Bourse

The "Stock Exchange Square" is definitely the center of the Bordeaux waterfront. It is one of Bordeaux's most recognizable sights. On its own, it is grand and spectacular. In front of the **Miroir d'Eau**, the pairing of the two becomes the most picturesque setting in the city, serving as the backdrop for millions of photos annually.

Place de la Bourse is a huge multi-building development designed by King Louis XV's primary architect from Paris. It took 25 years to build (1730-1755). For centuries, Bordeaux used to be surrounded by walls to protect itself from endless attacks. Many of these landmarks I have been showing you are arched gateway doors so the Bordelais can isolate entrances better to defend their city. This square symbolizes their opportunity to finally be free and to expand beyond the medieval walls.

⑭ Monument aux Girondins

This is a dramatic fountain with a towering column erected to honor, commemorate and remember the Girondins. The Girondins were a loosely formed political group from the French Revolution. The Girondins' name is from the department of the Gironde. They are remembered for fighting politically on behalf of Bordeaux

The Girondins were originally part of France's Legislative Assembly, supporting the French Revolution up until October 1793. Subsequently, they were executed (22 heads guillotined in 36 minutes) under the orders of one of the leaders of the Revolution they opposed.

This monument was built in the early 20th century in Place des Quinconces, the largest square in Europe (12 hectares). Quinconces is a term referring to the way trees are planted in staggered rows. It looks really cool walking underneath.

Monument aux Girondins depicts a woman standing atop a large pillar, representing liberty as she breaks free from her chains. At its base are two pools containing spectacular bronze fountains. The base represents the city of Bordeaux, the Garonne and Dordogne Rivers. The bronze fountains symbolize the triumph of the republic whose chariots are pulled by sea horses.

Monument aux Girondins is a striking memorial to the Reign of Terror.

⑬ Grand Théâtre de Bordeaux

Built in 1780 during the height of wealth here, the Grand Théâtre became the center of entertainment: ballet, opera, plays, concerts, and soirées. Today it is the stage for the Bordeaux National Opera.

They have a large permanent team of artists: 110 musicians from the Bordeaux National Orchestra, 38 dancers from the Bordeaux National Ballet, and 37 artists from the Bordeaux National Opera Choir. Each season they have guest artists, conductors and acclaimed soloists. On opening night, we saw two of the best ballet performances we have ever seen.

Of course tickets are available for events. They also have tours to show off the magnificence of this building and its ornate interior of Corinthian columns, sculptures of the Muses and Bohemian-crystal chandelier. Its grand staircase is said to have inspired the one in Palais Garnier in Paris.

⑮ Basilique Saint-Seurin

If you would like to see a real live crypt (okay, it's dead), the basement of this church is as eerie as it gets. This church dates back to the origins of Christianity in Bordeaux on a site dating from antiquity. According to legend, when King Charles the Great won the Battle of Roncevaux, he deposited the oliphant of their leader plus his knights here. And, this Palaeo-Christian crypt still has the tomb of the legendary Saint Fort.

⑯ Palais Gallien

This site is the remains of an amphitheater from the Roman city of Burdigala, the original name of Bordeaux when the Romans made it their city here. It is a short walk north of the current city center.

This amphitheater was built by the Romans during the 2nd century. Remember, the Romans brought the grapes here originally, ultimately leading to the grand wine regions of today. And now these ruins are the only visible remnant of the Roman city of Burdigala.

The amphitheater held 20,000 spectators, twice the population of the city, on their wooden benches. What remains today are several walls and massive arches of the stadium. Some of the walls are now incorporated into the surrounding houses and even their basements! Go see it. Maybe you will hear a lost echo of a roaring lion or shouting victorious gladiators.

⑰ Saint-Louis Church

The Church of Saint-Louis is a Roman Catholic church located in the Chartrons district in the north part of Bordeaux. It is a Gothic Revival church dedicated to Saint Louis, King of France.

Saint-Louis Church was built between 1874 and 1880. It is 60 meters long, 23 meters wide and 22 meters high. The ceilings are dramatically vaulted. It has two high towers, 58 meters tall, visible from all over the city. The stained-glass windows are particularly remarkable as they were made by two men in the choir.

MUSEUMS

There are quite a few excellent and diverse museums in Bordeaux. Some quite unusual and different from other museums you have seen in the world. They are spread out around the city. Check hours and display dates as I found several of them closed when I arrived. There are three very interesting museums that I will share with you in the coming pages, plus one below. The others are well marked on the map to make them easy to find.

⑪ Musée Mer Marine

Part history, part exploration. See the maritime history of Bordeaux in its heyday as the largest port of Europe. Actual artifacts and scaled models with tremendous detail. Super interesting especially if you like ships (photo left).

The other part of the permanent exhibition is about exploring the ocean, to discover the evolution of oceans from their formation to today. Gain a greater understanding of the marine ecosystems, see unknown ocean environments, the fragility of the ocean, the marine life it contains, and ideas for its preservation.

They had an interesting Da Vinci exhibit while I was there. More temporary exhibits are planned.

SOPHISTICATED & REGAL HOTEL

Now that you get a glimpse of how beautifully historic this city is, let me introduce you to one of the grandest hotels in Bordeaux. Le Grand Hotel is just that, grand! Sophisticated in every sense. Their total transformation in 2014 into regal magnificence is exemplified by the ultimate of five-star hospitality their exceptional staff exudes.

The Grande Théâtre and The Grand Hôtel are like bookends, mirroring each other across the Place de La Comédie (Golden Triangle), the hub of Bordeaux that leads into multiple directions of the city. They are truly reflections of each other as they both share the same architect and his vision. Both were built in the 18th century with the same neoclassical fronts with Corinthian style colonnades and the same excessive interiors with astonishing marble.

All the rooms are spacious suites decorated in 18th century luxury. Magnificent and comfortable is how I describe our room. Each room is distinguishingly unique in its layout, with lavish furnishings and views of the city. Upstairs is a two-star Michelin restaurant. I cannot tell you much as it was unavailable when I was there. Regardless, surrounding the hotel are numerous exceptionally great restaurants. I will tell you about many of them in the upcoming pages.

Their spa, Spa Guerlain, is one of my favorite parts of this property. Check out the indoor pool on the left page. An inviting pool for any princess, and her knight (with or without his shining armor). This is a relaxing, sensual, majestic place to spend an afternoon. Spa treatments are available too.

BORDEAUX **CITY CENTER** (Central)

Historic Hotel & Spa
**INTERCONTINENTAL
GRAND HÔTEL DE BORDEAUX**

2-5 Place de La Comédie
33000 Bordeaux, France

+33 (0)5 57 30 44 44
Info.Bordeaux@IHG.com

Bordeaux.InterContinental.com

English, French

FOOD AND WINE

One of the most exciting aspects of Bordeaux is its culinary scene. There are a whopping 1,400 restaurants. With a population of 256,000 people, this means that Bordeaux has 5.47 restaurants per 1000 people. A greater number of restaurants per capita than Paris or Lyon (France's gastronomical capital), 4.13 and 1.68, respectively. As food and wine lovers, this is a delicious paradise!

I have reviewed 15 Bordeaux restaurants in this chapter for you. Some are very fancy, others are simple hole-in-the-wall greats. I have highlighted both French traditional and unique contemporary fusion cuisines. I also cover Italian, Argentine and Japanese restaurants out of the many international options here.

While I ate at many more than the 15 restaurants included in this book, the one thing I can say is that we never had a bad meal. Some were good, some were great and some were extraordinary. Restaurants (and hotels) are grouped by area: central, followed by south, then north.

Keep in mind: The concept of restaurants being open for only two hours at lunch and two hours for dinner applies to Bordeaux City Center. Don't worry, I show you alternatives so you don't starve.

I was fortunate to meet many of the chefs and proprietors of these restaurants to discuss the concepts of their cuisine. Pierre Martin (photo above), proprietor of Le 1925, sat down at our table with his favorite wine, a 1968 Riveyrac Rivesaltes, where we discussed three of our favorite subjects: food, wine and Bordeaux.

■ BORDEAUX **DOWNTOWN** CENTRAL

Restaurant, Bar & Tea Room
COMPTOIR CUISINE & SALON DE THÉ

2 Place de la Comédie • 33000 Bordequx, France
+33 (0)5 56 56 22 33 • Contact@ComptoirCuisine.com
Open: Everyday, 12:00pm-10:30pm, Fridays & Saturday, Until 11:00pm

ComptoirCuisine.com • (Reservations available on their website)

Comptoir Cuisine is located in the front of **InterContinental Grand Hôtel de Bordeaux**. Its highly visible location and super good food makes this a bustling spot. Make reservations or sit at the bar, which worked out well for me.

They create seasonally fresh dishes with imaginative combinations of ingredients that are full of flavors. The atmosphere is business casual with indoor, outdoor and bar dining. Laurent Mougenot is quite the meticulous chef with how he designs his plates to be full of rich savory tastes.

The wine list is perfect. I counted 27 wines by the glass, and an entire wine list for the just 2009 vintages (an extraordinary year!), all of which were Grand Crus from each of the Bordeaux appellations. True to its name, "Salon de Thé" (translates to "Tea Room"), they have a variety of fine teas.

BORDEAUX CITY CENTER (Central)
Brasserie Restaurant
LE 1925

4 Place des Quinconces • 33000 Bordeaux, France
+33 (0)5 56 52 84 56 • Contact@Le1925.fr
Open: Everyday, 10:00am-10:30pm

Le1925.fr • (Reservations available on their website)

Le 1925 is located on the western edge of the Place des Quinconces square, facing the spectacular **Monument aux Girondins**. As the name suggests, this brasserie was originally opened in 1925. It was recently renovated to bring back the opulence of the Roaring Twenties. When you walk through the door, you feel the ambiance of the grand old times of this era.

The cuisine is traditional French befitting of the times. The wine list has over 700 bottles, beautifully hand-picked from all over France. Proprietors, Gaëlle & Pierre Martin, had a dream of creating a beautiful brasserie that offers an extensive selection of the finest wines of Bordeaux. Their dream has definitely come alive here.

BORDEAUX CITY CENTER (Central)
Le Grand Théâtre Brasserie Restaurant
LE QUATRIÈME MUR

2 Place de la Comédie, 33000 Bordeaux, France
+33 (0)5 56 02 49 70 • Contact@Quatrieme-Mur.com
Open: Everyday, 12:00pm-2:30pm & 7:15pm-11:00pm

Quatrieme-Mur.com (Reservations only, and only by telephone)

Located in the front of the **Grand Théâtre de Bordeaux**, Le Quatrième Mur (the fourth wall of the theatre), is a quiet unassuming place with extraordinary food inside where Philippe Etchebest earned a Michelin star. He is one of Bordeaux's most celebrated chefs, with multiple Michelin starred restaurants.

Dining is Table d'Hôtes (table of the host) where chef Etchebest serves you a seven-course masterpiece each evening. And literally, the chef team delivers the courses directly to you and presents their marvelous creations.

The square between Saint-André Cathedral (left) and Le Café Français (far right)

BORDEAUX **CITY CENTER** (Central)
Traditional Brasserie Restaurant
LE CAFÉ FRANÇAIS

5 Place Pey Berland, 33000 Bordeaux, France
+33 (0)5 56 52 96 69 • Contact@Le-Cafe-Francais.com
Open: Everyday, 8:00am-11:00pm

Le-Cafe-Francais.com
(Reservations by email or phone)

BORDEAUX **CITY CENTER** (Central)
Japanese Noodle Bar
FUFU RAMEN

37 Rue Saint Rémi, 33000 Bordeaux, France
+33 (0)5 56 52 10 29 • Contact@RestaurantFufu.com
Open: Everyday, 11:30am-10:30pm

RestaurantFufu.com
(Walk-ins only, no reservations here)

BORDEAUX **CITY CENTER** (Central)
Steak Restaurant
LA BRASSERIE BORDELAISE

50 Rue Saint-Rémi, 33000 Bordeaux, France
+33 (0)5 57 87 11 91 • Contact@Brasserie-Bordelaise.fr
Open: Everyday, 12:00pm-3:00pm & 7:00pm-2:00am

Brasserie-Bordelaise.fr
(Reservations available on their website)

Located in front of the **Saint-André Cathedral** and City Hall, on one of the city's most beautiful pedestrian squares (photo left).

Le Café Français is an old style French brasserie that has been cooking traditional French food for more than a century (1899). Servers are formally dressed in black and white suits, as the tradition of formal service continues. Dining is primarily outside on their large terrace (holds 250 people) looking right at the cathedral.

Le Café Français serves generous portions of traditional recipes from the Gironde region.

Located one block south of the **Grand Théâtre** on Rue Saint Rémi, a most popular shopping and restaurant district. They also have a location in the northern part of Bordeaux in the Chartrons district.

It is a simple menu here. Primarily noodle soups. And it is a noodle bar, only three small high-top tables. The restaurant is primarily a bar facing the kitchen (see photo below).

They have a few different kinds of ramen that are ever so delicious. This is the kind of food to crave for more. And I have been back for more. Plus, they have yakisoba, gyoza and hiyashi chuka.

Located one block south of the **Grand Théâtre**, on Rue Saint Rémi, a most popular shopping and restaurant district.

This is the first restaurant of Maison Lascombes (see page 480) where his style of style of quality and impeccable service began.

La Brasserie Bordelaise is an institution here known for its high-quality meats: regional pork including exceptional ham, delicious grilled beef and typical Gascony dishes. They also have a huge wine cellar of 700 bottles from Grand Crus to small producers from all over the world.

Exploring Wine Regions | **Bordeaux** | 39

BORDEAUX **CITY CENTER** (Central)
Late Night Steakhouse & Bar
BAR DU BOUCHER

5 Rue Parlement Sainte-Catherine, Bordeaux
+33 (0)5 56 81 37 37
Open: Everyday, 11:00am-midnight, Sat & Sun 2:00am

BarDuBoucher.com
(Reservations available on their website)

Located two blocks south of the **Grand Théâtre**, just off of Place du Parlement (a big open square filled with outdoor restaurants).

"Boucher" translates to "butcher," and that is exactly how you order your meat here. You choose your meat and the butcher will cut it to your size specifications and send it to the kitchen to be prepared. They pride themselves on being a 100% carnivore restaurant. Like a butcher shop, they have a wide range of steaks and other meats.

I discovered this place upon leaving an event late one evening, being told they are open late – 2:00am!

BORDEAUX **CITY CENTER** (Central)
Hamburger Stand
BIG FERNAND

5 Rue Guiraude, 33000 Bordeaux, France
+33 (0)5 57 14 94 77
Open: Everyday, 12:00pm-10:30pm

BigFernand.com
(Walk-ins only, no reservations here)

Located three blocks south and one block west of the **Grand Théâtre**, in the Sainte Catherine Promenade (a multi-level outdoor shopping center).

Their first location was in a small Parisian neighborhood where they learned that fresh baked bread with high-quality meat and interesting sauces romanced a regular clientele.

They have six very delicious recipes to tempt you. If not salivating already, they claim there are 3,840 burger combinations possible for you to create your own special burger. Super good fries too. And a micro-brew on tap.

BORDEAUX **CITY CENTER** (Central)
Italian Restaurant
OSTERIA DA LUIGI

23 Rue du Pas-Saint-Georges, Bordeaux
+33 (0)5 56 81 03 80
Open: Tues-Sun, 12:00pm-2:40pm & 7:00pm-10:30pm

OsteriaDaLuigi.fr
(Reservations available on their website)

Located four blocks south, and two blocks east, of the **Grand Théâtre**. I discovered this amazing Italian restaurant on my first trip to Bordeaux.

So delicious that with each subsequent trip I kept trying to find them again. On my sixth trip to Bordeaux, I could not be happier to finally find them down a little alley. I was thrilled to be sitting in this restaurant again. Now you have the address.

First time, I had homemade pasta with a generous portion of thinly sliced truffles. I was captivated. Second trip, I had quail lasagna with mushrooms and chestnuts. I am craving a third meal with them now!

BORDEAUX **CITY CENTER** (Central)
Restaurant
LE CHAPON FIN

GASTRONOMIC GROTTO

Located two blocks west of the **Grande Théâtre** in an area that was developed just after the French Revolution into a mecca for high society. Le Chapon Fin opened its doors here in 1825 and became the destination of the rich and famous, including kings and queens coming from all over Europe. Ultimately in 1933, Le Chapon Fin became one of the first ever three-star Michelin restaurants.

Through the centuries, the owners and chefs may have changed, yet Le Chapon Fin maintained its reputation as the theatre of gastronomic productions. Today, the dining room is surrounded by coral reef walls giving you an underwater feel. The service is very attentive. Each dish is presented with captivating details.

The food is very well crafted with a great variety of flavors and textures. Each dish arrived with deliciousness beyond our imagination. Their chef, Cédric Bobinet, is one very talented guy. We arrived just a month after he began and saw him warming up to the greatness he is establishing here.

Their 200-year-old cellar has wines from all over the world, an assemblage of good wines both in terms of price and enjoyment. And some crazy greats: I saw a 1928 d'Yquem, 1955 Lascombes, 1985 Dom Perignon and 1986 Pétrus. Wow!

5 Rue Montesquieu
33000 Bordeaux, France

+33 (0)5 56 79 10 10
Contact@Chapon-Fin.com

Chapon-Fin.com

English, French

*Open: Tuesday-Saturday
12:00pm-2:00pm & 7:30pm-9:00pm*
(Reservations available on their website)

Food photography from top to bottom:
Shrimp with a citrus vinaigrette
Potato squares filled with cream and caviar
Lobster with seasonal vegetables
Bass in fish broth with leaks and crispy seaweed

Interior photography from left to right:
Breathtaking entrance of Le Chapon Fin
Intimate table tucked in coral reef
Underground 200-year-old wine cellar

MAISON DU VIN DE BORDEAUX • LE BAR À VIN
1 Cours du 30 Juillet, 33000 Bordeaux, France
+33 (0)5 56 00 43 47
Open: Monday-Saturday, 10:00am-10:00pm

BarAVin.Bordeaux.com

Le Bar à Vin takes over the ground floor of an unusual triangle-shaped 18th century building of the Maison du Vin de Bordeaux, the headquarters of the Bordeaux Wine Council (the CIVB representing wine winegrowers, merchants and brokers).

This is a nice contemporary environment to enjoy a glass of wine with light bites. Updated frequently and always 30 wines by the glass, the intent is to show the diversity of Bordeaux wines: reds, clairets, dry and sweet whites, rosés, and sparklings. The wines are served by sommeliers in quality crystal stemware complete with the wine's information sheet. A place to come back to often.

BORDEAUX CITY CENTER (Central)
Cave À Vins (Wine Merchants)

Each of the four caves (wine merchants) I introduce to you here are all within two blocks to the north of the **Grand Théâtre**. These caves are what I call serious merchants of wine. They each have their own twists and very different inventories. With these four caves you should be able to find everything you need. And do some tasting too!

L'INTENDANT
2 Allées de Tourny, 33000 Bordeaux, France
+33 (0)5 56 48 01 29 • Contact@Intendant.com
Open: Monday-Saturday, 10:00am-7:30pm

Intendant.com

L'Intendant has a unique way of displaying its 15,000 exclusively Bordeaux wines: along the walls of a circular five-level stairway tower 12 meters high (photos left and below). They also sell by mail order from their multi-million bottles offsite wine cellar.

BORDEAUX MAGNUM
3 Rue Gobineau, 33000 Bordeaux, France
+33 (0)5 56 52 12 86 • Magasin@Bordeaux-Magnum.fr
Open: Monday-Saturday, 10:00am-7:30pm

Bordeaux-Magnum.fr

Bordeaux Magnum has 1,500 wines from Bordeaux as well as from most of the French wine regions. I found the staff to be very knowledgeable and offering good prices. They invite a Grand Cru Classé château to do a tasting each month.

LA VINOTHÈQUE DE BORDEAUX
8 Cours du 30 Juillet, 33000 Bordeaux, France
+33 (0)5 56 52 32 05 • Noemie@La-Vinotheque.com
Monday-Saturday 10am-7:30pm, Sunday 11am-7:30pm

La-Vinotheque.com

Two connecting retail spaces make up this large cave. It is very well organized by regions and appellations: 40 Bordeaux appellations, 50 Burgundy, 27 Champagnes, and 28 others in France. And 18 other countries. Prices range from $10 to over $10,000.

BORDEAUX CITY CENTER (Central)
Wine Educator
JEAN-MARC QUARIN

10 Allé de Ginouilhac • 33320 Le Taillan Médoc, Bordeaux, France
+33 (0)9 51 06 75 42 • JMQuarin@Quarin.com
Available as a conference speaker; and half/full day wine educational trips

Quarin.com

It all started at a fancy party thrown by Bernard Arnault (LVMH) at his Chateau d'Yquem estate in Sauternes. So much great wine was served. A notable vintage of a Grand Cru Classé of 1855 was being poured when Jean-Marc Quarin (seated next to me) made a controversial comment about a well-known wine critic's "big mistake" rating this wine. I was intrigued with this outspoken man. Come to find out he has tasted and profiled over 35,000 wines in Bordeaux. He has strong opinions and his credentials reinforce such. Plus, we are both authors (Jean-Marc's book: *Guide Quarin, The Wines of Bordeaux*).

Jean-Marc grew up in a winemaking family. He harvested his first grapes as a teenager and his family endlessly exposed him to different wines, training his palate. When he took a course at the University of Bordeaux to learn about taste defects in wine, he knew he had a talent for tasting, and went on to obtain a degree in Wine Tasting with distinction from the Faculty of Oenology.

On my next rip to Bordeaux, I met Jean-Marc at a Grand Cru Classé in Pauillac where he arranged a private room to taste a dozen or so wines. Complete with a whiteboard, he started by saying we were forbidden to smell any of the wines that day. Aromas were not to get in the way of his course to enhance our palate's understanding of the quality of the wine by how it evolves in our mouths. He has a specific way to taste the tannins in the wines, young or old, and we did both. We observed when the tannins would start, peak and fall off in our mouths. This exercise was eye-opening and it led to some great intellectual conversations. I know a lot about wine and this greatly added to my wine knowledge and tasting skills. Jean-Marc has a lot to offer in navigating the wines of Bordeaux.

Jean-Marc prefers to spend a day with you (or half day), arranging and taking you to a few wineries to introduce you to some great wines and teach you how to distinguish their quality and how to best find and enjoy wines you like.

BORDEAUX CITY CENTER (Central)
Wine School
L'ÉCOLE DU VIN DE BORDEAUX

3 Cours du 30 Juillet, 33000 Bordeaux, France
+33 (0)5 56 00 22 85 • Ecole@Vins-Bordeaux.fr
Open: Monday-Saturday, 10:00am-10:00pm

EcoleDuVinDeBordeaux.com

Located on the 2nd floor of the **Maison du Vin** and **Bordeaux Wine Council** building, L'Ecole du Vin is a unique opportunity to learn the basics or advance your knowledge of Bordeaux, its wines and its châteaux. It is really helpful to attend a course upon arriving in Bordeaux. This is great preparation for exploring the wine regions with knowledge and skill. It will a make a difference.

L'Ecole du Vin was started 30 years ago (1989) by the winemakers and négociants of Bordeaux to introduce a fun approach for novices to understand wine, and more specialized and in-depth studies for professionals. These are hands-on workshops with wines, activities and lessons.

• **Wine Essentials**. Understand Bordeaux, the art of wine tasting, terroirs and varietals, appellation features, winemaking techniques, sustainable developments, etc.
• **Immersive Activities**. Food and wine pairings, lunches, comparative tastings, red and white blendings, blind tastings, olfactory profiles, wine and chocolate pairings, role playing, etc.
• **Professional Expertise**. Food and wine pairings, wine fairs, wine by the glass, wine lists, sales, trends, etc.

In 2019 L'Ecole du Vin started online wine studies with workshops run by instructors worldwide. Very soon they will be introducing live video courses online. Now you can take classes prior to arriving in Bordeaux. Check out their catalog and register for courses on their website.

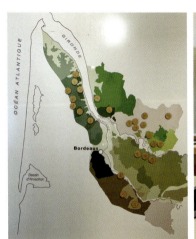

BORDEAUX CITY CENTER (Central)
SHOPPING AREAS OF BORDEAUX

Shopping in Bordeaux is special. Excellent shops. Many local French brands that you will love. And big fancy brands too. What makes shopping here so good is that the stores are concentrated primarily in a small area.

From the main road in front of the **Grand Théâtre** heading west, you will find shop after shop, big and small, galleries with specialty shops (photo left), and big luxury brands like Louis Vuitton (photo below left). This is a clean spacious street with the tram running through it.

From the **Grand Théâtre** heading south takes you onto Rue Sainte-Catherine, the longest pedestrian street in Europe (1.2 km, 3/4 mile). This is the main shopping street in Bordeaux and ends at the **Place de la Victoire**. Chain stores, both American and European, plus individual brands and small specialty shops, are all on this street (photo below).

From the **Grand Théâtre** heading south on Rue Sainte-Catherine to the first cross street. Turn east and you are on Rue Saint-Rémi, a street lined with restaurants. Turn west and you are on Rue de La Porte Dijeaux with endless shops. Galerie Bordelaise and Galeries Lafayette (France's largest department store) are at this intersection. I found so many good stores in this area. Great quality and the prices are much better than what you would expect and definitely better than prices of French brands in the U.S.

Bordeaux Wine Festival and Tall Ships Regatta

BORDEAUX CITY CENTER (Central)
Garonne River Cruises
BORDEAUX RIVER CRUISE

19 Rue Esprit des Lois, 33000 Bordeaux, France
+33 (0)5 56 39 27 66 • Contact@Bordeaux-River-Cruise.com

Bordeaux-River-Cruise.com
(Reservations available on their website)

With nice boats on the river (photo below), the Bordeaux River Cruise offers excellent options.
- **Wine Tasting Cruise.** Their wine tasting cruise takes you on the rivers to the famous appellations: Médoc, Saint-Émilion, Graves and Sauternes.
- **Lunch or Dinner Cruise.** Delicious meals are served while you cruise the Garonne River and enjoy amazing sites from a different perspective.
- **Estuary Island Cruise.** Cruise the Gironde archipelago visiting Margaux Island, a traditional wine growing estate, Patiras Island for lunch and views from the top of a lighthouse, and see the Fortifications of Vauban, one of the fortified buildings that formed a defensive ring around France.

BORDEAUX CITY CENTER
ANNUAL EVENTS

Bordeaux has numerous events throughout the year, many of which are directly related to wine. Here, I have included events that are annual and should be available any year you visit. Many concerts as well if you are so inclined.

January - **Bordeaux Rock** - Four days of 80s rock concerts and festival with international musicians, since 2005. BordeauxRock.com

March/April - **Primeur** - 5,000 wine professionals from all over the world sample the previous year's vintage from the barrel and reserve these wines at preferential prices. UGCB.net/en/professionals

April - **International Wine Challenge** - The largest and oldest wine competition in France with more than 5,000 wines from 38 countries tasted over two days in Bordeaux. ChallengeDuVin.com

May/June - **Vinexpo** - Held every odd year. Historically, a huge four-day display and tasting of over 500 exhibitors from 20 plus countries presenting their wines to 11,000 visitors from 50 countries. VinexpoBordeaux.com

June - **Bordeaux Wine Festival** - Europe's largest wine festival celebrating the **Tall Ships Regatta** race (from Liverpool to Dublin to Bordeaux) of the world's largest and most eye-catching sailboats on the quays of Garonne River. **Union des Grands Crus** also organizes over 120 Grand Crus for tasting followed by a Dragon Fireworks display on and over the Garonne River. Bordeaux-Wine-Festival.com

September - **Médoc Marathon** - 4,000 people dress up in the annual theme to take part in a race or a walk from château to château with tastings and music at each stop, followed by dinner, entertainment and fireworks. MarathonDuMedoc.com

December - **Bordeaux Tasting** - A festival of 7,000 people over two days of tasting the great wines of Bordeaux with workshops, panel discussions, music, food, and a big party at the Palais de la Bourse. TerreDeVins.com

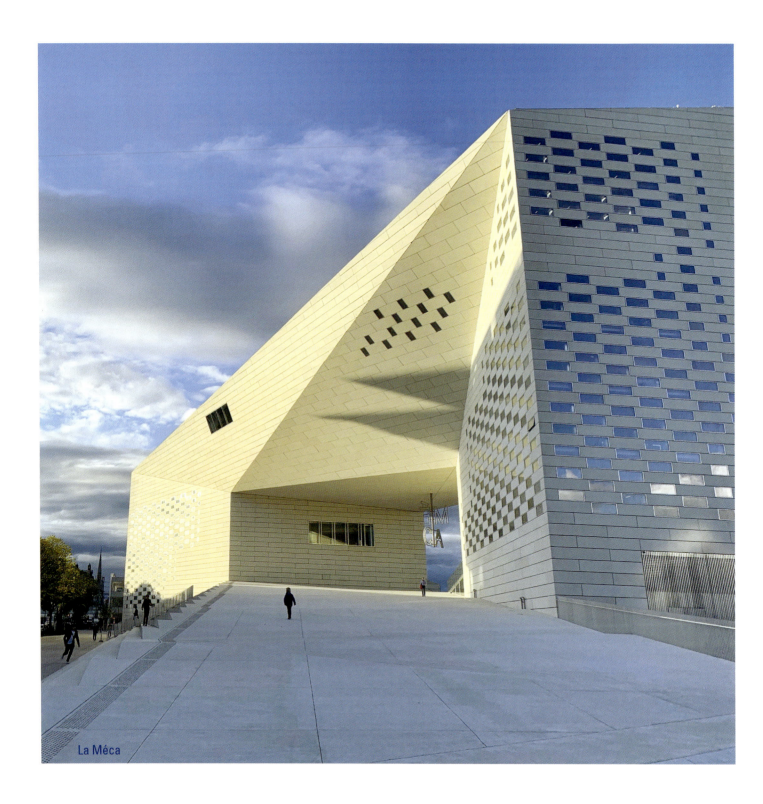
La Méca

BORDEAUX CITY CENTER (South)
Museum
LA MÉCA

Parvis Corto Maltese, Quai de Paludate, Bordeaux
+33 (0)5 47 30 34 67 • Contact@La-Meca.com
Open: Tuesday-Saturday, 1:00pm-6:30pm
Every 1st Sunday and 3rd Thursdays, Until 9:00pm

La-Meca.com

La MÉCA moved and built this new artistic building (left page) as innovative as the art inside. La MÉCA is an incubator for emerging artists. They find unique talent and display their work. They create projects for them to work on and then showcase their works within the museum walls. And further, they fund these artists to help jumpstart their careers.

Everything here is a collection of contemporary art in movement. A laboratory of local artists of the Aquitaine. The work here is progressive. Innovative. An interesting afternoon. I promise.

BORDEAUX CITY CENTER (South)
Group of Restaurants
LA BOCA FOODCOURT

Euratlantique, Quai de Paludate, Bordeaux
Open: Monday-Saturday, 10:00am-Midnight
Sunday, 10:00am-11:00pm

LaBocaFoodCourt.eu

This is an exciting hall of food purveyors. All 13 restaurateurs are local and independent operators. The quality of food is fresh and creative, and the cuisine varies with each restaurant. There is French, Italian, Thai, Japanese, Spanish, seafood, meat bar and burgers, Asian fusion, rotisserie, and pastries.

In the center of the hall are long tables for family-style dining. The concept is for everyone to talk about what they are eating. In the very center is a four-sided cocktail bar. Plus a wall of eight micro-beers on tap. Of course, great wine, as this is Bordeaux!

BORDEAUX CITY CENTER (South)
Hôtel & Restaurant
HILTON GARDEN INN

17 Allée de Rio, Quai de Paludate,
33800 Bordeaux, France
+33 (0)5 64 37 15 10

NaosHotelBordeauxCentre.com

In this south area of Bordeaux, there are extensive new developments (I counted 25 cranes), including this brand new Hilton with all the amenities, designs and cleanliness of new hotel. The hotel is on the Garonne River and only a 10-minute walk to the Bordeaux Saint-Jean train station.

Next to the Hilton is the La Boca FoodCourt and next to La Boca is La MÉCA museum. Across the street is a well-established center of night clubs. This is the new place to be! This is a neighborhood of a different ambiance and offers entertainment unique to those in historic downtown Bordeaux.

BORDEAUX **CITY CENTER** (North)
Modern Hôtel
SEEKO'O HÔTEL DESIGN

54 Quai de Bacalan
33000 Bordeaux, France

+33 (0)5 56 39 07 07
Contact@Seekoo-Hotel.com

Seekoo-Hotel.com

English, French

UNIQUE DESIGNER HOTEL

It took Seeko'o Hôtel some time to get design approval from the city in this very historic town. The new modern residential high-rises nearby helped pave the way to approve this super cool contemporary building with exciting modernist design, inside and out. Adding the word "design" to their name is a spot-on message.

Located on the north side of town, almost in front of a tram stop, Seeko'o Hôtel puts you one tram stop away from La Cité du Vin, Les Halles Foodcourt and Musée Mer Marine. Two tram stops away to El Nacional, Sister café and the spectacular Saint-Louis Church. And a 10-minute tram ride south to the center of Bordeaux.

The service here is extra-attentive. They will even email you ahead of your trip to help with transportation and other arrival needs. Comes with a nice breakfast too.

This brand new hotel is of ultra-designer ambiance with cool sleek contemporary applications throughout the new building.

BORDEAUX **CITY CENTER** (North)
Argentine Restaurant
EL NACIONAL

23 Bis Rue Rode, 33000 Bordeaux, France
+33 (0)5 56 79 22 76 • Info@ElNacional.fr
Monday-Saturday: 12:00pm-2:00pm, 7:30pm11:00pm,

ElNacional.fr
(Reservations by email or phone)

This is the authentic El Nacional restaurant from Buenos Aires, Argentina. They only have one other restaurant and here it is in Bordeaux. I am a huge fan of Argentine Asado, meats cooked over wood, now in France. Do you have a copy of my book: *Exploring Wine Regions - Argentina*? I point you to the best of the best Asado. Plus, I detail how to make Asado yourself in the back of the book. You can take a break from the delicious Bordeaux wines here and drink some luscious Argentine Malbec.

BORDEAUX **CITY CENTER** (North)
Breakfast Café
SISTER

11 Place du Marché Chartrons, Bordeaux
+33 (0)5 56 52 74 90
Open: Monday-Saturday, 8:00am-6:30pm

This was a random find. It looked like a cute little café to satisfy our craving for a coffee and croissant. I ended up getting a very delicious café latté and some other fresh baked treats. This was an excellent find and a special treat.

BORDEAUX **CITY CENTER** (North)
Upscale Foodhall of Restaurants
LES HALLES DE BACALAN

10 Esplanade de Pontac, Bordeaux
+33 (0)5 59 58 11 67 • Contact@Biltoki.com
Tuesday-Wednesday: 8:00am-2.30pm, 4:30pm-8.30pm
Thursday: 8:00am-2.30pm, 4:30pm-10.30pm
Friday-Saturday: 8:00am-10:30pm, Sunday: Until 5:00pm

Biltoki.com/hallesbacalan

Located across the street from **La Cité du Vin**, this is a place that has taken the concept of food halls to a whole new level of excellence. The hours above are serious. I was able to find just one vendor that would feed us at 2:28pm. Black Duck, we love you! Check out their food. Gourmet sliders: duck, pork, chicken, and salmon with crazy delicious sauces. The duck was my favorite. Out-of-this-world yummy! The quality here is so good that there is even a Michelin and a Maison Lascombes restaurant in the food hall.

BORDEAUX CITY CENTER (North)
7th Floor Restaurant
LE 7 RESTAURANT

4 Esplanade de Pontac
33000 Bordeaux, France

+33 (0)5 56 39 07 07
Contact@Seekoo-Hotel.com
Open: Everyday, 10:00am-11:00pm

Le7Restaurant.com
(Reservations available through their website)

English, French

7th floor atop La Cité du Vin, Le 7 is a restaurant as unique and creative as the museum.

7TH FLOOR VIEW OF BORDEAUX

Le 7 doesn't just have great food – the view here is spectacular. From the 7th floor, you can see Bordeaux, its towering monuments and the Garonne River (photo top right).

The cuisine here is very creative. Just like the concepts of the museum. This is another restaurant designed and operated by Nicolas Lascombes (page 480). He did it again. Excellent!

As wine is the theme here, Le 7 has 500 different wines from 50 countries, and 32 wines by the glass.

This building offers the perfect pairing: food and museum. And wine too of course, in both venues. You can spend an endless amount of time experiencing La Cité du Vin, so Le 7 offers the ideal break any time of day or evening.

BORDEAUX CITY CENTER (North)
Innovative Museum
LA CITÉ DU VIN

Esplanade de Pontac, 134 Quai de Bacalan
33000 Bordeaux, France

+33 (0)5 57 16 20 20
Contact@LaCiteDuVin.com
Open: Everyday, 10:00am-6:00pm, Weekends 7:00pm

LaCiteDuVin.com

*English, French, Spanish, Italian,
German, Japanese, Chinese, Dutch*

MOST INNOVATIVE AND INTERACTIVE MUSEUM IMAGINABLE

La Cité du Vin is not really a museum. Yes, technically it is a museum by definition; however, this place is more about the present and future of wine. And it is hugely interactive! With headphones in eight languages.

There is a wine regions area (so appropriate for *Exploring Wine Regions*) with large interactive video displays arranged by country with notable winemakers from each region (example photo right) talking about the specific topics you select. The answer to your question will determine which winemaker responds.

Another area is filled with aromas bottled in glass jars for you to smell (photo below right). Other aromas are secret and you guess the scent. What is interesting is that more than one answer can be correct. For example, banana and raspberry have the same chemical structures. The answer you pick is more about your familiarity and experience with the scent. Interesting, isn't it?

In another area, you sit down at a dining table and speak with holographic people who discuss their wine knowledge with you.

Yes, there is a history section. And a library, which has the *Exploring Wine Regions-Argentina* and *Bordeaux* books on its shelves. And so many other reference materials on the subject of wine.

This place is extremely interesting with so much to learn. You could spend a day here; however, you will want to come back. I have been there three times and I still have more to learn.

■ BORDEAUX **CITY CENTER** (North)
Hôtel Castle & Restaurant
LA GRANDE MAISON

10 Rue Labottière
33000 Bordeaux, France

+33 (0)5 56 38 16 16
Reservation@LGMBordeaux.com

LaGrandeMaison-Bordeaux.com

English, French, Russian, Spanish, Portuguese

Located in the northeast area of Bordeaux about ten minutes by car to the city center of Bordeaux. Across the street is the Cultural Institute of Bernard Margrez.

A place of charm and elegance with the extra-attentive five-star service.

SIMPLY ELEGANT

This is an excellent address in Bordeaux. This elegant 19th century castle was renovated by Bernard Magrez in 2014 into an impressive home for his guests. There are six stunning guest rooms decorated in an extravagant Napoléon style: pink, green, flowery violet and striking red rooms (photos below).

Everything about this property is highly refined. The elegance is everywhere. Their staff is beautifully mindful and thoughtful, always at your service.

They offer a grand food experience, a Pierre Gagnaire Restaurant, which received two Michelin stars in its first year. Imagine this, Magrez has the wines from all the Crus Classés of Bordeaux: 259 references including 172 Grands Crus Classés.

So now you have been invited to live an exceptional experience in this magnificent residence where French savoir-faire and refinement are king.

EXPOSING THE BEAUTY OF STREET ART

Across the street from La Grande Maison, Bernard Magrez has transformed a castle into a cultural center with contemporary art, events, creative workshops, and classical music performances.

The ambition here is driven by Magrez's desire to share his love for art. He created an endowment to fund this private initiative of artistic patronage. It has become the number one cultural center for street art. You never knew how good street art could be until you visit here.

The Institute intends to be the bridge between the traditional and the unconventional, a platform of cultural exchanges and experiences.

The Institute hosts two major exhibitions a year, plus highly eclectic programs led by researchers, intellectuals and lecturers with the aim of encouraging interaction between artists and the general public. The Institute also houses an artists' residence and studios to support new artists.

BORDEAUX CITY CENTER (North)
Museum & Art Gallery
CULTURAL INSTITUTE OF BERNARD MAGREZ

Château Labottière
16 Rue de Tivoli,
33000 Bordeaux, France

+33 (0)5 56 81 72 77
Contact@Institut-Bernard-Magrez.com
Open: Friday-Sunday, 1:00pm-6:00pm

Institut-Bernard-Magrez.com

English, French, Chinese

BORDEAUX · MÉDOC (Left Bank)
Where Cabernet Sauvignon is King

In the vineyards of Saint-Julien with Pauillac in the distance.

T he magic of Cabernet Sauvignon comes alive here in the Médoc. Through centuries of tradition, passionate land caretakers, terroir of heavy gravel and sand, and notable winemakers mastering their blends... Bordeaux's Médoc has brought forth some of the finest, most powerful and complex wines the world has ever seen.

THE MÉDOC

Let's begin this journey through the Bordeaux wine regions by entering the Médoc first. Located just north of the city of Bordeaux, the closest point is only a 15-minute drive. The Médoc spans 60 kilometers (37 miles) of wine regions along the Left Bank of the Gironde Estuary, fed by the Garonne and Dordogne Rivers. It is arguably the most well known of the Bordeaux wine regions as a result of Napoléon's bestowment of the "first-growths" in 1855, and their subsequent high-profile wines. Here we find the notable Château Margaux, Château Lafite Rothschild, Château Latour, Château Haut-Brion, and Château Mouton Rothschild, among the many other high-profile Grand Cru Classés of 1855.

The reason Cabernet Sauvignon is "king" here is because the soil composition is ideal for this grape variety. Gravel, from small pebbles to large stones, embraces the topsoil here. During the day, these stones reflect the sun back onto the vines, giving them added sun for growth. Think of it like being in a pool and getting extra tanning. You get the sun directly plus you receive the reflection off the water, absorbed by your skin at a much quicker pace. This is the same for the vines.

Cabernet Sauvignon needs warmer temperatures and a longer growing cycle than most grapes. The stones offer this through the benefits of reflection, as well as by absorbing the heat of the day and then releasing the warmth back into the vines in the evening, extending the day's warmth. The soil is a mix of gravel and sand. Sand also provides excellent water drainage ideal for Cabernet Sauvignon.

Conversely, clay soil, more consistent with the Right Bank, keeps temperatures cool and moist, more conducive to Merlot vines. Pockets of clay can be found in the Médoc and the châteaux that are fortunate to have some take full advantage of this soil to produce better Merlot grapes for their blends.

This makes Cabernet Sauvignon the primary grape used on the Left Bank, while Merlot generally takes a second seat in the blend. The third Bordeaux varietal most commonly used in Médoc blends is Cabernet Franc, followed by Petit Verdot. Once in a while you will find Malbec or Carménère in the blends.

Petit Verdot

CRU BOURGEOIS A STRICT STANDARD OF QUALITY

The Cru Bourgeois de Médoc are châteaux exclusively located in the Médoc, that have met strict standards of production and excelled in blind tastings. Some châteaux were left out of the 1855 classification and others were not even born yet when Napoléon made the classification official. Cru Bourgeois became their opportunity to have their high-quality wines officiated.

Cru Bourgeois is not a one-time classification from 150 years ago. Each château that wants to be classified must submit to the process and be approved annually. In 1932, when the first Cru Bourgeois list was drawn up, the Bordeaux Chamber of Commerce and Chamber of Agriculture selected 444 estates for the classification. In 1962, a union of the Crus Bourgeois was created to support the interests of the Crus Bourgeois winemakers.

Then finally, in 2003, the government approved the first official classification of the Crus Bourgeois du Médoc which recognized 247 châteaux out of 490 candidates. The classification was established by a jury of 18 professionals who judged the wines based on nine criteria: the terroir, grape variety, approach taken in the vineyard, winemaking, management and presentation of the property, bottling conditions, consistency in quality, organoleptic qualities of the wine, and their wine's reputation. Through the years, the Cru Bourgeois has evolved in many directions. Today, they have developed the most sophisticated, effective and fair way to classify and present the excellence of Cru Bourgeois wines.

T he Cru Bourgeois alliance continues to evolve into a commanding organization that assures quality wines at excellent prices.

The future of Cru Bourgeois is very exciting. New higher standards were adopted for the years 2020 forward. Chateaux are graded in three hierarchical levels: *Cru Bourgeois, Cru Bourgeois Supérieur,* and *Cru Bourgeois Exceptionnel*. Each and every bottle is certified and marked with an unremovable authentication sticker (photo upper left).

Any Médoc château can apply and each applicant is assessed and given a score by a jury of independent professionals (of no association with the châteaux or Cru Bourgeois staff, including family members). All wine professionals, all independent! Rigorous blind tastings and site visits to verify high production standards, all conducted by the independent jury.

Plus, the Cru Bourgeois châteaux maintain their great prices during excellent vintages so we benefit from stable prices.

The **Cru Bourgeois Cup** is a competition among Cru Bourgeois wines to be the best of the best with a winner and 11 laureates chosen from a blind tasting. Yours truly was honored to be one of the Cup judges (photo left).

THE GRAND CRU CLASSÉS OF 1855

The Grand Cru Classés of 1855 are those red wine châteaux, exclusively in the Médoc (except Haut-Brion in Pessac), that were bestowed the best wines in the world by Napoléon III in 1855. Each of the châteaux were ranked first though fifth-growths. There are only five (of 61 châteaux) that are first-growths, known as the Premier Crus. They are the big famous names of Château Haut-Brion, Château Lafite Rothschild, Château Latour, Château Margaux, Château Mouton Rothschild (originally second-growth until 1973 when elevated to first-growth as the only major change occurring in 150 years). And other notable growths (second to fifth) are Château Cos d'Estournel, Château Pichon Baron and Château Lynch-Bages.

Only two of the five first-growths are open to the public, Château Margaux and Château Mouton Rothschild, both reviewed in this book on pages 81 and 163, respectively. There are several second through fifth-growths open to the public, which I have found and reviewed for you in this Médoc section.

The Grand Cru Classés of 1855 also include sweet wines exclusively from Sauternes and Barsac (located at the southern tip of Graves). This is where a very special and unique terroir of Noble Rot produces golden sweet wines. See the Sauternes chapter starting on page 274. There are a total of 27 châteaux here, with only first and second-growths, and one Superior First-Growth, Château d'Yquem.

Cultivating Château Latour vineyards with horses

T he Grand Cru Classés of 1855 châteaux are still today, 150 years later, some of the most sought-after, most-expensive wines in the world.

What is the backstory of how these châteaux became classified? In 1855, it was time for the Worlds Fair to be held in Paris France. Emperor Napoléon III wanted to make his fair, *1855 Exposition Universelle de Paris*, an expression of France's best commerce, and surpass *London's Great Exhibition of 1851*.

Napoléon ordered an official classification of Bordeaux wines through the Gironde Chamber of Commerce and the Wine Brokers Union of Bordeaux. These brokers ranked the wines according to the château's reputation and the wine's selling price, which was considered directly related to quality. This ranking then became the official classification of Grand Cru Classés of 1855 which has stood proud ever since.

In this book, I review and present to you 19 of these Grand Cru Classés châteaux, in all five growth categories, and in all four of the communal waterfront sub-appellations of the Médoc. I also include 11 of the Sauternes and Barsac châteaux. All 30 of these châteaux are open to visitors with varying tourism experiences which I outline for you.

TABLE OF WINES AND TOURISM

CHÂTEAUX	Classified	Number of Wines	Red Wine	White Wine	Rosé Wine	Sweet Wine	Wine Shop	Boutique	Accommodations	Restaurant	Food Options	Food & Wine Pairings	Tours	Castle Tours	Workshops	Activities	No Reservation Necessary	Tourism Award	Innovations
Haut-Médoc AOC																			
Château d'Agassac	CB	6	√	√			√	√		√	√		6	√	√	√	√	√	
Château du Taillan	CB	3	√	√	√		√	√		√			9	√	√		√	√	
Château Lamothe Bergeron	CB	2	√				√	√			√		5	√				√	√
Château Larose Trintaudon	CB	4	√				√	√					3	√				√	
Château Paloumey	CB	3	√					√			√		12	√	√			√	
Château Saint Ahon	CB	3	√		√		√		√				3	√	√			√	
Margaux AOC																			
Château Deyrem Valentin	CB	3	√				√						1						
Château du Tertre	GCC	2	√				√			√	√		3					√	
Château Giscours	GCC	4	√	√			√			√	√		4	√	√			√	
Château Lascombes	GCC	3	√				√	√					2				√	√	
Château Margaux	GCC	4	√	√									1						
Château Marquis d'Alesme	GCC	2	√				√	√			√	√	6	√	√		√		√
Château Marquis de Terme	GCC	3	√		√		√			√	√		2		√			√	
Château Paveil de Luze	GCC	3	√	√			√		√		√		2	√				√	
Château Prieuré-Lichine	GCC	4	√	√			√	√			√	√	5	√				√	
Moulis-en-Médoc AOC and Listrac-Médoc AOC																			
Château Baudan	CB	3	√		√		√						1						
Château Brillette	CB	4	√				√						1						
Château Cap Léon Veyrin	CB	3	√				√			√	√		1						
Château Moulin-à-Vent	CB	2	√				√						1						
Château Reverdi	CB	2	√				√						1				√		
Saint-Julien																			
Château Beychevelle	GCC	3	√				√			√	√		3	√					
Château Gruaud Larose	GCC	2	√				√				√		6	√	√			√	
Château Lagrange	GCC	4	√	√			√	√		√	√		3	√				√	
Château Léoville Poyferré	GCC	3	√				√	√					4						

TABLE OF WINES AND TOURISM

CHÂTEAUX Pauillac AOC	Classified	Number of Wines	Red Wine	White Wine	Rosé Wine	Sweet Wine	Wine Shop	Boutique	Accommodations	Restaurant	Food Options	Food & Wine Pairings	Tours	Castle Tours	Workshops	Activities	No Reservation Necessary	Tourism Award	Innovations
Château Batailley	GCC	2	√	√			√						1						
Château Bellevue-Cardon	n/a	1	√										0						
Château Lynch-Bages	GCC	3	√	√			√						1					√	√
Château Lynch-Moussas	GCC	2	√	√			√						1						
Château Mouton Rothschild	GCC	3	√	√			√						1	√					
Château Pédesclaux	GCC	3	√				√						1	√				√	√
Château Pichon Baron	GCC	3	√				√						1					√	

CHÂTEAUX Saint-Estèphe AOC																			
Château La Haye	CB	5	√		√		√						1	√					
Château Lafon Roche	GCC	2	√				√						1				√		
Château Le Crock	CB	2	√				√						5		√	√			
Château Ormes de Pez	CB	1	√				√		√				1		√	√			

CHÂTEAUX Médoc AOC																			
Château Castera	CB	1	√				√	√					3	√	√			√	√
Château Loudenne	CB	1	√	√			√						3	√	√		√		
Château Saint-Christoly	CB	1	√				√						1		√	√			
Château Tour Castillon	CB	1	√		√		√						6		√	√			

CB = Cru Bourgeois
GCC = Grand Cru Classés of 1855

Château La Tour Carnet,
a Bernard Magrez property in the Haut-Médoc

BORDEAUX · MÉDOC APPELLATIONS

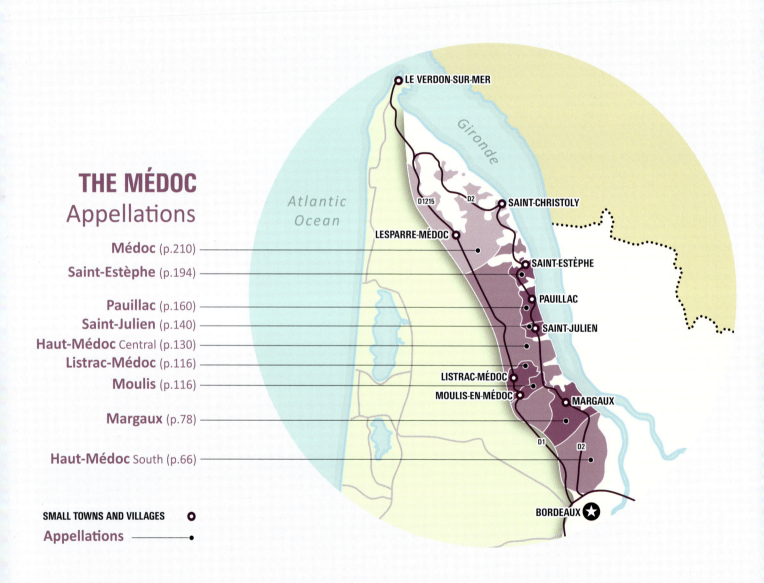

THE MÉDOC
Appellations

- Médoc (p.210)
- Saint-Estèphe (p.194)
- Pauillac (p.160)
- Saint-Julien (p.140)
- Haut-Médoc Central (p.130)
- Listrac-Médoc (p.116)
- Moulis (p.116)
- Margaux (p.78)
- Haut-Médoc South (p.66)

SMALL TOWNS AND VILLAGES ○
Appellations ●

W andering through the Médoc wine regions is as relaxing as it is inspiring. Ancient towns. Spectacular castles. Modern wineries.

APPELLATIONS OF THE MÉDOC

One of the things I love about the Médoc is the huge properties with castles, or châteaux as they call them. Many of these castles were built on their massive properties to show off the wealth of the owners. Today, we get to enjoy their grandeur, tour many of them, and even stay the night in some of them. I point out which are which, and you definitely want to go see them!

The other castles here were built for defense. There have been many battles fought in the Médoc and real fortresses still exist here, including moats and other fighting features.

The Médoc is where all the red wine Grand Cru Classés of 1855 are located; except one, Château Haut-Brion, which is in Pessac. The only other place for Grand Cru Classés of 1855 is in Sauternes (page 274) for the golden sweet wines.

The Médoc is also where all the Cru Bourgeois wines are located, exclusively. In the pages ahead, I bring to you only Cru Bourgeois and Grand Cru Classé châteaux. And only those châteaux that are open for visitors, and especially those who put on excellent tourism experiences.

The entire Médoc appellation is known as the "Left Bank" and covers an area over 16,500 hectares (40,772 acres) that are actual AOCs authorized for producing Médoc identified wines. The map on the left identifies the Médoc wine region in the different shades of purple.

Within the larger Médoc appellation there are eight sub-appellations, which include a Médoc sub-appellation as well as an Haut-Médoc sub-appellation. I have separated the Haut-Médoc into south (very close to the city) and central (mid way up the Médoc) for easy reference. There are six communal appellations: Margaux, Moulis-en-Médoc, Listrac-Médoc, Saint-Julien, Pauillac, and Saint-Estèphe.

Since the Médoc is north of the city of Bordeaux, I present these appellations from south to north, as you would arrive and traverse the Médoc traveling from the city of Bordeaux.

There are two highways running north and south through the Médoc wine regions. D2 is the local route, through the little villages, running closely along the estuary. D1 is inland and is faster traveling, turning into the D1215, and advantageous for reaching the farther appellations quicker. They are both marked on the map to the left.

Below are the distances and times (without traffic) to reach each appellation from the Bordeaux city perimeter.

Driving on the D2...
- **Haut-Médoc** (South) 11km/7mi (14 minutes)
- **Margaux** 22km/14mi (26 minutes)
- **Haut-Médoc** (Central) 33km/14mi (40 minutes)
- **Saint-Julien** 36km/22mi (44 minutes)
- **Pauillac** 43km/27mi (51 minutes)
- **Saint-Estèphe** 50km/30mi (58 minutes)
- **Médoc** 60km/35mi (70 minutes)

Driving on the D1...
- **Moulis-en-Médoc** 24km/15mi (25 minutes)
- **Listrac-Médoc** 28km/17mi (29 minutes)
- **Saint-Estèphe** 48km/30mi (49 minutes)
- **Médoc** 54km/35mi (55 minutes)

BORDEAUX · MÉDOC HAUT-MÉDOC AOC (South)
Closest Médoc Wine Region to Bordeaux City

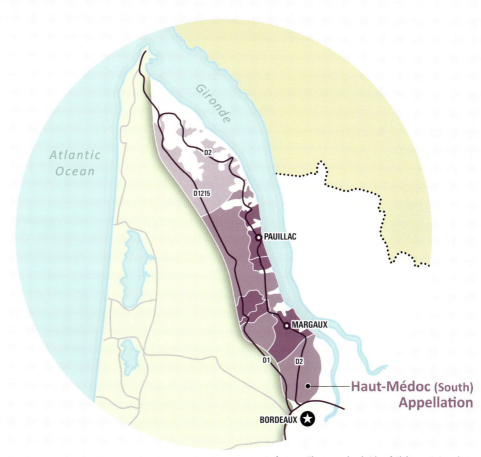

Left page: The moat backside of Château Saint Ahon

EASY DAY TRIPS FROM THE CITY

The Médoc has a sub-appellation called Haut-Médoc, the largest of all the sub-appellations. I was puzzled why "Haut" means "high" in French, and yet the top Médoc is at the bottom of the Médoc? Even locals did not have an answer. I realized it was not about north and south being top and bottom, it was upstream versus downstream. The upstream (upriver of the Gironde) is higher, meaning the Haut-Medoc. Voilà!

Being such a large area, I decided to separate the southernmost part of the Haut-Médoc, south of Margaux, as it has châteaux which are so close to the city of Bordeaux that they make for easy day trips. You can reach any of the châteaux here in less than a 30-minute drive from the city of Bordeaux.

Since the Haut-Médoc has only five of the 1855 classified châteaux (two are in this southern area), it has become the mecca of the greatest number of Cru Bourgeois châteaux. Many châteaux here are producing volume wines, so choosing Cru Bourgeois or Grand Cru Classé châteaux will keep you out of trouble. I am introducing you to four excellent Cru Bourgeois châteaux that not only have great wine, they also have great tourism experiences, including culinary opportunities.

Château d'Agassac has a gourmet restaurant in their castle, **Château Paloumey** has a wine and cheese rooftop, and **Château du Taillan** is an excellent picnic spot and can create a luxurious dinner. Here are the châteaux...

- Château d'Agassac, page 69 *(La table d'Agassac)*
- Château Paloumey, page 73
- Château du Taillan, page 75
- Château Saint Ahon, page 77

MÉDOC **HAUT-MÉDOC** (South)
Winery (Château) and Restaurant
CHÂTEAU D'AGASSAC

Quality Certification
Cru Bourgeois du Médoc
Winner: Best Of Wine Tourism

15 Rue du Château d'Agassac,
33290 Ludon-Médoc, France

+33 (0)5 57 88 15 47
Contact@Agassac.com

Agassac.com

English, French & Chinese

*Open: All Year, Everyday
In September, Monday-Saturday
Tours: Hourly, No Reservations Needed*

Knowing your terroir leads to excellence. Diversity of terroir creates unique wines.

THREE DISTINCT TERROIR WINES

This is a perfect château to obtain a greater understanding of the gravel and sandy soils of the Médoc. At Château d'Agassac, they have three different vineyards of three different soil compositions based on the density and size of stones. The smaller and fewer the stones, the lighter and fresher their wine. Their heaviest stone-concentrated soil, accompanied by much larger sized gravel, produces grapes of much deeper concentration and complexity. It is used for their top-level first label wine, which is quality certified by Cru Bourgeois through strict requirements and independent blind tastings.

Their location is ideal for a day trip from the city of Bordeaux, just a 15-minute drive. They have an entertaining and educational tour through their 43-hectare (106 acres) vineyards using an iPad to explain the terroir and how each is uniquely used to create three different wines. Plus, learn how they have been converting the vineyards into sustainable viticulture farming over the past 10 years.

In their barrel room, you can experience and learn from their many fishbowls (below) that express the various aromas found in the wines.

At the end of the tour, they have wine tastings in their ancient pigeon house where you will taste the differences in the wines from their vineyards. Afterwards, I highly suggest you plan to have lunch or dinner in their 13th century castle where you can enjoy more of their delicious wines, as well as others from around the world, paired with a gourmet meal in a beautiful ancient setting.

Collection of Wines
Château d'Agassac
(First Label - Cru Bourgeois)

Précision d'Agassac
L'Agassant d'Agassac
(Second Wines)

Château Pomiès-Agassac
Château Pomiès-Agassac Tête de Cuvée
La Rosé d'Agassac

MÉDOC HAUT-MÉDOC (South)
Winery (Château) Restaurant
LA TABLE D'AGASSAC

The Restaurant of Château d'Agassac

In Season: Lunch and Dinner Everyday
Except Sunday Evenings

Winner: Best Of Wine Tourism

15 Rue du Château d'Agassac,
33290 Ludon-Médoc, France

+33 (0)5 57 88 89 50
Contact@Agassac.com

Agassac.com

DINE IN A 13TH CENTURY CASTLE

The castle of Château d'Agassac was built in 1238 by Lord Gaillard d'Agassac to defend Bordeaux from the French while under British rule, complete with a moat surrounding the castle and a dovecote. The dovecote (pigeon house) whose size was proportionate to the owner's power and dates from this same period, was home to about 600 hundred pigeon couples. Château d'Agassac was an important fortress serving as the communication hub for the area with its pigeons.

Today, the castle of Château d'Agassac serves as a beautiful dining space for both lunch and dinner in an elegant historic setting. La Table d'Agassac is run by a sommelier passionate about creating an international food and wine experience. Wines from all over the world are offered by the glass and paired with gourmet delicacies newly inspired everyday.

The kitchen here can serve large events inside or outside on their expansive lawn in a wooded park setting. They have hosted many weddings, seminars and even concerts. They can accommodate up to 200 people for dinner in the castle, 2,000 people in the park and 277 people for a banquet in the cellar. Several other small rooms are also available.

MÉDOC **HAUT-MÉDOC** (South)
Winery (Château)
CHÂTEAU PALOUMEY

Quality Certification
Cru Bourgeois du Médoc
Winner: Best Of Wine Tourism

50 Rue Pouge de Beau
33290 Ludon-Médoc, France

+33 (0)5 57 88 00 66
Accueil@ChateauPaloumey.com

ChateauPaloumey.com

English, French

*Tours, Tastings & Workshops
Open: All Year, Monday-Friday
No Reservations Needed (except workshops)
April-October, Weekends By Appointment Only*

Educational tours and tastings, workshops in their vineyards, vatroom and cellars.

DO EVERYTHING. OR NOTHING.

There are so many different activities available (tours, tastings and workshops) that you can spend an entire day here and have so many interesting things to do. Or do nothing and sip wine on their rooftop patio overlooking the vineyards (photo left page). They are located just 15 minutes from the city of Bordeaux, making them ideal for a day trip.

Tours are interesting and educational. They take you on a walk through their vineyards and discuss the different terroir and how different grapes perform in different soils. Tours include tastings of their wines.

Tastings can go in many directions here depending on what you would like to experience. They own two other wineries, *Château La Garricq* and *Château La Bessane*, so a tasting across three wineries is interesting. They offer both vertical and horizontal tastings of Château Paloumey's three wines, with historical depth available. Or taste right out of the barrel of current aging wines.

Workshops are my favorite here...

• **Vineyard to Bottle Workshop.** This is an engaging experience to taste from the beginning, all the way through to the end, of the winemaking cycle. Start in the vineyard tasting the grapes, to the winery tasting from the vats, to the barrel room tasting wines as they are aging, and then for a tasting of the finished wines out the bottles.

• **Barrel Workshop.** Tour the property and then taste from the barrels to discover the influence brought on by different origins of oak.

• **Blending Workshop.** Blend your own wine.

• **Wine & Cheese Workshop.** Discover how traditional French cheese pairs with their wines.

• **Harvest Workshop.** Experience a hands-on harvest workshop in the vineyard, available at harvest time.

• **A La Carte, Customized Experiences.** Create your own customized experience from the many options you read about here.

• **Picnic & Rooftop Patio.** Enjoy fresh local foods, small bites, charcuterie and cheese platters prepared for a picnic in their park or rooftop patio.

Collection of Wines
Château Paloumey
(First Label - Cru Bourgeois)

Ailes de Paloumey
(Second Wine)

Plume de Paloumey
(Plot Specific Merlot & Cabernet)

MÉDOC **HAUT-MÉDOC** (South)

Winery (Château)
CHÂTEAU DU TAILLAN

Quality Certification
Cru Bourgeois du Médoc
Winner: Best Of Wine Tourism

56, Avenue de la Croix
33320 Taillan-Médoc, France

+33 (0)5 56 57 47 00
Info@ChateauDuTaillan.com

ChateauDuTaillan.com

English, French

*Open: All Year, Everyday
No Reservations Needed
Reservations Available On Their Website*

Hidden underground, secret cellars protected the wines from the German Nazi takeover of the property during World War II.

ANCIENT CELLARS

This property is filled with history. The château is a beautiful classic two-story building from the 18th century. The underground cellars, from the 16th century, are a magnificent piece of history (see the photographs to the left), which is now listed as a National Heritage Site of France.

The cellars are immense and meander deep underground. Fortunately, there were secret passageways that hid precious wines from the German Nazis who took over this château during World War II and drank all the wine they could find in these underground cellars. Tours take you through these secret passageways into the protected cellars where you will see older vintages dating back to the early 19th century.

With all this history and tradition, the fifth-generation sisters of this family have chosen a young cellar master to bring fresh and progressive ideas to their wines.

This is one of very few châteaux where you can count on to be open seven days a week, requiring no reservations, and located 15 minutes from Bordeaux city.

This property is perfect for buying a bottle of wine and sitting under their century-old trees in a beautiful park setting. They have delicious wines ideal for an afternoon outdoors. Stroll though the expansive property of vineyards and historic buildings. They can also host an intimate dinner in their château for up to 15 people, or 180 people in their winery.

Collection of Wines
Château du Taillan
(First Label - Cru Bourgeois)

La Dame Blanche
(White - Sauvignon Blanc)

Le Rosé du Taillan
(From a Blend of Red Grapes)

Wine in a Tube (100ml)
(Red, White and Rosé)

Les travaux vignerons
The Winegrowers' Working Cycle

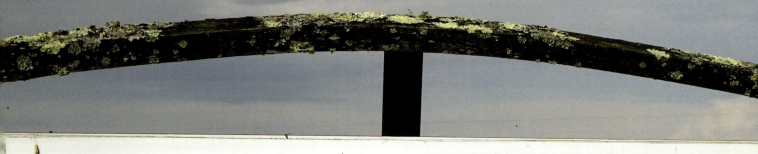

Septembre

Le château récolte l'essentiel du vignoble à l'aide d'une machine à vendanger. La machine enjambe le rang de vigne, le secoue avec ses bras «cueilleurs et secoueurs» et ramasse les baies de raisin qui tombent.

September: Most of the vine is harvested using a mechanical grape harvester. The harvester straddles a row of vine and shakes it with its "picker and shaker" arms and collects the fallen berries.

Octobre

Le Petit Verdot est vendangé à la main, compte tenu de sa fragilité. Les vendangeurs coupent les grappes de raisin entières à l'aide de sécateurs et les mettent dans un panier. Une fois le panier plein, le vendangeur le vide dans une hotte. Les vendanges continuent et durent environ 3 semaines.

October: The Petit Verdot grape is harvested manually because of its fragility. Grape-pickers cut off the whole grapes with clippers and place them in a basket on their back. Once the basket is full, they put the grapes in a bigger basket. The harvest continues and lasts about 3 weeks.

	Septembre 09	Octobre 10	Novembre 11	Décembre 12	Janvier 01	Février 02	Mars 03	Avril 04	Mai 05	Juin 06	Juillet 07	Août 08
	Vendanges / Harvest				Taille / Pruning					Epamprage		
					Pliage / Fastening					Levage / Tying-up		
			Epandage / Manuring	Broyage / Breaking			Travail du sol / Soil work				Effeuillage	Travail du sol / Soil work
			Sous-solage / Subsoil work						Sécaillage	Ecimage Rognage / Trimming Topping		
										Traitements / Treatments		

■ Travaux mécaniques Mechanical work
■ Travaux manuels Manual work
■ Travaux chimiques Chemical work

Novembre

La taille de la vigne commence dès la chute complète des feuilles et dure jusqu'en mars. Son but est de choisir les meilleurs rameaux pour limiter la quantité de raisins et ainsi en améliorer la qualité en concentrant les sucres dans un nombre limité de grappes.

November: Training the vine begins as soon as all leaves have fallen and lasts until March. It consists of selecting the best branches to yield fewer grapes of higher quality and higher grape sugar concentration.

Décembre

On épand de l'engrais et on réalise un travail du sol (sous-solage). Le sous-solage redonne de la perméabilité au sol en améliorant le drainage naturel. Il permet aussi de fragmenter les parties profondes du sol sans les ramener à la surface.

December: The fertilizer is spread and the land is tilled (subsoiled). Subsoiling restores soil permeability by improving natural drainage. It also helps to disintegrate the deeper parts of the soil without bringing them back to the surface.

Janvier

Le pliage et l'accanage consistent à lier les rameaux au fil de fer du palissage afin de diriger et orienter la pousse de la vigne.

January: Thinning and training of the vine consists of linking branches to the trellis wire to direct and guide the growth of the vine.

Février

Une fois la taille réalisée, il faut tirer les sarments et les broyer. Les bois broyés sont enfouis dans le sol apportant ainsi de l'humus.

February: Once the training of the vine is completed, the vine shoots are pulled and ground down. They are then buried into the soil, thus providing humus.

Mars

D'après le proverbe : « Taille tôt, taille tard rien ne vaut la taille de mars ».

March: The French have a proverb that is roughly translated as: "Prune early, prune late, nothing beats pruning in March".

Avril

Après la taille et avant que la vigne ne pousse, on réalise le sécaillage, c'est-à-dire remplacer les piquets et les fils de fer du palissage abîmés. Les plantations sont réalisées au mois d'avril.

April: After training the vine and before the grapes are cultivated, trellising must be carried out, whereby the damaged stakes and iron trellises are replaced. Plantation is carried out in April.

Mai

L'épamprage consiste à retirer les pampres, jeunes pousses situées au pied de la vigne. Cela permet d'orienter la vigueur de la vigne vers les rameaux choisis en hiver et non dans les pampres.

May: Suckering consists of removing the branches and young shoots at the base of the vine. This helps to direct the strength of the vine towards the chosen branches in the winter, and not those bearing the grapes.

Juin

Le relevage des fils permet une meilleure exposition des grappes au soleil des grappes. Il évite d'avoir une végétation désordonnée et facilite le passage aisé des tracteurs dans les rangs.

June: Lifting the training wires can provide better exposure of the grapes to the sun. It avoids having disorderly vegetation and helps to ease the passage for tractors.

Juillet

Les travaux en vert : rognage, écimage et effeuillage permettent une bonne aération de la vigne et un meilleur ensoleillement des raisins. Les années de fort rendement, on réalise l'éclaircissage ou vendanges vertes. Cela consiste à enlever certaines grappes pour favoriser la croissance des autres.

July: Green work: trimming, topping and removing leaves enables better aeration of the vine and the grapes have better exposure to the sun. Years that have produced a strong yield have usually been preceded by the thinning process or green harvesting. This involves removing some grape clusters to encourage the growth of others.

Août

Les traitements sont réalisés de mai à août pour prévenir la vigne des maladies (oïdium, mildiou, pourriture grise...).

August: Treatment is carried out from May to August in order to prevent infection of the vine (oïdium, mildew, grey mould...).

MÉDOC HAUT-MÉDOC (South)
Winery (Château)
CHÂTEAU SAINT AHON

Quality Certification
Cru Bourgeois du Médoc
Winner: Best Of Wine Tourism

57, Rue de Saint Ahon
33290 Blanquefort, France

+33 (0)5 56 35 06 45
Info@SaintAhon.com

SaintAhon.com

English, French

Open: All Year, Monday-Saturday
By Appointment Only

When donkeys flew and forests walked, grapes grew upon vines, and moments were born. The notion of wine is magical and ever evolving.

JARDINS DE MIRABEL

Something oddly special about that donkey poem, now twisted into a wine narrative. At Château Saint Ahon, Mirabel is their mascot donkey who accompanies you on a self-guided tour of their estate. Stroll freely along the dirt roads of their vineyards. Meander through their forest of tall dense trees and see the farm animals on this property, including Mirabel, who finds herself on the many signs throughout your journey. And go around the backside of the beautiful castle (pages 66-67) where the owners, Count and Countess Bernard de Colbert, reside. They are direct descendants of the famous King Louis XIV.

Jardins de Mirabel (Gardens of Mirabel) is an entertaining and educational journey through nature around this property. Signs are posted throughout your journey with Mirabel giving a quiz at each stopping point. Fun for the entire family, kids included.

The Jardins de Mirabel tour also has QR Codes provided so you can get further information on your smartphone. Innovations like this contributed to them being awarded the *Best Of Wine Tourism* award for *Discovery and Innovation*.

The terroir here is particularly good for Cabernet Sauvignon with gravel and sand soil (no clay). 60% of their vineyards are Cabernet Sauvignon. The balance is shared by Merlot, Cabernet Franc and Petit Verdot.

Befitting their natural environment and forest, it was only logical that they began sustainable farming in 2005 and received certification in 2013. In 2009, they became Cru Bourgeois certified, a quality standard they are very proud to achieve each year.

Although only a 20-minute drive from Bordeaux city, they have three rooms available on the property for overnight accommodations. The rooms are simple and very affordable. They have a nice gift shop as well.

Collection of Wines
Château Saint Ahon
(First Label - Cru Bourgeois)

Colbert Cannet
(Second Wine)

Mirabel
(Rosé)

BORDEAUX · MÉDOC MARGAUX AOC
Magical Margaux, A Soft Beautiful Appellation

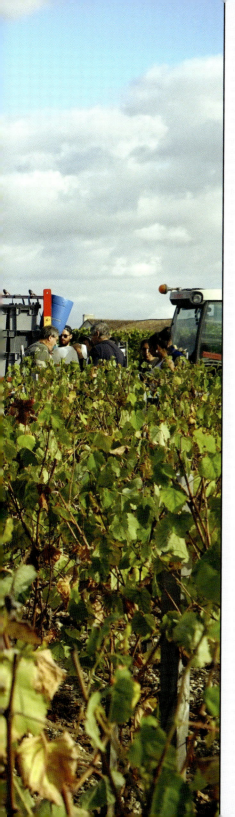

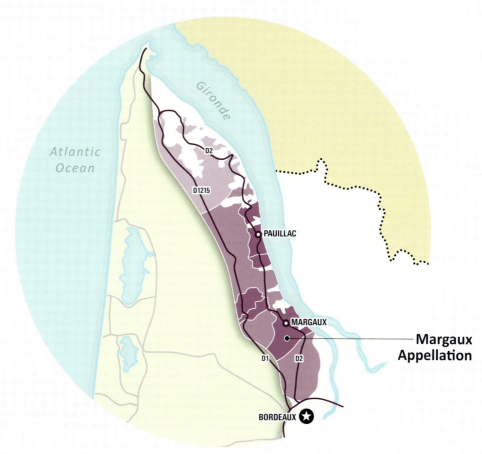

Margaux Appellation

Left page: Harvest at Château du Terte

SOFT FEMININE MARGAUX

In the land of big bold Cabernet Sauvignon of the masculine Médoc, Margaux is a unique sub-appellation with the bigness of everything we love about Cabernet Sauvignon, yet possessing a delicate softness that I can best call feminine. I find it enchanting. And the Château Margaux "magic" I tasted in their wine is real!

Looking back, the Margaux appellation was the first Bordeaux area cultivated for vineyards. There is evidence that the Romans planted grapes here 2,000 years ago. How did the Romans know of such superior land, of all the lands in the Médoc?

Margaux boasts the thinnest topsoil in the Médoc with the highest proportion of gravel that generates significant heat in the evenings and allows the soil to drain very well. Special terroir.

There are more classified growths in Margaux (21) than any other appellation. Encompassing several villages (Arsac, Cantenac, Labarde, Soussans, and Margaux) there is much charm to be found here, including numerous restaurants such as **Le Savoie** and **Restaurant Nomade**. Plus, some excellent caves (wine shops).
- Château Margaux, page 81
- Château Lascombes, page 87
- Château Marquis d'Alesme, page 89 *(in the village)*
- Château Giscours, page 93
- Château Prieuré-Lichine, page 95
- Château Marquis de Terme, page 99
- Château du Tertre, page 101
- Château Paveil de Luze, page 107
- Château Deyrem Valentin, page 111

MÉDOC **MARGAUX**
Winery (Château)
CHÂTEAU MARGAUX

Premier Cru (First-Growth)
Grand Cru Classé of 1855

33460 Margaux, France

+33 (0)5 57 88 83 83
Visite@Chateau-Margaux.com

Chateau-Margaux.com

English, French, Japanese, Mandarin

*Open: Monday-Friday, By Appointment Only
Reservations Available On Their Website
No Direct Sales of Wine*

P ractice makes, 850 years, perfect. Centuries. Generations. Evolution. Knowledge. Passion. Mastery might be lengthy, yet the magic is real.

MAGICAL FIRST-GROWTH WINE

The Margaux Magic. I am partial to the Margaux appellation and the magic of the appellation's name sake Château Margaux. There is something quite enchanting about this property when you taste how seriously luscious their wines are to drink. Yes, they are pricey, and I guess that's what you get when you're a first-growth Grand Cru château with a magical taste that is unforgettable and always leaves you longing for more.

So how did it all come about to be so good? Well, the Romans were the first to come here about 2,000 years ago and planted grape vines. The Romans loved their wine and were attracted to Margaux, resulting in the first appellation being planted in Bordeaux. Then in the 12th century, the Margaux estate became officially established as **La Mothe de Margaux** (the Margaux mound). The very best location was chosen, as this slight hill's elevation was perfect for fending off the French. Plus, its slopes created the drainage ever so important for making the highest quality wines. This location was the best for multiple reasons: a fortified castle was established on the hilltop known as La Mothe (from "motte," a small rise in the land), and vines were planted on the slopes with wine produced under the name of *Margou* through the 14th century.

Now add **850 years of practice** to this great location! That is a lot of vintages to constantly improve. Many passionate people contributed to the excellence of this estate along the way.

Collection of Wines
Grand Vin du Château Margaux
(First Label - Grand Cru)

Pavillon Rouge du Château Margaux
(Second Wine)

Margaux du Château Margaux
(Third Wine)

Pavillon Rouge Blanc
(White - Sauvignon Blanc)

And this long history is fascinating.

Product demand (the wine) was created by the King of England in the 12th century establishing the British term "Claret" as the table wine of England coming from Bordeaux. This was a huge benefit to Bordeaux during England's rule of this territory in France for 300 years (1152 to 1453). Once the British developed a taste for Bordeaux wines, the demand grew and wineries were quickly established in Margaux as well as the rest of the Médoc. Even after the French Revolution, the British still wanted their Bordeaux Claret. The industry was born and the growth continued beyond their 15th century loss of power.

Along came Pierre de Lestonnac in the 16th century, as the Lestonnac family now owned the estate. Pierre focused a decade (1572 to 1582) on completely restructuring the property as well as expanding the vineyards in anticipation of the continued demand for the Bordeaux Claret.

The Margaux lineage continued in the Lestonnac family though the women, eventually marrying into the Pontac family of Château Haut-Brion in 1654. This union became crucial 200 years later towards Château Margaux being included among the four first-growths of 1855.

By the end of the 17th century, the estate established its full size of 265 hectares (650 acres), a third devoted to vines (nearly identical to today's layout). At this time, châteaux were competing for quality reputations, and Château Margaux was born and revered as the epitome in the art of winemaking.

The 18th century then saw Claret develop from a pale watery drink that faded within a few years, to the dark complex wine being stored in cellars. This transformation was due to a man named Berlon who started an era of modern winemaking here at Château Margaux. He revolutionized the winemaking process through such techniques as banning harvest in the early mornings to avoid dew-covered grapes and the subsequent dilution of color and flavor. Berlon was the first to vinify red wine and white wine grapes separately. Imagine that! At the time, the red and white vines were co-planted in the same vineyard plots. He went on to identify the importance of unique soil qualities and differences in terroir found in the various parcels, as each imparted a significantly different characteristic.

During the 18th century, exciting things happened acknowledging the Château Margaux quality. In 1705, *The London Gazette* offered the first sale of leading Bordeaux wines which included 230 barrels of "Margoose." In 1771, Château Margaux became the first Bordeaux wine to be sold by Christie's (British auction house). In 1787, Thomas Jefferson, the United States ambassador to France (before becoming President) visited Bordeaux making notes that Château Margaux is one of the "four vineyards of first quality" and "there cannot be a better bottle of Bordeaux wine" than their 1784 vintage.

Then came the French Revolution, which brought much anguish and suffering to Château Margaux. The owner, Lord of Margaux Elie du Barry, was executed by guillotine and the estate seized by the state and sold at auction. Neglect followed. Multiple sales of the property ensued.

In 1801, the estate was ultimately purchased by the Marquis de la Colonilla, Bertrand Douat, for 654,000 francs (a little more than $100,000 US dollars). From Basque Spain, Douat was not likely to be beheaded. He tore down the estate's old château and completely rebuilt all the buildings on the property. Douat commissioned one of Bordeaux's foremost architects, Louis Combes (owner of the adjacent Château Lascombes), to create the 19th century Neo-Palladian style villa, often nicknamed the "Versailles of the Médoc" which still stands proudly today.

1855 marks the very special year when the Emperor Napoléon III bestowed the first-growth status to Château Margaux, naming this winery one of the top four wineries in Bordeaux. Today, Château Margaux continues to fulfill such an honor to be a Premier Grand Cru Classé of 1855 by producing one of the finest wine experiences in the world.

Ups and downs continued for Château Margaux. Some owners were only interested in the property as a business investment. Some wanted the prestige and luxury of living in the magnificent castle. And then there were those who had passion for the wines and contributed significantly towards the progress of excellence in winemaking.

In 1977, André Mentzelopoulos bought Château Margaux for 72 million francs ($16 million dollars). Mentzelopoulos was Greek, which caused quite the stir in France and all over the wine world. The idea of a Greek running one of France's greatest wineries was hard for many people to accept.

It turned out Mentzelopoulos fell in love with Margaux and proceeded to restore its grandeur with a determination to make the best wines possible. He installed better drainage in the vineyards. He hired the famed oenologist Emile Peynaud to produce magic in the winery. A second wine, Pavillon Rouge was introduced. Unfortunately Mentzelopoulos died just three years later at only 65 years old. His daughter Corrine stepped in immediately and took over. As one of the wealthiest women in France, Corrine poured cash and lots of love and passion into the excellence and magic of Margaux. Corrine is the sole shareholder and remains at the helm today.

MÉDOC MARGAUX
Winery (Château)
CHÂTEAU MARGAUX

HAVING 2ND & 3RD WINES MAKES THE MAGIC POSSIBLE

Understanding the concept behind a second wine is very important. Winemakers get to select only the very best juice to make their number one magical wine. Without wasting already great wine, the unused portion becomes the second wine, allowing the first label to be refined to the ultimate of excellence. While a second wine may be common for this quality technique, Château Margaux creates a third wine. The same concept applies, because of the third wine, the second wine can also be refined to excellence. Don't think their third wine is low quality. They still refine and then sell off the balance of juice to other wineries.

I believe this is why, even in challenging years, the Château Margaux Grand Cru has the excellence, the magic flavors, which grabs our attention. And their second wine, it's oh-my-gosh delicious!

I was fortunate to experience this first-hand by tasting an exceptionally great vintage (2009) of the second wine side by side with a challenging year (2004) for the Premier Grand Cru Classé. The second wine, *Pavillon Rouge du Chateau Margaux* (priced around $200) was quite sexy, with blackberry aromas and soft, rich notes of cherry and licorice on the palate. It was enlightening to discover that the magic of the Grand Cru still occurs in such an off year. Velvty. Silky. Delicate magic in the cheeks. A big Cabernet, yet ever so femininely soft. Layers and layers of berries, dark fruits and minerals result in a youthful vitality that becomes vibrant in the mouth. The magic happens! It's only befitting that a first-growth with such delicate femininity would come from a winery with a woman at the helm.

There are only two first-growth Grand Cru Classés of 1855 that open their doors to visitors. Château Margaux is one. No wine for sale though, just tastings. Private tours are by appointment only and are customized based on what you want to see and do. This is a completely self-contained property with an in-house blacksmith, electrician, painter, roofer, gardener, and even a cooper making their own oak barrels to their exact specifications.

This is a winery you definitely want to visit. Their wines will rock your palate. Magically!

MÉDOC **MARGAUX**
Winery (Château)
CHÂTEAU LASCOMBES

Deuxième Cru (Second-Growth)
Grand Cru Classé of 1855
Winner: Best Of Wine Tourism

1 Cours de Verdun
33460 Margaux, France

+33 (0)5 57 88 70 66
Contact@Chateau-Lascombes.fr

Chateau-Lascombes.com

English, French

*Open: All Year, Monday-Saturday
Reservations Not Needed
Visits Are Available By Appointment*

Because we are number two, "we try harder" is certainly inspiring; however, did Napoléon really put them up to it a 150 years ago?

SOFT DELICATE RICH WINES

Can you imagine being a second-growth knowing you were that close to first? And adjacent to the first-growth Château Margaux where your previous owner was their brilliant architect? Château Lascombes takes this challenge seriously!

Ten generations of owners since its inception in 1625 have contributed to the growth of this estate. Especially the last two, which infused great amounts of capital into modernizing the technical aspects of the winery, hired notable Michel Rolland as their consulting oenologist, and maximized terroir (also on a knoll, possibly higher than their neighbor).

Lascombes is focusing on Cabernet Sauvignon and Petit Verdot in their gravelly soil, common for the Médoc where these grapes thrive. Merlot is planted in clay limestone soil where it expresses itself magnificently. This is a uniquely sizable amount of clay for the Médoc which dominates their final blend. This is special!

I believe this clay limestone Merlot influences a distinctly supple soft richness in their wines, a delicateness that makes their wines drinkable earlier and yet still ageable for 30 plus years.

Their classic tour is available year round, Monday through Saturday, including harvest time, even without an appointment. As long as they have room, you are in. They also have private tours and a blending workshop by appointment as well.

The tour is a historical presentation of the winery, through the vineyards, around the castle, inside the vat room, all the way down into the cellars to see the historical wine collection. The best part is tasting both their beautiful wines: Château Lascombes and Chevalier de Lascombes. If you want to customize a unique tour, just ask. They want to accommodate.

Collection of Wines
Château Lascombes
(First Label - Grand Cru)

Chevalier de Château Lascombes
(Second Wine)

Le Haut Médoc de Lascombes
(Third Wine)

MÉDOC MARGAUX
Winery (Château) Light Foods
CHÂTEAU MARQUIS D'ALESME

Troisième Cru (Third-Growth)
Grand Cru Classé of 1855

7 Rue de la Trémoille
33460 Margaux, France

+33 (0)5 57 81 13 20
Contact@Marquis.wine

MarquisDAlesme.wine

English, French, Chinese

*Open: May-October, Monday-Friday
By Appointment Preferred
Casual Drop-Ins Are No Problem*

French-Asian fusion, an estate run by women delivering excellence in hospitality.

LOCATED IN MARGAUX VILLAGE

This is a special place for many reasons. First of all, they are located in the middle of the little Margaux village, right on the main road (D2). Entering their property is a promenade of beautiful architecture and gardens. It is a village in and of itself.

The property was completely rebuilt over a five-year period, opening in 2017. A stroll down the promenade leads to a brand new winery, many gardens of herbs, fruits and flowers, all designed for an educational experience. The promenade leads to the vineyards where a restored events building stands with views of the adjacent property (Chateau Margaux), the gently rolling hills of vineyards and the historic Margaux church.

At the entrance to the promenade is *Le Hameau* (Hamlet), their welcoming place of inspiration into the fine art of living. This is considered the soul of Marquis d'Alesme, a place to relax, shop, eat, drink wine, and it is the starting point for all their tours.

Le Hameau is an inspiration of Marie-Antoinette's pavilion at the Versailles, a beautiful French setup for refined living, a friendly spot that provides luxurious relaxation and delicious discoveries.

INVITING HOSPITALITY

Hospitality is most special here! An all-women team brings out the best of everything feminine. They have a focus on hospitality and family, nurturing the finest experiences possible. They are always welcoming, arms open, anytime May through October, even without an appointment.

To reflect the owner's heritage (French father and Chinese mother), Nathalie Perrodo chose classical French architecture throughout the pavilion exteriors. Inside, an elegant Asian feel is created by moon-shaped doorways into the barrel room (photo left), wavy brass panels resembling a stylized dragon tail (inside of the winery), and moon gates illustrated with Tao symbols. Countless aesthetic and technical details live together in the harmony of Yin and Yang. Perfect acoustics provides the wines with soft vibrations for exquisite aging. And the vintages live in their own space, maturing at their own pace, with odd and even years on separate floors to separate multiple vintages.

Numerous interesting and unique tours have been created for us to experience the wonder and magic of this special place.

Collection of Wines
Château Marquis d'Alesme
(First Label - Grand Cru)

Marquise d'Alesme
(Second Wine)

MÉDOC **MARGAUX**
Winery (Château) Light Foods
CHÂTEAU MARQUIS D'ALESME

THE MAGICAL INTERLUDE

This is the name of their magical tour experience throughout their property. In addition to the winery and barrel rooms discussed on the previous page, you will venture through the many Asian influences on French classicism with their insightful guide.

This is truly an educational experience. The different gardens will awaken and enlighten your awareness as you discover the property and learn about the many senses of wines and foods… smells, tastes, touch, sights and sounds. All encompassing.
• **La Cour des Simples** (Suspended in time). A medieval garden of serenity and privacy, discovering the senses of medicinal and fruit-bearing plants.
• **Garden of Contemplation** (Meandering interlude). Imagine the Garden of Eden, symmetrical and green, and contemplate the Yin & Yang of Earth and sky.

• **Garden of Euphoria** (A romantic interlude). Scents from diverse varieties of roses under apple trees permeate, colors abound, alivening your senses.
• **Garden of Senses** (A musical score for the senses). Sight and touch take over when trees crackle in the wind and we feel unusual foliage, rough-textured vegetation and thorny plants.
• **Petit Marquis** (A child's experience). The entire family is welcomed here. Designed to entertain your kid's curiosity and sharpen their senses through imagination, old-fashioned games and surprises.
• **Grand Cru Classé Tasting**. Delicious French specialties are served inside *Le Hameau* or outside on *La Cour des Simples*. Enjoy the art of living, relax and appreciate their wines, and spend two to three hours of indulgence here.

MÉDOC **MARGAUX**
Winery (Château)
CHÂTEAU GISCOURS

1855
GRAND CRU CLASSÉ

Troisième Cru (Third-Growth)
Grand Cru Classé of 1855
Winner: Best Of Wine Tourism

10 Route de Giscours
33460 Labarde, Margaux, France

+33 (0)5 57 97 09 01
Receptif@Chateau-Giscours.fr

Chateau-Giscours.com

English, French

Open: All Year, April-October, Everyday
November-March, Monday-Saturday

E njoying excellent wines in their park setting is a beautiful way to spend the afternoon.

Collection of Wines
Château Giscours
(First Label - Grand Cru)

La Sirène de Giscours
(Second Wine)

Le Haut-Médoc de Giscours
(Haut-Médoc AOC)

Le Rosé de Giscours
(Cabernet Sauvignon Rosé)

GREAT WINES, GREAT VISITS

Since 1552, Château Giscours has been producing wine on this property. Classified in 1855 as a third-growth Grand Cru Classé, the wines here are beautiful and full of the delicate rich fruit for which the Margaux appellation is known.

The terroir is extra special here: three hilltops of heavy gravel conducive to excellent Cabernet Sauvignon (reflecting the sun during the day and warming the vines in the evening) and east-west facing slopes offers the best sun exposure and a gentle climate. This results in beautiful wine.

Experiences are with a professional guide who will customize your visit to your level of knowledge and interest (vineyards, terroir, winery, cellars, the château, their history, winemaking process, etc.). After the tasting, enjoy a picnic in their park. They have bottles, and glasses, of wine for sale in their boutique. In addition to their **Classic Visit**, they have interesting themed visits...

• **The Gourmet Visit** (Wine & Cheese). This is a private experience of the Classic Visit, followed by a gourmet workshop of wine and fine French cheese pairings.
• **The Entertaining Visit** (Wine Workshop). This is also a private experience of the Classic Visit (minimum of 10 people), followed by an entertaining and very educational tasting course on all of the wine aromas and flavors from different wines and vintages from the estate.
• **The Private Visit** (Exclusive and Customized). This visit goes beyond the Classic Visit. Their professional guide works with your knowledge of wine (novice or connoisseur) to create a unique visit to discover the chateau, its history, its vineyard and the wine-making process. The best part of this visit is the private tasting inside the château (the castle). You will enjoy one of the private living rooms for a fully discussed and analyzed tasting of three wines.

MÉDOC **MARGAUX**
Winery (Château)
CHÂTEAU PRIEURÉ-LICHINE

Quatrième Cru (Fourth-Growth)
Grand Cru Classé of 1855
Winner: Best Of Wine Tourism

34 Avenue de la 5ème République
33460 Cantenac, Margaux, France

+33 (0)5 57 88 36 28
Contact@Prieure-Lichine.fr

Prieure-Lichine.fr

English, French, Spanish, Danish, German, Japanese

*Open: All Year, April-October, Everyday
November-March, Monday-Saturday
Reservations: Visit@Prieure-Lichine.fr*

T he monks somehow knew when they planted this estate in the 11th century that they had discovered something very special.

EXCEPTIONAL TERROIR

In the 1000s, monks came to the Margaux area and discovered this unique property and started planting grapes. Up through the 18th century, the monks held religious services with the parish and worked the fields of vines and other crops surrounding their now-gone Romanesque church on this 20 hectares (49 acres) estate.

During the French Revolution (1789-1799), this property was not subject to requisition as it was a church with a very active priest. No aristocratic head removals here! Not so for the other older noble estates or newer bourgeoisie estates. Its ancient monastic and medieval roots provided Château Prieuré-Lichine exception from this nasty part of the revolution.

The monks loved this property and knew, somehow, that they could produce good wine here. Over the centuries this has been proven correct. In 1855, Napoléon classified Château Prieuré Lichine as one of 10 fourth-growth properties.

Margaux is known for its mixed terroir of gravel and sand, which is ideal for Cabernet Sauvignon and special to the Médoc, and clay soils that are ideal for Merlot, which are not as prevalent in the Médoc. And this property has special pockets of each that have been planted with meticulous refinement.

The quality rose dramatically on this property to the point that the Bordeaux Royal Administration awarded them the rank of third-growth of Margaux on several occasions. The priest, proud and smart, took 98% of his tithe income in wine, creating the highest ecclesiastic income in the Médoc.

Today, the property is part of the Ballande Group, who has invested significantly into modernizing the winery. Fifteen new cement tanks and ten stainless tanks are used to vinify in specific batches separately, controlling the perfection of each harvest. Other modern techniques include planting the rooftop to help regulate humidity. This is definitely an interesting tour to check out.

Collection of Wines
Château Prieuré-Lichine
(First Label - Grand Cru)

Confidences de Prieuré-Lichine
(Second Wine)

Le Blanc du Château Prieuré-Lichine
(Sauvignon Blanc 60% and Sémillon 40%)

Le Clocher du Prieuré
(Haut-Médoc Merlot)

MÉDOC **MARGAUX**
Winery (Château)
CHÂTEAU PRIEURÉ-LICHINE

BEAUTIFUL MODERN WINEMAKING FACILITIES • EXCELLENT GIFT SHOP • INTERESTING TOURS

In addition to the new modern facilities for winemaking, architects designed a beautiful wine shop for tastings and a whole variety of gifts. Everything for enjoying wine and the culinary arts. Interesting books too.

Several tours are available by appointment.
• **The Discovery Visit** is their standard tour, in six languages, taking you through the different stages of producing their wines and into the cellars, plus tasting of two wines.
• **The Historical Visit** is an extensive history of their estate and of Margaux, plus the history of Bordeaux and the 1855 classification. Wine tasting also includes older vintages.
• **The Terroir Visit** is focused on the vineyards looking at their different soils and how each varietal does best in each environment. The tasting then examines each individual varietal alongside their blends in an interesting and practical exercise.
• **The Saveur Visit** is the Discovery Visit followed by a food and wine pairing, and an introduction into proper wine tasting techniques.
• **The Challenge Your Wine Tasting Powers Visit** is a fun, interactive and educational way to challenge your tasting skills. Everything revolves around how much you learn and improve. Three different steps are designed to test your tasting abilities and prepare you for better tasting techniques.

Exploring Wine Regions | **Bordeaux** | 97

MÉDOC **MARGAUX**
Winery (Château)
CHÂTEAU MARQUIS DE TERME

Quatrième Cru (Fourth-Growth)
Grand Cru Classé of 1855

3 Route de Rauzan
33460 Margaux, France
Global Winner: Best Of Wine Tourism

+33 (0)5 57 88 30 10
Tourisme@Chateau-Marquis-de-Terme.com

Chateau-Marquis-de-Terme.com

English, French, Italian

*Open: All Year, Everyday
By Appointment Preferred
Reservations Available By Email and Website*

A ge is beauty. Magnificent vines planted on this property in 1958 (photo left) offers the ultimate expression of special Margaux wines.

TRANSFORMATION

So it goes, 1958 was a great year, and this special vineyards (left) expresses its history and maturity with amazing wines. Just wait until you try this Grand Cru Classé. Aromas of fresh fruit. On the palate, black fruit, licorice and vanilla. You can really taste the terroir and maturity of these vines.

In the winery it is a very different story. A new modern addition was built for destemming and sorting on the upper level for a gentle gravity feed into the tanks. They use pressurized barrels and concrete tanks for an integral vinification. No pump-overs. The pressure provides for no harsh movements of the juice and gives them smoother tannins and more extraction from the skins. Ever so gently they make their wine. They simply ferment and age.

Bicycle and electric scooter tours offered, meandering the back streets of Margaux with stops to observe the magnificent care of the vines. Always educational and experiences differ with seasons.

Collection of Wines
Château Marquis de Terme
(First Label - Grand Cru)

La Couronne de Marquis de Terme
(Second Wine)

Le Rosé de Marquis de Terme
(Rosé of: Grenache 60%, Tibouren 25%, Cinsault 10%, Syrah 5%)

MÉDOC MARGAUX
Winery (Château), B&B
CHÂTEAU DU TERTRE

Cinquième Cru (Fifth-Growth)
Grand Cru Classé of 1855
Winner: Best Of Wine Tourism

14 Allée du Tertre
33460 Arsac, Margaux, France

+33 (0)5 57 88 52 52
Receptif@ChateauDuTertre.fr

ChateauDuTertre.fr

English, French, Spanish

*Open: All Year, April-October, Everyday
November-March, Monday-Saturday
By Appointment Only
Reservations Preferred By Email*

F or a thousand years, this estate has been loved, and it will continued to be loved for a thousand more.

THE HIGHEST GRAVEL HILL TOPS

This thousand-year-old estate is possibly best known for its unique terroir. Claiming to be at the highest point in Margaux, Château du Tertre has the superb soil of gravel and sand on these hilltops, supreme for Cabernet Sauvignon. It is deliberate that 70% of their vines are planted with Cabernet Sauvignon. With lower pockets of clay and limestone, Merlot adds 20% to their estate. Plus, 7% Cabernet Franc and 3% Petit Verdot.

This elevation also helps protect the vines from late spring frost, which has been devastating to other neighboring properties.

Add to this, a beautiful spring that runs through their property that provides natural drainage from the gravelly hills, protects them from excess water and drought, and gives them cooler temperatures essential for their development.

Since 2007, Château du Tertre has been converting their vineyards to organic and biodynamic farming. Every year, two hectares (of their 52-hectare estate) are replanted to organic and biodynamic from the beginning.

In the winery, they have converted to all wood and concrete vats. They gravity fill their tanks for optimum delicate handling. The concrete vats are truncated cone tanks of small capacity allowing them to vinify plot by plot with the best grapes separated as they come into the winery.

Attention to detail, as in any business, is essential to producing the very best. No wonder they proudly treasure their 1855 Grand Cru Classé classification.

Collection of Wines
Château du Tertre
(First Label - Grand Cru)

Les Hauts du Tertre
(Second Wine)

MÉDOC **MARGAUX**
Winery (Château), B&B
CHÂTEAU DU TERTRE

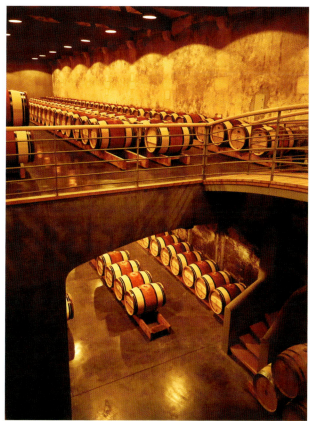

TASTINGS IN THE UNDERGROUND BARREL ROOM

Tours at this property are beautiful in a dramatic and eye-catching way. The vineyards, the château grounds, the winery, each equally spectacular in their own unique ways.

Tastings underground in the aging cellars among the barrels is a special way to enjoy their wines. And tasting directly from the barrels takes you to an even greater level of appreciation.

Tours are available by appointment.

• **The Classic Guided Tour** includes the history of the château, the wine making facilities and underground barrel cellars. They will adapt to your interest and focus on either history, technical explanations or other specific subjects concerning winemaking. Plus tasting their wines of course.

• **The Wine & Cheese Visit** adds to the tour an original tasting that pairs three wines of the property with fine French cheese.

• **The Private Tour** is an intimate experience for as little as two people, tailor-made for you, and with a special château guide. You choose your interest, and based on your knowledge, they will focus on certain themes: history and architecture, the vineyards, winemaking or a tutored tasting of three wines in their private tasting room. Adding fine French cheese is an option.

Open: All Year, April-October, Everyday
November-March, Monday-Saturday
By Appointment Only (preferred by email)
Receptif@ChateauDuTertre.fr

MÉDOC MARGAUX
Winery (Château), B&B
CHÂTEAU DU TERTRE

BED & BREAKFAST • ABOVE THE WINERY

Imagine waking up to the sun shinning across vineyards and into your bedroom window. This is the experience here. Magnificent! On the second floor, above the winery, you get vast views across this estate. You see the property come alive as workers arrive in the vineyards and to the winery. This is a truly unique experience to stay overnight in a Grand Cru Classé working winery. Six individually unique rooms are decorated in an elegant style with antique furniture. It was built in 1855.

Rooms are grand with a separate bedroom from the large living room and work-space. Fireplace ambiance. Large private bathroom with double sink, claw-foot tub and separate shower. In the European land of small accommodations, this is living it up in grand style and spaciousness at a reasonable price.

Ever seen a pool (left page) this impressively beautiful, elaborate and extravagant? Lounge by the magnificent pool. Take a long swim. Take in the history. Allow your senses to absorb the aesthetics, qualities, shapes, colors, and pleasing forms. Rest in the beautiful poolhouse with a peaceful summer setting of luxury.

In Bed & Breakfast style, hot, made-to-order breakfast, is served in the 18th century castle (or in your room) alongside a beautiful spread of freshly baked breads, cheese, meats and other delicious French goodies.

MÉDOC MARGAUX
Winery (Château), Castle Rental
CHÂTEAU PAVEIL DE LUZE

Quality Certification
Cru Bourgeois du Médoc
Winner: Best Of Wine Tourism

3 Chemin de Paveil
33460 Soussans, Margaux, France

+33 (0)9 75 64 57 97
Contact@ChateauPaveilDeLuze.com

ChateauPaveilDeLuze.com

English, French

*Open: All Year, By Appointment Only
April-November, Tuesday-Saturday
December-March, Monday-Friday*

Collection of Wines
Château Paveil de Luze
(First Label - Cru Bourgeois)

Petit Paveil
(Second Wine)

Paveil de Luze Blanc
(Sauvignon Blanc Wine)

S even generations of passion and love for a castle they call home.

A FAMILY AFFAIR

In 1862, the Luze family began their wine passion here with Baron Alfred de Luze buying the vineyards of Paveil from the Lords of Bretonneau, a family associated by marriage under the reign of King Louis XV. This resulted in the merger of Paveil and Luze, with the Baron now creating prominence of Château Paveil de Luze wines all over the world.

Today, seven generations later, 32 hectares of vines lay in front of the castle. Their cherished garden, a passion inherited from their fathers, carry a deep sense of belonging to this property. Every man and woman in this family has put their hands on the expression of their property and quality of its wines.

Behind the castle spans a massive and beautiful park, lake and forested backdrop of this wooded estate. Just taking a seat on a park bench to relax and gaze, with a nice glass of wine, is a delightful way to enjoy an afternoon.

Speaking of wine, Château Paveil de Luze has earned the Cru Bourgeois designation of quality wines certified each year through blind tastings and other important criteria. Plus, Château Paveil de Luze wines are an excellent value in comparison to the other increasingly expensive wines in this Margaux appellation.

Exploring Wine Regions

ExploringWineRegions.com

Exploring Wine Regions
BOOK SERIES

EXPLORING THE WORLD

One Region at a Time...

- Argentina - 2016
- Bordeaux France - 2020
- California USA - Coming Soon!
- New Zealand
- Italy
- South Africa
- Portugal
- Spain

TRAVEL WITH US

COME JOIN US...
On Extraordinary Trips

Uncover the best wines
on one-of-a-kind exclusive trips!

JoinUs@ExploringWineRegions.com

ALL THIS AND MORE AT
ExploringWineRegions.com

MÉDOC **MARGAUX**
Winery (Château), Castle Rental
CHÂTEAU PAVEIL DE LUZE

EXPERIENCE AUTHENTIC CASTLE LIVING

Join one of the château owners in a complete takeover of this castle. Reserve through AirBnB and it comes with a full-time staff, including a gourmet chef. Château Paveil de Luze can accommodate eight guests, in four bedrooms, with five beds and three bathrooms. The guest rooms have not been remodeled; they are a genuine piece of history to experience authentic castle life in Bordeaux.

Château Paveil de Luze is the family's way of life, which revolves around common passions. Here, you will be welcomed by a host member of the family. Gourmet breakfasts, lunches and dinners will be prepared by their chef and served in the large ornate dining room. The wines of their château, as well as neighboring Grand Cru Classé wines, are included in the experience.

The property has beautiful grounds. Not just surrounded by vineyards, the property is forested with a park setting, lake and a grand pool.

The stay here is designed to immerse you in fine wines and gastronomy, arts and culture, sightseeing and relaxation. Depending on your interest, they can arrange a private visit to the cellars and vineyards, as well as neighboring Grand Cru Classés.

This is a unique property to learn about a family and their history, their way of life and the sweetness of castle life at Château Paveil de Luze.

They really do invite you to discover their true family saga.

MÉDOC **MARGAUX**
Winery (Château), B&B
CHÂTEAU DEYREM VALENTIN

Quality Certification
Cru Bourgeois du Médoc

1 Rue Valentin Deyrem
33460 Soussans, Margaux, France

+33 (0)5 57 88 35 70
Contact@Chateau-Deyrem-Valentin.com

Chateau-Deyrem-Valentin.com

English, French, Italian, Spanish

*Open: All Year, Monday-Friday
By Appointment Only
Reservations Through Their Website or Call
Tours: Conducted By The Owner/Winemaker*

T erroir. It's all about the terroir. On a tiny plot of land in a sea of Grand Cru Classés of 1855, amazing wine comes from this property.

ELEGANT BEAUTIFUL WINE

Let's just get right to the point. This wine is beautiful, elegant and delicious. This is a tiny property of just 13 hectares surrounded by big name properties; the Grand Cru Classé properties classified in 1855. Terroir is everything!

Everything about this place is straightforward and perfect. Attention to detail is meticulous. It is family run. Owner and winemaker, Christelle Sorge, is practically a one-woman show, taking over from her father after returning from Australia and Chile, where she worked in the wine regions. She is young, innovative, and has exceptional terroir as her primary ingredient.

With seven levels of soil depth here, Christelle knows her terroir like no other. She identifies the dark stones that came from the Pyrénées Mountains millions of years ago, and pink stones from the Garonne River, noting the deeper we go the smaller the stones. The large stones on the surface hold the warmth of the day for the vines at night.

All work in the vineyard is by hand (the cutting, pruning, leaf removal, harvesting). Everything is handpicked one block at a time and fermented one block per tank. Meticulous. Exacting. Perfection.

The results are Cru Bourgeois certified wines that are rich, elegant, feminine, fruity, floral, with silky tannins. This is a place to come see the magic, meet the owner (she gives the tours) and buy some wine (excellent pricing). By appointment only, seven days a week. If she is there, she will gladly welcome you.

Collection of Wines
Château Deyrem Valentin
(First Label - Cru Bourgeois)

Château Soussans
(Second Wine)

Château Valentin
(Haut-Médoc)

DOWNTOWN MARGAUX

Margaux is a small village of just 1,500 people, sharing the same name as, and located in the Margaux wine region. Margaux is one of five little villages in this appellation (neighboring villages being Arsac, Labarde, Soussans, and Cantenac).

Located right on the main road, highway D2, it is only a few blocks long with excellent restaurants such as **Restaurant La Savoie**, caves (wine shops) such as **La Cave d'Ulysse** and **Cave l'Avante Garde**, the chocolate manufacturer **Mademoiselle de Margaux**, châteaux adjacent to the highway such as **Château Marquis d'Alesme**, and the **Maison du Vin de Margaux** where you can find the wines from all over the Margaux appellations.

■ MÉDOC **MARGAUX** DOWNTOWN
Wine Merchant and Tourism
MAISON DU VIN DE MARGAUX (DU TOURISME)

7 Place de la Tremoille • 33460 Margaux, France
+33 (0)5 57 88 70 82 • Syndicat.Margaux@Wanadoo.fr

MaisonDuVinDeMargaux.com

Maison du Vin translates to "House of Wine" (of Tourism). This is the syndicate of wineries of the Margaux appellation making their wines available all in one place. It is also the Tourism Office for Margaux.

Most of the well-known appellations have a Maison du Vin. With Margaux being a very important and prominent appellation in the Médoc, they make a very impressive presentation of the wines. They have first and second labels, Grand Cru Classés and Cru Bourgeois. And good prices.

They also have the Margaux Tourism Office to help you with your château visits. Go to their website for a detailed map and lots of information.

■ MÉDOC **MARGAUX** DOWNTOWN
Chocolatier Manufacturer and Retail
MADEMOISELLE DE MARGAUX

1 Route de l'Ile Vincent • 33460 Margaux, France
+33 (0)5 57 88 39 90 • Contact.Web@MademoiselleDeMargaux.fr

MademoiselleDeMargaux.com

Mademoiselle makes very creative chocolate here with unique designs and flavors. Need I say more? Open to the public and located in Downtown Margaux.

Sarments du Médoc (French for "branches of Médoc") is a spectacular outcome from a big mistake. Kind of like how the peanut butter got into the chocolate and we ended up with peanut butter cups. Here, the chocolate-making machine went haywire and the chocolates came out in wavy pieces looking like grapevines. How perfect is that for the Médoc wine region. Branches of Médoc are grapevines, how appropriate. So a star was born. Plus the flavors are to die for!

Imagine gourmet chocolate made with sweet blackberry, enhanced with the lemony verbena and looks like a grapevine. Wow!

MÉDOC **MARGAUX** DOWNTOWN
Cave (Wine Merchant)
LA CAVE D'ULYSSE

2 Rue de La Tremoille • 33460 Margaux, France
+33 (0)5 57 88 79 94 • Commercial@CaveUlysse.com
CaveUlysse.com

A cave is a wine shop, merchants who sell all types of wines from the Médoc. This cave is very fancy! They have the first-growth wines, in many vintages, including older vintages. It is a big shop with much variety, located in downtown Margaux, and ships all over the world.

MÉDOC **MARGAUX** DOWNTOWN
Cave (Wine Merchant)
CAVE L'AVANT GARDE

17 Rue de La Tremoille • 33460 Margaux, France
+33 (0)5 57 88 76 71 • Contact@Cave-Margaux-LAvantGarde.fr
Cave-Margaux-LAvantGarde.fr

This cave (wine shop) carries wines from all over the Médoc. They are a no-nonsense wine shop, with good pricing, and ships to the USA, Europe, Hong Kong and Japan. They have the big names, as well as unusual local finds. Nice friendly people, a very casual atmosphere, located right in downtown Margaux.

■ MÉDOC **MARGAUX** DOWNTOWN
Restaurant
RESTAURANT LE SAVOIE

1 Place Trémoille
33460 Margaux, France

+33 (0)5 57 88 31 76

LeSavoie.net

English, French

*Open: Monday-Saturday
Lunch & Dinner*

A beautiful and elegant restaurant in downtown Margaux with a big wine list coming from their in-house cave.

ELEGANT HISTORIC SETTING

Choosing wine here is a treat. Many Grand Cru Classé wines throughout the Médoc. Older vintages too. Priced fair. English speaking staff is limited, so they have an English menu.

Lobster claws topped with caviar, fresh mango, basil dressing (photo right). Scrumptious!

Beef Fillet Tournedor Rossini style, glazed with foie gras, truffles, and boulangerie style potatoes (photo far right).

Creme brulée (photo below).

MÉDOC MARGAUX
Restaurant
RESTAURANT NOMADE

3 Route des Château
33460 Labarde, Margaux, France

+33 (0)5 56 35 92 38
Contact@Restaurant-Nomade.fr

Restaurant-Nomade.fr

English, French

Open: Everyday
Lunch: 12:00pm-2:00pm
Dinner: 8:00pm-9:30pm
Reservations Through Their Website or Call

Trains, trains and no more trains. Now a beautiful setting for gourmet meals.

CREATIVELY DELICIOUS

La Gare (French for "train station") is the old Margaux station converted into a restaurant with a very cute addition. A husband (chef) and wife (she speaks very good English) team.

Imagine Mackerel Rillettes with vegetables (photo left). Crazy delicious and unique.

Cod and leeks (photo below left) cooked to perfection. Flaky, fresh with an unimaginable buttery sauce.

Peach and nectarine, vanilla ice-cream (photo below) with all the fruit juices to mix with home-made creamy vanillaness.

BORDEAUX · MÉDOC MOULIS & LISTRAC-MÉDOC AOC
Exploring the Inland Appellations

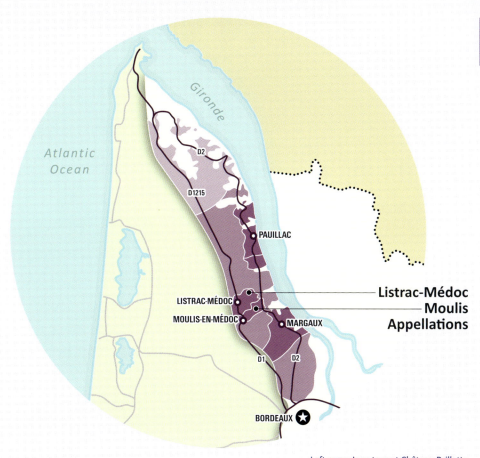

Left page: Jeep tour at Château Brillette

THE TWO INLAND APPELLATIONS

As we continue to travel from south to north within the Médoc, **Moulis** and **Listrac** are adjoining appellations, south to north respectively, in the middle of the Haut-Médoc, inland along the very western edge farthest away from the Gironde River. You can easily imagine the terroir here is different from the other appellations along the river's edge.

As you can see on the map, these are very small appellations. They have unique microclimates very special for winemaking, specifically characteristics which create more fruit-forward wines that are drinkable much earlier than the other appellations of the Médoc.

The terrain is slighter higher with sloping hills of gravel and sand, providing excellent water drainage conducive to Cabernet Sauvignon of the Left Bank.

However, Merlot does very well here too. Many châteaux will have greater proportions of Merlot than Cabernet, further allowing the wines here to be softer, earlier drinkable wines. Plus, these two appellations are just northwest of Margaux, which has softer, more elegant, feminine types of wines.

The châteaux listed here are all Cru Bourgeois certified and excellently priced. Their wines are high quality as determined by the organization's blind tastings.
- Château Brillette, page 119
- Château Moulin-à-Vent, page 121
- Château Baudan, page 123
- Château Reverdi, page 125
- Château Cap Léon Veyrin, page 127

Exploring Wine Regions **Bordeaux**

MÉDOC MOULIS
Winery (Château)
CHÂTEAU BRILLETTE

Quality Certification
Cru Bourgeois du Médoc

Route de Peyvignau
33480 Moulis-en-Médoc, France

+33 (0)5 56 58 22 09
Contact@Chateau-Brillette.fr

Chateau-Brillette.fr

English, French

*Open: All Year, Monday-Friday
By Appointment Only*

Collection of Wines
Château Brillette
(First Label - Cru Bourgeois)

Hauts-Brillette
(Second Wine)

B de Brillette
(Combination of Château Brillette and Haut-Brillette)

Oscar de Brillette
(The Family's Celebration Wine)

T he terroir of slippery slopes here make for superb drainage in this soil, magnificent for a fruit-forward Moulis appellation.

THE BRILLETTE SLOPES

This 100-hectare estate is located on one of the highest hills in Moulis, with 30% of their land on dramatic slopes providing excellent drainage to the heavily rocky and sandy soil, and creating a unique personality for their wines. Since Merlot does very well on their property, this is their primary grape. Terroir is always critical to the quality of the grapes, and with the unique slopes here, their name Brillette came from its landscape ("brillette" means "slope" in French).

This property was originally used for raising animals until the 1830s when the château was built and vineyards were planted. In 1976, the Flageul family began three generations of modernizing the winery and introducing new procedures and techniques to improve the winemaking process, ultimately creating such high-quality wines to earn the Cru Bourgeois certification.

They are deliberate with their blends. The estate is composed of 48% Merlot (50-year-old vines), 40% Cabernet Sauvignon, 9% Cabernet Franc, and 3% Petit Verdot. They choose to be Merlot dominant for its softness and roundness, allowing it to be enjoyed in as early as a few years.

They use Cabernet Sauvignon and Cabernet Franc to give the wine structure and for aging many years. They also use Petit Verdot (a variety unique to the Médoc region of Bordeaux) to bring richness and depth of color to the wine. The relatively high percentage of Merlot grapes marks a defining characteristic of Château Brillette in this region where the terroir favors Cabernet Sauvignon.

The wines here are fruit-forward, easy to drink young, even just a few years after the harvest date. The wines are priced surprisingly low, considering their Cru Bourgeois certification.

MÉDOC MOULIS
Winery (Château)
CHÂTEAU MOULIN-À-VENT

Quality Certification
Cru Bourgeois du Médoc

72 Avenue du Médoc
33480 Moulis-en-Médoc, France

+33 (0)5 56 58 15 79
Moulin@Moulin-A-Vent.com

Bordeaux-Vineam.com

English, French

Open: All Year
May-September, Monday-Saturday
October-April, Monday-Friday
By Appointment Only

O rganic agriculture. A natural ecosystem. The balance of nature in their vineyards produces extraordinary quality in grapes and wines.

FEMININE WINES FROM AN ALL-WOMAN TEAM

Château Moulin-à-Vent is an all-woman team producing the utmost in feminine qualities in their wines. Naturally. Their soil characteristics of sand, clay and limestone is most conducive for the femininity of Merlot, which is 73% of their vines. This is unusual for the Left Bank, where Cabernet Sauvignon is predominant. Also unusual is the all-female team, which gives them a soft touch to all their wines.

Château Moulin-à-Vent is part of a family of six châteaux in the Bordeaux Vineam group. CEO, Jean-Baptiste Soula is obsessed with organic farming and creating a sustainable ecosystem within all his properties. As of 2019, he successfully achieved this at all six locations.

The ecosystem he has created is a remarkable community of plants, animals, birds, insects, living organisms, and non-living components, all working in harmony. They are all linked together through nutrient cycles and incredible energy flows, working together to create allies, and interacting as a self-sustaining environment. That is surely a mouthful; however, truly remarkable. And not just your typical lists of beneficial insects. They have integrated an extensive array of flowers, grass, hedges and soils for worms, even bees, bats, and endangered species, such as the European mink. This is the perfect place to live! Imagine just how healthy that makes everything.

This environment is taking the concept that you must start with excellent grapes in order to make excellent wine. To the ultimate degree. And just wait until you taste their wines. I found their Cru Bourgeois label, Château Moulin-à-Vent, to be a beautiful expression of Merlot, fruity and supple, big, yet elegant, and with soft tannins, making the wine drinkable early, yet still ageable.

Tours, especially around their property learning about their biodynamic ways, are very interesting. Reservations required.

Collection of Wines
Château Moulin-à-Vent
(First Label - Cru Bourgeois)

Château Moulin de Saint Vincent
(Second Wine)

MÉDOC LISTRAC-MÉDOC
Winery (Château)
CHÂTEAU BAUDAN

Quality Certification
Cru Bourgeois du Médoc

2 Route de Taudinat
33480 Listrac-Médoc, France

+33 (0)5 56 58 07 40
Chateau.Baudan@Wanadoo.fr

ChateauBaudan.com

English, French

*Open: All Year, 10:00am-4:30pm
Monday-Friday, Reservations Not Needed
Weekends, By Appointment Only*

A fter 60 years of dormancy, from out of the dust emerges a new breed of wines.

A BEAUTIFUL RENAISSANCE

How exciting it must have been for Alain Blasquez to resurrect his great grandfather's property, which laid dormant for 60 years after his untimely death, and for his wife Sylvie to join him in this exciting venture. And look what they have turned Château Baudan into: An estate that has earned Cru Bourgeois certification as verification of their outstanding work.

Inside are nostalgic, ancient cellars with innovative modern equipment. They use conical tanks turned upside down, with the large end at the bottom. This changes the form and structure of the juice from pump-over, achieving greater extraction, concentration and tannins. The results are excellent. Rich color, bold flavors, great structure, and round soft tannins. And elegant with freshness in the fruit. This is really a very nice wine.

A visit to this property offers more than just a tour. They have a beautiful grass park with large mature trees in their backyard aside the vineyards... perfect for a picnic. They have a nice indoor space in their modern tasting room. They have private rooms too. They can also provide lunch or dinner if you give them advance notice.

This is a small château where you get to visit with the owners and experience their renaissance firsthand. Call or write them ahead of time and arrange what you would like. They are very nice people and you will thoroughly enjoy their company, and not to mention their wines!

Collection of Wines
Château Baudan
(First Label - Cru Bourgeois)

Matibon de Baudan
(Second Wine)

Partage de Baudan
(A Fruity Wine)

MÉDOC **LISTRAC-MÉDOC**
Winery (Château)
CHÂTEAU REVERDI

Quality Certification
Cru Bourgeois du Médoc

11 Route de Donissan
33480 Listrac-Médoc, France

+33 (0)5 56 58 02 25
Contact@ChateauReverdi.fr

ChateauReverdi.com

English, French

Open: All Year, Monday-Saturday
Sundays, By Appointment Only

M aking your own Bordeaux blend gives you great appreciation for winemakers, plus you get to take a bottle home with you.

STUDYING YOUR OWN BLEND

Château Reverdi is a family business. Brother and sister, Mathieu and Audrey Thomas, farm 32 hectares (79 acres) in this inland appellation of Listrac-Médoc. They are the third generation here, since the 1950s, focusing on three of the six Bordeaux varietals: Merlot, Cabernet Sauvignon and Petit Verdot.

What makes this a special visit is being able to taste these three varietals as separate wines, then discussing their nuances with one of the owners. Next, you make your own personal blend. You are the judge of perfecting your finished wine.

They age only 25% of the wine in new oak, allowing the terroir to come forward and allowing each grape to stand out with little oak influence.

To Mathieu and Audrey, their Merlot (from 35-year-old vines) gives pinky red fruit aromatics, lots of tannins and cherry flavors; their Cabernet Sauvignon adds the structure to the blend and more depth to the red cherry; and the Petit Verdot gives the wine its deep inky purple color.

With their help, you get to make your creation, complete with a customized label with your name on the bottle.

Collection of Wines
Château Reverdi
(First Label - Cru Bourgeois)

Château L'Ermitage
(Second Wine - Cru Bourgeois)

MÉDOC **LISTRAC-MÉDOC**
Winery (Château) and Hotel
CHÂTEAU CAP LÉON VEYRIN
Château Julien & Château Bibian

Quality Certification
Cru Bourgeois du Médoc

54 Route de Donissan
33480 Listrac-Médoc, France

+33 (0)5 56 58 07 28
Contact@Vignobles-Meyre.com

Vignobles-Meyre.com

English, French

*Open: All Year, Monday-Friday
Reservations Not Needed
Saturday, By Appointment Only*

200 years of family care and devotion, the sixth generation continues a legacy of beautifully hand-crafted wines.

THREE CHÂTEAUX

Château Cap Léon Veyrin is the merger of the Cap Léon and Veyrin estates by the Meyer family in 1810. "Cap" originally meant "head" or higher land, which is a very important aspect of the terroir here with lots of sun and natural hillside drainage.

Everything here is handled with delicate care to create the best possible wines. Both old and young vines are hand-harvested from numerous parcels across the Listrac appellation.

Nathalie and Julien Meyre are now the 6th generation of this family to manage this property, the oldest continuously-owned estate in Listrac. And there are three boys, all under 10 years old, being nurtured to take over this historic estate.

Their wines have qualified for Cru Bourgeois every year since 1932, with their 2015 vintage (a super great year) winning the prestigious Coupe de Crus Bourgeois award in Paris. And imagine this wine winning the award, then receiving 91 points and costing only 16€. Stock up!

In 1985, the Meyres purchased Haut-Médoc property of Château Julien, and in 1990, bought Château Bibian (also Cru Bourgeois certified).

This means that you can taste all three wines, all in one place. And they can arrange for you to visit their other properties as well.

Collection of Wines
Château Cap Léon Veyrin
(First Label - Cru Bourgeois)

Château Bibian
(Sister Property - Cru Bourgeois)

Château Julien
(Sister Property in Haut-Médoc)

MÉDOC **LISTRAC-MÉDOC**
Winery (Château) and Hotel
CHÂTEAU CAP LÉON VEYRIN

CHAMBRES D'HÔTES
Bed & Breakfast

+33 (0)5 56 58 07 28
Contact@Vinobles-Meyre.com

FOUR ROOMS OF BORDEAUX WINE

Befitting for accommodations in the vineyards to be named after the four most common Bordeaux varietals: Cabernet Sauvignon, Merlot, Cabernet Franc, and Petit Verdot.

Chambres D'Hotes is the B&B of Château Cap Léon Veyrin with each room offering double beds, private bathrooms and breakfast in the morning.

This is a great way to see the activity of the winery in action. Plus they have two other châteaux nearby (Château Bibian and Château Julien) where they can arrange visits for you. Enjoy their gardens and, of course, the vineyards.

Tastings can be of three châteaux in one place. Two are Cru Bourgeois, one of which was awarded the Cru Bourgeois Cup for their superior excellence. And they have old vintages to taste as well.

BORDEAUX · MÉDOC HAUT-MÉDOC AOC (Central)

Surrounding Margaux, Pauillac and Saint-Julien Appellations

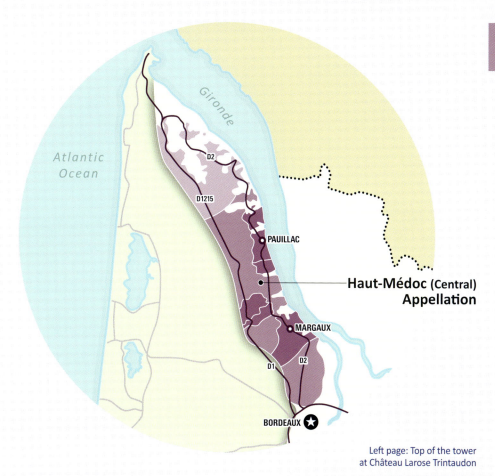

Left page: Top of the tower at Château Larose Trintaudon

NEIGHBORING TERROIR

The Haut-Médoc is a large area, as you can see on the map, so I have centralized this part in the book (especially since I am presenting the châteaux from south to north in the Médoc). And even further, the two wineries I want to introduce to you while in the Haut-Médoc appellation are very close to the Pauillac and Saint Julien appellations. Rather than define the terroir for the widespread Haut-Médoc, it might be better to consider these wineries based on their closest famous appellation.

Château Larose Trintaudon is directly west of the Saint-Julien village and close to the intersection of the Pauillac and Saint-Julien appellations. Although they are in a different appellation, they are so close to these two famous appellations that it might be more correct to say they share characteristics of their terroirs. They are Cru Bourgeois and surrounded by classified growth properties.

Château Lamothe Bergeron is just south of the Saint-Julien appellation and close to the river (between D2 and the river). The terroir is much more representative of their Saint-Julien neighbor and of vineyard properties close to the river than châteaux inland, a long ways across the Haut-Médoc.

Just a few blocks south of Lamothe Bergeron on the D2 is a roadside cafe **Le Bontemps**. Located in a strip center looking very unassuming, yet the food inside is gourmet and delicious.

A little further south in the village of Arcins is **Le Lion d'Or**. Visit this local's hangout for a taste of local cuisine and an environment without tourists.
- Château Larose Trintaudon, page 133
- Château Lamothe Bergeron, page 135

MÉDOC **HAUT-MÉDOC** (Central)
Winery (Château)
CHÂTEAU LAROSE TRINTAUDON

Quality Certification
Cru Bourgeois du Médoc
Winner: Best Of Wine Tourism

D206 Route de Pauillac
33112 Saint Laurent Médoc, France

+33 (0)5 56 59 41 72
Adminventes@VignoblesDeLarose.com

Chateau-Larose-Trintaudon.fr

English, French, German

Open: All Year, Monday-Friday
Reservations Not Needed
Reservations Available Through Their Website

W e have not inherited our land from our parents; instead we are borrowing it from our children.

REAL SUSTAINABLE AGRICULTURE

Have you ever considered that the quality of ingredients used by a chef has everything to do with the resulting quality of food prepared? Freshness. Organic. Flavor. In winemaking, it is said that you can't make great wine from bad grapes. True. The vineyard and the quality of its farming is paramount to superior winemaking characteristics.

At Château Larose Trintaudon, they are obsessed with sustainable agriculture. Their quest for ultimate health of the land has led them to an initiative that began in 1999 to adopt certification standards. This helped guide them to optimize their terroir in order for the grapes to fully reach its potential.

In just 11 years, they achieved the ultimate results of these policies, as they were rated Exemplary, the highest level of Sustainable Development by AFNOR (the official standardization and certification body in France under the French Ministry of Industry). This is the first European vineyard to ever obtain this level of recognition.

Even better though are the results in the bottle, where Cru Bourgeois certifies their wines for their superior quality through blind tastings every year.

Under the parent company, Vignobles De Larose, they have two other Haut-Médoc wines: Château Larose Perganson and Château Arnauld, both Cru Bourgeois certified wines.

This is a huge operation of three million bottles annually. They are just west of the Saint-Julien appellation and southwest of Pauillac, surrounded by classified-growth properties.

Visits and tastings start every 30 minutes, and are FREE. No reservations needed.

THE INSIDE SCOOP - The castle is not always open and they have only two visits per week up into the tower (Monday and Thursdays at 3:00pm) with 12 people maximum. Once a week, the cellar manager and vineyard manager conduct special visits where you get to meet the actual people involved with wine production.

Collection of Wines
Château Larose Trintaudon
(First Label - Cru Bourgeois)

Les Hauts de Trintaudon
(Second Wine)

Château Arnauld
Château Larose Perganson
(Both: First Label - Cru Bourgeois)

MÉDOC **HAUT-MÉDOC** (Central)
Winery (Château)
CHÂTEAU LAMOTHE BERGERON

Quality Certification
Cru Bourgeois du Médoc
Winner: Best Of Wine Tourism

49 Chemin des Graves
33460 Cussac-Fort-Médoc, France

+33 (0)5 56 58 94 77
Contact@LamotheBergeron.fr

LamotheBergeron.com

English, French, Spanish

*Open: All Year, April-October, Everyday
November-March, Monday-Friday*

B eauty in historic restoration, in modern applications and in technological wonders.

RESTORATION PERFECTION

Located just south of the Saint-Julien appellation, near the river along the wine route of D2, is a top-level Cru Bourgeois château with unique and interesting tourism.

Looking at this château photograph (left), the castle does not even look real, as it was restored to such absolute perfection. This is an undoctored photo. It is as though they sanded each stone back to its original beauty. And they did! The inside is clean and modern where the tours start. This is where you begin to experience their technological surprises (I won't give it away here).

This property began in the 18th century by scientist Jaques de Bergeron who was interested in everything nature; not just vines and agronomy. His interests included bugs, fertilizers and other congruent plants and trees. Ultimately, he published an important methodology for grafting the vines in Bordeaux. His Bergeron Method was used in Bordeaux through the 20th century.

As a result of the quality of this agronomy and winemaking techniques, Château Lamothe Bergeron rose to the superior level of quality with Cru Bourgeois certification. Today the property is owned by a Cognac house, which means you can taste and buy Cognacs here too.

Tours are of great fascination here with an innovative approach to understanding winemaking and wine tasting. They begin in the 19th century castle, meandering through the gardens to a observation deck to fully take in the vineyards' landscape and soils. Then, as you enter the winery and cellar, holographic images take over and present the winemaking process in a way you have never been able to experience until now.

Choose tastings from two to five wines, a vertical tasting experience, wine workshops, wine and macarons tasting, lunch and wine picnic or just a glass of wine and a nap in the garden (blanket provided) under century-old trees.

Collection of Wines
Château Lamothe Bergeron
(First Label - Cru Bourgeois)

Demoiselles de Bergeron
(Second Wine - Light Red)

Nove
(Limited Edition Since 2014 - A Powerful Red)

MÉDOC **HAUT-MÉDOC** (Central)
Winery (Château)
CHÂTEAU LAMOTHE BERGERON

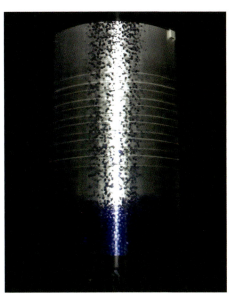

A HOLOGRAPHIC EDUCATION

This place is awesome. The technology, interactions, holograms, black-light visuals... all very cool. Unlike anything you will experience at any other château.

And educational. The holograms are designed to be very interesting, extremely educational, and visually stimulating. All true.

Out of the darkness, the tank above lights up holographically, showing the grapes filling the tank, gasses forming, pump-over occurring, berries floating, sugars turning to alcohol, tank emptying; something you could never see through stainless steel, concrete or wood vats.

Here, the visually exciting movement inside the tank tells the story of the winemaking process.

Far left, the winemakers appear three-dimensionally inside the barrel room and speak to you about the many considerations they make in producing a top-level Cru Bourgeois wine. They write on the glass (so it seems) as they consider each component and they explain as you watch.

This château has many more surprises, holographic and otherwise. These are the most amazing experiences you can imagine. Interesting, educational and with lots of innovation. Only at Château Lamothe Bergeron.

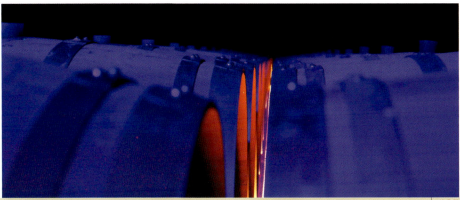

MÉDOC **HAUT-MÉDOC** (Central)
Restaurant
RESTAURANT LE LION D'OR

11 Route de Pauillac
33460 Arcins, France

+33 (0)5 56 58 96 79

LeLionDOr-Arcins.fr

French, English (little)

*Open: Tuesday-Saturday
Lunch & Dinner*

LOCAL HANGOUT

Located right on the D2 between Margaux and Saint-Julien in the little village of Arcins. This is a local's restaurant. The food is excellent and the prices even better. Reservations are a must. I tried walking in a few times, then I finally had someone call and book my table. So worth it.

I suggest their Discovery Menu of authentic cuisine, locally sourced foods from the land and estuary, prepared daily according to the owner/chef Michael Lemonnier's inspiration.

Flavorful salad topped with a variety of pork offerings (photo right). Interesting. Savory.

Locally raised beef shish kabob with chef's special glaze and potatoes (photo far right).

Vanilla bean ice cream, canelé, and Sarments de Mademoiselle chocolate (photo below).

This is a local's hangout. Experience a real French environment of eating, drinking and having good times with friends and family.

MÉDOC **HAUT-MÉDOC** (Central)

Restaurant
LE BONTEMPS

2 Place du Général de Gaulle
33460 Cussac Fort Médoc, France

+33 (0)9 83 02 14 16
RestaurantLeBontemps@Gmail.com

French, English (little)

Open: Monday-Friday: 10:00am-5:00pm

On the D2, centrally located in the Médoc, is a quick bite of casual gourmet food.

EXCELLENT WEEKDAY LUNCH

In the parking lot next to the church of Cussac, this unpretentious cafe is actually a delicious delight for lunch. This is a great weekday spot to grab an excellent meal indoors or outdoors.

Soft-boiled egg (photo upper left) on top of a bed of delicious green beans, topped with seeds and onions. Divine!

A lightly toasted bun filled with Pyrénées ham and fresh salad of shaved white radish, onions and greens (photo below left).

Lamb shanks, succulent and tender, cooked with herbs in its own juices (photo left).

Beef and foie gras sausage topped with caramelized onions and raisins. Plus, super-thin delicate homemade potato chips (photo below).

BORDEAUX · MÉDOC SAINT-JULIEN AOC
Lesser-Known Greatness of the Grand Cru Classés

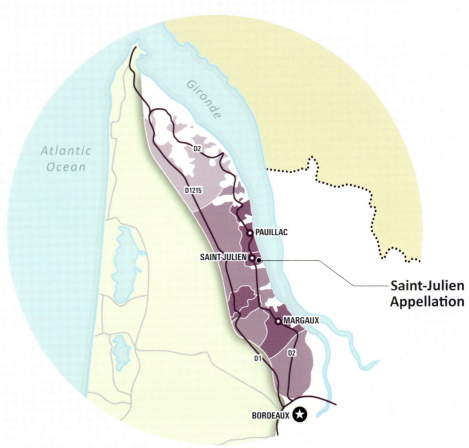

Left page: View from the observation tower at Château Gruaud Larose

A SMALL SPECIAL APPELLATION

Saint-Julien is a small appellation immediately south and adjacent to the famed Pauillac appellation of classified first-growths. Saint-Julien may be small in size; however, big on talent with excellent terroir.

The land here is covered with gravel and pebbles, which provides the naturally regulated soil temperature especially important for Cabernet Sauvignon, the primary grape grown here. The gravelly ridges, where the vineyards are planted, create excellent drainage very important for the vines. The vineyards lie on a bed of sedimentary rock with a mix of sand, clay and sedimentary deposits, creating the magic of the terroir here.

Saint-Julien is also a tiny cute little village in the middle of the appellation right on Highway D2. It has a nice lunch spot, **Bistrot Chez Mémé**, and an amazing gourmet restaurant for dinner, **Le Saint-Julien**. Plus, a cave (wine shop) that has some nice unexpected wines from small châteaux. Because they are wine distributors, **Vins de Saint-Julien** gets interesting wines at very good prices.

There are four very special châteaux I want to introduce you to in this appellation. They are all Grand Cru Classés of 1855. They really bring to light the quality and tourism opportunities of this little appellation and community.
- Château Gruaud Larose, page 143
- Château Léoville Poyferré, page 145
- Château Lagrange, page 147
- Château Beychevelle, page 151

Exploring Wine Regions **Bordeaux** | 141

MÉDOC **SAINT-JULIEN**
Winery (Château)
CHÂTEAU GRUAUD LAROSE

Deuxième Cru (Second-Growth)
Grand Cru Classé of 1855
Winner: Best Of Wine Tourism

33250 Saint-Julien-Beychevelle, France

+33 (0)5 56 73 89 43
GL@Gruaud-Larose.com

Gruaud-Larose.com

English, French, Spanish, German, Portuguese, Russian

Open: April-October, Monday-Saturday
November-March, Monday-Friday
By Appointment Only

Observation tower offers spectacular views over the vineyards, château and winery, across the Saint-Julien landscape.

VIOLENT STORMS, THOMAS JEFFERSON AND NAPOLÉON III

In February 1872, Marie-Thérèse set sail for Saigon, hitting a common and violent storm there, sinking her in the Straits of Gaspar. Just another common casualty... until 1992 when the ship was discovered and up came 2,000 bottles of Château Gruaud Larose. Despite spending 120 years in cold quiet dark submission, this noble wine showed its beautiful character over a century later.

In May 1778, prior to becoming President of the United States, Thomas Jefferson visited Bordeaux as Ambassador to France and ended up learning how old vines produced better wine. His vast knowledge and curiosity of wine led him to not only ranking Château Gruaud Larose high as a second Grand Cru, and it inspired the opportunity for him to create the acclimatization of the European vine for the distribution of wine worldwide.

In 1855, Emperor Napoléon III declared the official ranking of Grand Crus Classés with Château Gruaud Larose scoring as a 2nd classified growth.

Gruaud Larose is an extraordinary property where history has moulded the wine within the Saint-Julien appellation, a distinct appellation, with no comparison of any other district. History and terroir have made their marks.

Today, the winery uses modern technology to make better use of the harvest from this special land. A modern tasting room was built with a towering lookout to witness the magnificent terroir. Historic buildings also remain.

There are all types of tours and activities here. All tours include the Observation Tower, vineyards, winery, cellars and tastings. Plus, wine and cheese pairings, a chocolate and wine pairing, a harvest workshop, a wine tasting course, and a cooking course. Tastings also come with the opportunity for four different historical verticals of wines. I would choose the wines of great vintages: the 1995, 2000, 2005, and 2010. There are several concepts of choice. Reservations required.

Collection of Wines
Château Gruaud Larose
(First Label - Grand Cru)

Sarget de Gruaud Larose
(Second Wine)

MÉDOC SAINT-JULIEN
Winery (Château)
CHÂTEAU LÉOVILLE POYFERRÉ

1855 GRAND CRU CLASSÉ

Deuxième Cru (Second-Growth)
Grand Cru Classé of 1855

38 Rue de Saint-Julien
33250 Saint-Julien-Beychevelle, France

+33 (0)5 56 59 08 30
LP.Visite@Leoville-Poyferre.fr

Leoville-Poyferre.fr

English, French, Mandarin, Cantonese

Open: All Year, April-October, Monday-Saturday
November-March, Monday-Friday
By Appointment Only (Walk-In Tastings accepted)
Leoville-Poyferre.fr/en/visits-and-tastings

From the largest property in the Médoc, to a Second Classified-Growth Grand Cru, Léoville Poyferré rises above as a premier wine producer of excellence.

THE HISTORY OF A GREAT WINE

This property began as noble heritage, nearly 400 years ago, with notable Château Margaux and Château Lafite. It was in 1740 that Alexandre de Gascq-Léoville created the Léoville estate by purchasing every great vineyard-planting property he could acquire, ultimately creating the largest vineyard estate in the Médoc at that time, and with four different château labels.

Through an inheritance to Baron Poyferré de Cerès, Château Léoville Poyferré was born the same year as the United States, in 1776. In 1855 Emperor Napoléon III bestowed Grand Cru status to them as a second classified-growth of the Médoc. Unfortunately, difficult times ensued due to finances, weather and disease. Château Léoville Poyferré was then fortunately purchased and now managed by the Cuvelier family since 1920.

For a 100 years now, numerous Cuvelier family members have contributed to the success of Château Léoville Poyferré. The vineyards have been completely restructured and replanted to maximize terroir per varietal. The winery has been modernized with the latest technology. The winemaking team has advanced the wine quality to a new level of excellence, which I hope you are ready to try. And there is a warm reception for wine tourism that will make you feel at home and educated. Your taste buds will be enlightened. Expert or novice, they will customize a tour and tasting based on whatever you want to see or learn.

If you love chocolate, they have a wine and chocolate pairing for indulging. Reservations for a tour are a must. They also have a great gift shop with more than just wine.

Collection of Wines
Château Léoville Poyferré
(First Label - Grand Cru)

Pavillon de Léoville Poyferré
(Second Wine)

Château Moulin Riche
(A Cru Bourgeois Wine)

MÉDOC SAINT-JULIEN
Winery (Château) and Hotel
CHÂTEAU LAGRANGE

Troisième Cru (Third-Growth)
Grand Cru Classé of 1855
Winner: Best Of Wine Tourism

33250 Saint-Julien-Beychevelle, France

+33 (0)5 56 73 38 38
Visites@Chateau-Lagrange.com

Chateau-Lagrange.com

English, French

Open: All Year
April-September, Monday-Saturday
October-March, Monday-Friday
By Appointment Only

Collection of Wines
Château Lagrange
(First Label - Grand Cru)

Les Fiefs de Lagrange
(Second Wine)

Le Haut-Médoc de Lagrange
(Haut-Médoc Wine)

Les Arums de Lagrange
(Sauvignon Blanc, Sauvignon Gris, Semillon)

S imply a beautiful expansive estate from the Romans through the Middle Ages and today.

A PROPERTY AS BEAUTIFUL AS ITS WINES

This property has even deeper history. It is one of those places the Romans discovered possibly as early as the first century B.C. There was not much documented detail to this history until 416 A.D. when planting vines in this terroir was paramount.

Although wine production continued through the Middle Ages with property ownership mostly untraceable, Lagrange became the largest wine producing estate in the Médoc.

The 18th century brought noble ownership and prestige to the property, elevating its wines. Baron de Brane, a member of the Bordeaux Parliament and owner of Château Mouton, brought obvious widespread fame to the wines.

Jean-Valère Cabarrus, an influential wine merchant, commissioned the construction of the Tuscan-style château, which is now the centerpiece of the property and emblem of Château Lagrange labels. Even Thomas Jefferson, as President of the United States, visited and deemed Lagrange an important classified growth. And the Count Duchâtel, who was a politician and secretary to King Louis-Philippe, expanded the property to 300 hectares, making their vineyards the largest in the Saint-Julien appellation.

Today, this massive property boasts over 300 species of trees, including a cedar tree that is three centuries old. There is a stream flowing into a natural lake attracting birds and wildlife of all sorts. This is a property to enjoy a glass of wine, Château Lagrange of course, while meandering the rich landscape for hours and hours.

The Japanese whisky company, Suntory, acquired the château in 1983 and commenced with a complete restructuring of the vineyards, an unbelievably spectacular renovation of the property and buildings, including the castle. They also modernized the winery to fulfill their ambition of producing a refined, elegant, expressive wine.

Imagine all this while producing over 700,000 bottles of wine, still hand-picking and hand-sorting every grape before they are touched by technology. This is true Grand Cru status in action.

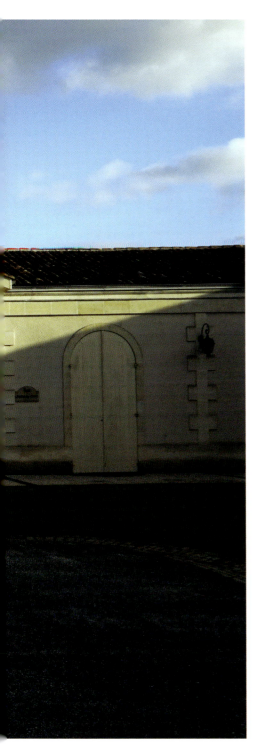

MÉDOC **SAINT-JULIEN**

Winery (Château) & Hotel
CHÂTEAU LAGRANGE

LES JARDINS DE LAGRANGE
The Gardens & Hospitality of Lagrange

12 ROOMS • 2 SUITES • GOURMET CHEF • SPECTACULAR LANDSCAPE

I am sure you have figured out that Saint-Julien is centrally located in the middle of the Médoc, making Château Lagrange a very convenient place for your accommodations. They have 12 beautifully appointed, modern rooms. And two spacious suites as well. All surrounded by extensive vineyards.

The rooms, as well as the dining and lounging areas, are located away from the tourists and wine production facilities of the property, providing privacy and serenity. You will totally enjoy the early morning cooked-to-order breakfast, followed by a stroll of the property before visitors arrive.

The property is spectacularly beautiful, both in landscape and in architecture. Meander the stone walkways, see the many French gardens, find the natural lake overlooked by the castle where the ducks will greet you with welcoming chatter.

Breakfast is included. Lunch and dinner can be arranged for 4+ people, guests or non-guests.

Gourmet Lunches and Dinners (wine pairings)
• **l'Authentique de Lagrange.** Terroir recipes cooked with local market products.
• **La Gourmandise du Chef** (on demand). A gastronomic menu revisiting key French dishes.
Tours & Tastings
• **The Classic Tasting**. Enjoy the beauty of their four different wines.
• **The Tailor-Made Tastings**. Horizontal tastings, vertical tastings, blind tastings, as well as wine and mature cheese tastings.
• **The Blending Workshop**. Make your own blend, your own Grand Vin.

All visits include a guided tour through the French gardens and among the vineyards where you will learn about their unique terroir. Then enter the massive state-of-the-art vat room to reach the underground tunnel to the massive cellar.

MÉDOC SAINT-JULIEN
Winery (Château) and Hotel
CHÂTEAU BEYCHEVELLE

Quatrième Cru (Fourth-Growth)
Grand Cru Classé of 1855

33250 Saint-Julien-Beychevelle, France

+33 (0)5 56 73 38 01
Visite@Beychevelle.com

Beychevelle.com

French, English, Italian, Spanish, Mandarin

*Open: All Year
May-September, Monday-Saturday
October-April, Monday-Friday
By Appointment Only*

T he contrast of history and the most modern winery imaginable, coexisting in harmony.

LEGENDS, LUXURY & LOVE

This is a property of extraordinary historical contrasts. The château is a magnificent castle of preserved antiquity from the 16th century. Yet, the winery has ultra modern architecture and the most current state-of-the-art technology. All working together on this beautiful property amongst French gardens and rolling vineyards.

The contrast of ownership is interesting as well. The château, the magnificent castle, was originally built in 1565 by the ordained Bishop from the Archdiocese of Bordeaux. In the next century, the first Duke of Épernon bought the property giving it much prestige. Then it was rebuilt 200 years later by Nobleman Marquis in 1757. Then another 200 years later, in the 20th century, two different families purchased the estate and both expanded the château into what has been endearingly called the *Little Versailles of the Médoc*.

This first Duke of Épernon had a huge impact on the estate. He was the Governor of the province and a Grand-Admiral with a great reputation, so when boats sailed along the Gironde passing by the property, they would lower their sails to show their allegiance. This gesture of respect gave rise to the château's emblem, a ship with a griffon-shaped prow; its name in Gascon, Bêcha vêla, meaning "baisse voile" ("lower the sails"). Later, the name evolved to become Beychevelle. It is interesting how names come to be.

In homage to the Grand-Admiral, the new modern winery was designed to behold the legend of this first Duke of Épernon and his important contribution to its name and great reputation. Architect Arnaud Boulain designed the new Château Beychevelle winery inspired by elements of tall ships, sails, and the movements of sailing the globe. See the waves aside the building in the photo above. The chandelier in the photo left is a mast with sails protruding from the ceiling in majestic and simplistic beauty. The next page's spread of their aging cellar makes you feel you are in the bowels of a ship.

The design is inspiring, you really must visit, and the technology and modern concepts incorporated into the winery are most impressive. Innovation is at its ultimate with the latest and most sophisticated advancements in technology to further their quality of winemaking.

We really must not forget the wine as we get wrapped up in the romance of this property. The terroir of Saint-Julien is special, and particularly this estate, located just one kilometer from the river. Deep gravelly soil that drains well and resists spring frost produces a wine with a delicate bouquet, fine structure, soft yet full tannins, bringing out an elegance of luscious fruit and beautiful color.

They received the Grand Cru Classé of 1855 distinction of excellence with a great reputation all over the world, further elevating their mastery of excellence with the new technology in the winery.

Collection of Wines
Château Beychevelle
(First Label - Grand Cru)

Amiral de Beychevelle
(Second Wine)

Les Bruliéres de Beychevelle
(Haut Médoc Wine)

Barrel Cellar, aging the wine at Château Beychevelle

MÉDOC **SAINT-JULIEN**

Winery (Château) and Hotel
CHÂTEAU BEYCHEVELLE

LE TABLE DE BEYCHEVELLE
The Table of Beychevelle
Extraordinary hospitality of luxury accommodations, gourmet dinners and special wines of new and old vintages at this Grand Cru Classé of 1855.

LIVE THE LIFE OF FRENCH ARISTOCRATS (FOR A FEW DAYS)

This 16th century castle is restored (redecorated and modernized) to beautiful authentic perfection. They have 11 rooms and two suites for rent! Check out the pictures. This place is amazing. Plus two reception rooms, a meeting room and a grand dining room for elaborate dinners, which they customize for their guests, complete with the general manager dining with you. This is a remarkable experience!!!

Le Table de Beychevelle is a unique opportunity to experience life like the aristocrats did in this authentic castle, with service just as opulent as the nobles received.

And "Le Table" takes on a much deeper meaning as they put on a dinner of grand proportions. This is like living in a family home, not a guest house, and definitely not a hotel. Here, you will feel welcomed and like royalty!

This is a food and wine lovers' paradise in every respect, from the hors d'oeuvres in the foyer, through dinner and dessert, with a historical vintage experience of their Grand Cru Classé wines.

The 21st century winery brings contrast to this marvelous estate. Tours are interesting as they take you through six centuries of history up to the most current of modern technology in winemaking. You will visit the historic castle and the modern winery and cellar. And taste, of course, their excellent wines.

• **The Admiral's Tour**. Property tour with a guided tasting of their wines

• **The Secrets of the Winegrower**. Learn their secrets here alongside a winemaker, full immersion of the inner workings of the winery and cellar. Plus a mystery tasting of four of their wines.

• **The Masterclass**. You are considered "Special Guest Status" with a personal guide for an in-depth look at their legendary history through modern times, seeing the full property inside and out, with a guided tasting of five of their finest wines.

MÉDOC **SAINT-JULIEN**
Restaurant
LE SAINT-JULIEN

11 Rue de Saint-Julien
33250 Saint-Julien-Beychevelle, France

+33 (0)5 56 59 63 87

Restaurant-Le-Saint-Julien.com

English, French

Open: Everyday
Lunch: 12:00pm-2:00pm
Dinner: 7:30pm-9:30pm
Reservations Through Their Website or Call

A beautiful setting of gourmet delights, open for lunch and dinner every day.

FRESH TRUFFLES ANYONE?

Imagine a basket of truffles brought to your table to choose from, like you would a cut of meat or fish. Owner and Chef Claude Broussard is obsessed with truffles of many creative sorts.

Imagine a creamy soup topped with thinly sliced truffles (photo left page), so uniquely rich and flavorful.

How about a salad of buffalo mozzarella and truffles (below left), with fresh dressing.

And even more. Local Médoc oysters, duck liver ravioli, roasted lamb, beef back steak, monkfish on the bone, and a crawfish pot.

Homemade vanilla ice-cream, atop crushed nuts, and fresh whipped cream with a chocolate stick (photo below).

DOWNTOWN SAINT-JULIEN

Saint-Julien is a very small village of just 600 people, sharing the same name as, and located in the Saint-Julien wine region. Saint-Julien is open and spacious, with a nice little square and park in the middle of the village.

Located right on the main road, highway D2, it is only a couple of blocks long with an extraordinary restaurant **Le Saint-Julien** (previous page) and a small casual lunch spot **Bistrot Chez Mémé** (next page). There is also a unique wine shop **Via Vinum** stocked with Saint-Julien and other Bordeaux wines that you would not normally find. This is a great place for wine discovery as the mother-and-son team knows their châteaux and finds quality undiscovered wines.

■ MÉDOC **SAINT-JULIEN** DOWNTOWN

Wine Merchants
VIA VINUM - VINS DE SAINT-JULIEN

6 Rue des Platanes • 33250 Saint-Julien-Beychevelle, France
+33 (0)5 56 59 60 86 • Mathieu@Via-Vinum.com • Open: Monday-Saturday

Via-Vinum.com

Vins de Saint-Julien is a unique wine shop in that they collect wines from lesser known producers of very high quality. Madam Isabelle Lassalle-Cherbonneau, owner of this wine shop, is also a wine negotiant with 20+ years in the wine trade. Isabelle knows how to find the under-discovered wines and make them available to us. You can find extraordinary wines with much lower costs than the big names. And they have the big names too!

Her English-speaking son Mathieu runs the wine shop and is very knowledgeable and friendly. They will also ship your wines home for you if you do not want to carry them.

MÉDOC **SAINT-JULIEN**
Restaurant
BISTROT CHEZ MÉMÉ

30 Rue de Saint-Julien
33250 Saint-Julien Beychevelle, France

+33 (0)5 56 73 85 32

BistrotChezMeme.Overblog.com

English, French

Lunch: Monday-Saturday, 12:00pm-2:00pm

Casual bistro with a creative delicious menu. A local's hangout, just for lunch, on the D2 in the little Saint-Julien village.

A LOCAL TRADITION

In the square of the Saint-Julien village, this is the local's hangout for tasty lunches. It is a small place with both indoor and outdoor dining and creative foods. Open just two hours per day with service that is serious and prompt. They have daily specials, which were the best dishes at our table.

Imagine a hamburger (photo below), with a waffle as the bun. Delicious.

Super delicious chicken leg (photo left), juicy tender and full of flavor. Served over mashed potatoes and vegetables.

BORDEAUX · MÉDOC **PAULLAC AOC**
The Boldness of First-Growths Maturing Here for Centuries

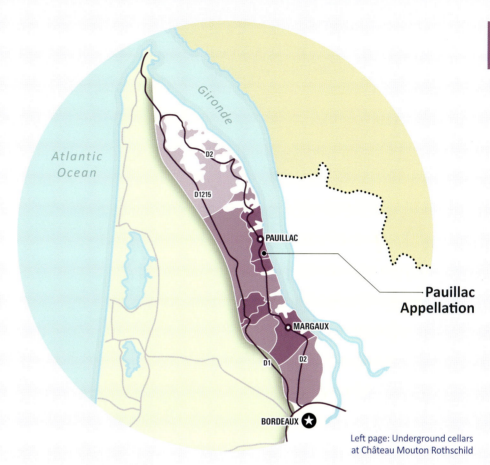

Left page: Underground cellars at Château Mouton Rothschild

MOST PRESTIGIOUS

We started this book by considering that Bordeaux was the center of the wine universe. Once we drill down into the wine regions here, we recognized the Médoc as the key appellation of the grand estates, the Grand Cru Classés of 1855 and Cru Bourgeois wines. Drilling further, Pauillac is the sub-appellation that is most recognized appellations, deemed by many as the undisputed capital of the Médoc.

Pauillac wines are some of the most prestigious in the world, giving rise to 18 Grand Cru Classés in 1855, including three (of only five) first-growths (Lafite-Rothschild, Latour and Mouton-Rothschild). The terroir here is unique, especially the soil, and is considered the ultimate for Cabernet Sauvignon. Deep concentrations of large gravelly stones on top of sand (with clay in the sub-soils) and vineyards planted on slopes and hillsides, allow for good water drainage. At the same time, this causes the roots to grow deep, struggling to reach the water-absorbed clay during crucial dry spells. Not good for most crops; however, these are the optimum conditions for Cabernet Sauvignon. The magic of Pauillac.

This is an appellation where all the Grand Cru Classés are competing heavily to have first-growth qualities. And succeeding. In 1990, for example, many consider Pichon Baron and Lynch-Bages to have made better wines than the first-growths! This is the place to explore Cabernet Sauvignon.

- Château Mouton Rothschild, page 163
- Château Pichon Baron, page 169
- Château Bellevue-Cardon, page 173
- Château Pédesclaux, page 175
- Château Batailley, page 179
- Château Lynch-Moussas, page 181
- Château Lynch-Bages, page 185

Exploring Wine Regions Bordeaux

MÉDOC **PAUILLAC**
Winery (Château)
CHÂTEAU MOUTON ROTHSCHILD

Premier Cru (First-Growth)
Grand Cru Classé of 1855

33250 Pauillac, France

+33 (0)5 56 73 21 29
Chateau-Mouton-Rothschild.com/contact

Chateau-Mouton-Rothschild.com

English, French

Open: All Year, Monday-Friday
By Appointment Only
Reservations Available On Their Website

Collection of Wines
Château Mouton Rothschild
(First Label - Grand Cru)

Le Petit Mouton de Mouton Rothschild
(Second Wine)

Aile d'Argent
(White Wine)

It is those with grand ambitions, willing to take bold steps outside of tradition that transform an industry, who deserve the highest honor.

INNOVATION AND WINE

Château Mouton Rothschild is more than an extraordinary wine, more than a first-growth Grand Cru Classé, and more than the illustrious Rothschild family... Mouton Rothschild is an innovator of grand proportions in the wine industry. They forged new directions, redefining the wine business, especially the marketing and distribution system, which has dramatically reshaped the industry.

It all began in 1853 when Baron Nathaniel de Rothschild purchased what was called then "Château Brane-Mouton" from British royalty. Why? Because he needed high-quality wines to serve his prestigious guests. So he bought the best he could find and immediately changed the name to his: Château Mouton Rothschild.

My understanding is that Baron Nathaniel was active in the movement for classified-growth wines, the Premier Cru status for first-growths, working with Emperor Napoléon and his *Exposition Universelle de Paris*, which lead to the Grand Cru Classés of 1855... except Château Mouton Rothschild was left out of first-growth premier position. Mouton was sorely named second growth. For the next 65 years, all was quiet with the Rothschilds, they didn't even visit their own estate.

For generations, the Rothschilds have enjoyed the extraordinary wines and nice profits of the château. It was not until 1922, that Baron Philippe de Rothschild (Baron Nathaniel's great-grandson) inherited the estate at age 20 and moved to Bordeaux.

MÉDOC PAULLAC
Winery (Château)
CHÂTEAU MOUTON ROTHSCHILD

And moved to Bordeaux he did.

Baron Philippe made this his lifelong passion.

Can you imagine taking the reigns of this massive and prestigious estate at age 20? Well, it turned out to be the best thing that ever happened to Château Mouton Rothschild.

Just two years later Baron Philippe made a huge bold move to take on the all-powerful wine merchants who controlled the wine industry. Wine merchants used to negotiate with châteaux for their wines, which were delivered in barrels. The merchants bottled the wine in their own facilities with labels they created and with their own names on them. The Baron bucked the system big-time; bottled his own wine and hired well-known artist Jean Carlu to design his labels. In 1924, the Chateau Mouton Rothschild vintage was released by the winery. The outrage was intense. The uproar was tremendous.

And the Baron did not back off. He summoned the other top-growths to take quality control into their own hands by bottling themselves in their own facilities. And it happened. They followed suit. Soon wineries realized they needed to create their own brands, labeling and bottling their own wines, all within their quality control. Baron Philippe inspired an entire industry, significantly revolutionizing the world of wine.

The new artistic label might have been ahead of its time, he thought, and went back to a traditional label design (his of course) the next year and waited 20 years before he took on this idea again. In 1945 and thereafter, the labels for each vintage were original artwork specially created for Mouton by a famous contemporary artist. Some highlights are: Miró, Chagall, Picasso, Dali, Warhol, and so on.

Speaking of Picasso, the 1973 label was created by Picasso to celebrate another major achievement by Baron Philippe. The Baron conducted Mouton as though it was a first-growth, continually enhancing the image and quality of wine, and fought vigorously for more than 20 years to officially secure its elevation to first-growth status. This has never happened since the establishment in 1855. Some châteaux may have deserved elevation, some a demotion, and maybe some ousted. Baron Philippe finally triumphed in 1973, when Mouton was officially decreed as one of only five Premier Grand Cru Classés of 1855.

Baron Philippe de Rothschild was truly a visionary genius, a man of commitment and action during his 66 years of reign (1922-1988). He changed a winery, and at the same time, changed the world of wine.

MÉDOC **PAUILLAC**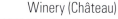
Winery (Château)
CHÂTEAU MOUTON ROTHSCHILD

BARON PHILIPPE THE POET

THE MOTTO OF MOUTON ROTHSCHILD

1855	*Premier ne puis,* *Second ne daigne,* *Mouton suis.*	*1855*	*First I cannot be,* *Second I do not deign to be,* *Mouton I am.*
1973	*Premier je suis,* *Second je fus,* *Mouton ne change.*	*1973*	*First I am,* *Second I used to be,* *Mouton does not change.*

Baron Philippe was also an expressive poet. These poems reveal the emotional impact between him and wine. Above is how he felt before and after his achievement of elevating Mouton to first-growth status. Below, well, I think we can all relate and appreciate.

> *" Wine, it is born, then it lives,*
> *but die it does not,*
> *in man it lives on. "*

Baron Philippe was an artist and lover of the arts and, with his second wife, maintained strong relationships between Mouton and the arts. They collected important pieces from all over the world that related to grapes and wine. Some rare items included: 17th century German jugs, cups and goblets from the kings of Naples; Medieval tapestries, paintings, ivories, and glassware; and Chinese, Japanese and Persian porcelain.

All of this culminated into the opening of a museum on the Mouton property. The **Museum of Wine and Art** opened in 1962, transforming the winery into one of the leading Bordeaux tourist attractions. It was extremely unusual for a château in Bordeaux to accept visitors. They made wine, not entertain guests. The Baron continued his bold moves with the museum as well as opening an art gallery, displaying the original paintings created by famous artists for the labels of each year's Château Mouton Rothschild bottles. Today, Mouton Rothschild offers a beautiful tourism experience. By appointment only, a curated tour takes you through the vineyards and gardens, into the spectacular winery (photo left and below) and the Grand Chai aging cellar (photo four pages previous), through the museum and art gallery, and to a tasting of their extraordinary wines. All a beautiful experience.

Baron Philippe made another bold move by forging a partnership with a California winery in 1979. Remember in 1976 at the Judgement of Paris, a blind tasting declared a California wine winning the best wine against the French (for which the French have never forgotten). Nonetheless, Bordeaux's distinguished Baron Philippe joined with Napa's distinguished Robert Mondavi to create **Opus One** just three years later. This is the first ever Franco-Californian ultra-premium wine, planted, made, matured, and blended in the traditional Bordeaux manner, yet in Napa California.

Baron Philippe de Rothschild was a man of innovation, determination, creativity, and maybe above all else, full of bold ideas with the guts to take them on. Today, we have a legacy of extraordinary wines, unique and interesting tourism experiences, and an industry forever changed and inspired.

MÉDOC PAUILLAC
Winery (Château)
CHÂTEAU PICHON BARON

Deuxième Cru (Second-Growth)
Grand Cru Classé of 1855
Winner: Best Of Wine Tourism

33250 D2, Pauillac, France

+33 (0)5 56 73 17 17
Contact@PichonBaron.com

PichonBaron.com

English, French, Spanish, Portuguese, Czech, Chinese

Open: All Year, Everyday
By Appointment Only

L ocation. Location. Location. Not just a retail thing, supreme terroir is everything to making top-quality Grand Cru Classé wines.

SUPERIOR TERROIR. SPECTACULAR CHÂTEAU. SYNCHRONOUS WINERY.

The concept of terroir could not be more noticeable in the creation of this estate. Château Latour, one of the five Premier First-Growth Grand Cru Classés, has terroir of unquestionable quality and distinctive characteristics. Their steward in the 17th century, Pierre Desmezures de Rauzan, began purchasing many plots of land neighboring Latour with the intentions of giving them to his daughter upon marriage. In 1694 she married Baron Jacques Pichon de Longueville and thus the Pichon Baron estate was born. Achieving second-growth Grand Cru Classé status in 1855 I believe directly correlates to the quality of the extraordinary first-growth neighboring terroir.

The spectacular château you see towering in the center of the property (photo left page) was built in 1851. The Renaissance architecture, with its two emblematic turrets, was a sign of wealth and became the inspiration for the name of their second wine. The château stands proudly and imposing, reflecting the prestige of the wines here.

After many generation in the family, Château Pichon Baron was eventually sold to AXA Millésimes in 1987, who infused a tremendous amount of capital into the restoration of the château and the modernization of the winery. While the château went through a beautiful meticulous restoration, the winery received a total reconstruction.

The reconstruction of the winery was a lot more than a full modernization and work-flow efficiency. The design and usability of the space is part of what makes this winery visit so interesting and visually awe-inspiring. Now spanning the front of the château is a beautiful reflection pool in between the two winery buildings (photo above), also of impressive architecture.

Under the reflection pool reveals an expansive underground aging cellar between the two winery buildings. It is designed to make you feel you are in *Twenty Thousand Leagues Under the Sea* with views of both water and sky.

Collection of Wines
Château Pichon Baron
(First Label - Grand Cru)

Les Tourelles de Longueville
(Primarily Merlot, from their Sainte-Anne vineyard)

Les Griffons de Pichon Baron
(Primarily Cabernet Sauvignon, from their gravelly vineyards near the Gironde estuary)

MÉDOC **PAUILLAC**
Winery (Château)
CHÂTEAU PICHON BARON

TERROIR IS THE LEGACY OF THIS GRAND CRU

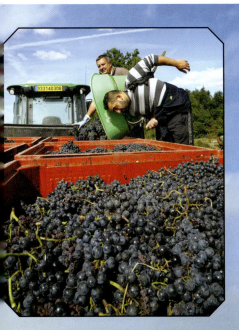

Here reveals this beautiful estate. See the amazing terroir, high on the plateau that Pierre Desmezures de Rauzan obtained for his daughter in the 17th century. Today, the vines have an average age of 35 years and are used to make their wonderful first-label Grand Cru Classé.

On tour here is a museum (so to speak) of their older vintages. Find your birth year. Was your birthday in a great year for Bordeaux? Mine wasn't. Tasting that 1907 (photo right) sure would be a treat! Can you imagine the 1881 vintage? Wow!

I was fortunate to experience a side-by-side tasting of the 2015 vintage (an excellent year) of all three tiers of that year's wines. While their Grand Cru Classé was of expected extraordinary deliciousness, the other two wines are really not seconds; they are unique exquisite blends at much better prices.

The **Les Tourelles de Longueville** is primarily Merlot of a softer and more distinctive difference to their Grand Cru (and drinkable much younger). They have a special vineyard, Sainte-Anne vineyard, where the terroir is conducive to growing Merlot.

The **Les Griffons de Pichon Baron** is a Cabernet Sauvignon blend from grapes grown near the Gironde Estuary (that is towards the direction of Château Latour) on very gravelly soil.

Don't miss experiencing **Château Pichon Baron** and all its glorious deep black fruits and subtle spice notes. It is more than everything you would expect of a second-growth Grand Cru Classé of 1855.

They have daily tours here all year, including weekends, holidays, summer and winter. You must have an appointment though.

Exploring Wine Regions **Bordeaux**

MÉDOC PAUILLAC
Winery (Château)
CHÂTEAU BELLEVUE-CARDON

33250 Pauillac, France

+33 (0)5 56 59 32 18
Chateau@Bellevue-Cardon.com

No Website

English, French, Dutch

Not Open - This is a Private Residence
Tastings and Sales at Château La Haye (page 203)

T erroir! Terroir! To be adjacent to the land of a first-growth Grand Cru means everything!

A FAMILY'S DREAM

Imagine you come to Bordeaux to participate in the wildly exciting *Marathon of the Médoc Châteaux*. This is a run, or a walk, along the D2 stopping at Grand Crus for a glass of wine to make the marathon much more interesting. That was 2008 for the Cardon family.

Two years later, they buy a château in Pauillac, the former home of the priest of Pauillac. Four years later, they acquired the vineyards (once used for making wine labeled as *adjacent to Château Latour*) surrounding their home (photo right).

Impressive, obtaining .6 hectares of first-growth, Premier Grand Cru Classé of 1855 vineyards... oh my gosh wow! That is the acquisition of a dream! Three years later in 2015, they released their first vintage as Château Bellevue-Cardon.

The story goes deeper. These vineyards originally belonged to the château and wine was produced dating back to the 1850s. Then, the frost of 1956 put that to an end. The vineyards were sold off and no longer part of the château.

Today, they have added their family name to the label and removed Latour (see photo right) and are bringing us the most incredible wine at a fraction of the price. How do you get some? The family also purchased *Château La Haye* in 2012 in the neighboring appellation of Saint-Estèphe (see page 203) where they have tastings and bottles for sale. Plus, Château La Haye is Cru Bourgeois classified with excellent wines of their own.

Collection of Wines
Château Bellevue-Cardon
(First Label)

MÉDOC PAUILLAC
Winery (Château)
CHÂTEAU PÉDESCLAUX

Cinquième Cru (Fifth-Growth)
Grand Cru Classé of 1855
Winner: Best Of Wine Tourism

33250 Route de Pédesclaux, Pauillac, France

+33 (0)5 57 73 64 64
Contact@Chateau-Pedesclaux.com

Pedesclaux.com

English, French, Japanese, German

Open: All Year, April-October, Monday-Saturday
November-March, Monday-Friday
By Appointment Only

U ltra modern brilliantly progressive winery, with forward-thinking technology, all on a historic Grand Cru Classé property.

HISTORIC CHÂTEAU WITH AN ENLIGHTENED NEW WINERY

Stand there! Take it all in. A historic château made of ancient limestone blocks, now encased in a modern glass structure designed by a visionary, the renowned architect Jean-Michel Wilmotte. Like no other château you will ever see. It is representative of the historic 1855 classification property wrapped with a modern design. Look through the glass on the right side and discover that even the historic birdhouse is encased in this glass palace.

History saw choice properties achieving the status of the Grand Cru Classé in 1855. Real estate became treasured here in Pauillac, especially with the fame of three first-growth Grand Crus. Château Pédesclaux is fortunate to have exceptionally great vineyards, neighboring both Rothschild properties, and Mouton owning them for a short time.

In 2009, Françoise and Jacky Lorenzetti acquired Pédesclaux from Chateau Mouton Rothschild with a grand plan to expand the vineyards and bring in the most innovative approaches to modern winemaking. They expanded the vineyards to 48 hectares through deliberate acquisitions adjacent to both Mouton and Lafite. Terroir is everything and Pédesclaux set itself up with this rich heritage.

With the construction of a brand new winery (photo below), they had a blank slate to create anything they wanted, including the impressive aging cellar (photo left) deep beneath this new building. Let's look at the precious care they give to their fruit when it enters and lives in the winery.

Collection of Wines
Château Pédesclaux
(First Label - Grand Cru)

Fleur de Pédesclaux
(Second Wine)

MÉDOC **PAULLAC**
Winery (Château)
CHÂTEAU PÉDESCLAUX

NO PUMPS, ONLY WINE ELEVATORS

OK, so some wineries claim they do not use pumps; however, this winery takes this concept to the very extreme. When grapes arrive at this winery, they are cared for with such delicateness and love you might expect with Japanese Kobe cows. Great heritage and even greater love.

Don't you just love the modern design (photos left)? Clean lines. Simple colors. Mood lighting. If I were a grape, this is where I would love to live. And they would love me back!

This is a totally new gravity-fed multi-level winery where everything has been designed to preserve the beautiful qualities of the grapes. This is mastery of gravity flow to the highest degree. Wine elevators (people use stairs) transport the wine gently up through the facility to the levels it needs to flow. Gentleness is magical in making wine.

It all begins when the grapes arrive at the top level of the winery, then sorted and placed in cold storage for very slow extraction to enhance the true aromas and color. Later, the grapes are gently added to the vats by gravity. They have 58 double compartment conical tanks (lower left) to be able to micro-vinify the various vineyards separately, as Pédesclaux has vineyards throughout the Pauillac appellation, with varying terroir, allowing them to select the nuances when blending to perfection.

Now for the clever pumpless pumpovers. The fermenting juice is gently released by gravity from its vat by hose into elevator tanks (upper left). They have four elevator tanks that go up and down, lifting the juice above the vinification tanks, then gently releasing the juice, again by gravity, through a hose back into the tank. Brilliant.

When the wine eventually leaves its tank for barrels, once again hoses are used to gently take the wine by gravity to the lower aging cellar to gently fill the oak barrels. In the end, the barrels take the elevator back up to the top of the winery for pump-free bottling.

This is like no winery tour you have ever experienced. And the wine is extraordinary. You will taste the gentleness in the smooth delicate tannins. You will see the beautiful color, smell the ripe fruit aromas and taste the flavorful deliciousness that fills your mouth with long lingering and developing nuances. Make a reservation and you will be happy you did.

MÉDOC PAULLAC
Winery (Château)
CHÂTEAU BATAILLEY

1855
Grand Cru Classé

Cinquième Cru (Fifth-Growth)
Grand Cru Classé of 1855

33250 D206, Pauillac, France

+33 (0)5 56 59 01 13
Domains@Borie-Manoux.fr

Batailley.com

English, French, German

*Open: May-July & September-December
Monday-Friday, By Appointment Only*

> History can be fascinating and even more compelling with delicious old wines.

NO BATTLE WINNING WINE EXCELLENCE

History can be so interesting and Château Batailley's is no exception. The Médoc is filled with castles, some for grandeur and some for defense. Batailley was one of the very first châteaux here, dating back to the 15th century and was quite well known because it was one of the oldest wine estates in Bordeaux.

And most significantly, in 1453, it got its name from the word "battle" with the end of the Hundred Years' War, the famous military battle where France defeated the British reign here.

The 19th century marked Napoléon III classifying Château Batailley as a Grand Cru Classé in 1855. And further, with Napoléon's landscape architect Barillet-Deschamps (a famous horticulturist responsible for planting many of the great gardens of Paris), they designed the beautiful park surrounding this property.

Then in 1961, the Castéja family, owners of nearby Château Lynch-Moussas (next page) and other wine estates in Bordeaux, purchased this special estate. The castle has been completely renovated, quite beautifully I must say, and is now their family home (photo above).

Philippe Castéja runs the family estates, their wine merchant business and serves as the President of the *Conseil des Grand Cru Classés en 1855*. He has invested considerably in the vineyards, winery and cellars, as well as his team, to elevate the quality of the wines here significantly.

Look at the cellar on the left page. Underground, Château Batailley keeps 1,200 bottles of each vintage. Such discipline! And I had the special opportunity to sit down with Philippe over lunch and share his 1959 vintage Grand Cru (below) and learn of his passions for excellence in pursuing greatness in all his wines.

Collection of Wines
Château Batailley
(First Label - Grand Cru)

Lions de Batailley
(Second Wine)

MÉDOC **PAUILLAC**

Winery (Château)
CHÂTEAU LYNCH-MOUSSAS

Cinquième Cru (Fifth-Growth)
Grand Cru Classé of 1855

33250 Madrac, Pauillac, France

+33 (0)5 56 00 00 70
Domains@Borie-Manoux.fr

Lynch-Moussas.com

English, French, German

*Open: May-July & September-December
Monday-Friday, By Appointment Only*

The boldness of a Cabernet Sauvignon with the softness of a Merlot; just the two of them in harmony as a Grand Cru Classé.

A SPECIAL ESTATE, WITH AN INTERESTING HISTORY

Here is another château owned and improved upon by the Castéja family. Originally the property was know as *Château Lynch,* as it was owned by the Lynch family. Prominence came through Count Jean-Baptiste Lynch, who was the Mayor of the City of Bordeaux and Earl of the Empire. When Jean-Baptiste Lynch died in 1835, Château Lynch was divided in half. Being located in Moussas, the name became Château Lynch-Moussas. The other half of the property was in Bages and became the well-known Château Lynch-Bages (see page 185). Lynch-Moussas kept the castle. Both properties became Grand Cru Classé in 1855.

The Castéja family bought the estate in 1919 and I feel fortunate to have been introduced to them on their 100th anniversary. When Philippe Castéja became involved in the year 2000, he quickly moved to introduce a second label the next year so they could dramatically increase the quality of the Grand Cru (for better blending of the finer quality juice, giving the seconds to the second wine).

Philippe Castéja invested a lot of time and money into restoring the vineyards, modernizing the winery, renovating the château, and adding superior talent to the team. This has made a huge difference in elevating the quality of the wine. It is considered that with the 2010 vintage forward, the Château Lynch-Moussas wines have achieved their best quality in centuries.

This is a massive estate. Not only are 62 hectares (153 acres) planted to vines, there are another 140 hectares (346 acres) devoted to forest and park land on the estate. This property is beautiful! Enjoy a glass of their wine upstairs overlooking the vineyards and forest. It is breathtaking!

Château Lynch-Moussas only grows Cabernet Sauvignon (75%) and Merlot (25%), and is one of the very few Médoc classified properties to only plant two grape varietals. I also found that the soil here is uniquely rich clay (see left page photo) conducive to growing Merlot, bringing an extra special quality to their wines.

Collection of Wines
Château Lynch-Moussas
(First Label - Grand Cru)

Les Hauts de Lynch-Moussas
(Second Wine)

PAUILLAC VILLAGE BAGES

This little hamlet as they call it, Bages, is a tiny restored village adjacent to **Château Lynch-Bages**. In 1749 Thomas Lynch began planting the vineyards here on the Bages land, thus creating the Château Lynch of Bages. Today, owner Jean-Michel Cazes salvaged his childhood village and conducted a full renovation of the village to beautiful historic excellence, with a lively food and wine theme around its central square.

Surrounding the square is the **Café Lavinal** restaurant, **Bages Bazaar** gift shop, **L'Atelier Vélo** bicycle rentals, **Boucherie de Bages** butcher shop with homemade specialties, and **Viniv** where you can make your own customized barrel of wine with the expertise of the Château Lynch-Bages winemaker and his team. And, just outside of the village is **Château Cordeilla-Bages**, a four-star hotel and Michelin-star restaurant in a historic château. All part of the luxury experience created by the Cazes family.

■ MÉDOC **PAUILLAC** BAGES
Boutique
BAGES BAZAAR

33250 Village Bages, Pauillac, France
+33 (0)5 56 59 15 40 • Contact@BagesBazaar.com
Open: Monday-Saturday, 10:00am-7:00pm

A must-visit discovery for your world of food and wine. A large two-story gift shop filled with so many interesting home decorations, personal items, cookware, tableware, numerous cooking and wine books, and local wines.

■ MÉDOC **PAUILLAC** BAGES
Bicycle Rental Shop
L'ATELIER VÉLO: LE COMPTOIR D'ANDRÉA

33250 Village Bages, Pauillac, France
+33 (0)5 56 09 76 62 • Info@FunBike.fr
Open: Thursday-Monday, 10:30am-6:00pm (July & August, Open Everyday)

Pauillac is a beautiful place to ride bicycles with its gentle sloping hills and spectacular scenery through the vineyards. Visit châteaux, the harbour, shops, and the carrelets (colorful wooden fishing huts along the river built on stilts). L'Atelier Vélo has all types of bicycles available, including electric, chainless and mountain bikes. They also have organized bike tours.

MÉDOC **PAUILLAC** BAGES
Restaurant Bistro Brasserie
LE CAFÉ LAVINAL

Passage du Desquet
33250 Village Bages, Pauillac, France

+33 (0)5 57 75 00 09
Contact@CafeLavinal.com

CafeLavinal.com

English, French

*Open: Monday-Saturday
12:00pm-2:00 pm & 7:00pm-9:00pm*

C asual 1930's style French gourmet brasserie with 120 bottles, 8 by the glass, of local wines.

LOCALS HANGOUT

In the village of Bages, adjacent to Château Lynch-Bages, Café Lavinal is a casual French bistro with gourmet cuisine in a lively ambiance of red moleskin seats and attentive service. On beautiful days, I recommend enjoying their outside terrace. This is a popular hangout to watch the local wine trade and winemakers gather and mingle.

Taste this: Amuse Bouche (photo left) a carrot veloute with cumin cream. Divine.

A Pumpkin Tart, so unique, with vegetables and vegetable shavings (below left).

Peach Vacherin (below) with verbena from their garden. Decadent.

Exploring Wine Regions **Bordeaux**

MÉDOC **PAUILLAC** BAGES
Winery (Château)
CHÂTEAU LYNCH-BAGES

Cinquième Cru (Fifth-Growth)
Grand Cru Classé of 1855
Global Winner: Best Of Wine Tourism

33250 Pauillac, France

+33 (0)5 56 73 19 30
Visit@LynchBages.com

LynchBages.com

English, French

*Open: March-November
Monday-Friday, By Appointment Only*

A completely new Grand Cru Classé winery with roots deep in tradition and hospitality.

GRAND CRU NEW

Have you ever seen a giant crane in the vineyards before? Me neither! Just a short distance from Highway D2, I could not miss the cranes towering into the sky. Cranes in an agriculture wine region, what is possibly being built? I thought, maybe a lofty resort? Could it be a high-rise office building? What? Little did I expect a Grand Cru Classé of 1855 winery being built, all new, from the ground up!

When you dig deeper, you find out that Jean-Michel Cazes, owner of Château Lynch-Bages, is quite the innovative forward-thinking entrepreneur in the wine regions. He is building a state-of-the-art winery to optimize the Grand Cru Classé terroir that has earned his wines a stellar reputation. Now, just think how much better their wines are going to get with the new technology and better facilities!

And even better for us, the new winery will be open for tours and tastings. Entering from the central square of the Bages Village, the entire complex will be integrated as Jean-Michel began restoring the village in 2000 and has created the ultimate mecca of food and wine magnificence.

This is where Jean-Michel grew up playing in the tiny streets of Bages. Restoring its charm and bringing in purveyors that make food and wine a passionate part of life (page 182) is very important to him. Bages has become a significant local and tourist destination. This has earned him the prestigious title of *Wine Tourism Pioneer* in 2010 by the French Superior Council of Wine Tourism (Conseil Supérieur de l'Œnotourisme).

The entire complex of the winery and the central square are integrated for a full-day experience here. The new winery began with the harvest of 2019 and opened to the public in 2020. They have created different experiences to learn about their winery and wines.

There is an entire day of enjoyment to be had here at Village Bages and Château Lynch-Bages. They are known for displaying modern art and the village is a restored historic beauty. Enjoy a gourmet lunch, shop for interesting gifts and wine accessories, take in the winery experience, go for a stroll or bike ride, and take away great wines.

Collection of Wines
Château Lynch-Bages
(First Label - Grand Cru)

Echo de Lynch-Bages
(Second Wine)

Blanc de Lynch-Bages
(Sauvignon Blanc, Sémillon and Muscadelle)

MÉDOC **PAULLAC** BAGES
Winery (Château)
CHÂTEAU LYNCH-BAGES

GRAND CRU TERROIR

We must not forget the historic terroir here that gives Château Lynch-Bages its magnificence of a Grand Cru Classé. They took no break in producing their wines (using their existing winery) while building anew.

It all began here with Thomas Lynch, a wine merchant, who believed in the quality of Pauillac terroir and particularly this property. He amassed a very large estate of vineyards at that time (1749-1824). Ultimately estates can get divided, which is why you see other châteaux bearing his name, as in Chateau Lynch-Moussas, also a Grand Cru Classé in Pauillac (page 181). Being in Bages, it was natural that his *Cru de Lynch* became *Chateau Lynch-Bages* in its new delineation.

Then, in 1939, a new era was born with the ownership by the Cazes family taking the reigns and masterfully introducing hospitality, tourism and the art of food and wine living. Many also believe they improved the quality of their wines above its fifth-growth classification. I agree.

In search of perfection, Lynch-Bages presorts their grapes right in the vineyard immediately upon picking (photo left page) before bringing them into the winery for further sorting. Here you see a Petit Verdot vineyard, such black inky grapes that add depth of color to their wines and complexity to the flavors and tannins.

I had the wonderful opportunity to have lunch with the Cazes family and their team during harvest. They are quite hospitable and generous people, providing lunch to their entire staff, during this special and busy time.

Little did I know, though, they had a blind tasting planned for me during lunch. Two decanters (photo below) with the winery and date hidden from me. Could I pick the château and vintage. Château was straightforward for me, as two different terroir gave them their unique distinction. Ormes de Pez (page 205) is a Cru Bourgeois château they own and have the same winemaker. Vintage, I was close. The process to figure this out is always so interesting.

Note, 2005 and 2009 were exceptionally great years in Bordeaux, so these wines were off-the-chart excellent. If you visit one of their wineries, you will be able to taste both château's wines.

MÉDOC **PAUILLAC** BAGES

Winery Hotel & Restaurant
CHÂTEAU CORDEILLAN-BAGES

A Relais & Châteaux Luxury Property
Global Winner: Best Of Wine Tourism

Route des Châteaux
33250 D2, Pauillac, France

+33 (0)5 56 59 24 24
Contact@CordeillanBages.com

CordeillanBages.com

English, French

*The Hotel is Open:
March-November*

*The Restaurant is Open:
March-November, Wednesday-Sunday
Lunch: 12:00pm-1:30pm
Dinner: 7:30pm-9:00pm
Reservations Available Online*

F our-star luxury in the middle of vineyards at a 17th century château

PAUILLAC LUXURY VIEW

Château Cordeillan-Bages is a gem among the Cazes family group of luxury food and wine experiences. Located just down the street from their Château Lynch-Bages winery (page 184) and Village Bages (page 182), alongside highway D2.

This is a boutique hotel with 28 luxury rooms and a Michelin star restaurant (next page), providing ultra-personalized service catering to their guests. Since 1992, they have been part of the Relais & Chateau hotel group, an association of restaurateurs and innkeepers who are passionate about the fine art of living. That is exactly what you will find here.

The main building is a historic 17th century château on two hectares of the original vineyards. They continue to make wine here (photo far right) and serve it in their restaurant. The rooms are of modern stylish comfort, especially their deluxe bathrooms, with fresh flowers! And views of the vineyards or quiet secluded courtyard (photo left).

Wine tasting, breakfast buffet and traditional breakfasts are available. They have a gym, sauna, heated outdoor pool, and patio seating.

Collection of Wines
Château Cordeillan-Bages

MÉDOC **PAUILLAC** BAGES
Winery Hotel & Restaurant
CHÂTEAU CORDEILLAN-BAGES

MICHELIN STAR RESTAURANT IN THE VINEYARDS

Let's start with lunch. They know you don't want to take too much time for lunch because you have wineries to visit. So they created a **one-hour gourmet three-course lunch!** Yes, it's for real. They are on top of it. And centrally located in the Médoc! You get gourmet cuisine and onto the next winery. That sure makes me very happy.

And yet I highly recommend you take your time and enjoy an evening with Chef Julien Lefebvre for dinner here. In just one year after his arrival in 2017, Julien earned his first Michelin star. Not surprising, as he trained under a three-star chef in Paris. He is a young guy with big aspirations, and Château Cordeillan-Bages is just the right place to appreciate his passion for food artistry and the joy of food and wine experiences.

Julien will stimulate your senses in many ways. Visually, his presentations are creative and interesting, serving in wooden boxes and tree branches (left), for example. In your mouth, the sensations of deliciousness will be an evening of magic. He is inventive with his ingredients and preparations, with fresh local ingredients from the region. Chef Julien is on a mission to be one of the best great chefs of the world, and you can find him here, in Pauillac, at Château Cordeillan-Bages.

Chef Julien says, "Cooking is all about wine." Good thing their cellar has 1,500 wines, including Bordeaux Grand Crus, and a talented sommelier for the pairings. There are several fantastic chef's tasting menus, plus his uniquely designed seven-course Ayurvedic cuisine, and the special one-hour gourmet lunch. So much to enjoy here!

DOWNTOWN PAUILLAC

Pauillac is a larger village in the Médoc (population 5,000), sharing the same name and located in the Pauillac wine region. It has a beautiful marina (sunrise picture to the right) and a street lined with restaurants across from the harbor, many of which have outdoor seating with views of the harbor.

Hotel Restaurant de France et d'Angleterre and **La Salamandre** (right page) offer great foods at great prices. **Maison Bellet** is simply a treat in decadence of French pastries.

A visit to the **Maison du Tourisme et du Vin** is a good place to start, as they can help you set appointments for the châteaux you read about in this book. Don't miss the upstairs for an excellent education in wine aromas.

■ MÉDOC **PAUILLAC** DOWNTOWN
Wine Merchant and Tourism
MAISON DU TOURISME ET DU VIN DE PAUILLAC

La Verrerie • 33250 Pauillac, France
+33 (0)5 56 59 03 08 • Open: Everyday, 9:30am-7:00pm

"Maison du Tourisme et du Vin" translates to "House of Tourism and Wine." This is the syndicate of wineries of the Pauillac appellation making their wines available all in one place. It is also the Tourism Office for Pauillac.

Many of the Pauillac châteaux have made their wines available for purchase here. There are many wine accessories, books and souvenirs available too. Their team will also call and make appointments for you at châteaux, restaurants and accommodations.

Upstairs is an interactive exhibit to learn about the aromas of wine. It is very well done; professional, interesting and educational for all levels of knowledge and interests.

■ MÉDOC **PAUILLAC** DOWNTOWN
Artisan Boulanger - Pâtissier (Bakery)
MAISON BELLET

Three locations in Pauillac • 33250 Pauillac, France
- **17 Rue Aristide Briand** • +33 (0)5 56 59 00 61
Open: Everyday, 6:00am-1:00pm & Tuesday-Saturday, 3:00pm-7:00pm
- **5 quai Albert de Pichon** • +33 (0)5 56 59 84 83
Open: Monday-Saturday, 7:00am-7:00pm
- **115 Route de Cagnon** • +33 (0)5 56 09 14 46
Open: Monday-Friday, 7:00am-1:00pm, 4:00pm-7:00pm, & Saturday, 8:00am-1:00pm

For 23 years Mr. Thierry Ballet has been baking in Pauillac and is the talk of the town when it comes to a bakery (boulangerie). A must go-to for creative snacks, sandwiches, and so many beautifully crafted sweet French pastries.

MÉDOC **PAUILLAC** DOWNTOWN
Restaurant
LA SALAMANDRE

15 Quai Léon Perrier • 33250 Pauillac, France
+33 (0)5 56 59 24 87

This is a casual place, open 7:15am to 10:00pm everyday with indoor and outdoor terrace seating overlooking the harbor. Very casual environment with excellent steaks (see photo below). Plus, a nice wine selection and very reasonable pricing.

MÉDOC **PAUILLAC** DOWNTOWN
Restaurant (and Hôtel)
HÔTEL RESTAURANT DE FRANCE ET D'ANGLETERRE

3 Quai Albert-Pichon • 33250 Pauillac, France
+33 (0)5 56 59 01 20 • Contact@HotelDeFrance-Anglette.com
HotelDeFrance-Angleterre.com

Delicious cuisine in a casual environment with excellent prices. As part of a hotel (I have not seen inside the hotel), this restaurant is open for breakfast, lunch and dinner. With nice weather, sit on the terrace and enjoy the sunrise over the marina (photo left page). Lunch is equally beautiful outside. The terrace is covered. Service attentive. The cuisine is traditional southwestern French, everything hand-made with fresh local ingredients. They have over 100 wines from all regions of France and always more than 15 wines available by the glass.

BORDEAUX · MÉDOC SAINT-ESTÈPHE AOC
Discovering the Elegance of Clay and Merlot, Unique to the Médoc

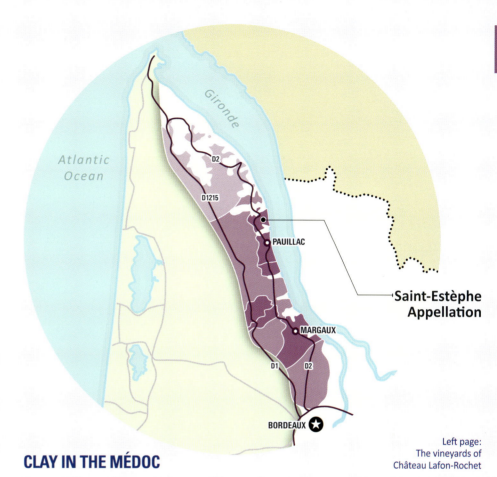

Left page:
The vineyards of Château Lafon-Rochet

CLAY IN THE MÉDOC

Saint-Estèphe is the most northern communal appellation in the Médoc along the gravelly western shores of the Gironde Estuary. There was Margaux, Saint-Julien, Pauillac and now here is Saint-Estèphe.

While Saint-Estèphe is just north of Pauillac, only separated by a stream, the soil composition changes here, giving this appellation its own distinctive AOC. Five classified growths of 1855 are located here and numerous Cru Bourgeois.

The soil distinction is rather significant. Being farther downstream from the Garonne River, there is much less gravel and the stones are smaller. Plus, there is clay in the soil here! Clay brings out the Merlot and this is exactly what the châteaux are planting. And they continue to plant greater and greater ratios of Merlot as they discover how well it performs. Further, the clay retains water which becomes extremely helpful in drought years.

The benefits to us from this Merlot-rich ratio in the Saint-Estèphe wines is the beautiful palate of softness and elegance, which also allows for earlier consumption of their wines. While 10 years is typical for minimum aging (and these wines will still go the distance), they can be approachable in as little as a few years, especially with decanting.

In exploring the Médoc, Saint-Estèphe is an important appellation. You may just love these wines the most. Or, like me, it expands your palate to different wines for different occasions, moods and cuisine. I bring you one Grand Cru, three Cru Bourgeois, two of which are owned by Grand Crus.
- Château Lafon-Rochet, page 197
- Château Le Crock, page 201
- Château La Haye, page 203
- Château Ormes de Pez, page 205

MÉDOC **SAINT-ESTÈPHE**
Winery (Château)
CHÂTEAU LAFON-ROCHET

Quatrième Cru (Fourth-Growth)
Grand Cru Classé of 1855
Winner: Best Of Wine Tourism

Blanquet Ouest
33180 Saint-Estèphe, France

+33 (0)5 56 59 32 06
Lafon@Lafon-Rochet.com

Lafon-Rochet.com

English, French

Open: All Year, Everyday
By Appointment Only

L ike great masters of music, sculpture and painting, wine is known through its experience.

SCREAMING GOLD

A golden castle? Really! And a golden winery too? Crazy you might think. And others will definitely agree with you. For Michel Tesseron, he wants your attention and has made a bold move. Michel has put a lot into modernizing the winery and making this Grand Cru Classé wine exceptional.

A golden cow sculpture too, kind of deconstructed into modern parts that flow with the wind. I think cheese. Wine and cheese! Let's explore wine first.

Inside the golden walls is a fully modernized winery worth your visit. A stunning display of stainless tanks (left page), perfectly aligned barrels elegantly aging their wines, and aesthetically stained concrete block tanks (photos on next two pages) shows us the commitment and passion Michel and his family have for their wines produced.

Beyond the great capabilities of the modern winery, they study the soil intensely in the vineyard. They have 40% Merlot growing (quite unusual for the Médoc) and by knowing their soil composition well, they are bringing out the best in their varietals. They dig pedologic pits in and around their vineyards.

They dig deep, as much as 10 feet into the soil to understand and create exacting profiles of their vineyards. The subsoil is very important to them. Clay components are valuable to the Merlot. And knowing the density of gravel enhances the Cabernet Sauvignon. Knowing this plays a huge role in their viticulture success.

In 2007 Michel gave his château to his son Basile, who has taken on the sensory qualities of their wine with a passion. Basile gives credit to his grandfather teaching him how to smell, savor and taste. To Basile, wine is an experience. It is everything to him.

Three-star Michelin Chef Michel Guérard said it best when he said that knowing Basile evokes emotions that moves him. He sees a sensitive passionate guy in love with the food and wine experience and is making wine with the kind of refinement you see with masters of great music, painting and sculpture.

I guess we have hit food now. And it's making me hungry. I want something special to go with a bottle of Château Lafon-Rochet. Joining me?

Collection of Wines
Château Lafon-Rochet
(First Label - Grand Cru)

Les Pélerins de Lafon-Rochet
(Second Wine)

Le saviez-vous ? / Did you know ?

Une barrique bordelaise contient 225L de vin, soit 300 bouteilles.

A Bordeaux-type wine barrel contains 225L of wine, or the equivalent of 300 bottles.

Enigme 6 / Riddle 6

La fin est proche, vous chauffez, mais attention à ne pas vous brûler.

The end is near, you're getting warm, but be careful not to get burnt!

MÉDOC **SAINT-ESTÈPHE**
Winery (Château)
CHÂTEAU LE CROCK

Quality Certification
Cru Bourgeois du Médoc

1 Rue Paul Amilhat
33180 Saint-Estèphe, France

+33 (0)5 56 59 73 05
LP.Visite@Leoville-Poyferre.fr

ChateauLeCrock.fr

English, French

Open: All Year, No Reservations Needed
July & August, Everyday
June & September, Monday-Saturday
October-May, By Reservations Only
ChateauLeCrock.fr/en/tours-and-tastings
Tours & Tastings: No Charge

G ot kids? Are you a kid? Want to play? Mystery, fun and an interesting education awaits.

TRESOR Ô CROCK • ESCAPE Ô CROCK

Only two families have cared for this property over the last three centuries. The Merman family started here at the beginning of the 19th century and built the beautiful château (above) and planted the vineyards. The Cuvelier family purchased the property in 1903 and has kept it in their family ever since. In 1920, they purchased Châteaux Léoville Poyferré (page 145), a second-growth Grand Cru Classé in the Saint-Julien appellation.

Bringing Grand Cru Classé expertise to this property, Château Le Crock became a Cru Bourgeois Superior wine in 1932. Both properties are managed with these high standards by Cuvelier family today.

Enough of the seriousness of good wine. Now for the fun. This place is fun! Games. Tough enough for adults, interesting for the kids. Total family fun.

• **Tresor Ô Crock** is a treasure hunt, Crock style. The challenge, if you accept the mission, goes like this… The ghost of Pierre Merman, the first owner here, has stolen the recipe for the wines. This is serious. A series of treasure maps take you throughout the property, inside and out, through the park, the château, the vineyards, fermentation room, and barrel room to find and follow clues, which ultimately lead you to the recipe; saving Château Le Crock and its recipe for their fine wines.

Be the hero. Out prank the prankster Merman. The clues are challenging, making you think, and the discovery leads you to a fun understanding of the winemaking here. No doubt, the most unusual experience and adventure at a winery.

• **Escape Ô Crock** is the popular new escape experience. Check with them for event dates.

• **Dégust'Ô Crock** is a delicious food and wine pairing experience. French cheese, charcuterie and chocolates are paired with both their wines. The best way to taste them.

They also have regular tours of their property, tasting of their wines, and children are served grape juice so they can feel part of the experience.

Enjoy a glass or a bottle of wine in their beautiful park or on the patio in front of the château. It's a very romantic setting. Croquet too. No reservations needed and no fees.

Collection of Wines
Château Le Crock
(First Label - Cru Bourgeois)

Château La Croix St-Estèphe
(Second Wine)

MÉDOC SAINT-ESTÈPHE
Winery (Château)
CHÂTEAU LA HAYE

Quality Certification
Cru Bourgeois du Médoc

1 Rue de Saint-Affrique
33180 Leyssac, Saint-Estèphe, France

+33 (0)5 56 59 32 18
Info@ChateauLaHaye.com

ChateauLaHaye.com

English, French

*Open: All Year, April-September, Monday-Saturday
No Reservations Needed and No Charge
October-April, By Appointment Only*

Collection of Wines
Château *La Haye*
(First Label - Cru Bourgeois)

Le Cèdre de Château La Haye
(Second Wine)

Château Bel-Air
(Aged in Fermenting Vats)

Majesté de Château La Haye
(Special Release Only in Great Years)

Rosé La Haye
(Cabernet Franc, Merlot, Cabernet Sauvignon)

Noble roots, a romantic getaway for royalty, and the goodness of unique winemaking.

THE LEGEND OF KING HENRY II

It is true, King Henry II came to Bordeaux often to this remote area of Saint-Estèphe with his mistress Diane de Poitiers. This was their "hunting lodge" as they escaped Paris for their romantic journeys of some 20 years. Their presence was cast in stone at the entrance to the château with their initials intertwined, as were these lovers. This became a royal monogram of Château La Haye, now their logo, found on their wine labels and burned into the caps of their oak aging barrels.

Château La Haye is one of the oldest castles in Saint-Estèphe, with the property remaining in the Bernard family for 370 years. Nobility struck this property in 1821 when Louis Bernard was ennobled and became Baron Bernard de Saint Affrique. His noble coat of arms graces the bottles and is engraved into the front door of the castle.

I particularly like some of the unique things they do in winemaking. They cultivate yeast directly from the vineyards they harvest, and grow it in a special laboratory. This is almost like natural fermentation, just giving the juice a little more of the same yeast it already possesses.

While some winemakers like to micro-vinify in small batch tanks to fine tune higher quality, here they micro-age their wines. They have 280 oak barrels from many different coopers, different forests, different oak grains, and different toasts. Imagine the different aroma and flavor profiles they taste to find the perfect wines to blend for their first label, a Cru Bourgeois wine. Definitely worth your tasting. And they have five different wines to explore, which is quite uncommon in Bordeaux.

Also, ask to taste their Château Bellevue-Cardon, from a propery adjacent to Chateau Latour. Excellence at 10% the cost (see page 173).

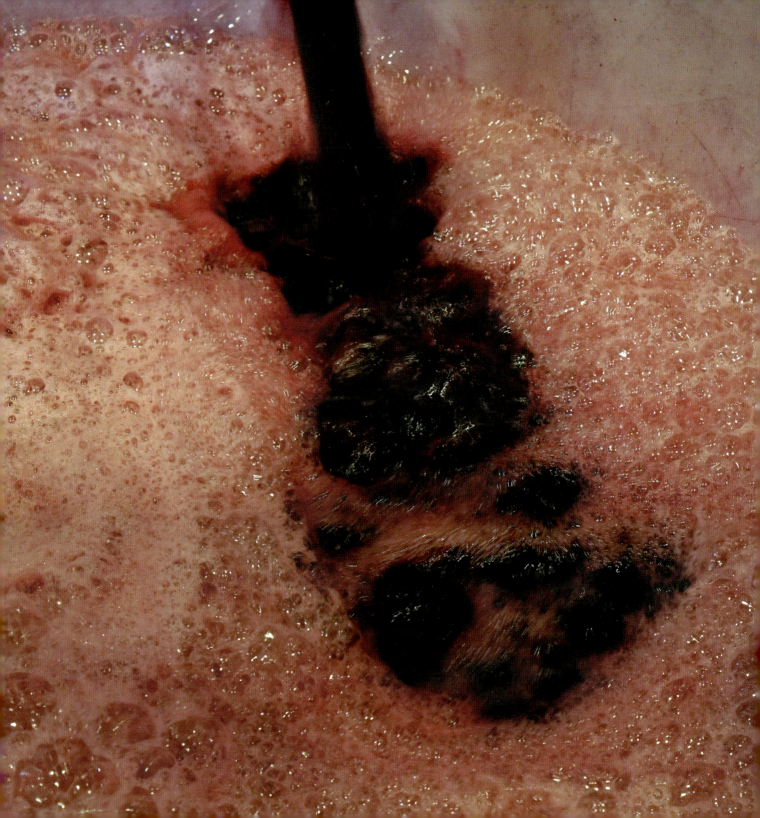

MÉDOC SAINT-ESTÈPHE
Winery (Château) B&B
CHÂTEAU ORMES DE PEZ

Quality Certification
Cru Bourgeois du Médoc

29 Route des Ormes de Pez
33180 Pez, Saint-Estèphe, France

+33 (0)5 56 73 19 30
Visit@Lynch-Bages.com

OrmesDePez.com

English, French

Open: Monday-Friday, By Appointment Only
Tours and Tastings: No Charge

Cru Bourgeois Exceptionnel wines made by a Pauillac Grand Cru Classé of 1855.

THE BEST OF BOTH

Château Ormes de Pez is part of the Cazes family of luxury hospitality in the Médoc alongside its sister château, Château Lynch-Bages (page 185), located in the Pauillac appellation. Château Ormes de Pez benefits from Grand Cru Classé winemaking expertise and quality vineyard management that Château Lynch-Bages brings them.

Here, in the northwestern part of Saint-Estèphe, there is more clay in the soil giving them the opportunity to enhance their wines with more Merlot. This gives them a softer more approachable wine early in its aging. Please taste. You will be impressed. It is no wonder this château was certified for their high quality as one of only nine Cru Bourgeois Exceptionnel wines blind tasted in 2003.

The history of this property dates back to the 18th century with several owners. By the end of the 19th century the winery was managed by the Cazes family, ultimately purchased by Jean-Charles Cazes in 1940 and has stayed in the family ever since. In 1980 Jean-Michel Cazes fully modernized the 18th century buildings to optimize current winemaking.

Their château here has also been renovated into a beautiful B&B of five rooms (next page). It is a nice place to stay to fully enjoy their property and for exploring the northern areas of the Médoc.

The terroir here is particularly special with the cool clay soil in the northwest of the Saint-Éstephe appellation where they are located. This is soil conducive to Merlot, which is not common in the Médoc. They cultivate 41% Merlot, and as I said earlier, this give a soft elegance to their wines, making them drinkable much earlier than most Médoc wines. And they also have plots of the traditional Médoc soil of gravel, stones and pebbles where Cabernet Sauvignon loves to grow.

They have just one wine: the Château Ormes de Pez. It is Cru Bourgeois Exceptionnel. It is truly a vineyard wine representing the four varietals they grow on their property. You really want to experience the uniqueness of this wine when exploring the full range of Médoc wines. Plus, they have all the other Cazes family wines here at this château to taste.

Collection of Wines
Château Ormes de Pez
(First Label - Cru Bourgeois)

MÉDOC SAINT-ESTÈPHE
Winery (Château) B&B
CHÂTEAU ORMES DE PEZ

B&B Open: March-November, Everyday

Booking: via.eviivo.com/en-GB/ormesdepez33180
+33 (0)5 56 59 30 05 • Visit@OrmesDePez.com

BED & BREAKFAST • IN THE CASTLE • AT THE WINERY

This is the original 18th century castle on the property, lived in by the previous owners through the centuries, including Mr. Cazes. Today, it has been completely restored and modernized to beautiful luxury. They have five elegant rooms that are spacious with private baths. The decor is a mix of antique and modern. Lots of charm.

Views are to either the vineyards or the massive park setting of the backyard with a 100-year-old walnut tree standing majestically. During the summer months you can also use the swimming pool. Such a joy to wake up to a picturesque setting. A quiet, peaceful morning coffee outside on the back patio overlooking the park.

For breakfast, they create a big meal of both buffet and hot cooked-to-order items. Fresh baked pastries and, if you are there during harvest like I was, a fresh glass of "just squeezed" Cabernet Sauvignon grape juice from the winery.

This is the perfect place to hang your hat for a few days as you explore the Saint-Estèphe appellation and its little village; a short walk on quiet roads by rolling vineyards (next page). Ormes de Pez also provides nice bicycles for their guests to use.

DOWNTOWN SAINT-ESTÈPHE

Saint-Estèphe is a very small village, surrounded by vineyards in every direction, in this northernmost communal appellation of the Médoc. It shares the same name and is located in the middle of the Saint-Estèphe wine region along the river (photo right). The population of barely 1,500 gives this little hamlet a quiet quaint feel. In the center of the village is the **Église Saint-Étienne de Saint-Estèphe** (upper right photos next page), an 11th century historic monument and a church of Romanesque architecture.

The village is a short and beautiful stroll from **Château Ormes de Pez** (page 205), and they have many bicycles you can borrow to roam the area and explore the village. You will find quiet streets meandering through vineyards with several other châteaux you can visit. Making the Ormes de Pez B&B your home is a great way to relax and take in this beautiful area.

BORDEAUX · MÉDOC **MÉDOC AOC**
The Northernmost Appellation of the Médoc

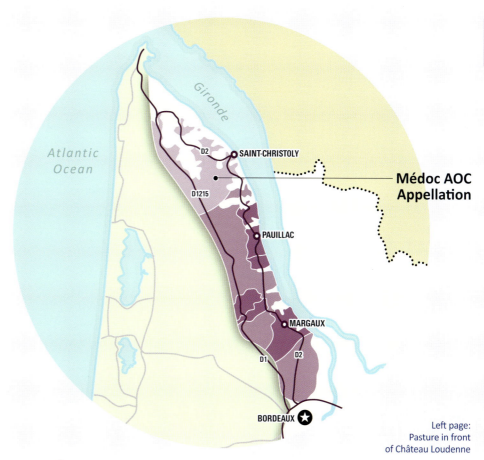

Left page:
Pasture in front of Château Loudenne

THE MÉDOC WILDS

The Médoc is both the entire Médoc Appellation, which included the seven sub-appellations, and also its own separate sub-appellation at the northern most tip of the Médoc, beyond Saint-Estèphe. This is the end of the Médoc before reaching the ocean.

This is the last stop for the deposits brought down from the Garonne River, Dordogne River and the Pyrénées Mountains, held back by the strength of the Atlantic Ocean as it pushes into the Gironde Estuary. Here lies the prominent gravel and stones from the Garonne River conducive to Cabernet Sauvignon in the Médoc, as well as clay and limestone from the Pyrénées and Dordogne River most special for growing Merlot. And the soil varies dramatically throughout this appellation, giving distinction to each châteaux's wines; a special expression of their own terroir.

If you want to get away from it all, here is the countryside farthest from the city. The châteaux are spread apart from each other and the vineyards are less dense than those further south. Welcome to the Médoc. The land of serenity. A peaceful intermingling of vineyards with other types of agriculture and animals. This is what I call *The Wilds of The Médoc*.

On my way to **Château Loudenne**, I found myself peacefully off a country road, entranced by cows, in this painting-like setting of the grassy meadow (photo left). Here I present to you...
- Château Castera, page 213
- Château Loudenne, page 217
- Château Tour Castillon, page 219
- Château Saint-Christoly, page 221

MÉDOC **MÉDOC AOC**
Winery (Château)
CHÂTEAU CASTERA

Quality Certification
Cru Bourgeois du Médoc
Winner: Best Of Wine Tourism

Rue du Bourg
33340 Saint-Germain-d'Esteuil, France

+33 (0)5 56 73 20 60
Chateau@Castera.fr

Chateau-Castera.com

English, French

*Open: All Year
Monday-Friday, No Appointment Needed
June-August, Saturdays By Appointment Only*

A property of long rich history, cherished and restored to magnificence today.

AN IMPORTANT LEGACY

This is a very cool place to spend the day. There is so much history here. And the entire property has been restored to historic perfection. Even the vineyards are manicured impeccably, reflective of the beauty of their wines. Mix in modern art to arouse your attention and enlighten your senses, like the wine bottle sculpture (photo right) scattered around the beautiful park-like property.

Dating back as far as 900 AD, records show that the Lords of Castera built the church of Saint-Germain. Today the little chapel stands beautifully in restored grandeur on the Castera grounds. In 1121, a recorded deed shows the ownership and reference to the castle described as a fortress defending the area.

Imagine this though: King Henry IV decides to confiscate Castera and messes with the wrong family. Having deep pockets and influence through their large wine export business, they launched a court battle, which lasted for centuries (oddly makes our court system look fast) to retain their ownership of Castera. The Castera legacy lives on.

Collection of Wines
Château Castera
(First Label - Cru Bourgeois)

Marquis de Castera
(Second Wine)

MÉDOC **MÉDOC AOC**
Winery (Château)
CHÂTEAU CASTERA

GREAT WINES, GREAT TOURS, GREAT HISTORY, GREAT FUTURE

Even with its fortress castle, this property gets seized yet again, goes through many ups and downs during the centuries, and finally rests in the hands of Thomas Press today. Thomas recently finished a 25-year project to fully restore every building on the property, including modernizing the winery and substantially improving the vineyards.

Estate Manager and Technical Director, Philippe Grynfeltt, comes to Castera from first-growth Grand Cru Classé Château Margaux and has made it his mission to visit the vineyards every day to optimize Castera's superb terroir. Yes, every day. That is where I found him when I visited Château Castera. And when you taste his wines, you will know what I am talking about and appreciate Philippe's dedication and the experience he brings to this Cru Bourgeois wine.

The tours here are extensive, educational and interesting. Their **Discovery Tour** takes you through the history of the Médoc and this ancient estate. You will learn about viticulture, winemaking and barrel aging, all critical to producing wine. Plus, of course, a tasting of their delicious wines. Their **Heritage Tour** adds the history of the most famous owners and includes a special private tour of the tower (photos on this page and previous page) displaying the château's valuable archives. Their **Premium Tour** also includes the two aforementioned tours, plus barrel tasting with the cellar master, followed by a vertical tasting of several vintages. The last two tours require reservations and are well worth it.

MÉDOC MÉDOC AOC
Winery (Château)
CHÂTEAU LOUDENNE

Quality Certification
Cru Bourgeois du Médoc

33340 Saint-Yzans-de-Médoc, France

+33 (0)5 56 73 17 88
Contact@Chateau-Loudenne.com

Chateau-Loudenne.com

English, French, Chinese

Open: All Year, Reservations Not Needed
April-October, Tuesday-Saturday,
November-March, By Appointment Only

B eauty surrounds the elegance of eras gone by. You can still feel the liveliness of the wild parties and happy guests.

GLAMOUR AND HISTORY UNTOUCHED

Little did I expect to be greeted with a bottle of white wine in this predominantly red wine region. So refreshing and elegant like the parties they held. We reminisced about the prestigious guest list and fun times. And the wine, a Sauvignon Blanc and Sémillon blend, was worthy of all the attention. I was inspired.

Felt like Vaudeville, a bit more refined, as we sat in the living room sipping. I was looking for the seductive dancers, celebrities and maybe Frank Sinatra. The vibe is still here. And the wine was certainly celebratory deliciousness. I was enchanted. I was ready to put on my tux and dance with the glamorous ladies.

Even further back in time, the magnificence of this 17th century castle is reflected as it sits along the shore of the Gironde Estuary near the mouth of the ocean. With its own docks, the ships would arrive and the parties would begin. It was owners Alfred and Walter Gilbey, who in 1875 made this their residence, and invited distinguished guests to enjoy the finer things, as lovers of living life.

With vineyards overlooking the estuary of ideal climactic conditions, the location is perfect for receiving foreign guests. The estuary acts as a thermal regulator and the Atlantic Ocean provides the vineyards with a temperate oceanic climate. Tasting the terroir, you will find uniqueness and elegance in the glass.

Loudenne welcomes you for tours and workshops. Take a vineyard stroll with the ocean breeze on their 326-acre estate. Experience the castle and cellars. Participate in winemaking and other workshops. Sip their magnificent wines.

Collection of Wines
Loudenne Le Château - Médoc
(First Label - Cru Bourgeois)

Loudenne Le Château - Bordeaux
(White Wine - Sauvignon Blanc & Sémillon)

Loudenne Les Folies
(Second Wine - Red)

Loudenne, Les Folies
(Second Wine - White - Sauvignon Blanc & Sémillon)

MÉDOC **MÉDOC AOC** SAINT-CHRISTOLY
Winery (Château)
CHÂTEAU TOUR CASTILLON

Quality Certification
Cru Bourgeois du Médoc

3 Rue du Fort de Castillon
33340 Saint-Christoly-Médoc, France

+33 (0)5 56 41 54 98
Contact@VignoblesPeyruse.com

VignoblesPeyruse.com

English, French

Open: All Year, Monday-Friday
July-August, Reservations Not Needed
September-June, By Appointment Only
Tours and Tastings: No Charge

A location that attracted nobility, battles and terroir for producing Cru Bourgeois wines.

RELAXED AND CASUAL WITH UNIQUE ACTIVITIES

This property comes from a long lineage of nobility. Ownership has been associated with lords, kings, governors, knights, and admirals as far back as the 11th century. The château name comes from the Castillon site of many battles where the British defended Bordeaux from France and Spain. Not just a strategic location for battle along the Gironde Estuary, it has forever gained the reputation for magnificent terroir.

In modern history, Theobal Peyruse purchased the property 1914 and it has remained in the Peyruse family ever since. Today great-great-grandson and daughter, Sébastien and Laure, continue the tradition of this great property.

This is a very casual place where you can get to know the owners who conduct the tours that are personal and insightful. There is more than just vineyards facing the estuary, like this huge garden of sunflowers (photo above) and alfalfa fields, and more. This is the great terroir of the estuary's thermal regulation and the Atlantic Ocean's temperate oceanic climate.

Not just tastings here. They have created numerous unique and creative moments for you to remember at their property. Plus special wines from this terroir, typically 40% Merlot, 40% Cabernet Sauvignon, 15% Cabernet Franc, 3% Petit Verdot, and 2% Carménère.

- **Guided Walks in the Vineyard**. Interesting moments discovering the life-cycle of the vines along the estuary, enjoying wine and local foods.
- **Visit and Tasting in the Barrel Cellar**. Visit their cellar to discover the terroir of this appellation by tasting the wines of Château Tour Castillon.
- **Music and Wine Evenings**. Jazz and tapas served on the banks of the estuary (in the cellar if bad weather), music around the wines of the château.
- **Carrelet on the Estuary**. This is a unique moment to enjoy the estuary with wine and charcuterie on an authentic carrelet (fishing platform).
- **Hot Air Balloon Ride**. Float above the vineyards in a hot air balloon, launched from their property with wines to enjoy the birds-eye view.

Collection of Wines
Château Tour Castillon
(First Label - Cru Bourgeois)

La Révélation de Castillon Médoc
(Vineyard Select, Only 3,600 bottles)

La Tentation de Castillon
(Rosé of 50% Cabernet Sauvignon & 50% Merlot)

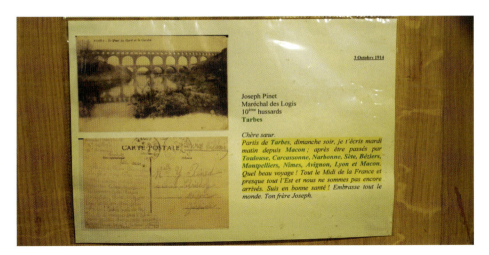

MÉDOC **MÉDOC AOC** SAINT-CHRISTOLY

Winery (Château)
CHÂTEAU SAINT-CHRISTOLY

Quality Certification
Cru Bourgeois du Médoc

1 Bis Impasse Mairie
33340 Saint-Christoly-Médoc, France

+33 (0)5 56 41 82 01
Chateau.St.Christoly@Wanadoo.fr

ChateauSaintChristoly.com

English, French

Open: All Year
Monday-Friday, Reservations Not Needed
Weekends, By Appointment Only

P ostcards from the war expressing love and fear, and longing to come home to winemaking.

SEVEN GENERATIONS

This is seven generations of the same family owning and running this château. Rather unique that no other person or family has been involved with this winery. It all started in 1850 when Peirre Moreau, the blacksmith of Saint-Christoly, bought some vines and named the vineyard after the village as his cellar was in this charming village.

Château Saint-Christoly is immediately behind the historic church, Église de Saint-Christoly-Médoc, (photo right) in the center of the tiny village of just 200 people. Saint-Christoly is on the estuary with a port for shipping their wines around the world. In 1924, they won their first gold medal in Paris. In 1932, they obtained the quality certification as a Cru Bourgeois wine.

Down the street is La Maison du Douanier (next page), a beautiful B&B and excellent gourmet restaurant on the beach next to the port. This makes for a nice stop on your journey through the Médoc wine regions.

The cellar room (photo left) has an art exhibit on the walls and a very interesting Historic Postcard Exhibit on the barrel ends (photo above). Fourth-generation Joseph Pinet served in the war and sent postcards to his sister every day. They have an archive of 400 postcards they rotate in the cellar.

Joseph wrote his sister about the places where he was stationed and the different people that he met along the way.

He also wrote her about being in a boat while German submarines launched bombs around him as he watched the boats sink.

Joseph survived the traumatic war. Three weeks later, he died from a mosquito bite.

A unique and heart-warming experience wandering the cellar reading postcards on barrels. And a tasty experience enjoying the softness to their wines of 60% Merlot and 40% Cabernet Sauvignon. The seventh generation includes two sisters, Sandrine and Cathy, who deliberately work to create a more feminine style with their wines.

Collection of Wines
Château Saint-Christoly
(First Label - Cru Bourgeois)

Château La Rose Saint-Bonnet
(Second Wine)

■ MÉDOC **MÉDOC AOC** SAINT-CHRISTOLY
Restaurant
LA MAISON DU DOUANIER

Open: July & August, Everyday
April-June & Sept-Oct, Wednesday-Sunday
November & December, Thursday-Sunday

Reservation on their website
Under "Restaurant" click on "Book A Table"

A SPECIAL TREAT

On the beach in Saint-Christoly, inside or patio dining of gourmet yumminess.

Located inside La Maison Du Douanier's historic B&B (page right) in a beautiful modern elegant setting. Large dining room (photo top right) and spacious terrace with unobstructed views of the estuary. Right on the beach, this is a very special spot to enjoy a gourmet meal.

Chef Jean-Luc Beaufils has an impressive career with several prestigious restaurants in Paris. Now he brings his talent to this tiny village of 200 people and the many guests who travel from afar for his creative gourmet dishes.

Turbot & Oyster, with onions and leeks in a rich and savory oyster sauce (photo right top).

Prawns & Cannelloni, stuffed and oozing with vegetables from their garden. The sauce is to die for; a reduction of prawns, vegetables, garlic onion, and herbs (middle photo).

Partridge (bird), with cauliflower, mushrooms and other vegetable, and a delicious meat reduction sauce (photo bottom right).

Figs & Chocolate of all sorts (photo below).

MÉDOC **MÉDOC AOC** SAINT-CHRISTOLY

Hotel B&B
LA MAISON DU DOUANIER

2 Route de By
33340 Saint-Christoly-Médoc, France

+33 (0)5 56 41 35 25
Contact@LaMaisonDuDouanier.com

LaMaisonDuDouanier.com

English, French, German

*Open: April-December
Reservation On Their Website
Under "Rooms" Click On "Availability"*

A B&B on the shores of the estuary, in the wild backcountry of the Médoc appellation.

AN OFF-THE-GRID ESCAPE

So quiet. So remote. So nice to get away from it all in this very relaxing environment of the vastly remote wine region of the Médoc appellation in the far north. This is the perfect escape.

Only four rooms and an amazing restaurant (left page) in this historic building renovated with a hip modern interior. The rooms are light, bright and clean. Each room is named after Médoc appellations. I chose the Estèphe, upstairs, corner room, with views over the estuary. In the little village is the historic church and Château Saint-Christoly to visit (page 221).

The owners, Jean-Luc, Vincent and Romain, Chef, Hotel Manager and Hospitality Director, respectively, are very talented and welcoming guys. They have injected a wonderful passion into this property, inside and out, from infrastructure to hospitality, making this a fabulous and complete getaway. I can't wait to be back!

BORDEAUX · MÉDOC MÉDOC ATLANTIQUE

Escape to the Beaches of the Médoc's Atlantic Ocean

Left page:
Sandy beach
of Lacanau-Océan

THE MÉDOC BEACHES

As we reach the northern tip of the Médoc, let's continue counterclockwise and proceed down the coast of the Atlantic Ocean. Being near the wine regions, this is a great escape to the beaches of Bordeaux. It's beautiful. The beaches are expansive and full of lots of sand. There is much to do here, or nothing at all, if you want an escape.

There are cute little villages to discover, with plenty of history and lots of character. There are sand dunes everywhere along the coast, small and large; and a huge one just south of the Arcachon Bay.

The forests were planted here to retain the sand dunes, which they have successfully done, and now the trees have matured into a gigantic landscape perfect for hiking, horseback riding and bicycling. The bicycle paths are excellent and plentiful.

At the top of the Médoc, Le Verdon-sur-Mer has the ferry-crossing harbor plus a yacht harbor with water sports and the delicious restaurant **Le Belem**.

Soulac-sur-Mer is quaint and full of history.

Montalivet is where the large naturist resorts reside, offering lots of naked sunbathing and spas. There is also horseback riding on the beach!

Lacanau-Océan is beach town extraordinaire. Lively. Great surfing. Beautiful people. Miles of bicycle paths along the beach and in the forest.

Arcachon Bay is for delicious oysters, huge sand dunes and a great restaurant in Cap-Ferret.
- Le Verdon-sur-Mer, page 226
- Soulac sur Mer, page 228
- Montalivet naturist resorts, page 230
- Lacanau-Océan, page 233
- Arcachon Bay & Cap-Ferret, page 238

Exploring Wine Regions | **Bordeaux** | 225

MÉDOC ATLANTIQUE **LE VERDON-SUR-MER** PORT-MÉDOC

At the northern-most tip of the Médoc, where the Gironde Estuary and the Atlantic Ocean meet, is a beautiful area known at **Le Verdon-Sur-Mer**. On this peninsula you will find four ports and three lighthouses.

Three lighthouses stand at the point of this peninsula. **Cordouan Lighthouse** is the active lighthouse of this main entrance to Bordeaux. From April to November, it is open to the public as the last remaining offshore lighthouse in the world open for visits. Tours depart through Port-Médoc across from **Restaurant Le Belem**. Also, **Grave Lighthouse** is a maritime museum to visit. **Saint-Nicolas Lighthouse** marks the entrance to Saint-Nicolas beach.

Port-Bloc is where the ferry crosses the Gironde Estuary (there is another ferry crossing in the middle of the Médoc from Lamarque to Blaye). The **Grand Port Maritime** of Bordeaux is for the commercial ships. **Port aux Huîtres** is in the village where the oysters are famous. **Port-Médoc's** yacht harbor is home to many beautiful luxury boats. Enjoy an afternoon or evening at the **Restaurant Le Belem** overlooking the yacht harbor.

Port-Médoc is where you can enjoy all kinds of water sports. **Le Paddle Center** (paddlecenter33.com) has stand-up paddle boards for rent and classes for all levels. Jet skis and flyboards can be found at **FlyJet33** (Flyjet33.com). For sightseeing boats and fishing excursions contact **Vedette La Boheme** (Vedette-LaBoheme.com). Sailboats and powerboats of many sizes can be rented, with or without a skipper, from **Ocean Serenity** (OceanSerenity.com).

MÉDOC **PORT-MÉDOC**
Restaurant & Bar
RESTAURANT LE BELEM

Le Verdon sur Mer
33123, Port-Médoc, France

+33 (0)5 24 23 61 25

RestaurantLeBelem-Port-Medoc.fr

English, French

Open: Everyday for Lunch & Dinner

Overlooking the yacht harbor, this gourmet casual restaurant has the best outdoor dining.

BEAUTIFUL LUNCH

Such a beautiful way to spend the afternoon, enjoying a wonderful lunch, sipping delicious Médoc wines, overlooking the yacht harbor, and taking in the warm tranquil sunny day as the sailboats quietly sail along. This husband/wife team here spoils you with personality and excellent service (Bruno) and lots of delicious treats from the kitchen (Stéphanie).

Taste this: Smoked Salmon Salad (photo left) with whole shrimp and fresh sweet oranges.

Flying Fish Wing (below left) steamed in a special butter from Normandie, with leaks and potatoes. Rich. Tender. Flakey. Yum.

Duo of Carmel and Mango Ice Cream (below). Very rich and flavorful. Decadent.

Exploring Wine Regions | **Bordeaux** | 227

MÉDOC ATLANTIQUE SOULAC-SUR-MER

Soulac-sur-Mer is a cute little oceanside village of just 2,700 people in this northern Atlantic Médoc beach region. It has tiny little streets lined with interesting architecture and expansive sandy beaches. There are several good restaurants to check out and B&Bs to experience the local flavor of the area.

The Little Tourist Train is a must ride: a slow-paced, mini railway that runs 7km from Soulac-sur-Mer along the beaches and through the forest to the Cordouan Lighthouse at the tip of the peninsula. The **Museum of Art & Archeology** has over 300 works to see. There are street art shows in the summer. Bicycle lovers (rentals available) will love the well-developed paths that run north and south along the coast and inland into the forest.

■ MÉDOC ATLANTIQUE **SOULAC-SUR-MER** ■
Restaurant
LB RESTAURANT CRÊPERIE

6 Rue Fernand Lafargue • 33780 Soulac-Sur-Mer, France
+33 (0)5 56 09 92 60 • English, French
Open Everyday: 12:00pm-2:30pm and 7:00pm-11:00pm

LB, as they are known, is the local steak house. Just one block off the main street and open for lunch and dinner. They are well stocked with wines to pair with your steaks, and a wine wall where you can go choose your bottle for the evening. Large portions at good prices with excellent service.

■ MÉDOC ATLANTIQUE **SOULAC-SUR-MER** ■
Hotel (B&B)
HÔTEL L'ÉCUME DES JOURS

4 Rue du Perrier de Larsan • 33780 Soulac-Sur-Mer, France
English, French • +33 (0)5 56 09 81 34
HotelEcumeDesJours.com

Just a few blocks from the ocean, Hotel L'Écume des Jours is a B&B with 11 rooms in this little town. It is not fancy, just very clean and charming. Very much a local flavor with a nice spread for breakfast. They have bicycles to rent so you can take to the many bike paths available here.

MÉDOC ATLANTIQUE **NATURIST RESORTS**

MÉDOC ATLANTIQUE **MONTALIVET**
Naturist Resort
EURONAT

IN THE NAKED SUN, NAKED

The French love being naked outdoors in the sun. In fact, there are 2.6 million active nudists in France. And France attracts another 3.5 million visitors from around the world to their 500+ officially authorized nude destinations. The Médoc has the oldest and largest naked resorts.

Along the northern coast of the Médoc, there are two very large naturist resorts. Beyond your imagination huge! CHM Montelivit, the worlds first naturist resort, is 175 hectares (432 acres) with homes, cabins, mobile homes, campsites... and, get this, more than 10,000 people are there during the peak season of July and August.

Euronat is the world's largest resort with 335 hectares (828 acres) of homes, cabins (photo below), campsites, shopping center, also with 10,000 people at the resort during peak season. When I was there in September, I was told it was quiet with only 3,000 people. Wow!

This is like a city with dozens of businesses: shops, restaurants, bars, wine shop, bakery, coffee shops, fish market, grocery stores, and the typical general store. Plus, Euronat has a world-class spa with a focus on health and sensory experiences from the ocean.

Speaking of the ocean, Euronat has more than two miles of spacious beach to enjoy nude sunbathing, playing in the water (photo left), swimming or just strolling along their wide sandy beaches feeling the salty breeze and warm sun on your body. A natural and liberating experience.

THALASSOTHERAPY SPA

This is a very interesting spa. Imagine treatments where there is no massage, no acupressure, no physical manipulation whatsoever... and yet when I was done with a few treatments, my body and muscles felt worked over and sore. What happened I wondered. Thalassotherapy is what they told me.

Thalassotherapy is considered a sensory treatment using seawater and marine trace elements to bring about revitalization of the body. First, I was covered with algae from head to toe to be absorbed by the skin for 30 minutes. Then I was immersed in a hot bath of seawater and other ocean elements. This was followed by a hot marine shower raining all over my body while I lay in bliss. I was invigorated. Alive! They tell me that this provides a remineralization of the body and boosts the immune system. A healthy wellbeing emerges.

While we believe the ocean offers so much to mankind, this magical experience offered by Euronat's Thalassotherapy Spa supports this belief of our ocean's gifts. I can't wait to go back and do this again.

And there is more. You will also find a large indoor seawater swimming pool at 31°c (88°f), outdoor sun deck (photo below), indoor sun room, two saunas, steam room, whirlpool, water aerobics, water Taî Chi, and so much more.

33590, Grayan-l'Hôpital, Montalivet, France

+33 (0)5 56 09 33 33
Info@Euronat.fr

Euronat.fr

Open: All Year, Everyday

THALASSOTHERAPY at EURONAT

+33 (0)5 56 73 24 50
Thalasso@Euronat.fr

Open: April-October, Everyday

HORSEBACK ON THE BEACH

Ride horses through the pine forests, along the sand dunes, out into the ocean breeze, and into the ocean waves. This is a magical experience just north of Euronat in Soulac-sur-Mer.

LES PETITS CHEVAUX
(the little horses)

+33 (0)5 56 73 24 50
Info@Les-Petits-Chavaux.com

Les-Petits-Chevaux.com

MÉDOC ATLANTIQUE LAKE HOURTIN & LAKE LACANAU

LAC (LAKE) D'HOURTIN

The Médoc Atlantique has two very large lakes, Lake Hourtin and Lake Lacanau. Lake Hourtin is the largest freshwater lake in France (21.88 sq. miles). It is surrounded by a beautiful dense forest, the *Médoc Regional Nature Park*. Between the lake and the ocean, on the northwestern shore, are 8.3 sq. miles of sand dunes and marshland known as the *Dunes et Marais d'Hourtin*, which has been designated as a nature reserve. There are roads, hiking trails and well planned bicycle paths surrounding most parts of the lake.

Just east of the lake is the town of Hourtin. **Restaurant d'Hourtin** is a nice casual place for lunch or dinner. It is located in the center of town across from a charming little park and beautiful church.

ÉTANG (POND) DE LACANAU

One-third the size of d'Hourton (7.66 sq. miles), Lake Lacanau is definitely not a pond as its name suggests. Full of water sports and tranquil areas to get away and enjoy the peaceful outdoors. Fresh air, birds, turtles and other wildlife live in this enchanting environment.

The town of Lacanau is five minutes to the east of the lake. The Lacanau-Océan village and its beaches are five minutes to the west on the Atlantic Ocean. At the north shore of Lake Lacanau are many vendors for water sports, boat excursions and even paddleboard yoga! Plus, you can stay in cabins or tents outdoors at **Lodging Le Loc** (page 235) right on this north shore. Or be pampered in four-star luxury at **Vitalparc Hôtel & Spa** (page 237), just a mile west of the lake.

MÉDOC ATLANTIQUE **LACANAU-OCÉAN**

LACANAU-OCÉAN

Lacanau-Océan is likely the most well-known of the beach destinations along the Médoc Atlantique. The beaches are expansive as you can see in the photo above and the little village is charming with many outdoor restaurants, bars and ice cream shops lining its one main street (photo left). This is the closest Médoc Atlantic destination to the city of Bordeaux (less than an hour's drive). Summer has a lively festive atmosphere here, with their population growing from 4,500 to more than 80,000 people during peak summer season.

The beautiful sandy beach is vast and wide open, with nearly 10 miles of beaches, and lifeguards. The Atlantic Ocean is delightfully warm in the summer (68 to 77°F) and the waves extra perfect for surfing. In August, Lacanau-Océan hosts the world's top surfers for *Lacanau Pro* on the professional circuit for the world surfing championship! Plus, you can rent surfboards yourself and even get a professional surfer to teach you how to ride the waves.

There is a beautiful golf course meandering through the sand dunes and pine forests. Inland is an extensive network of more than 60 miles of cycling paths though the forest, to both lakes, as well as along the beaches. Electric and traditional bicycles are available to rent.

MÉDOC ATLANTIQUE **LACANAU-OCÉAN**
Cabins & Tents
LODGING LE LAC

30 Avenue de La Plage
33680 Le Moutchic, Lacanau, France

+33 (0)5 56 03 00 26
Contact@LodgingLeLac.com

LodgingLeLac.com

English, French

*Open: February-November, Everyday
Reception: 9:30am-12:30pm and 2:00pm-7:00pm*

SIXTY MILES OF CYCLING PATHS

A cyclist's and outdoor adventurer's dream! A network of over 60 miles of cycling paths winding through the massive pine forest, connecting with both lakes. The path meanders along the beaches and through the sand dunes, and connects with the Lacanau-Océan village. You can get yourself an electric bike – **Vitalparc Hôtel** has many to rent – so you can see more without being worn out.

MAGICAL OUTDOORS

Outdoor accommodations with 50 cabins, canvas tents like those in Africa, American Indian teepees, and tree houses all designed to experience the outdoors. See the Milky Way, hear the sounds of nature, smell the fresh air, and still have free WiFi and breakfast included.

Located directly on the north shore of Lake Lacanau and a five-minute drive to Lacanau-Océan village and beach, it has numerous water sports available on the lake. Cook your own food outdoors or enjoy one of the restaurants nearby.

MÉDOC ATLANTIQUE **LACANAU-OCÉAN**
Hotel & Spa
VITALPARC HÔTEL & SPA

33680 Route du Baganais, Lacanau, France

+33 (0)5 56 03 91 00

VitalParc.com

English, French

Resort Open: All Year, Everyday
Restaurant Open: Breakfast, Lunch and Dinner

A HEALTHY RETREAT

Renovated in 2018, Vitalparc Hotel & Spa has 57 rooms on four floors in a four-star establishment. It is just five minutes from the beach and the Lacanau-Océan beach village. They have electric bike rentals to take you to the village, beach or into the forest with miles and miles of scenic bike paths. The hotel has an outdoor heated pool, indoor jacuzzi and a pool with dramatic blue mood lighting (photo left). It also has a healthy restaurant and unique spa.

THE SENSORY UNIVERSE

This is a super cool, modern, innovative spa, that goes beyond the body massage treatment. Casually enjoy an indoor heated swimming pool, whirlpool with bench and hydromassage jets, a heated jacuzzi, steam room, dry sauna, an ice grotto, and a sensory polar shower.

Fresh chilled shrimp on a bed of lightly grilled tomatoes with an assortment of vegetables; Ocean Salad, fresh fish with mixed greens and vegetables; Salmon Back, cooked on the skin, with a sauce of red peppers and vegetables.

Indoor Heated Swimming Pool (left page)
Steam Room and Dry Sauna (below middle)
Sensory Polar Shower (top middle)
Ice Grotto (below)

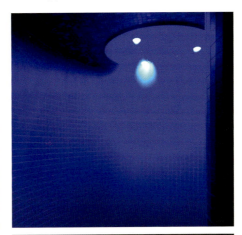

Exploring Wine Regions | **Bordeaux** | 237

ARCACHON BAY'S SAND DUNES

To the south of the Médoc Atlantique is Arcachon Bay, about an hour directly east of the city of Bordeaux, with two important destinations to check out. Northwest of the bay is Cap-Ferret, a quaint little beach town popular for their oysters right out of the water. To the south of the bay is "La Dune du Pilat" (a "heap" or a "mound" in English), a massive sand dune, the tallest in all of Europe.

It's a hike, so get ready. Check out the stairs. The Dune du Pilat is 106 meters high (348 feet). And it is moving up to 16 feet per year! One of the reason the forest was planted in the Medoc was to stop the erosion of the shoreline and sand dunes along the entire coast. Here, the wind keeps this sand dune growing and moving, and its stabilization is no longer anticipated. As archaeologists study the effects of this movement, they are discovering more about the dunes dating back 4,000 years.

In the photo below you can see this massive sand dune with blue ocean on the right and green forest to the left. This beautifully sculpted sand dune stretches 2,700 meters (and 500 meters wide), making it the tallest sand dune in Europe. It is free and open all year. Climb to the top and walk this amazing wonder of nature.

+33 (0) 5 56 22 12 85 • LaDuneDuPilat.com
Pyla-sur-Mer • La Teste-de-Buch, France

ARCACHON BAY'S CAP-FERRET

THE BEST OF ARCACHON BAY

The mouth of the bay enters from the south with a protective peninsula along the west shore. This headland is 25 km and is known as Cap-Ferret. Beautiful sandy beaches line the ocean side where some of the most delicious oysters line the inside bay where oysters can be found.

An hour west of Bordeaux city on highway D106, Cap-Ferret is a super cute community of villages. A step back in time to a beatnik France of sandals, surfing and sun. This is a hidden gem attracting wealthy residents and talented chefs. One such place, in a super casual beach vibe environment, is **L'Hôtel de La Plage**.

Find this little street, Ave de l'Herbe, along the water. The street is so tiny, you must park outside and walk in. You will find Hôtel de La Plage as soon as you enter from the waterside. The village is filled with shops and restaurants along the narrowest of streets. So romantic, peaceful and full of charm.

L'Hôtel de La Plage is a *Maison Lascombes* restaurant (page 480) so you can expect an extraordinary dining experience of food and wine!

You must start with a dozen on the half shell! Arcachon Bay is one of the largest oyster centers in Europe, and with four terroirs (yep, not just for wine), and Cap-Ferret is known for growing the most delicious oysters in the bay!

Don't let the casual beach environment fool you, this restaurant is delicious. The fish you see here is fresh out of the bay, served whole with so many flavors to enjoy. This ribeye steak was one of the best steaks we experienced in Bordeaux on this trip (also visit Maison Lascombes' steak restaurant in downtown Bordeaux, **La Brasserie Bordelaise**, on page 39). And coffee comes with many morsels of sweet decadence.

MÉDOC ATLANTIQUE **ARCACHON BAY**
Hôtel & Restaurant
HÔTEL DE LA PLAGE

1 Avenue de l'Herbe
33680 Lége-Cap-Ferret, France

+33 (0)5 56 60 50 15
Contact@HotelDeLaPlage-CapFerret.fr

HotelDeLaPlage-Cap-Ferret.fr

English, French

Open: April-October
Breakfast, Lunch and Dinner

OYSTER FARMING

Arcachon Bay, particularly in Cap-Ferret, offers ideal conditions for growing these delicious oysters.

The salinity of water is the perfect mix of salt from the Atlantic Ocean and freshness from the Landes Forest that covers 70% of the land and purifies the water that runs off into the bay.

The bay has its own microclimate with lots of sunshine throughout the year and no heat waves in the summer (average summer temperature in 22-24°c / 72-75°f), providing the optimal conditions for oyster production.

The bay's shallow water enables light to penetrate to the bottom, which combined with freshwater and its accompanying food, results in areas (especially Cap-Ferret) with a high production of phytoplankton and algae.

If you cannot make it here, the restaurants throughout Bordeaux serve these oysters.

BORDEAUX · GRAVES (Left Bank)
Graves, Pessac-Léognan, Sauternes & Barsac Appellations

Exploring Wine Regions **Bordeaux** | 241

Gravelly Graves' magical terroir for Cabernet Sauvignon is in the lesser known Left Bank region of Bordeaux, extending into Sauternes where botrytis results in one of the worlds most unique sweet wines.

Above: A stunning view of Château d'Yquem from the back patio of Château Sigalas Rabaud in Sauternes.
Previous & Left page: The gravelly soils of Château Smith Haut Lafitte growing Cabernet Sauvignon in Pessac-Léognan.
Below: Grapes ripe and ready for harvest in Graves.

THE GRAVES REGION

Now let's journey through the Graves wine region, located immediately south of the city of Bordeaux. "Graves" [gräv] is a French word meaning "gravelly land." Graves actually starts within the city metropolis of Bordeaux, as Pessac is the second largest suburb of Bordeaux with a population of 60,000 people. The downtown Bordeaux tram connects with Pessac, making it easy to access while staying in the city.

Graves spans 50 kilometers (31 miles) along the Left Bank of the Garonne River. From north to south, Graves starts at the city of Bordeaux and the Pessac-Léogran sub-appellation, through the Graves appellation, the Sauternes/Barsac sub-appellations, and ultimately to the city of Langon.

Pessac is home to many important Bordeaux universities (along the tram route) and prestigious wineries. Two definitely worth mentioning here are: first-growth Grand Cru Classés of 1885 Château Haut-Brion and Grand Cru Classés of Graves Château Pape Clément (page 251).

Graves is also a Left Bank wine region, left of the Garonne River (Médoc is also Left Bank to Garonne River; primarily Left Bank to the Gironde Estuary.) Graves is south of Bordeaux city, while the Médoc is north of Bordeaux city, all of which are on the Left Bank. This puts Graves upstream where the first gravelly stones landed from the river. It is these stones and gravel that offer Cabernet Sauvignon an optimal terroir for growing.

While the focus here is on the production of Cabernet Sauvignon, Graves is the only Bordeaux sub-region which produces all three high-quality types of Bordeaux wines: reds, dry whites and sweet wines. All three being of superior quality. This is a beautiful and diverse region worth exploring.

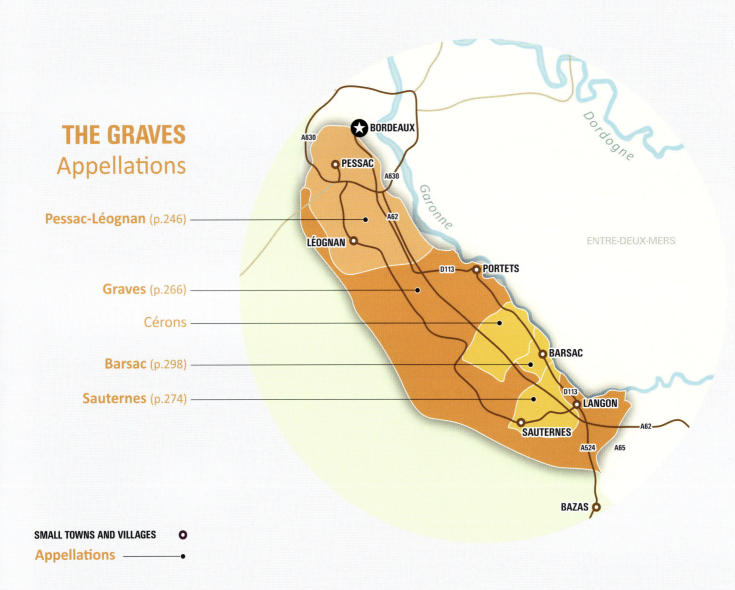

Exploring the Graves wine regions is an opportunity to discover the excellence of all three types of wines produced in Bordeaux.

Above: Château Rayne Vigneau in Sauternes

APPELLATIONS OF GRAVES

Graves is the overall appellation of the Graves wine region, with sub-appellations of Pessac-Léognan and Sauternes/Barsac, which I separate into chapters and distinguish here in the book.

The Graves appellation extends 50 kilometers (31 miles) south of the city of Bordeaux along the Left Bank of the Garonne River. Graves, and its sub-appellations, covers an area of roughly 7,200 hectares (17,800 acres) of vineyards. The map on the left identifies the Graves wine regions in the different shades of brown. Across the river is Entre-deux-Mers and a whole host of sub-appellations with differing terroir and numerous châteaux.

Graves and Pessac-Léognan are the appellations producing red wines here. And with the gravelly soil, the wines are primarily Cabernet Sauvignon followed by Merlot for their blends. Petit Verdot and Cabernet Franc, depending on the estate, may or may not be added in very small amounts.

Sauternes and Barsac are the appellations here that produce the sweet golden wines made from a unique microclimate which causes botrytis, affectionately known as Noble Rot, to grow. The three main grapes here are Sémillon, Sauvignon Blanc and Muscadelle. The Cérons sub-appellation also produces the sweet wine; however, the Noble Rot is not significant here and there are no notable producers, so I have left them out of the book.

All of Graves, including the sub-appellations of Pessac-Léognan and Sauternes/Barsac, produce dry white wine. And they are excellent dry white wines, primarily Sauvignon Blanc. Also, Sémillon.

Graves is where wine production took off in Bordeaux as the birth of Clairet's huge export business to England. Eleanor of Aquitaine (Bordeaux) married King Henry II (England) in the 12th century, launching 300 years of British rule over Bordeaux and its flourishing wine trade. When the Médoc marshland was drained by the Dutch in the 17th century, the fame of Bordeaux wines shifted to the Médoc estates we know today.

Not to be mistaken, extraordinary wines are produced in Graves. Wines that rival any other region of Bordeaux! I will impress upon you several great wine-producing châteaux here, as well as fun, interesting and educational tourism.

Since Graves is south of the city of Bordeaux, I will unveil these appellations from north to south, as you would arrive and traverse Graves traveling from the city of Bordeaux.

There is one highway running north and south through the Graves wine regions. A62 is a fast moving highway with a toll crossing (credit cards accepted). There are many local roads, which are quite picturesque, however there is no main road to follow as they keep changing from one road to another. Using GPS for local roads works just fine.

Below are the distances and times (without traffic) from the Bordeaux city perimeter.

From Bordeaux city center...
- **Pessac** (tram)   6km/4mi   (30 minutes)
- **Pessac** (driving)   6km/4mi   (20 minutes)

Driving from Bordeaux perimeter...
- **Léognan**   7km/4mi (14 minutes)
- **Graves/Portets** 16km/10mi (14 minutes)
- **Barsac**   30km/19mi (25 minutes)
- **Sauternes**   38km/24mi (30 minutes)
- **Langon**   37km/23mi (25 minutes)

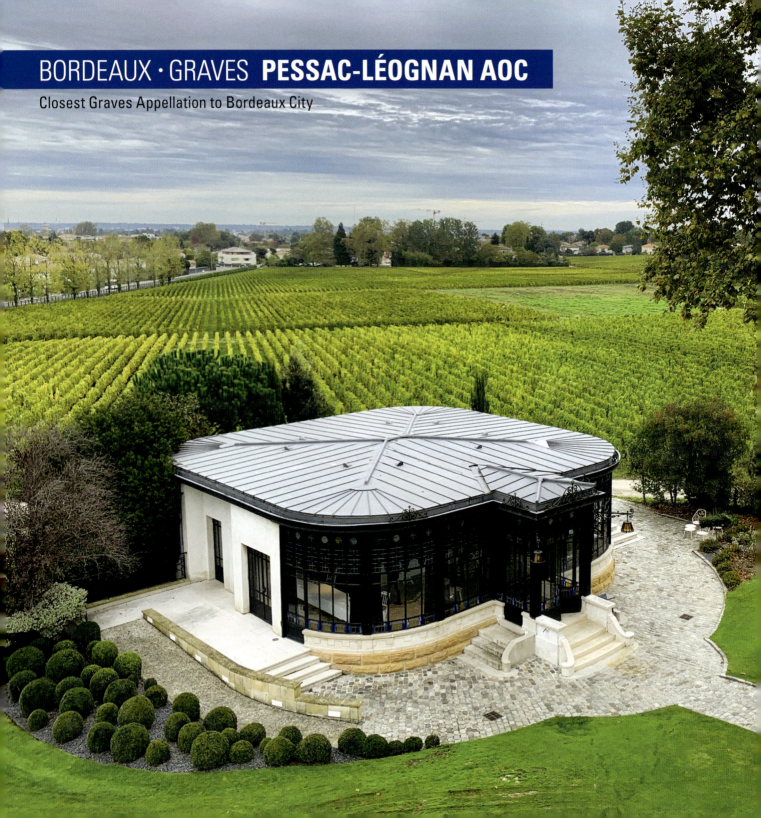

BORDEAUX · GRAVES PESSAC-LÉOGNAN AOC
Closest Graves Appellation to Bordeaux City

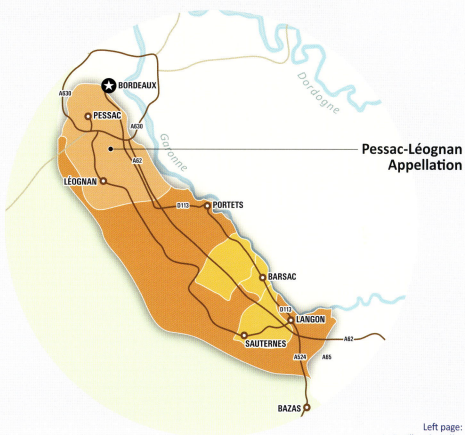

Pessac-Léognan Appellation

Left page:
Le Pavillon du Prélat
at Château Pape Clément
built by Gustavo Eiffel (Eiffel Tower)

EASY DAY TRIPS FROM THE CITY

Pessac-Léognan collectively is a special appellation defined by its unique terroir in Graves that produces excellent wines and superior Grand Cru Classé châteaux established by a 1959 classification. They are equally famous for their dry white wines as their red (which is still the predominant production).

Pessac-Léognan is adjacent to the city of Bordeaux, with Pessac being part of the metropolis, connected by the Bordeaux tram system.

Pessac has a nice restaurant at the tram stop **Brasserie de l'Hôtel de Ville**, then a 30-minute beautiful stroll (or 5-minute drive) to **Château Pape Clément**, which has excellent luxury tourism experiences, accommodations in their castle, and an extraordinary dinner.

Léognan is also close, with all of the wineries within a 20-minute drive from Bordeaux. And the winding roads are ideal and enticing for a beautiful drive out of the city.

Since the forest extends into Pessac-Léognan, the landscape here is beautifully dramatic with rolling hills of vineyards and towering pine forest, and roads that meander through it all.

Here are the châteaux...
- Château Pape Clément, page 251
- Château de Rouillac, page 257
- Château Haut-Bailly, page 259
- Château Le Pape, page 261
- Château Smith Haut Lafitte, page 263

Exploring Wine Regions **Bordeaux** 247

GRAND CRU CLASSÉ **OF GRAVES** — CLASSIFIED WINES

Graves has been producing wine for 2,000 years; long before the Médoc existed as a wine region. During the 300 years that the British ruled Bordeaux (12th to 15th centuries), the wines of Graves were exported to the UK. These are the Bordeaux Clairets that became so popular and successful. The Clairets came from Graves.

Then came the success of the Médoc. The Dutch drained the marshland expanding usable property. Forests were later planted, further improving the Médoc. And then came the classification of 1855 whereby Napoléon III confirmed the Grand Cru Classés of 1855 which gave validation and prestige to those châteaux that were exceptionally great wineries.

Now, if you were producing excellent wines in Graves, you would not be very happy about being left out. The only château in Graves included in the 1855 classification was Château Haut-Brion. So the wineries joined together and formed the Syndicat Viticole des Graves de Bordeaux, and officially petitioned the Institut National des Appellations d'Origine (INAO) to classify the wines of Graves. A professional jury was established to determine the quality and pricing of the wines in the region and ultimately chose 16 châteaux in the northern third of Graves and the INAO enacted a Graves classification. This classification was officially approved in 1953 and the number of estates was slightly increased in 1959. This classification stays in effect today. It is said that if a château can show that the quality and price of their wines are on par with the classification, they can be added.

Unique in Bordeaux, the classification includes both red and white wines, 22 labels in total. Some châteaux are classified for only white wine, some only for red, and others for both. The white wines from Graves are notably some of the best in all of Bordeaux. Some are so good they are more expensive than the reds. I can attest. You really must try them.

Since all of the Cru Classés of Graves were located in the Pessac and Léognan area, further definition of exceptional quality was established by creating the sub-appellation of Pessac-Léognan AOC in 1987.

The conclusion of all of this is that the Pessac-Léognan AOC and the Cru Classés of Graves are defined and classified as exceptionally great wines, producing wines that stand proud against any Médoc Grand Cru Classé of 1855 wine.

Château Pape Clément uses "Grand Cru Classé de Graves" on their classified wine labels and "Grand Vin de Graves" for their non-classified wine labels. Notice that all the labels below are identifying the Pessac-Léognan AOC quality appellation.

On the left is a "Grand Cru Classé de Graves" wine and is labeled both "Grand Cru Classé" and "Grand Vin de Bordeaux". Grand Vin de Bordeaux is just a marketing name as it is not a classified term. On the right is a non-classified winery. They are using the Pessac-Léognan AOC to define their quality appellation. While not a Cru Classé, Château de Rouillac is an excellent wine worth trying.

Château Smith Haut Lafitte uses both "Grand Cru Classé" and "Grand Cru Classé de Graves" on their label. Both are correct ways to identify the wine as Cru Classé classified. Their white wine is not classified so they are using a common label phrase "Grand Vin de Graves."

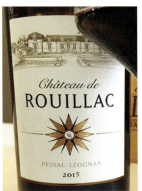

TABLE OF WINES AND TOURISM

CHÂTEAUX Pessac-Léognan	Classified	Number of Wines	Red Wine	White Wine	Rosé Wine	Sweet Wine	Wine Shop	Boutique	Accommodations	Restaurant	Food Options	Food & Wine Pairings	Tours	Castle Tours	Workshops	Activities	No Reservation Necessary	Tourism Award	Innovations
Château Haut-Bailly	GCC	4	√	√			√			√	√		1	1				√	
Château Le Pape	GCC	1	√						√	√									√
Château Pape Clément	GCC	7	√	√	√		√	√	√		√	7	7	√	7	7	√	√	
Château de Rouillac		5	√	√			√	√			√		1				√	√	
Château Smith Haut Lafitte	GCC	6	√	√			√	√		√			3	3	2		√	√	

CHÂTEAUX Graves AOC	Classified	Number of Wines	Red Wine	White Wine	Rosé Wine	Sweet Wine	Wine Shop	Boutique	Accommodations	Restaurant	Food Options	Food & Wine Pairings	Tours	Castle Tours	Workshops	Activities	No Reservation Necessary	Tourism Award	Innovations
Château de Portets		4	√	√			√			√			4		2		√	√	
Château de Roquetaillade													1	√					
Château Venus		6	√	√			√						2		7		√	√	√

GCC = Grand Cru Classé

Château Smith Haut Lafitte in Pessac-Léognan

GRAVES PESSAC-LÉOGNAN
Winery (Château) & Hotel
CHÂTEAU PAPE CLÉMENT

Grand Cru Classé of Graves
Winner: Best Of Wine Tourism

216 Avenue du Docteur Nancel Pénard
33600 Pessac, France

+33 (0)5 57 26 38 34
Visite@Pape-Clement.com

Pape-Clement.com

English, French

Open: All Year, Everyday
Call, Email or Book On Their Website

Tradition and innovation at its finest. Leading tourism experiences. Meet Bernard Magrez: Ahead of his time while keeping tradition.

HORSES AND DRONES AND TED

Walk through a Château Pape Clément vineyard one day and witness horses plowing the soil as it was done centuries ago. The next day see drones flying over the vineyards monitoring its evolution, collecting data for vine health and harvest times.

Bernard Magrez has created a technology lab, *The Vine Science Centre*, to bring scientific innovation into vine growing. It is led by Doctor of Oenology, Arnaud Delaherche, to develop more sustainable, high-precision approaches in each of their four Grand Cru Classé vineyards.

Meet TED, another *Science Centre* innovation. TED is a self-contained electric 4WD robot. He manages grass and weeds in the vineyards, both under the vines and between the rows, using mechanical rather than chemical methods.

As one of the oldest Grand Crus of Bordeaux, this property has an interesting history. Their first harvest dates back to 1252 with the help of nobility bringing them into the limelight. At the time, its owner, Bordeaux Archbishop Bertrand de Got, became Pope in 1305 under the name of Clement V. Add "Pape" (means "Pope" in French) to the name and you get Château Pape Clément and the iconic brand known thereafter.

While Magrez's vision and dedication are evident in his Grand Cru Classé red wine that is deservingly famous for its beautiful structure, his white wine, pictured here is so magnificent beyond imagination and is the most expensive wine he produces. Sauvignon Blanc, Sémillon, Sauvignon Gris, and Muscadelle. Simply divine.

Collection of Wines
Château Pape Clément
(First Label - Red Wine - Grand Cru Classé)

Château Pape Clément
(First Label - White Wine)

Le Clémentin du Pape Clément
(Second Wine - Red)

Le Clémentin du Pape Clément
(Second Wine - White)

GRAVES **PESSAC-LÉOGNAN**

Winery (Château) & Hotel
CHÂTEAU PAPE CLÉMENT

Open: All Year, Everyday

Booking Available On Website: Pape-Clement.com
Or Call: +33 (0)5 57 26 43 06
Or Write: Reservation@Pape-Clement.com

A NEW ERA IN WINE TOURISM

Bernard Magrez has always been ahead of his time innovating tourism experiences at a time when other châteaux in Bordeaux typically kept their doors closed. Forty years later, Magrez continues to create better and better tourism experiences while others try to follow in his success. Château Pape Clément is the epicenter of his experiences.

At Château Pape Clément, you can stay in an authentically restored castle from the 13th century thar was the home of Pope Clément V. This is not just a room; it is an experience. Quite a luxurious experience.

The caretaker of the castle maintains the grand home impeccably as if it were her own home. When it comes to breakfast, she will proudly serve you delicious treats she made herself with enthusiasm and pride. There is nothing like a home-cooked meal for breakfast. And you get it here.

Be sure to request their grand dinner in their opulent dining room (photo upper left) under their magnificent Baccarat chandelier. The food and wine pairing will be extraordinary. The elegant dinner is served by formal butlers.

BERNARD MAGREZ **LUXURY WINE EXPERIENCES**

*My life, forty years of passion dedicated to the vineyard.
My goal is to pass down excellence.*

— BERNARD MAGREZ

With either a helicopter or a Bentley, Bernard Magrez is all about the *Luxury Wine Experience*. It is his motto – and he delivers. Bernard is the only person who owns four Grand Cru Classé châteaux in Bordeaux. And they are in four different appellations. By helicopter, you can visit all of them in one day. A very cool experience indeed.

In Pessac-Léognan - Château Pape Clément
In Sauternes - Château Clos Haut-Peyraguey
In Haut-Médoc - Château La Tour Carnet
In Saint Émilion - Château Fombrauges

MÉDOC **SAINT ÉMILION** PESSAC **SAUTERNES**
BERNARD MAGREZ
LUXURY WINE EXPERIENCES

+33 (0)5 57 26 43 06
Contact@Pape-Clement.com

LuxuryWineExperience.com

Available 7/365. Everything is well planned, by reservations

HANDS-ON WORKSHOPS

One of the greatest pleasure of wine is that it is ever-learning, forever interesting. Magrez has created a whole host of interesting workshops, classes and participatory experiences in and around the winery and vineyards.

• THE KEYS TO WINE TASTING
Did you know that raspberry and banana have the same molecule? Yes, and while I smell raspberry and you smell banana, we are both correct. It is about what you are most familiar. Guess what, I love raspberries! Consider a class with an experienced sommelier and learn things like this.

• B WINEMAKER
The French always blend their wines. Here you get to taste the individual grape varietals and determine how you would blend to your taste. You are the chef. And you get to bottle, personalize your label and take it home.

• CALENDAR OF THE WINEMAKER
What is a green harvest and why is it important? When do the buds break? How is the leaf-thinning process strategized each year? Wood, concrete, clay, or stainless? And their effects on the wine? Learn the critical stages winemakers address in the vineyard, winery and cellars.

• FOOD AND WINE PARING
Did you know that a rosé is the perfect starter because it is more acidic and gets the saliva going? Sauvignon Blanc is also acidic working well with seafood and creams. Big tannin wines work with proteins, hence the well-known beef and Cabernet Sauvignon pairing. And Sauternes pair very well with birds, foie gras, and light and fruity desserts. We have all experienced the magic of a great pairing... the wine and food taste even better together. Each sip leads you to another bite, and each bite leads you to another sip. Here, a sommelier reveals how to create this magic.

• AND MORE...
Caviar & Wine, Cheeses & Wine, Wine Tasting Basics, Perfecting Wine Tasting, Testing your Senses, Blind Tastings, Understanding Terroir, Picnics, Picnic in a Rolls Royce, The Secrets in Bernard Magrez's Cellars, and so much more.

All workshops come with lots of wine tasting. Everything is pre-planned just for you so you can customize an experience exactly the way you desire.

GRAVES PESSAC-LÉOGNAN
Winery (Château)
CHÂTEAU DE ROUILLAC

Global Winner: Best Of Wine Tourism

12 Chemin du 20 Août 1949
33610 Canéjan, France

+33 (0)5 57 12 84 63
C.Lestable@ChateauDeRouillac.com

ChateauDeRouillac.com

English, French

*Open: All Year -
Monday-Friday, By Appointment Only
Saturday, By Special Appointment*

B alance, finesse, elegance, and power...the wine as well as the horse.

AN EQUESTRIAN HISTORY

Back in the day, Baron Georges Eugene Haussmann, the architect famous for the elegant Champs Elysées in Paris, was the original owner of Château de Rouillac. Baron Haussmann was passionate about horses and wine so this château was designed around an equestrian center, where it still remains today. Its newest owners, Laurent and Sophie Cisneros, also passionate about horses and wine, took over in 2009 and are continuing the love and tradition of horses and wine.

Baron Haussmann was fortunate enough to introduce his wines to Napoléon Bonaparte who loved them so much that he visited the property in Bordeaux many times, bringing the wines home to his table in Paris. Laurent Cisneros was also fortunate enough to introduce his wines to oenologist Eric Boissenot, who is a consulting winemaker to the first-growths of the Médoc: Château Margaux, Mouton Rothschild, Lafite Rothschild, and Latour. AND he convinced Boissenot to help him elevate the Château de Rouillac wines.

Keep in mind, this winery is not a Grand Cru Classé even though it is located on the same soil of Pessac-Léongan where all of the Grand Cru Classé of Graves are located. Think value! Without the "hood ornament" of Grand Cru Classé, yet with the same exceptional terroir and extraordinary consulting oenologist, the Château de Rouillac excellence can be had at a great value.

Collection of Wines
Château De Rouillac
(First Label - Red Wine)

Château De Rouillac
(First Label - White Wine)

Le Baron De Rouillac
(Second Wine - Red)

Le Dada De Rouillac
(Second Wine - White)

Le Dada De Rouillac
(Third Wine - Red)

GRAVES PESSAC-LÉOGNAN
Winery (Château)
CHÂTEAU HAUT-BAILLY

Grand Cru Classé of Graves
Winner: Best Of Wine Tourism

103 Avenue de Cadaujac
33850 Léognan, France

+33 (0)5 56 64 75 11
Mail@Haut-Bailly.com

Haut-Bailly.com

English, French

Open: All Year, Monday-Friday
By Appointment Only

100 points from Robert Parker.
-year-old vines.

IN AGE IS BEAUTY

Visits here are simply beautiful. A winemaking team that produces quality vineyards that exceed 100 years in age, and a terrace where you can sit and enjoy the elegant wines and beautiful view.

Robert Parker made a grand statement about this château in honoring them with 100 points for their 2009 vintage.

If you love the Robert Parker big bold style of wines, you are going to love Château Haut-Bailly. This wine comes with lots of elegance and finesse. Balanced and luscious. I love the big flavor style wines. The richness is very attractive to me. And when they are elegant, like this one, it melts in your mouth with yumminess. It's the perfect combination!

Parker is definitely in love with this property. He gave them 96 points in 2005 and again in 2008. Then a perfect score in 2009, followed by 97 points in 2010. Then in 2018, they earned 98 points.

If anything, you really must try this style of wine. It may be your thing.

It has been said that Château Haut-Bailly has the best chef in Bordeaux. Well, I cannot confirm. What I can tell you is that they do weekday lunches in the elegant 1872 château. Starting with a Champagne aperitif, and onto a handcrafted pairing of their wines with a four-course seasonal menu.

You can further immerse yourself in their kitchen with a cooking workshop with their chef. They focus on French gastronomy by producing traditional recipes, such as Burgundy gougères or Bordeaux canelés. Then enjoy your creations with a glass of their Grand Cru on the terrace.

Collection of Wines
Château Haut-Bailly
(First Label - Red Wine - Grand Cru Classé)

Haut-Bailly.II
(Second Wine - Red)

HB Haut-Bailly
(Third Wine - Red)

Rosé de Haut-Bailly
(Rosé of Cabernet Sauvignon)

GRAVES **PESSAC-LÉOGNAN**
Winery (Château) and Hotel B&B
CHÂTEAU LE PAPE

25 Chemin Le Thil
33850 Pessac, France
Winner: Best Of Wine Tourism

+33 (0)5 56 64 75 11
Hospitality@Haut-Bailly.com

ChateauLePape.com

English, French

*Open: All Year, Everyday
Reservations On Their Website*

Collection of Wines
Château Le Pape
(First Label - Red Wine)

A castle, a home.
Château living.

A PRIVATE MANOR HOUSE

Right down the street from Château Haut-Bailly is this private property devoted strictly to hospitality. Château Le Pape is owned by Haut-Bailly, so the grapes from the magnificent nine hectares surrounding the château are quietly taken away to Haut-Bailly for winemaking.

This is an elegant 18th century house which was entirely renovated according to heritage conservation rules. It is stunning. Six different suites, spacious, with private modern baths. And a big spread of food for breakfast in the morning. With nice weather, you can have breakfast on the terrace (photo left) overlooking the serene park atmosphere. The chef at Haut-Bailly is also available for your needs at Le Pape.

Exploring Wine Regions **Bordeaux**

GRAVES **PESSAC-LÉOGNAN**
Winery (Château)
CHÂTEAU SMITH HAUT LAFITTE

Perfection. A beautiful story of 19 years in pursuit of excellence, achieving the perfect 100 points.

Grand Cru Classé of Graves
Global Winner: Best Of Wine Tourism

Château Smith Haut Lafitte
33650 Martillac, France

+33 (0)5 57 83 11 22
Visites@Smith-Haut-Lafitte.com

Smith-Haut-Lafitte.com

English, French

Open: All Year, Everyday
Tours: By Appointment Only

A PASSION FOR EXCELLENCE

Four-time Olympic ski champions, Florence and Daniel Cathiard, parlayed their medals into a sporting goods business that afforded them to purchase Smith Haut Lafitte in the year 1990. Dilapidated and without any charm for the wines, they spent the next ten years completely renovating and restructuring Smith Haut Lafitte from the vineyards to the winery and cellars, and especially the winemaking methodology.

I have never seen such meticulous perfection going into each and every aspect of achieving perfect grapes. They only want perfect specimens; perfect size, not bruised, crushed or broken in any manner. The vineyards are hand picked, vine by vine, as the exact moment of ripeness is critical.

Sorting begins in the vineyard, then in the winery, followed by an advanced optical sorter that chooses each berry based on preselected ripeness criteria: size, sugar content, etc. Can you picture their perfect ski maneuvers that put them fractions of a second ahead of their competition to win the gold?

They are winning the gold here as well. In 2009 Robert Parker discovered their wine and initially gave them 98 points for this vintage, saying the wine was "nearly perfect." Two years later, retasting the evolution of the '09 in the bottle, Parker was willing to say they had achieved perfection and rescored the wine a perfect score of 100 points!

Optical sorting. Hand sorting. Berries on dry ice. Perfect grapes ready for perfect wine.

Collection of Wines
Château Smith Haut Lafitte
(First Label - Red Wine - Grand Cru Classé)

Château Smith Haut Lafitte
(First Label - White Wine)

Le Petite Haut Lafitte
(Second Wine - Red & White)

Les Hauts de Smith
(Third Wine - Red & White)

FOREST OF THE **FIVE SENSES**

CLOSE YOUR EYES AND ENTER THE FOREST...

GRAVES **PESSAC-LÉOGNAN**
Winery (Château)
CHÂTEAU SMITH HAUT LAFITTE

Incredible how much our senses are heightened when our eyes are closed. We get tuned in, tapped in, and open for discovery. Plan for at least two hours for an excursion through the Chateau Smith Haut Lafitte *Forest Of Senses*. All five senses will be stimulated. All along the path, you will be faced with sensory stimuli. Take it in. Feel what it brings you. Smith Haut Lafitte has won tourism awards for this.

Photo to the left, step down to the platform. Pull yourself across the water with the rope to the island. Discover sculptures hanging from the trees. Dangling sticks, carved beautifully. Hear the breeze and how the wooden ovoids tap the planks. A moment. Another. Take it all in.

Now go discover the goat, he will greet you towards the end.

Your perception of the forest will never be the same.

SO MUCH GOING ON HERE...

Plan to spend the day. The property is huge. Many impressively grand sculptures. Several tours of the vineyards, winery and cellars. Hands-on workshops of vineyard management, cellar master activities and a winemaking masterclass. A cooperage. Watch them make their own wine barrels. Visit the underground historic cellar to see century-old vintages of their wine. Taste their wines outdoors, fireside in the winter. By the way, all tours and workshops include tasting their spectacular wines. How about a wine and chocolate pairing? Yum! And don't forget to climb their tower for a panoramic view of the vineyards and forest.

ANOTHER BEAUTIFUL FAMILY STORY – OF GRAPE SKINCARE

The Cathiard's daughter, Mathilde, came home after graduating from business school only to discover that there were valuable nutrients, specifically that grape seeds contain polyphenols with anti-ageing properties, in the grape seeds and skins that her parents were discarding. The now famous Caudalie French skincare company was born specializing in anti-aging products. Further, Mathilde opened her first Vinothérapie Spa adjacent to Smith Haut Lafitte, including Les Sources de Caudalie, a five-star hotel and Michelin star restaurant. Get a copy of our "Extra Chapters" (Page 483) for a six-page review of Les Sources de Caudalie and Vinothérapie Spa.

NATURAL FARMING FOR HEALTHY GRAPES AND ENVIRONMENT

This entire property is its own ecosystem. Surrounded by forest on all sides, with deep gravelly soil, reaching clay 20 feet below. They have converted to all natural farming practices, including hand-harvesting and horses for plowing the vineyards.

Exploring Wine Regions | Bordeaux | 265

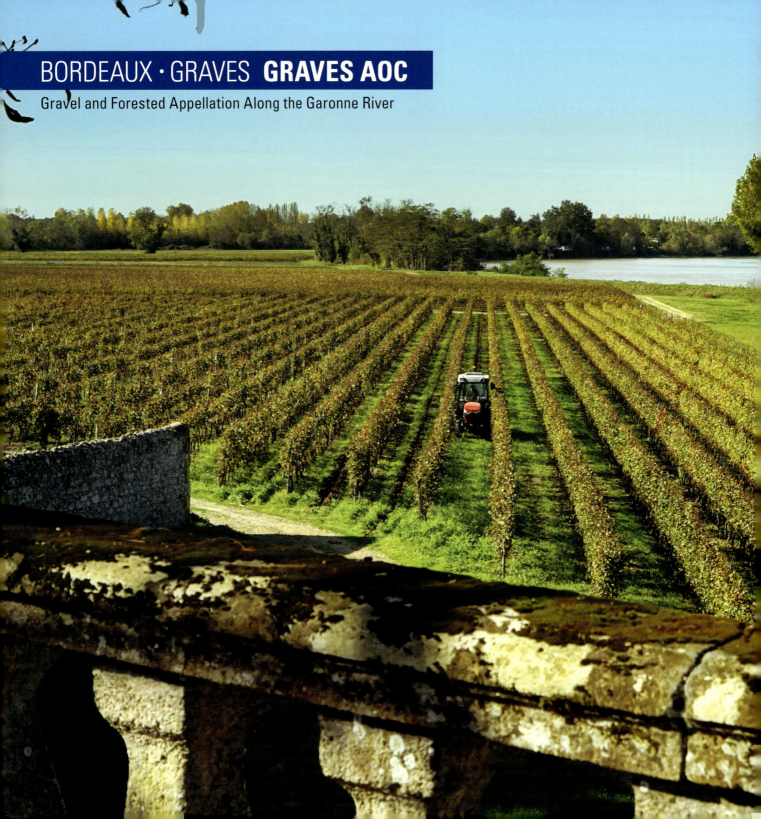

BORDEAUX · GRAVES GRAVES AOC
Gravel and Forested Appellation Along the Garonne River

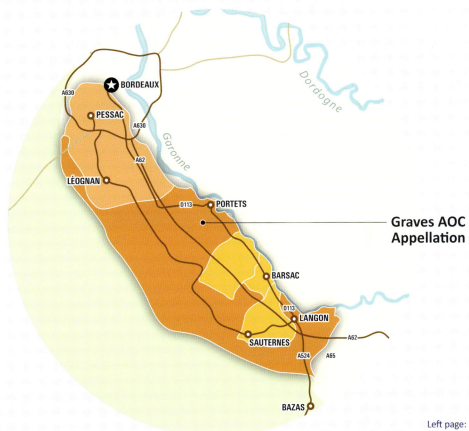

Graves AOC Appellation

Left page:
The vineyards of Château de Portets along the Garonne River flowing in the background

BEAUTIFUL TERROIR

First, we should distinguish between Graves, the entire appellation including Pessac-Léognan and Sauternes/Barsac, and Graves AOC (Appellation d'Origine Contrôlée) as a sub-appellation. This is analogous to the entire appellation of the Médoc, and Margaux AOC as a sub-appellation. This chapter is devoted to the Graves AOC sub-appellation.

Graves AOC as its own appellation can sometimes be overshadowed by the fame of the Pessac-Léognan and Sauternes/Barsac sub-appellations. Let that not deter you. I have a couple of châteaux to show you that are very much worth visiting. One is historic along the river, **Château de Portets**, and the other is new, modern and can take you flying over the regions, **Château Vénus**. Plus, a real fortress castle that you can visit, explore and feel its history.

Remember, Graves is where it all began for wine in Bordeaux with the birth of Clairet. Eleanor of Aquitaine, King Henry II, and British rule over Bordeaux, gave rise to a flourishing wine trade. Today, the Graves AOC châteaux are very competitive, delivering high-quality wines at very good prices and coming up with excellent tourism experiences to encourage visits.

Also, this is forested land with magical rocky soil, beautiful for the vines, and picturesque for your exploring.

Here are the châteaux...
- Château de Portets, page 269
- Château Vénus, page 271
- Château Roquetaillade, page 273

GRAVES **GRAVES AOC**
Winery (Château)
CHÂTEAU DE PORTETS

Winner: Best Of Wine Tourism

Rue de Mongenan
33640 Portets, France

+33 (0)5 56 67 12 30
Oenotourisme@ChateauDePortets.fr

ChateauDePortets.com

English, French

Open: All Year
April-October, Monday-Saturday
November-March, Monday-Friday

O n the river where the stones from the Pyrénées Mountains gathered heavily.

NAPOLÉON WAS HERE

It all began 1000 BC when the Romans built the Port of Portets to develop a viniculture trade along the Garonne River. The community of Portets became an important town and ultimately today there are 35 or so wineries here.

Actually it started 25 million years ago after two continents collided and rivers brought gravel and stones from the Pyrénées Mountains to the Left Bank Graves regions. The larger stones are closer to the river and Château de Portets could not be any closer to the river as their vines practically kiss the water on the bank of the river.

Being on the water has even further advantages beyond the gravelly soil so special to Cabernet Sauvignon. When Napoléon traveled from Spain to Bordeaux, he would stop at Château de Portets for lunch prior to making his ceremonial visits to Bordeaux. De Portets was an important fortified castle until the 16th century. Today they offer games for children around the castle, like counting how many chimneys they can find.

After the 2nd World War, the château was in shambles. Jules Theron, an agronomy engineer, purchased the property in 1956 and resurrected the property with the help of his son. His granddaughter Marie-Helene Yung-Theron is continuing with improvements and has created innovative tourism opportunities to go with their stellar wines. I must tell you that her Sauvignon Blanc is extraordinary and at a great price!

Marie-Helene has created a beautiful film and seasonal sculptures in her theatre. Plus, she has injected technology into the tourism experiences by creating an interactive tactile table to discover at your own pace: the Graves terroir, what happens in each of the four seasons in their vineyards and cellars, and many interesting wine facts organized for both a fun and educational experience.

You will love their *Back From The Market* visit where you get to taste their estate wines paired with local savory dishes or an aged cheese and charcuterie pairing.

Collection of Wines
Château De Portets
(First Label - Dry White Wine)

Grand Vin Château De Portets
(First Label - Red Wine)

Château De Portets
(Second Wine - Red Wine)

Château Port Du Roy
(Bordeaux Supérieur - Red Wine)

> **GRAVES GRAVES AOC**
> Winery (Château)
> **CHÂTEAU VÉNUS**
>
> *Winner: Best Of Wine Tourism*
>
> 3 Pertigues Lieu dit Brouquet
> 33720 Illats, France
>
> +33 (0)6 03 17 91 39
> Contact@ChateauVenus.com
>
> **ChateauVenus.com**
>
> *English, French*
>
> *Open: All Year, Monday-Saturday
> Reservations Not Required*
>
> *Reservations are Required for Flying*

Feminine wines from the goddess of Venus. A modern approach to soft beautiful wines.

A BEAUTIFUL STORY

Before we go flying, let's enjoy the story of Bertrand and Emmanuelle Amart. They met in college when he was studying oenology and viticulture and she was studying wine trade. They decide to take their diplomas, get married and travel the world to learn more about wine.

When they returned to Bordeaux, they bought four hectares of land, planted one hectare with vines, and rented a house with an old cellar. Château Vénus was born. As time passed and people discovered and loved their wine, they bought more land. Today, they have nine hectares planted, a brand new winery built, and the cutest little girl, Leonie, added to the family. You will find her dancing in their Vénus videos making the wine more beautiful.

And now for the best part. Bertrand and I are pilots. Bertrand built a grass runway right down the middle of his vineyards, bought an airplane and keeps it in the farming hangar. We brought out that fine bird and took to the skies. We flew Graves, Sauternes, Saint Émilion and Pomerol. And he will do the same for you. Seriously. Go there!

When you see beautiful aerial photographs in this book, please think of Bertrand. He helped make it happen. I love to fly, and this was an extra special treat to see and capture Bordeaux from the air.

Let's not forget about the wines. The Château Vénus wines are just like the goddess... soft and elegant, delicate and beautiful, seductive and ready. This is a new style of wine, drinkable now, very feminine (so different from the masculine Médoc), and made with love and passion, as their beautiful story goes.

Collection of Wines
Château Vénus
(First Label - Red Wine)

Château Vénus
(First Label - White Wine)

Château Vénus Tentation
(Second Wine - Red Wine)

Apollon
(Premium Red Wine)

Les Délices d'Apollon
(Fourth Wine - Red and White Wines)

GRAVES **GRAVES AOC**
Medieval Castle
CHÂTEAU DE ROQUETAILLADE

33210 Roquetaillade, Mazères, France

+33 (0)5 56 76 14 16
Roquetaillade@Hotmail.com

Roquetaillade.eu

English, French

Open: All Year
Every Afternoon, 2:30pm-5:00pm

A real castle. A fortress. Capable of holding off the enemy for two years straight.

STRATEGIC FORTRESS

As Sébastien de Baritault, owner of Château de Roquetaillade (in his family for 700 years), explained to me, there are two ways to take a castle. One is by force. Generally you do not do so well. Or two, by waiting them out, as the inhabitants will eventually need food and water. Makes sense.

The property of Roquetaillade has a natural defense being on top of a limestone plateau, with cliffs to hold off the enemy. Wooden fortresses were known to be built here as early at the 8th century, possibly much earlier.

With permission from King Edward, Gaillard de la Mothe and his uncle Pope Clement V (Château Pape Clement) built a new style of castle in 1306. A deep moat surrounds the castle constructed of limestone blocks with balistraria (arrow slits) on all sides and levels. Not likely anyone would try to take this castle. Little did any enemy know this castle was built on a well so the water was endless and they stored food to last two years. To try and wait them out, everyone would eventually give up.

This was the last English castle built in France. And most amazing is that it has stayed in the same family for these past 700 years. After the wars, the Roquetaillade was redesigned to be a comfortable home. Windows were installed on the lower floors and the arrow slits were taken out. The inside became quite lavish for the family of this castle.

Today, no one lives in the castle and it is open for tours.

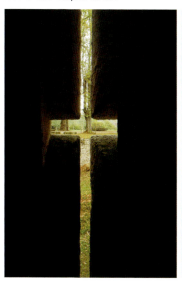

BORDEAUX · GRAVES **SAUTERNES AOC**

Golden Wines of Noble Rot

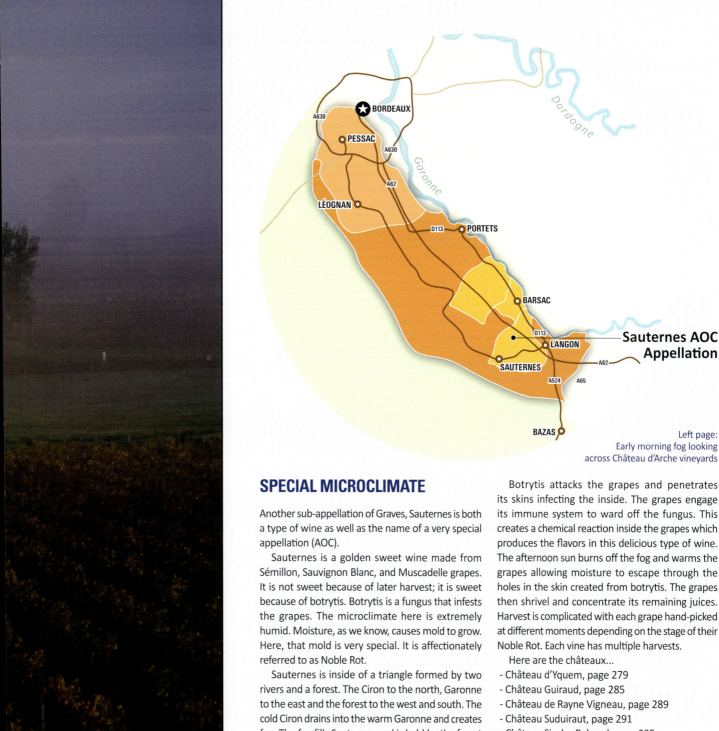

Sauternes AOC Appellation

Left page:
Early morning fog looking across Château d'Arche vineyards

SPECIAL MICROCLIMATE

Another sub-appellation of Graves, Sauternes is both a type of wine as well as the name of a very special appellation (AOC).

Sauternes is a golden sweet wine made from Sémillon, Sauvignon Blanc, and Muscadelle grapes. It is not sweet because of later harvest; it is sweet because of botrytis. Botrytis is a fungus that infests the grapes. The microclimate here is extremely humid. Moisture, as we know, causes mold to grow. Here, that mold is very special. It is affectionately referred to as Noble Rot.

Sauternes is inside of a triangle formed by two rivers and a forest. The Ciron to the north, Garonne to the east and the forest to the west and south. The cold Ciron drains into the warm Garonne and creates fog. The fog fills Sauternes and is held by the forest creating the perfect environment for fungus to grow.

Botrytis attacks the grapes and penetrates its skins infecting the inside. The grapes engage its immune system to ward off the fungus. This creates a chemical reaction inside the grapes which produces the flavors in this delicious type of wine. The afternoon sun burns off the fog and warms the grapes allowing moisture to escape through the holes in the skin created from botrytis. The grapes then shrivel and concentrate its remaining juices. Harvest is complicated with each grape hand-picked at different moments depending on the stage of their Noble Rot. Each vine has multiple harvests.

Here are the châteaux...
- Château d'Yquem, page 279
- Château Guiraud, page 285
- Château de Rayne Vigneau, page 289
- Château Suduiraut, page 291
- Château Sigalas Rabaud, page 295

Exploring Wine Regions **Bordeaux** | 275

GRAND CRU CLASSÉ OF SAUTERNES & BARSAC

Even though Sauternes may be tucked away in the southern part of Bordeaux, in the very south of the Graves appellation, they are not a secret to the fans of quality wines around the world; nor were they hidden from the classification of 1855. Most people think of the Grand Cru Classés of 1855 as being exclusively red wine and exclusively in the Médoc (except first-growth Château Haut-Brion being in Pessac-Léognan, Graves).

Even more interesting is that there are more first-growths in both Sauternes and Barsac than there are in the Médoc. The Médoc has five first-growths, and they are super famous (Chateaux Margaux, Mouton Rothschild, Lafite Rothschild, Haut-Brion and Latour). Sauternes and Barsac have 11 first-growths and 15 second-growths. And then you may ask, what about Château d'Yquem? Well, I had an even more complex questions. Why three levels of growths and the second level is a first-growth? Why wouldn't d'Yquem be a first-growth, the second level be second-growths and the third be the third? So here is the interesting answer: The 11 first-growths are on par with the first-growths of the Médoc (including pricing), so that is why they are first-growths. Château d'Yquem was far superior to the first-growths, so it was bestowed as a superior first-growth (Premier Cru Supérieur).

Let's review the history of the classification of 1855, which defined these châteaux. Napoléon wanted to show the world that France has the very best wines at his *Exposition Universelle de Paris* in 1855 to surpass *London's Great Exhibition of 1851*. Napoléon ordered the official classification of Bordeaux wines through the Gironde Chamber of Commerce and the Wine Brokers Union of Bordeaux. These brokers ranked the wines according to the château's reputation and the wine's selling price, which was considered directly related to quality. Imagine these Sauternes wines having the similar reputations and selling prices as Château Latour for example. And that Château d'Yquem out-priced everyone at that time.

This ranking then became the official classification of Grand Cru Classés of 1855 which has stood proud ever since. The sweet wines from Sauternes and Barsac were very much included with 28 châteaux classified. In this book, I review and present to you five Grand Cru Classé châteaux in Sauternes and two in Barsac. Plus a non-classified château in Barsac worth your exploration.

On the Château Suduiraud first label they identify "Premier Grand Cru Classé en 1855," where the second label is not classified and the markings were left off. Château Guiraud identifies their classification a little differently as "1er Grand Cru Classé en 1855" Premier and 1er essentially mean the same thing. Château Sigalas Rabaud does it slightly differently dropping the "en." All are correct.

Château d'Yquem does not put any classification on their label. A bold move in their most superior position and belief in public knowledge.

TABLE OF WINES AND TOURISM

CHÂTEAUX Sauternes AOC	Classified	Number of Wines	Red Wine	White Wine	Rosé Wine	Sweet Wine	Wine Shop	Boutique	Accommodations	Restaurant	Food Options	Food & Wine Pairings	Tours	Castle Tours	Workshops	Activities	No Reservation Necessary	Tourism Award	Innovations
Château Guiraud	GCC	3	✓	✓		✓				✓	3		3		3		✓	✓	
Château de Rayne Vigneau	GCC	4	✓	✓		✓	✓					✓	3		2	3	✓		
Château Sigalas Rabaud	GCC	5	✓	✓		✓			✓	✓			2		1				
Château Suduiraut	GCC	7	✓	✓		✓						✓	1		1	1			
Château d'Yquem	GCC	2	✓	✓		✓							3						

CHÂTEAUX Barsac AOC	Classified	Number of Wines	Red Wine	White Wine	Rosé Wine	Sweet Wine	Wine Shop	Boutique	Accommodations	Restaurant	Food Options	Food & Wine Pairings	Tours	Castle Tours	Workshops	Activities	No Reservation Necessary	Tourism Award	Innovations
Château Climens	GCC	2	✓	✓		✓					3		3		3		✓	✓	
Château Coutet	GCC	3	✓	✓		✓					✓		✓		1				
Château Gravas		4	✓	✓	✓	✓					3		3		3		✓		

GCC = Grand Cru Classé of 1855

Château d'Yquem in Sauternes

GRAVES **SAUTERNES**
Winery (Château)
CHÂTEAU D'YQUEM

Premier Cru Supérieur (Superior First-Growth)
Grand Cru Classé of 1855

Château d'Yquem
33210 Sauternes, France

+33 (0)5 57 98 07 07

ChateauYquem.com

English, French

*Open: All Year, Everyday
By Appointment Only
Reservations Available On Their Website*

Collection of Wines
Château d'Yquem
(First Label - Superior Grand Cru)

No second wine here. If the year does not meet their standards, then they do not make the wine

Yquem Y
(Dry White Wine)

SIMPLY YQUEM

Château d'Yquem wine can be simply stated as the premier wine of Bordeaux. It is considered to be superior to the first-growths of the Médoc. It is owned by Bernard Arnault, Chairman & CEO of LVMH (Louis Vuitton Moët Hennessy) and the wealthiest man in Europe. The wine is so good it is coveted, collected and consumed at some of the most prestigious events in the world.

Eloquently, it is Yquem.

GRAVES SAUTERNES
Winery (Château)
CHÂTEAU D'YQUEM

PERFECT GRAPES MAKE SUPERIOR WINES

Let's explore how the best of the best does it. We should probably start with terroir, as that is what Bordeaux is all about. We buy Bordeaux wines based on the château's unique terroir that creates their flavor profiles.

Sauternes in and of itself has very unique terroir. They get an average of 92 days of fog. It is so humid that botrytis cinerea (Noble Rot) grows and creates this magical wine (see pages 275). Further, Yquem is located on one of the highest plateaus in Sauternes with soil of prehistoric limestone fossilized oysters, with gravel and pebbles that accumulate heat (this is still Graves), which creates warm and dry conditions in this very humid environment. Below, in the subsoil, is clay. Clay retains water in the right place, deep below where the roots grow and drink, and at the right time for the vines when they need water from dry spells, which often happen. And, there are numerous springs on the estate to feed water into the clay; Yquem built over 100 km (62 miles) of drainage pipes to prevent over saturation of the soil. This is great terroir.

Yquem has a very large estate with 113 acres of vines. This is important as it gives them diversity in the terroir for greater complexity in their wines. Just look at their beautiful property and château on the left page. They harvest these vineyards with unbelievable meticulous attention. They truly harvest grape by grape. Imagine, each vineyard is harvested an average of six times, and in certain years as many at ten times. Each individual grape is analyzed for its botrytis and concentration, and is either harvested, discarded for having other types of fungus, or kept for the next round of harvest. Harvest occurs over a six-week period during September to November, depending on weather conditions.

Can you imagine the training that goes into each picker to assure the harvest of the right grapes happens properly? Yquem has 200 pickers sorted into four groups of 50 people. New people must go through three days of extensive training before they are allowed to harvest. And new pickers are not allowed to harvest the first round on a vine.

Château d'Yquem also has 20 full-time female vineyard workers who manage their own separate plots on the property; they are engaged and intimately knowledgeable of each vine, responsible as the singular person watching after their vineyards all year. One master vineyard manager oversees these ladies and the entire 700,000 vines of this estate.

Yquem only grows two grape varieties: Sémillon (75%) which produces a rich wine with body and structure, and Sauvignon Blanc (25%), infusing aromas and finesse. Upon harvest, grapes are immediately brought into the winery and pressed three to four times with a pneumatic winepress. Juice from the various pressings are blended before fermentation; however, each day's wine is aged separately for the first six to eight months. Taste and lab analysis determine which wines meet Yquem's strict standards.

Fermentation takes place in only new French oak barrels. Since Yquem allows the fermentation process to stop naturally, it can take up to six weeks for completion, depending on the yeast/sugar activity. Preliminary blends are made and then moved to the aging cellar where they will stay for 20 months. A rigorous selection process continues in the cellar, removing the lees and light sediments, clarifying the wine on a regular basis. Towards the end of aging, blind tastings are conducted to assure the best possible final blend.

My perfect pairing with Château d'Yquem... Oysters!

GRAVES **SAUTERNES**
Winery (Château)
CHÂTEAU D'YQUEM

VISITING THE ESTATE

Yes, it is possible to visit this 400-year-old estate. Château d'Yquem wants you to discover its magic. By reservations only. They are ready.

They have three simple options, all including a tour of the vineyards, winery and cellars, followed by a tasting of your choosing. All tours are small and intimate, six people maximum.

- **The Discovery**

Tasting of Château d'Yquem and Y

- **The Trilogy**

Tasting of the three most recent vintages of Château d'Yquem

- **The From One 5 to Another**

A vertical tasting of vintages five years apart of Château d'Yquem

Might I add, their wines are everything magical beyond what you can imagine. I have personally tasted many different vintages, and they always delight. They are a bouquet of tropical fruit salad, with mango richness and pineapple freshness in the mouth. Now I want a glass!

A party at Chateau d'Yquem is a very special treat. Especially when hosted and attended by owner Bernard Arnault. Typically private and not open to the public, as this one was by invitation only. These grand parties exemplify the magnificence and quality of this estate and the people behind it.

Yquem makes a dry white wine simply called: Y. It is a blend of their Sauvignon Blanc and Sémillon

Their beautiful tasting room below.

GRAVES SAUTERNES
Winery (Château) & Restaurant
CHÂTEAU GUIRAUD

Premier Cru (First-Growth)
Grand Cru Classé of 1855
Winner: Best Of Wine Tourism

Château Guiraud
33210 Sauternes, France

+33 (0)5 56 76 61 01
Accueil@ChateauGuiraud.com

ChateauGuiraud.com

English, French

*Open: All Year, Everyday
Reservations Not Required
Reservations Available On Their Website*

T otally organic and the first Premier Grand Cru Classé of 1855 to have its own ecosystem and be awarded Agriculture Biologique certification.

THE ECOSYSTEM

This is a very special property. It is an ecosystem in and of itself. They are located on the same plateau as Château d'Yquem, directly behind them at a higher elevation up against the forest. The forest surrounds them for an isolated ecosystem which allows them to be organic and self-contained. Thanks to current owner, Xavier Planty, this property has undergone a complete transformation, resulting in extraordinary wines.

Planty built hotels throughout the property. Bug hotels (photo left). And bugs book rooms. Even move in permanently. Nesting boxes are provided for birds, and hives are built to attract pollinating insects. In 2010, an entomologist counted 635 species of insects and spiders in the vineyards, including seven species of bumblebees. If you allow nature to take its course, it will express its full potential.

In 2001, Château Guiraud created a unique conservatory of white grape varieties. And now there are 175 different strains of Sémillon and Sauvignon Blanc. It is the only one of its kind in the world. The objective is to select only the most robust and the specimens most representative of Sauternes for the nursery. This guarantees the exceptional biodiversity of future vineyards.

Speaking of diversity: This large estate of 128 hectares (316 acres) has dozens of different soil composites and microclimates. This heterogeneous soil creates a wide range of diversity in the wines, which are then blended into their uniquely different Grand Cru Sauternes. This gives them a great degree of balance and complexity with numerous aromatic nuances and unique flavors.

For me, Château Guiraud is a beautifully romantic wine of gentle sweetness and aromatic elegance. I find delicious minerality (no doubt representing the terroir of this unique property) with apricot flavors and white flower aromas. Ever so wonderful.

Collection of Wines
Château Guiraud
(First Label - Premier Grand Cru)

Petit Guiraud
(Second Wine)

Guiraud G
(Dry White Wine)

GRAVES **SAUTERNES**
Winery (Château) Restaurant
CHAPELLE DE GUIRAUD

FIRST GRAND CRU RESTAURANT

I was fortunate to dine here with Nicolas Lascombes (photo left), the man behind this extraordinary restaurant, soon after they opened. Nicolas is responsible for creating many unique gourmet restaurant in and around Bordeaux (see page 480).

The setting is adjacent to Château Guiraud overlooking their vineyards inside an 1874 chapel situated next to the castle. You might feel the ambiance of a French Tuscany setting. And the cuisine is as natural, local, wholesome and organic as the landscape of Château Guiraud's natural ecosystem of a vineyard farm.

Sitting at the table with Guiraud owner, Xavier Planty, and Nicolas was an amazing treat in itself, beyond sampling their impressive cuisine and tasting wines from Guiraud and other local Graves châteaux. The wine list here is said to exceed 500 labels from all over Bordeaux and beyond. Big names, as well as small family producers, which these two men know how to find.

Nicolas had a vision to create a cuisine of local and natural origins to reflect the restaurant's location. Check out the pictures of fresh local truffles, mussels, steaks, and a creamy dessert. This is the first restaurant at a Premier Grand Cru Classé of 1855 in all of Bordeaux. And they have already qualified as a Michelin Plate.

While I chose to sit outside on the patio amongst the trees, flowers, wild grasses, and vineyards, inside is just as beautiful with space for 200 guests, including private rooms (big and small).

Winner: Best Of Wine Tourism

Château Guiraud
33210 Sauternes, France

+33 (0)5 40 24 85 45
Contact@LaChapelleDeGuiraud.com

LaChapelleDeGuiraud.com

English, French

Open: All Year
Lunch: Everyday
Dinner: Friday and Saturday Nights
Reservations Available On Their Website

Guiraud G, a dry white wine of 50/50 Sauvignon Blanc and Sémillon

One of many small producer served here

O n top of the hill, with many entertaining and educational activities to enjoy.

GRAVES SAUTERNES
Winery (Château)
CHÂTEAU DE RAYNE VIGNEAU

Premier Cru (First-Growth)
Grand Cru Classé of 1855
Winner: Best Of Wine Tourism

4 Le Vigneau
33210 Bommes, France

+33 (0)5 56 76 61 63
Chateau@RayneVigneau.fr

RayneVigneau.fr

English, French, Italian, German, Spanish

Open: All Year
April-November, Everyday
December-March, Monday-Friday
For Visits: +33 (0)5 56 76 64 05

Collection of Wines
Château de Rayne Vigneau
(First Label - Premier Grand Cru)

Gold de Rayne Vigneau
(Limited to Exceptional Vintages '05, '09, '14)

Madame de Rayne
(Second Wine)

Le Sec de Rayne Vigneau
(Dry White Wine)

SO MUCH TOURISM FUN HERE

Before we get into all the fun, let's not forget this winery is a Premier Grand Cru Classé of 1855 whose reputation is recognized beyond the classification, as well-known wine brokers rank Rayne Vigneau second only to Yquem. The estate is located on the third highest spot in Sauternes, behind Yquem.

Their hill of 84 hectares (207 acres) is planted with three grapes, the typical Sémillon and Sauvignon Blanc, plus 2% Muscadelle. And surprisingly, their property has precious stones mixed with the gravel: agates, onyxes, amethysts, and sapphires. Imagine what these stones do to enhance the aromas and flavors of their wines.

Is a Sauternes just a Sauternes just a generic sweet golden Sauternes? No. Each château has its own terroir, with unique soils that are reflected in the diversity of their wines. Château de Rayne Vigneau has this originality and is a worthy treat.

This château offers a lot of activities. Three tours (and tastings), three fun activities, two educational workshops, and a customized food and wine pairing.

TOUR & TASTINGS
Vineyard, winery and cellar tour with tasting of:
- **Three wines**. Sec de Rayne Vigneau, Madame de Rayne, Château Rayne Vigneau
- **Three verticle wines** of Château de Rayne Vigneau
- **Six vintages** of Château de Rayne Vigneau

ACTIVITIES
- **The Sweet Escape**. An escape game
- **Tasting on a Tree Top**. Atop a cedar tree with panoramic views
- **Rayne Vigneau on Horseback**. Vineyard stroll

WORKSHOPS
- **The Five Senses Awake**. Workshop and tastings
- **Blending Workshop**. A unique experience blending wines by varietal to understand the crucial steps of blending a great wine. And you will leave with your own personalized Grand Cru Classé.

MEALS AT THE CHÂTEAU
- **A Food & Wine Pairing**. Customized and priced to your request (from 4 to 55 people).

GRAVES SAUTERNES
Winery (Château)
CHÂTEAU DE SUDUIRAUT

Premier Cru (First-Growth)
Grand Cru Classé of 1855

Château Suduiraut
33210 Preignac, France

+33 (0)5 56 63 61 92
Contact@Suduiraut.com

Suduiraut.com

English, French

Open: All Year, Monday-Saturday
By Appointment Only

An atmosphere of aromas and colors. Smell 19 common aromas of Sauternes and see the color darken with age through the decades.

COLORS & SCENTS

Not a lot of tours here. Or workshops. Or other activities. Instead, the tasting room is a potpourri of knowledge to be absorbed.

First, let's distinguish the Suduiraut blend from the typical 75/25 blend, as they are 94% Sémillon with a 6% splash of Sauvignon Blanc. Sémillon is wildly fragrant after infected with botrytis and makes the flavorful aromatics in this wine special.

The tasting room is the place to be. They have 19 clear glass jars with the fruits, spices, herbs and flowers we commonly smell and taste in Sauternes (photo left). This is a great experience to familiarize yourself with these aromas while tasting their wines at the same time.

In the tasting room, there is a long row of their Grand Cru bottles displaying vintage after vintage. You will see the color dramatically changing year after year for decades. So do the flavors. These wines were meant to be aged and they taste better the longer you can store them.

I had the opportunity to experience a pairing of three wines with seven year gaps: 2013, 2006 and 1999 (see photo right). You can do this too. The tasting room is filled with their different wines and in many different vintages. And even better, you can buy the older bottles here if you like.

The 2013 was fresh, lively with tropical fruits, not too dense, easy to approach and drink.

The 2006 was more intense without being heavy, with flavors of orange-saffron, caramel and mango.

The 1999 was a real treat. It was powerful, elegant and not too sweet. Beautiful complexity. It had marmalade, bitter orange and smoky on the finish. This is sip-on-its-own wine for the den.

I also had the opportunity to taste the first label and the second wine of the same 2008 vintage. I was surprised by the excellence of the second label. Beautifully expressive. Just as big and full bodied, with vanilla and fruits of apricot and orange. I want some now just thinking about it.

Collection of Wines
Château Suduiraut
(First Label - Premier Grand Cru)

Castelnau de Suduiraut
(Second Wine)

Lions de Suduiraut
(Young Vines Fresh Label)

S de Suduiraut Vieilles Vignes
(Old Vines, Dry White Wine)

Blanc Sec de Suduiraut
(Young Vines, Dry White Wine)

GRAVES SAUTERNES
Winery (Château) and Hotel B&B
CHÂTEAU SIGALAS RABAUD

Premier Cru (First-Growth)
Grand Cru Classé of 1855

Rabaud-Sigalas
33210 Bommes, France

+33 (0)5 57 31 07 45
ChateauSigalasRabaud@gmail.com

Chateau-Sigalas-Rabaud.com

English, French

Open: All Year, Everyday
By Appointment Only
Reservations Available On Their Website

T he best things come in small packages. This is the smallest of all the Premier Grand Crus, making wine of superb craftsmanship!

Collection of Wines
Château Sigalas Rabaud
(First Label - Premier Grand Cru)

Lieutenant de Sigalas
(Second Wine)

Demoiselle de Sigalas
(Dry Wine Wine)

Sémillante de Sigalas
(Second Wine - Dry White Wine)

Le 5 de Sigalas
(Without Sulfites - Semi Sweet White Wine)

FOURTEEN HECTARES OF GRANDEUR

This is the smallest of the Premier Grand Crus. And we all know good things come in small packages. This château is no exception.

At one time, this estate was much larger. A previous generation feared the vineyard and sold off most plots, keeping just the 17th century chartreuse (country home, photo above) and a small 14-hectare plot still in the family today. Sixth generation winemaker Laure de Lambert Compeyrot is excited to work this plot of land, as she sees that the best of the very best terroir was kept. And her belief was confirmed in 2017 when many estates lost most or all of their vineyards to frost. Sigalas Rabaud lost none. Now that could be considered great terroir!

Let the wine speak for itself though. Very impressive, I discovered. Even second labels, like her Lieutenant de Sigalas, is magnificent. Others have also classified the quality of the Sigalas Rabaud wines at the level of Yquem and Rayne Vigneau.

Laure comes from a science background in oenology and has worked hard to retain the heritage of the great vines of the estate. She has also added cultivation methods, which suppress all herbicide use and replaces insecticides with sexual confusion (a deliberate process to prevent moths from mating in the vineyards). Now she sees increases of auxiliary fauna beneficial to the health of the vineyard environment. This is a beautiful and healthy place to visit.

GRAVES SAUTERNES
Winery (Château) and Hotel B&B
CHÂTEAU SIGALAS RABAUD

ACCOMMODATIONS BOOKING
...by phone or website form

ChateauSigalasRabaud@Gmail.com
+33 (0)5 57 31 07 45 • Booking.com

Chateau-Sigalas-Rabaud.com

B&B Open: April-October, Everyday

PRIVATE CHARTREUSE

This 17th century chartreuse, the home of the family, has four charming rooms decorated beautifully by the owner Laure de Lambert Compeyrot. Enjoy breakfast in the morning on the terrace or in the formal dining room. You are being welcomed into their home.

This is truly an opportunity to live amongst the vines in a small intimate setting. Instead of a big castle, it is a small, warm country family home. It is authentic vineyard life.

They are a very generous and hospitable family. If you would like lunches or dinners planned, just give them some notice and they will be happy to accommodate. If you would like a special tour or experience on the property, they will be delighted to create something with you.

Relax in the calm of their park setting – a lawn with large mature trees and swimming pool surrounded by vineyards.

TOURS & WORKSHOPS
Reservations available on their website

• **Sigalas Discovery**
A stroll through the vineyards learning about Sauternes and this special terroir, followed by a tasting of three of their wines.

• **Sigalas History**
A historical tour of the vineyards, winery and cellars with the owner of Sigalas Rabaud including a tasting of three of their wines.

• **Sigalas Sensory**
A workshop discovering your tasting skills while engaging your five senses in evaluating three of Sigalas Rabaud wines.

• **Sigalas Gourmand**
Enjoy a specialty plate and a glass of Sauternes on their terrace or in their living room.

• **La Terrasse de Sigalas**
Enjoy an afternoon of small bites and wine on their expansive terrace.

• **Dinner at Sigalas Gourmand**
In the family's tradition of hospitality, enjoy a four-course gourmet dinner and three Sigalas Rabaud wines in the dining room of the 17th century chartreuse.

DOWNTOWN SAUTERNES

Sauternes is a small village of just 775 people, sharing the same name as their famous wine, and is located in the Sauternes wine region. Sauternes is one of five little villages in this appellation (neighboring villages being Bommes, Fargues, Preignac and Barsac). Barsac is also a sub-appellation of Sauternes.

The village has a nice little park in the center of town with benches for a peaceful pause. Across from the park is the **Maison du Sauternes** (below) where you can find, *and taste*, the wines from all over the appellation. Down the main road of Rue Principale are two excellent restaurants **La Saprien** and **Auberge Les Vignes** (see next page).

GRAVES **SAUTERNES** DOWNTOWN
Wine Merchant
MAISON DU SAUTERNES

14 Place de la Mairie • 33210 Sauternes, France
+33 (0)5 56 76 69 83 • Contact@MaisonDuSauternes.com
MaisonDuSauternes.com

"Maison du Sauternes" translates to "House of Sauternes." This is the syndicate of wineries of the Sauternes appellation that sell the region's wines all in one place at reasonable prices.

Most of the well-known appellations have a house of wine, and Sauternes has a particularly nice one. They have both first and second labels, and dry white wines, and a bar where they encourage you to sample the wines. An easy way to taste around Sauternes, all from one place.

They also have a boutique with books, wine accessories, aroma kits, clothing, kids stuff, and other cool items.

■ GRAVES **SAUTERNES** VILLAGE

Restaurant
AUBERGE LES VIGNES

23 Rue Principale • 33210 Sauternes, France
+33 (0)5 56 76 60 06 • AubergeLesVignes@Orange.fr
AugergeLesVignes.com

In the village of Sauternes, Auberge Les Vignes is a restaurant I wish was back at home. Incredible foods at super great prices. I would be addicted to the warm goat cheese salad with shaved duck, and the grilled steak filet over wood embers in the open fireplace, Asado! They also serve prime rib, duck breast and whole fish. The desserts are tempting.

Lunch: Tuesday-Sunday, 12-2:00pm • Dinner: Tuesday-Saturday, 7:30-9:30pm

GRAVES **SAUTERNES** VILLAGE ■

Restaurant
LE SAPRIEN

14 Rue Principale • 33210 Sauternes, France
+33 (0)5 56 76 60 87 • Contact@LeSaprien.fr
LeSaprien.fr

Also in the village of Sauternes, La Saprien has become a meeting place for gourmands, especially for local specialities like this beef tartare (photo above). White tablecloths contrast the stone walls and open beams. Sit under a Platanus tree on the outdoor terrace for a more romantic meal.

Here they serve the classics of French gastronomy, in a bistronomic spirit. Generous portions of simple seasonal ingredients. They have a very nice wine list from around Bordeaux.

Lunch: Tuesday-Sunday, 12:00pm-2:00pm
Dinner: Tuesday-Saturday, 7:30pm-9:00pm

Reservations: Call or go to LaFourchette.com

BORDEAUX · GRAVES **BARSAC AOC**

More Noble Rot

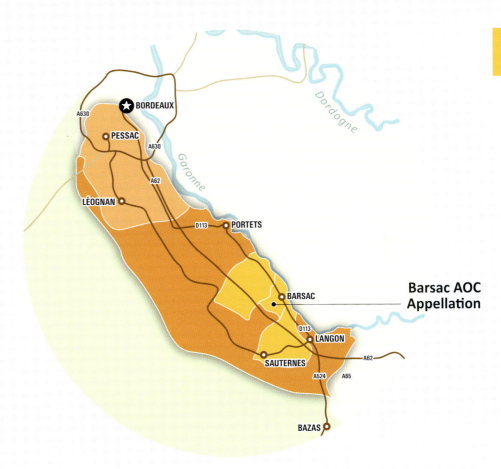

Left page: Harvesting at Château Climens

SPECIAL MICROCLIMATE

Sauternes is a village, an appellation and a type of wine. Barsac is also a village and an appellation, yet they produce Sauternes wines. Barsac lies within Sauternes, a sub-appellation, on the northeastern boundary of Sauternes along the Garonne River. Barsac is permitted to label their wines as either a Barsac appellation or Sauternes appellation.

Barsac is located at the point where the Ciron River's cold water meets the Garonne River's warm water, resulting in a fog that fills the area and makes it possible for the Roble Rot to develop. Botrytis is the same in Barsac. They also fall under the same classification of 1855 bestowed upon this area with Premier Crus and Deuxième Crus (first and second-growths) status.

The wines from Barsac are still a golden sweet wine made from Sémillon, Sauvignon Blanc, and Muscadelle grapes. The terroir is a little different though. Barsac has limestone in the soil, giving the wines greater freshness, lighter, more aromatic expression, and typically fruitier than Sauternes.

Barsac is winning top awards for its wines. In 2017, for example, *Wine Spectator* honored **Château Coutet** as the No. 3 best wine in the world. Barsac is worth discovering and here are three châteaux to explore.

Here are the châteaux...
- Château Coutet, page 301
- Château Climens, page 305
- Château Gravas, page 307

GRAVES **BARSAC**
Winery (Château)
CHÂTEAU COUTET

Premier Cru (First-Growth)
Grand Cru Classé of 1855

Château Coutet
33720 Barsac, France

+33 (0)5 56 27 15 46
Info@ChateauCoutet.com

ChateauCoutet.com

English, French

Open: All Year, Monday-Friday
By Appointment Only
Reservations Available On Their Website

Beauty is skin deep. And the skins here go very deep! 375 years of winemaking.

A SERIOUS WINNER

Things are serious here at Château Coutet. And maybe they should be. *Wine Spectator* named them the No. 3 "Best Wine in the World" in 2017 for their 2014 vintage of Château Coutet Premier Grand Cru. First, we have to recognize that 2014 was a stellar year for Sauternes/Barsac wines and so all the wines should be off-the-charts excellent. However, looking at the full list of the Top 100 wines that year, not one other château in Sauternes or Barsac made the list. Not even one of those big names. Bravo and cheers to you Château Coutet. Well deserved.

I enjoyed a nice lunch pairing with current and older vintages of their wine. Masterful. Both the cuisine and the wines.

This is a beautiful place. Unassuming on the outside. Stunning on the inside. From the living room, the pressing room (photo left) to the aging cellar (photo next spread). Elegant and beautiful perfection, just like their wine.

You could do a standard tasting here. Two wines. Three wines. Older vintages. Blind tastings as well.

However, a lunch or dinner here is an experience you will want at a place this serious about their wine. And they will pair the cuisine like you cannot imagine. Pricey, yet worth the experience. And you will be joined by one of the family members too.

Collection of Wines
Château Coutet
(First Label - Premier Grand Cru)

La Chartreuse de Coutet
(Second Wine)

Cuvée Madame Opalie
(White Wine)

GRAVES BARSAC
Winery (Château)
CHÂTEAU CLIMENS

Premier Cru (First-Growth)
Grand Cru Classé of 1855
Winner: Best Of Wine Tourism

Château Climens
33720 Barsac, France

+33 (0)5 56 27 15 33
Visite@Chateau-Climens.fr

ChateauClimens.com

English, French

*Open: May-October
Monday-Tuesday & Thursday-Friday
Saturday, By Appointment Only*

Exclusively the only certified biodynamic estate in Sauternes and Barsac.

NATURE AND HARMONY

You gain an appreciation for biodynamic farming here at Château Climens. They grow many different types of herbs, flowers and other plants, which they dry and make into teas. They use this tea to spray onto the leaves and soil, instead of using chemical herbicides and pesticides, as the tea naturally strengthens the vines and wards off pests. Such simple brilliance!

This all makes sense for farming. I am glad I got to see first-hand how the tea replaces all the chemicals and taste the extremely high-quality wines that results from this innovative process. They focus on great wine and deliver just their first label and a second wine. And 100% Sémillon too.

The tours are interesting as they include a visit and tutorial of the biodynamic herb drying room, the Tisanerie. Taste the current releases or enjoy a historical vertical tasting. Or try their super unique Yoga & Meditation Visit, relaxing in the Tisanerie and a tasting with a healthy lunch. Or, they can prepare a gourmet lunch experience with the perfect food and Sauternes pairing.

Current owner, Bérénice Lurton, has been in charge of this estate since 1992, taking control of its destiny with dedication, purpose and passion. You can see it in the way she works and the results of her wine.

Collection of Wines
Château Climens
(First Label - Premier Grand Cru)

Cyprès de Climens
(Second Wine)

GRAVES BARSAC
Winery (Château)
CHÂTEAU GRAVAS

Winner: Best Of Wine Tourism

6 Lieu Dit Gravas
33720 Barsac, France

+33 (0)5 56 27 06 91
Chateau.Gravas@Orange.fr

Chateau-Gravas.com

English, French

*Open: All Year, Everyday
By Appointment Only*

Stimulated by creativity in both modern art and delicious wine.

CENTURY-OLD VINES

While most châteaux speak of their old vines being 30 to 40 years old, here at Château Gravas, they have 13.5 hectares of 100-year-old vines which they use for the first label wine. Look at the gnarlyness of the vines in the photo. They show their age and the wine reflects the maturity. And the flavors are special. Rich as you might expect, evoking dried and candied fruits. And a beautiful soft nose of white flowers.

The soil is different here in the north part of the Barsac AOC, being so close to the river. Clay and limestone permeate the soil and gives the wine an added structure and minerality. 100% Sémillon!

To make the centennial vines even more special, they have bottled the wine in a carafe (photo far right). The presentation is elegant. It is like a large perfume bottle, befitting as Sauternes is such a beautiful aromatic wine. It makes for such a great gift with its attractive presentation!

Tours here are interesting. One of the owners will take you into the vineyards and talk about terroir, vine stocks, seasons, workers, winemaking, and cellar aging. There is art throughout the cellar; paintings, sculptures, and musicians from time to time, some extraordinary, others playful. This is a fun place to hang out as you don't know what you will find next around the corner.

Collection of Wines
Château Gravas
(First Label - Grand Vin de Sauternes)

L'Esprit de Gravas
(Second Wine)

Les Sensations de Gravas
(Dry White Wine)

La Tentation de Gravas
(Red Graves: Cabernet Sauvignon and Merlot)

DOWNTOWN BARSAC

Barsac is a small village of just 2,000 people, sharing the same name and located in the Barsac AOC wine region (Barsac is also a sub-appellation of Sauternes). The Barsac village is next to the Garonne River with a small port. Downstream is the city of Bordeaux. There is a beautiful rustic park on the river with tall trees and park benches to enjoy an afternoon.

This is a quiet little town with some coffee houses and nice restaurants. Just to the south of Barsac is the city of Langon (right page), the largest city and at the far southern tip of the Graves wine regions. There are many shops, stores and restaurants here.

■ GRAVES **BARSAC** DOWNTOWN

Wine Merchant
MAISON DES VINS DE BARSAC

Place de l'Eglise • 33720 Barsac, France
+33 (0)5 56 27 15 44 • MaisonDesVinsBarsac@Gmail.com
MaisonDesVinsBarsac.com • Open: Everyday, Except Wednesday

"Maison des Vins de Barsac" translates to the "House of Wines of Barsac." This is the syndicate of wineries for the Barsac Appellation that makes their wines available all in one place. This is a more extensive place than just Barsac wines, as they stock wines from Sauternes and also a few wines (red and white) from Graves AOC. There is also a boutique with many wine accessories, books and gift items. They have the big 54-aroma kit box and a box of Champagne aromas. And ugh, the box of bad aromas!

GRAVES **LANGON** DOWNTOWN
Restaurant
CLAUDE DARROZE

95 Cours du Général Leclerc • 33210 Langon, France
+33 (0)5 56 63 00 48 • Contact@Darroze.com
Darroze.com • Open: Everyday, Lunch 12-1:30pm, Dinner 7:30-9:30pm

A delicious story... In 1895, the Darroze family's great grandfather opened the Le Relais Inn at Villeneuve-de-Marsan in the Landes. After first being taken over by Jean, and then by Francis and Claude it ended up in the hands of Hélène Darroze, who was named the "Veuve Clicquot World's Best Female Chef of 2015" by the World's Best 50 Restaurants. Needless to say, the food at this Michelin rated restaurant is excellent. The cuisine is based on high quality seasonal ingredients. The four photos should say it all.

DOWNTOWN LANGON

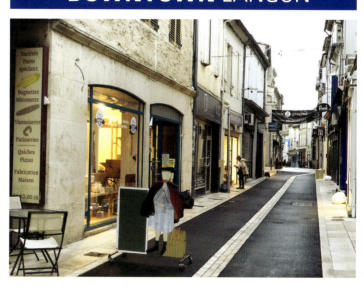

With a population of 7,700, the city of Langon is large enough to have the infrastructure for things you may need: grocery stores, salons, florists, restaurants, shops, etc. And lots of real estate offices.

Langon is located at the very southeast corner of the Graves appellation on the Garonne River with roads leading to both Barsac and Sauternes, about ten minutes drive from each.

In the center of town is a large roundabout with a spectacular fountain occupying the intersection. This is where so many of the shops, salons and restaurants are located, including Claude Darroze above. There are two small local restaurants just a couple of buildings west and east of this roundabout.

To the west is a semi underground bar/restaurant called **Le Cochon Volant**. They are open continuously from 9:00am-11:00pm, everyday. With short lunch and dinner hours at most restaurants, this place can be a lifesaver.
7 Place du Général de Gaulle, Langon • +33 (0)5 56 63 01 62

To the east is an Italian restaurant **Le Don Camillo**, with pizza, pasta, fish, and meat specialties. For a change of pace, they only have Italian wines, and a house wine for €3 a glass! Open Tuesday through Saturday
Lunch: 12:00pm-2:00pm
Dinner: 7:00pm-10:00pm
9 Rue du Baron, Langon
+33 (0)5 56 63 46 80

BORDEAUX · **LIBOURNAIS** (Right Bank)
Home of the Saint-Émilion, Pomerol and Fronsac Appellations

Above: The vineyards of Château Franc Mayne in Saint-Émilion
Left page: Perfect specimens of Merlot grapes hanging at Château Pavie

Three appellations of Merlot greatness. The magic of clay and limestone brings alive this grape's happiness.

THE QUEEN OF GRAPES

Saint-Émilion, Fronsac and Pomerol are three completely separate appellations, not subordinate to another, nor related in any way. They have very different terroirs as you will see. The one thing they have in common as Right Bank appellations is Merlot. This is a Merlot-concentrated region, as opposed to Cabernet Sauvignon on the Left Bank. Most of the blends from these appellations are primarily Merlot, followed by Cabernet Franc. A little bit of Cabernet Sauvignon or Malbec may be blended; however, not very common.

The reason for a Merlot concentration here is terroir. As we have discussed, it is all about terroir in Bordeaux. And Merlot loves it here; it thrives and tastes ever so good. Furthermore, Merlot loves the coolness of clay and the Right Bank is filled with it! While Cabernet Sauvignon is the King of the Left Bank, Merlot is the soft beautiful Queen of the Right Bank.

Merlot brings fullness and fruitiness to the wines (especially red and black fruits), while the Cabernet Franc brings the tannins, delicacy, elegance, and lots of aroma. Nice blend, wouldn't you say?

The terroir here is beautiful with its rolling hills and slopes for absorbing sunshine and facilitating water drainage so valuable for viticulture. The soils are different in each of these three appellations, alternating between combinations and densities of gravel, sand, types of clay, and various limestone.

Saint-Émilion terroir is built around a massive plateau of limestone; this is thick, deep and abundant limestone. The châteaux, homes and the entire village of Saint-Émilion were built out of large blocks of limestone dug out of the ground. As a result, many of the châteaux on the plateau have caves below their buildings and vineyards. There are four general terroir types: the plateau, the slopes (off the plateau), the foot (of the slopes) and the valley floor. Most of the Cru Classé châteaux are on the plateau and slopes.

Fronsac terroir is more dramatic with its hills (known as the Tuscany of Bordeaux) and more uniform in its clay and limestone mix in the soil. It is 1/5 the size of Saint-Émilion with a more consistent limestone terroir. The wines here are as beautiful as the landscape. Did you know that Fronsac is the appellation where Dany and Michel Rolland live and have their winery Château Fontenil? This is an appellation of too much undiscovered greatness.

Pomerol terroir is clay, with a distinctive blue clay vein that runs atop the plateau where the famous Pétrus grapes are grown. The blue clay spreads out across the plateau and travels south down a gentle slope into the Cheval Blanc property in Saint-Émilion. Hmmm, ever thought that Cheval Blanc tastes more like a Pomerol than Saint-Émilion wine? I do. This is a terroir of clay mixed with gravel and iron oxide, no limestone. The wines here are deep in color, rich in flavor, yet ever so elegant – I really love this combination.

BORDEAUX · LIBOURNAIS APPELLATIONS

The Famous Appellations of Saint-Émilion, Fronsac and Pomerol

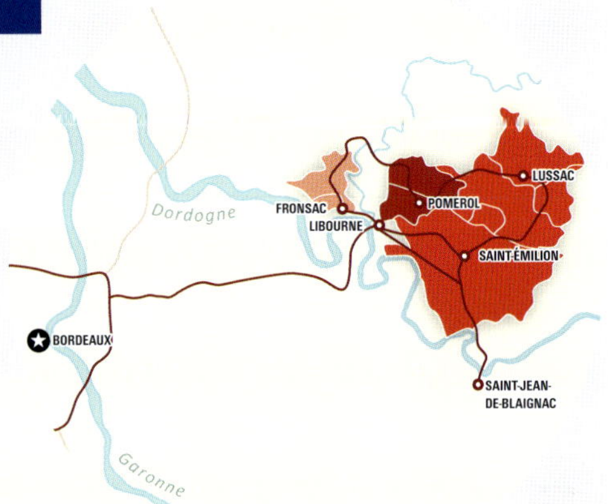

LIBOURNAIS
Appellations

- Lalande-de-Pomerol
- **Pomerol** (p.442)
- **Fronsac** (p.416)
- **Canon Fronsac** (p.416)
- **Saint-Émilion** (p.316)
- Saint-Georges-Saint-Émilion
- Montagne Saint-Émilion
- Lussac Saint-Émilion
- Puisseguin Saint-Émilion

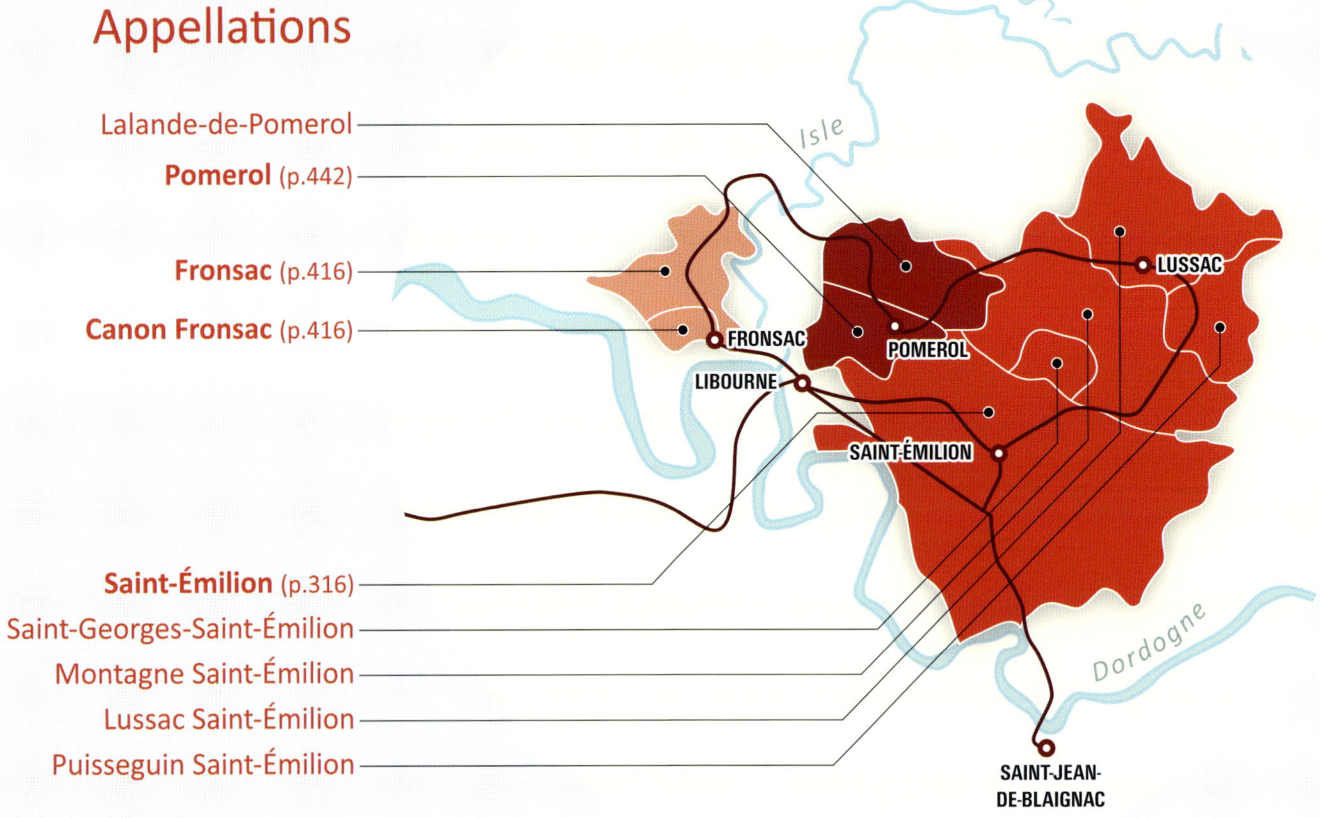

SMALL TOWNS AND VILLAGES ○
Appellations ———•

Above: Rooftop Château Cheval Blanc looking across the vineyard landscape of Saint-Émilion.

The right bank comes alive with Saint-Émilion, Fronsac and Pomerol.

THE LIBOURNAIS REGION

The word "Libournais" is derived from the name of the city, Libourne, the central point of the area. As the region's largest city, it is the business center with a shipping port used for the wines. Libournais is not the name of the people who live here, it is the name of the region containing the world-famous wine appellations of Saint-Émilion, Fronsac and Pomerol. Their borders are all within minutes of this city. Saint-Émilion is to the northeast, Pomerol is directly to the north, and Fronsac is immediately to the northwest of Libourne.

The map on the left will give you a good picture of the location of these appellations in relation to the Dordogne River, city of Libourne, and the distance to the city of Bordeaux. The map is to scale so you can get a good sense of the area. From Bordeaux city to Libourne is 38 km (24 miles) and takes about 45 minutes to drive without traffic. Add another 10 to 30 minutes depending on where you are going.

Best to stay in the wine region. And why not wake up to vineyards in the morning? I have found some very cool hotels, B&Bs and even some châteaux to spend the night. A night in a castle? Oh yes!

Note that each of these three appellations have satellite appellations: Saint-Émilion has four, Pomerol and Fronsac both have one each. In this book, I focus on the three primary appellations, with the one exception of Fronsac/Canon Fronsac.

The next column has the distances and time (without traffic) to reach each these appellations from Bordeaux, Libourne and Saint-Émilion.

From Bordeaux city center...
- **Libourne** 38km/24mi (45 minutes)

From Libourne city center...
- **Fronsac Village** 4km/2.5mi (8 minutes)
- **Pomeral Village** 5km/3mi (10 minutes)
- **Saint-Émilion Village** 9km/6mi (14 minutes)
- **Saint-Jean de Blaignac** 17km/11mi (22 minutes)

From Saint-Émilion village...
- **Pomerol Village** 6km/4mi (7 minutes)
- **Fronsac Village** 11km/7mi (15 minutes)
- **Saint-Jean de Blaignac** 11km/7mi (15 minutes)

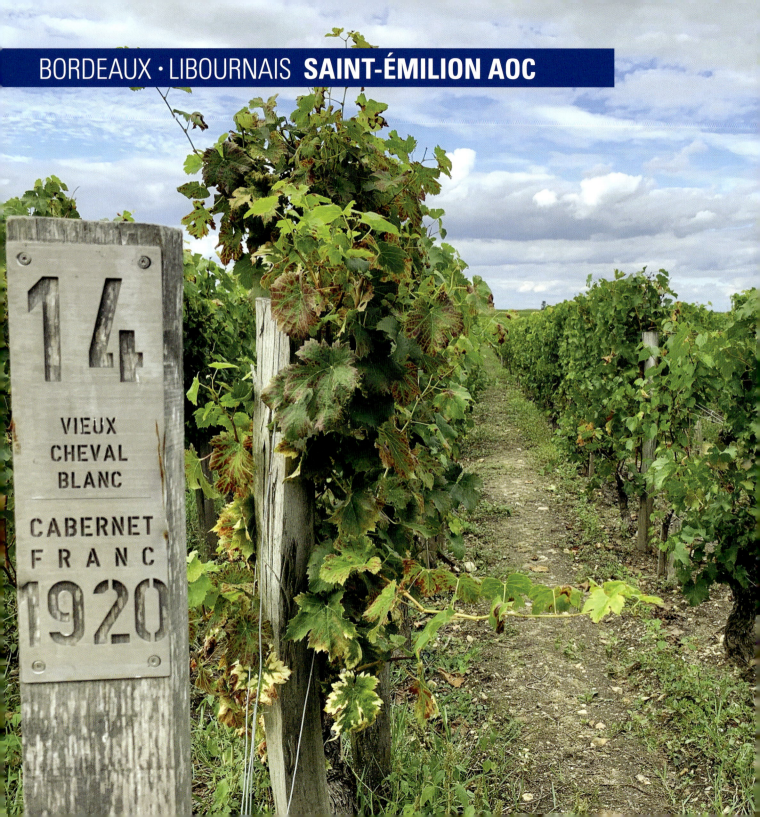

NORTHWEST

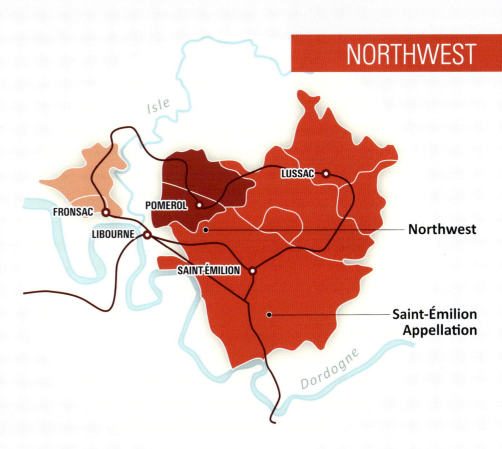

Northwest

Saint-Émilion Appellation

NORTHWEST SAINT-ÉMILION

Saint-Émilion is a very large appellation, four times the size of Fronsac. I present 24 châteaux to you here, plus restaurants and accommodations. Because it would be exceedingly cumbersome to lump them all together, I have broken down Saint-Émilion into quadrants, grouping the châteaux into areas.

In the other Bordeaux appellations of Graves and Médoc, they have sub-appellations to group them geographically. Here I have created areas that have common terroir.
- Northwest, page 317
- Western Slope, page 327
- South Slope, page 347
- Eastern Plateau, page 369
- Central Plateau, page 389
- Saint-Émilion Village, page 401

As we move across the Saint-Émilion appellaton, we will begin at closest point to Libourne, the very northwest part of this appellation. Located right on the border of Pomerol, the terroir of this part of Saint-Émilion shares many common characteristics with Pomerol's terroir. You will find the wines here taste similar as well.

There are two prominent châteaux here, plus an extraordinary gourmet restaurant, **La Terrasse Rouge**, on top of Château La Dominique that you must visit.

Here are the châteaux...
- Château Cheval Blanc, page 321
- Château La Dominique, page 323

GRAND CRU CLASSÉ OF SAINT-ÉMILION

On the Right Bank here in Saint Émilion, the qualifications for Grand Cru and Grand Cru Classé are very different from the Left Bank of Médoc, Graves and Sauternes. A big difference is that in Saint-Émilion, the classifications are not permanent. Every ten years, each château must re-qualify through a detailed strict process. This occurs in the second year of each decade. Previously it was 2012 and then 2022, 2032, etc. (Note: Pomerol and Fronsac do not have classifications.) Further, Saint Émilion's four satellites (Lussac, Saint-Georges, Montagne and Puisseguin) are not included in the classification either.

Saint-Émilion has four classifications (ranked from lowest to highest): Grand Cru, Grand Cru Classé, Premier Grand Cru Classé B, and Premier Grand Cru Classé A. The classifications are for red wines only and only for the first labels of a château.

Grand Cru - To be a Grand Cru, the château must be located within the Saint-Émilion boundaries (excluding satellites) and follow certain rules. The vineyards must be planted with a density of no less than 55 rows per hectare and yields must not exceed 49 liters per hectare. All vinification, aging and bottling must be on the château property. A sample of the wine must be provided to ensure it meets a minimum standard of quality determined by wine brokers, producers, negociants, and oenologists in blind tastings. Also, samples are randomly taken from store shelves to verify it is the same wine that was submitted. Of the 800+ wineries in Saint-Émilion, roughly 200 are classified as Grand Cru.

Grand Cru Classé - This is where the qualifications get serious and complex. Every ten years, the three classé levels must be re-classified. Châteaux must submit either 10, 15 or 20 consecutive previous years of wines for a independent third party (not related to Saint-Émilion in any manner: family, business, or otherwise) to conduct blind tastings and scoring. They must achieve a certain score level on a 20-point grading system. This is all set up, managed and officiated by the French government's Institut National des Appellations d'Origine (INAO). Here are the breakdowns.

Château Cheval Blanc and Château Angelus have two different styles to presenting their Premier Grand Cru Classé status. Both are correct and both mean the same thing ("Premier" means "first," and Premier is a 1er).

Above: Commonly, when the first label of a château is a classified wine (Grand Cru Classé), the second wine is generally a (Saint-Émilion Grand Cru). Here is how Château Troplong Mondot does it.

Below: MT Decoster owns all three of these chateaux so you can see how they identify their labels. The left two labels are the Château de Candale second and first label, which are both identified qualifying as "Saint-Émilion Grand Crus." The right two labels are both classified wines and are marked "Grand Cru Classé." And notice they are also marked qualifying as a "Saint-Émilion Grand Cru." Redundant, as all classified wines are also always Grand Crus. It is surely a marketing thing.

Grand Cru Classé	Premier Cru Classé - B	Premier Cru Classé - A
Submit 10 Years of Wine	Submit 15 Years of Wine	Submit 20 Years of Wine
Minimum 14 of 20 Points	Minimum 16 of 20 Points	Minimum 17 of 20 Points
- 50% Blind Tasting	- 30% Blind Tasting	- 30% Blind Tasting
- 20% Terroir	- 30% Terroir	- 30% Terroir
- 20% Public Reputation	- 35% Public Reputation	- 35% Public Reputation
- 10% Facilities Practices	- 5% Facilities Practices	- 5% Facilities Practices
63 Châteaux in 2012	**14 Châteaux in 2012**	**4 Châteaux in 2012**

Until 2012, there were only two Premier Cru Classé As: Cheval Blanc and Ausone. The two new Premier Cru Classé As are Pavie and Angelus, which I review and you will learn more about in this book. This system of classification started in 1955, ironically exactly 100 years after the Grand Cru Classés of 1855. From the beginning, both Cheval Blanc and Ausone have been classified continuously at the top slot of first-growths.

Keep in mind, Grand Vin de Bordeaux is only a marketing term and does not mean the wine is classified. Legally, only those châteaux with official classification by the INOA are allowed to use the Grand Cru Classé on their label, and only their first label; no second or other wines from the same château.

TABLE OF WINES AND TOURISM

CHÂTEAUX Premier Grand Cru Classé A & B	Classified	Number of Wines	Red Wine	White Wine	Rosé Wine	Sweet Wine	Wine Shop	Boutique	Accommodations	Restaurant	Food Options	Food & Wine Pairings	Tours	Castle Tours	Workshops	Activities	No Reservation Necessary	Tourism Award	Innovations
Château Angélus	GCC-A	3	√										1						
Château Beau Sejour Becot	GCC-B	2	√				√						1						
Château Cheval Blanc	GCC-A	3	√	√									1					√	
Château Pavie	GCC-A	2	√				√						2						
Chateau Troplong Mondot	GGC-B	2	√				√	√		√	√	√	2					√	
Château Valandraud	GCC-B	10	√	√	√		√	√					1					√	

CHÂTEAUX Grand Cru & Grand Cru Classé	Classified	Number of Wines	Red Wine	White Wine	Rosé Wine	Sweet Wine	Wine Shop	Boutique	Accommodations	Restaurant	Food Options	Food & Wine Pairings	Tours	Castle Tours	Workshops	Activities	No Reservation Necessary	Tourism Award	Innovations
Château Ambe Tour Pourret	GC	4	√	√	√		√	√		√	√	√	1	√					
Château de Candale	GC	5	√	√	√		√	√		√	√	√	6	√			√		
Château Cantenac	GC	3	√				√	√		√	√	√	1				√		
Château La Croizille	GC	2	√				√	√			√		3				√		
Château La Dominique	GCC	3	√	√			√	√		√	√	√	5		√			√	√
Château de Ferrand	GCC	2	√				√	√			√	√	22	√	√	√		√	
Château Fonplegade	GCC	2	√				√			√			1						
Château Fonroque	GCC	2	√				√						1						
Château Franc Mayne	GCC	2	√				√	√	√				1			√		√	
Château Frombrauge	GCC	4	√	√			√	√	√		√	√	8	√	√			√	√
Château La Grace Dieu	GC	1	√				√						1						
Château Guadet	GCC	1	√				√						1	√			√		
Château Haut-Sarpe	GCC	3	√	√	√		√			√		√	√	1					
Château de Pressec	GCC	3		√							√		4				√		
Château Soutard	GCC	2	√				√	√		√	√		8	√	√	√		√	√
Château Villemaurine	GCC	3	√				√	√		√	√		5					√	
Clos des Jacobins	GCC	1	√										1						
Union de Producteurs	GC	50+	√	√	√	√	√	√					1		√		√	√	

GCC-A/B = Premier Grand Cru Classé • GCC = Grand Cru Classé • GC = Grand Cru

SAINT-ÉMILION NORTHWEST
Winery (Château)
CHÂTEAU CHEVAL BLANC

Saint-Émilion Premier Grand Cru Classé - A

1 Cheval Blanc
33330 Saint-Émilion, France

+33 (0)5 57 55 55 55
Use "Contact" form on their website

Chateau-Cheval-Blanc.com

English, French

*Open to select interested parties only.
If you know an importer, distributor or notable retailer who can vouch for you as a Cheval Blanc consumer, you may be able to get an invite.
Or write us. We have connections.*

T radition and innovation at Château Cheval Blanc continues in grand style.

SIX CENTURIES OF WINEMAKING

Adjacent to Pomerol and sharing the same clay and gravel soils, Château Cheval Blanc defines perfection very differently than the other Premier Grand Crus of Saint-Émilion. No Saint-Émilion famous limestone here! Instead, the vein of blue clay runs from the Pomerol plateau, where Pétrus lives, and crosses the appellation line into the Cheval Blanc property. This estate used to be part of the larger Château Figeac property and is now recognized as one of the world's most prized vineyard estates.

During the 19th century when the first-growths of the Médoc were bestowed by the 1855 Napoléon classification, Cheval Blanc collected awards at the world's most important wine exhibitions. Medal after medal, gold after gold, the Château Cheval Blanc wine achieved its status, garnering the same price as Margaux, Latour and Lafite. It was not until the Saint-Émilion classification of 1955 that Cheval Blanc was officially recognized as a first-growth.

With Bernard Arnault (LVMH Companies) as its new owner, Cheval Blanc was launched into the future with ultra modern facilities. Contrasted by the traditional buildings, the futuristic structure designed by architect Christian de Portzamparc (winner of the 1994 Pritzker Architecture Prize), now houses the latest in winemaking technology and customized tanks designed for each and every individual vineyard plot (photo above).

There are exactly 54 customized tanks for each of their 54 vineyard plots, exactly sized to match each plot's yield. Each of these plots cannot be more meticulously managed to perfection prior to blending their iconic wines.

The 2012 vintage was an average year for Bordeaux. I took a glass of their Cheval Blanc 2012 up to their rooftop and pondered it for a while. A long while. The more I sat with this wine, the more beautifully rich and perfect it became. It should not be difficult to make a great wine in a great year – after all, it is about terroir. However, this tasting was a prime example of the importance of a great winemaking team. One with the skills to always create magnificent wines in any given year. And Cheval Blanc deserves its Premier first-growth status when you realize they have this ability.

Collection of Wines
Château Cheval Blanc
(First Label - Premier Grand Cru Classé A)

Le Petit Cheval
(Second Wine - A Saint-Émilion Grand Cru)

Le Petit Cheval Blanc
(Bordeaux Blanc - Dry White Wine)

SAINT-ÉMILION NORTHWEST
Winery (Château) & Restaurant
CHÂTEAU LA DOMINIQUE

Saint-Émilion Grand Cru Classé
Winner: Best Of Wine Tourism

1 La Dominique
33330 Saint-Émilion, France

+33 (0)5 57 55 20 73
Visite@Chateau-LaDominique.com

Chateau-LaDominique.com

English, French

Open: All Year
April-October, Everyday
November-March, Tuesday-Saturday
Reservations Available On Their Website

Excellent wines with many outstanding tourism experiences to enjoy the day here.

FLYING BLIND

Okay, I do fly with my eyes open! I have a very good friend who is blind and makes wine in California. Losing one sense has heightened others. Like a blind musician who can hear in exceptional ways, my friend David can smell and taste like we can only dream. His ability to take in the wine's nuances is remarkable. The proof is in the wine: Hunt Cellars, Paso Robles, CA.

How blind can you get for a blind tasting? Château La Dominique takes it to the extreme. They built an underground blind tasting room to neutralize all the senses (photo left). First, the elevator ride down gets you in a quiet state. Then contrasted by walking on a noisy floor of loose stones. The room is extra dark, with minimal mood lighting. By the time you get to the table and sit down, your senses are already heightened and confused at the same time. Now it is time to begin.

Bottles of wine, all the exact same shape and size, are covered with black socks. Wine glasses are all black and of the same shape and size. Are you blinded yet? Then they dim the lights even further and you hear the sound of wine being poured. Do you know what a Syrah sounds like filling a glass? Good, no Syrah here!

Notepad ready, it's time to smell what is going on in those black wineglasses. It would be natural for them to pour you their wine. But how? Verticals? A horizontal? Or what?

They were very tricky with me. Maybe they will be with you too. One wine just did not smell like a Bordeaux. I guessed otherwise and was correct. It impressed the socks off of me (and those bottles) to find out I could sense what was going on. This is a must-do experience here.

Next door to Cheval Blanc, with similar terroir, La Dominique wants you to enjoy their estate. Open all year with creative ideas in tours and tastings. They go beyond the standard tasting. Discover the three stages of winemaking with four of their wines. Or experience their cellar with a professionally led tasting. They have a gourmet rooftop restaurant with views of the vineyards. Plus, there is a large wine shop and a boutique here.

Collection of Wines
Château La Dominique
(First Label - Grand Cru Classé)

La Dominique
(Second Wine - Red and White Wines)

SAINT-ÉMILION NORTHWEST
Winery (Château) & Restaurant
CHÂTEAU LA DOMINIQUE

ROOFTOP RESTAURANT

Located on the rooftop of Château La Dominique, a Saint-Émilion Grand Cru Classé, this indoor and outdoor "Red Terrace" restaurant is a treat to be discovered. Stairs hidden behind a modern red wall on the side of the château lead to the rooftop. Up here you will find a large display of red glass stones covering most of the roof beyond the dining area and a view of magnificent vineyard landscapes.

This is just a stunning start to your upcoming gourmet experience. Created by Nicolas Lascombes (page 480), deliciousness is delivered with attentive service. Their menu oozes with temptations...

Calf's Sweetbread with grainy mustard sauce (super yum), sautéed mushrooms and potatoes (top left).

Fresh Oysters on the half-shell directly from the Arcachon Bay.

Meats too enticing to want just one. The rib steak, grilled and sliced, ever so juicy (lower left) or the grilled veal chop cooked to perfection, with seasonal vegetables (photos bottom left).

Imagine this: They have all ten Bordeaux first-growths on the wine list. Maybe this is where the Club of Ten has their secret meetings! They also have many other small local producers on the list for you to savor.

Desserts are to die for. Iced parfait with soft meringue shells and summer berries (bottom right). So good I could eat ten of them. And I seriously considered it.

LA TERRASSE ROUGE
Gourmet Dining By Maison Lascombes

Winner: Best Of Wine Tourism

1 Château La Dominique
33330 Saint-Émilion, France

+33 (0)5 57 24 47 05
Contact@LaTerrasseRouge.com

LaTerrasseRouge.com

English, French

Open: All Year, Everyday
Lunch: 12:00pm-3:00pm • Dinner: 7:00pm-11:00pm
November-April, Dinner, Friday & Saturdays Nights
Reservations Available On Their Website

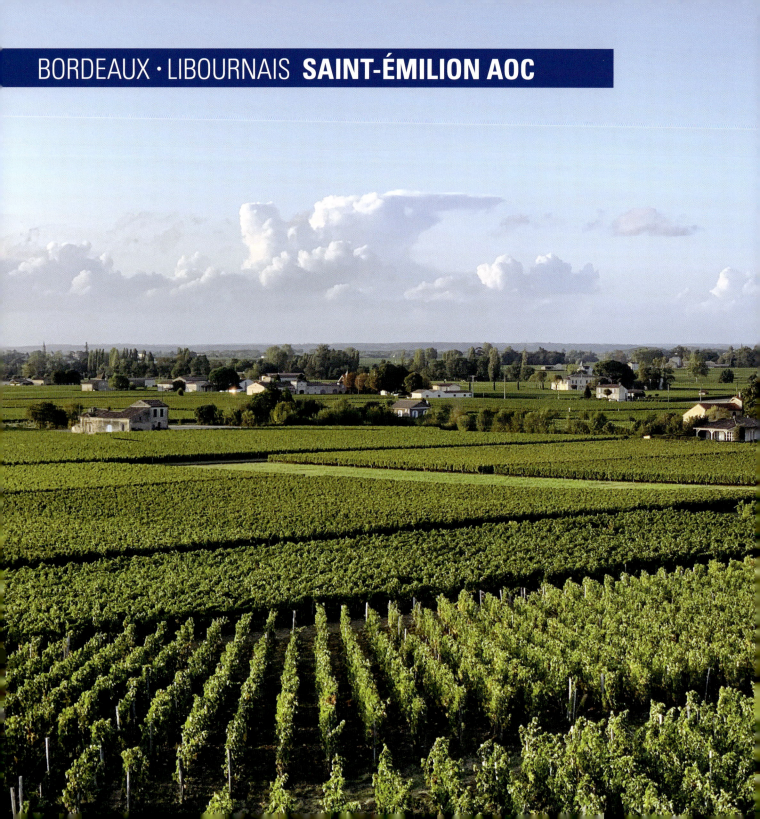

BORDEAUX · LIBOURNAIS **SAINT-ÉMILION AOC**

WESTERN SLOPE

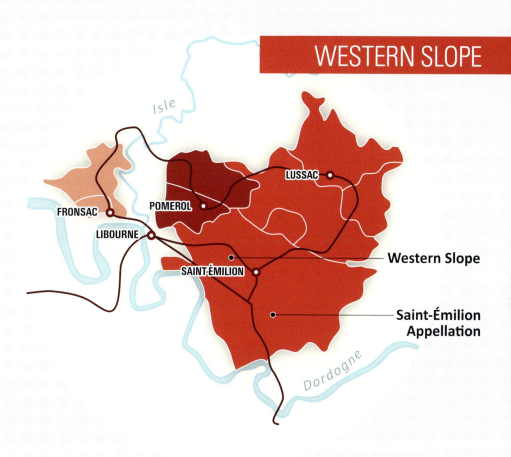

Western Slope

Saint-Émilion Appellation

Left page: The spectacular view from the Château Franc Mayne treehouse across their vineyards into the vineyards of Clos des Jacobins and the Clos des Jacobins château on the far right

SAINT-ÉMILION WESTERN SLOPE

This next quadrant of Saint-Émilion is the Western Slope. It is the slope that drops from the plateau of the Saint-Émilion village following the D243 highway that leads to Libourne.

Two super good places to stay the night here. First, **Hôtel Grand Barrail** is a castle surrounded by vineyards with a restaurant and a spa. Also, **Château Franc Mayne** offers rooms in their château, in a restored old village post office, and in a luxury treehouse, if you are so inclined. Being right off the highway, these two places offer you easy access to both Saint-Émilion and Pomerol.

Here are the châteaux…

Grand Crus Classés
- Château Franc Mayne, page 329
- Clos des Jacobins, page 333
- Château Fonroque, page 335

Grand Crus
- Château Ambe Tour Pourret, page 337
- Château La Grace Dieu des Prieurs, page 339
- Château Cantenac, page 341

SAINT-ÉMILION WESTERN SLOPE
Winery (Château) & Hotel
CHÂTEAU FRANC MAYNE

Saint-Émilion Grand Cru Classé
Winner: Best Of Wine Tourism

14 La Gomerie D243
33330 Saint-Émilion, France

+33 (0)5 57 24 62 61
Welcome@RelaisFrancMayne.com

RelaisFrancMayne.com

English, French

Open: All Year, Everyday
Reservations Not Needed, Although Helpful

Extensive underground caves with modern techno-holographic animated visuals.

DIVERSE TERROIR

Located just 3200 feet west of the Saint-Émilion village, Château Franc Mayne sits on the beginning of the gradual slope of this Western Slope of Saint-Émilion. They have the advantages of the plateau, slope and foot terroir on their small seven-hectare property. In Saint-Émilion, the estates are much smaller than the Médoc and Graves; the average is just seven hectares. They feel blessed to have all three terroirs.

This diverse terroir is important to the blending complexity of their Saint-Émilion Grand Cru Classé. With their new owner, they have begun the process of organic farming and have planted 100% Merlot grapes (it was previously 90% Merlot). They believe the diversity of their property lends best to blending the three different Merlot profiles, with distinctive limestone, gravel and sand terroirs, allowing them to achieve the very best Grand Cru Classé.

From the back side of Franc Mayne, it is a short walk to the village across the plateau. The front side offers some of the most beautiful views looking across the countryside, and a short walk to their neighbor Clos des Jacobins (review next page).

Franc Mayne has just one tour. It is extensive, interesting, educational, and is followed by wine tasting, of course.

They take you through 600 years of history, vineyards and terroir, vat room and underground. The massive caves resulted centuries ago when limestone blocks were dug out for construction.

Franc Mayne stores their barrels for aging in these ancient limestone quarries because it offers the perfect temperature and humidity. Their cave also offers the fun experience of meandering through five acres underground and through varying sizes of openings and levels of areas. On display are original mining equipment used centuries ago to cut out limestone blocks (photo below). What's most unique is their holographic display that is interesting, entertaining and educational.

Collection of Wines
Château Franc Mayne
(First Label - Grand Cru Classé)

Les Cedres de Franc Mayne
(Second Wine)

SAINT-ÉMILION WESTERN SLOPE

Winery (Château) & Hotel
CHÂTEAU FRANK MAYNE

Open: All Year, Everyday

+33 (0)5 57 24 68 54
Reservations: Info@RelaisFrancMayne.com

A NIGHT IN THE CHATEAU, POST OFFICE OR TREEHOUSE

Château Franc Mayne has three very nice choices for accommodations.

The Main Château has four luxurious bedrooms. This is the original family's 18th century home, which was completely restored in 2019, with the winery adjacent. The beautiful living room (photo center left), the dining room for breakfast (all stays include an array of delicious breakfast items), the outdoor terrace, the park and gardens, and the natural swimming pool are all spots to explore and enjoy.

The Old Village Post Office is the original Saint-Émilion post office on the Franc Mayne property. They have renovated it into two suites encompassing one floor each. The top floor bedroom is in the photo above and its bath is the bottom left photo. The rooms are spacious and upstairs suite has expansive views. You can even see the Saint-Émilion village church tower and fireworks on special occasions.

The Treehouse is an unusual treat here. Built into a 100-year old cedar tree, the room offers stunning views across the vineyards with direct access to the natural swimming pool. Luxurious bedroom (photo top left), bathroom and with a porch to enjoy the views.

SAINT-ÉMILION WESTERN SLOPE
Winery (Château)
CLOS DES JACOBINS

Saint-Émilion Grand Cru Classé

4 La Gomerie
33330 Saint-Émilion, France

+33 (0)5 57 51 19 91
Visite@MTDecoster.com

MTDecoster.com

English, French, German

Open: All Year, Monday-Friday

Tastings Also Available At Their Sister Winery: Château de Candale (page 361)
Reservations: MTDecoster.com/reservation

A beautiful property with characteristics worthy of being a UNESCO World Heritage Site.

SPEAKING OF TERROIR

It all started here by the monks who lived in the farm buildings on the property and worked the vineyards to earn money from the wine. These Dominican monks were known as the Jacobins, hence the name Clos des Jacobins. And "Clos" refers to the short rock walls built around vineyards to protect the grapes from theft and improve the climate within the vineyard.

While the walls are no longer here, the property is meticulously kept. Just look at the vineyards in the left photo. Even during harvest this is a beautifully manicured estate. No detail is overlooked. So much so that UNESCO has listed them as a World Heritage Site for their viticultural landscape. Its spectacular beauty is one of the reasons to visit this property (as you can see your photographer in the right picture capturing some magnificent images).

Clos des Jacobins is located next door to Château Franc Mayne at the foot of the slope. This foot provides a terroir of limestone rock and clay with limestone scree that has eroded from the plateau above. This is very consistent throughout their property, giving them one single block for making their wine. And just a first label. This is a specific style you are going to love, which is a wine that speaks terroir in its entirety.

Clos des Jacobins has been classified since their start in 1954 and won the Grand Cru Classés of Saint-Émilion trophy in 2006 after being semi-finalist twice. And with that, I say cheers!

Collection of Wines
Clos des Jacobins
(First Label - Grand Cru Classé)

SAINT-ÉMILION WESTERN SLOPE
Winery (Château)
CHÂTEAU FONROQUE

Saint-Émilion Grand Cru Classé

Château Fonroque
33330 Saint-Émilion, France

+33 (0)5 57 24 60 02
Info@ChateauFonroque.com

ChateauFonroque.net

English, French

*Open: All Year, Monday-Friday
By Appointment Only
Reservations By Phone or On Their Website*

B iodynamic principals in full bloom here, following the theories of Steiner and Goethe.

INNOVATIVE THINKING

Words by Fonroque's Oenologist Alain Moueix.

"Reading Goethe has helped me to find bridges between art and nature, aesthetics and science, environment and humans. His book, *Metamorphosis of Plants* changed my understanding of interconnections. Goethe demonstrates how plants can be used to heal plants. Steiner teaches us how to identify, understand and use a plant's psychological profile, rather than dissecting it and banishing it to a herbarium. Biodynamics cannot be undertaken with clever formulas and preconceived ideas, but rather requires observation and an understanding of interconnections, a holistic view of things. Goethe drew, composed poetry and prose, studied nature, and wrote about the fine arts and theory of color. *Metamorphosis of Plants* is therefore always within reach on my desk. Goethe criticized the arrogance of botanists of his time in the way they approached the plant kingdom – he wanted to understand nature, not dominate it. All of this had a strong influence on me, in both how I make my wine and how I lead my teams. I try to explain more and impose myself less. I compare my wines to paintings: they should be beautiful, and they should be beneficial and pleasing."

Need I say more? If you are not enthralled with how he makes wine, I do not know what to say.

Collection of Wines
Château Fonroque
(First Label - Grand Cru Classé)

Château Cartier
(Second Wine)

SAINT-ÉMILION WESTERN SLOPE
Winery (Château) & Restaurant
CHÂTEAU AMBE TOUR POURRET

Saint-Émilion Grand Cru Classé

D243, Secteur Pourret
33330 Saint-Émilion, France

+33 (0)5 57 55 23 28
Visite@Celene-Bordeaux.fr

Celene-Bordeaux.fr

English, French

Open: All Year, Everyday
Cooking Classes: Monday-Friday, Lunch & Dinner
Reservations Available On Their Website

F ood and Wine! This château is very much about the food and wine experience.

NEVER JUST WINE

Across the street (D243) from Château Franc Mayne and Clos Des Jacobins, their five hectares of vines are planted on ancient sand on clay soil, which they find produces wines with very fine tannins and a velvety mouth. The Merlot (75%) and the Cabernet Franc (25%) is organically farmed (certified since 2015). They make one wine, a Saint-Émilion Grand Cru.

The owner, Francoise Lannoye, owns three other wineries in Bordeaux. Tastings are always four wines including a sparkling wine, giving you a full experience to enjoy.

Château Ambe Tour Pourret is focused on food experiences with their wines. They have structured their remodel around this concept. Even their basic tour and tasting comes with a cheese plate specifically paired for you to taste from their four estates. And the more food experiences you want to try, the more interesting it gets here. Madame Lannoye wants you to experience "the art of living" by teaching you how to cook scrumptious treats and pair them with delicious wines. A restaurant is coming in 2020 above the winery.

They recently converted the kitchen at Château Ambe Tour Pourret to allow for 12 people to fully participate in cooking classes.

• **I Cook At The Chateau** is not a simple cooking class where you might eat some fancy bread. They do a full three-course menu: starter dish, main course and a dessert. And they do them every day of the week for both lunch and dinner.

Get a reservation and get involved. This is the place for food and wine. Isn't that what wine is all about?

Collection of Wines
Château Ambe Tour Pourret
(First Label - Grand Cru)

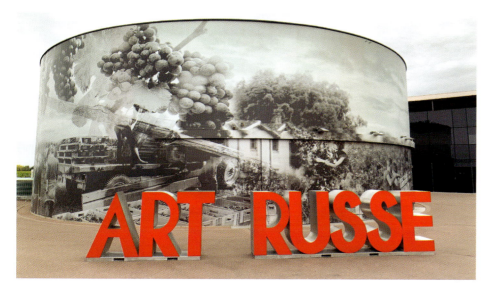

SAINT-ÉMILION WESTERN SLOPE
Winery (Château)
CHÂTEAU LA GRACE DIEU DES PRIEURS

Saint-Émilion Grand Cru

1 La Grâce Dieu
33330 Saint-Émilion, France

+33 (0)5 57 74 42 97
Web@LaGraceDieuDesPrieurs.com

LaGraceDieuDesPrieurs.com

English, French

*Open: All Year, Monday-Friday
By Appointment Only*

The passion for making great wine leads to the passion to promote great Russian art.

ANAMORPHOSIS

At Château La Grace Dieu Des Prieurs, there is a passion for both art and wine. And its excellence. This is a new winery that started in 2013 with very modern facilities, all works of art. The round building (above) spirals underground into the vinification room with what looks like abstract art painted all over the floor. You might even wonder who made a mess?

Anamorphosis is what it is. When walking above the tanks on the catwalk, you will see the abstract image on floor reflected onto the shiny stainless steel vats. The clear image of Yuri Gagarin, the Russian astronaut who became the first person to journey into outer space, will magically appear. A very cool effect (photo left page).

Art Russe, a foundation that owns the largest collection of 19th and 20th century Russian art, has granted this winery use of 12 images per year for their bottles. The bottles are a unique squatty shape. They only produce a first label Grand Cru wine; however, they have 12 different labels with Russian paintings. Now I need to buy a case!

And super cool packaging too. A six-bottle set is packaged in a chess box complete with chess pieces and game board. A single bottle in a concrete cylinder with a wood cap. And an elegant case made of luxurious soft leather holding three bottles in beautiful display.

Collection of Wines
Château La Grace Dieu Des Prieurs
(First Label - Grand Cru)

SAINT-ÉMILION WESTERN SLOPE
Winery (Château)
CHÂTEAU CANTENAC

Saint-Émilion Grand Cru
Winner: Best Of Wine Tourism

2 Lieu-dit Cantenac, D670
33330 Saint-Émilion, France

+33 (0)5 57 51 35 22
Reservation@Chateau-Cantenac.fr

Chateau-Cantenac.fr

English, French, Spanish, Cantonese

Open: All Year
Monday-Friday, Reservations Not Needed
Saturday-Sunday, By Appointment Only
Reservations Available On Their Website
Call, Email, Drop-Ins are No Problem

H aving a good time is only the beginning here. They win awards for their hospitality.

A FAMILY OF WINE AND FRIENDS

This château located on the D670, right out of Libourne as you enter Saint-Émilion, is a big family affair. Mom, Nicole Roskam-Brunot (pictured above), has three boys with three little girls each. There is so much cuteness running around this property. This is definitely a child (and dog) friendly place. And AJ, (also pictured above) married to one of her sons, has created hospitality and tourism experiences that has won them several awards.

Tours are friendly and informative about their history, family, terroir, and winemaking. They created a film of all four seasons at the château and offer an iPad to help guide you during the tour.

Château Cantenac has three excellent wines, no second labels. Their other two wines are actually special editions of their first wine. All of them are Saint-Émilion Grand Crus.

Château Cantenac is a classic style which they have been making for 150 years.

Château Cantenac ClimAt is an exclusive selection of the vintage, an exceptional blend of what they feel deserves their top "A" grade.

Château Cantenac Sélection Madame is mom's personal choice of the best grapes. She personally does the blend and signs every bottle. A very limited quantity is made.

Here is what Madame Nicole explained to me about wine... The fruit is the beautiful woman and the oak is her perfume. When she enters the room, you admire her beauty. And when she leaves, her perfume lingers behind. And that is the beauty of wine!

Collection of Wines
Château Cantenac
(First Label - Grand Cru)

Château Cantenac ClimAt
(Vintage Selection - Grand Cru)

Château Cantenac Sélection Madame
(The Proprietor's Selection - Grand Cru)

SAINT-ÉMILION WESTERN SLOPE
Château Hotel, Restaurant & Spa
HÔTEL GRAND BARRAIL

Route de Libourne D243
33330 Saint-Émilion, France

+33 (0)5 56 55 37 00
Contact@Grand-Barrail.com

Grand-Barrail.com

English, French

Open: All Year, Everyday
Reservations Available On Their Website
Or, Any of The Major Travel Booking Websites

Grand Barrail - Spa Saint-Émilion
Open: All Year, Everyday

Spa Reservations Available By Email or Phone
+33 (0)5 56 55 37 09 • Spa@Grand-Barrail.com

FIVE-STAR HISTORIC CASTLE

Located on the D243 highway halfway between Libourne and Saint-Émilion village, it is a very convenient location being just five minutes from either the Saint-Émilion village or Pomerol.

Grand Barrail is a five-star hotel with both a castle with historic rooms (bed and bath photos lower right) and a new wing with modern rooms (photo lower left). Beautifully contrasting choices. Either way they are luxurious rooms. A full American breakfast buffet is included.

The property is beautiful as you can see from the photo on the left page. They have forested areas, big open grass parks, flowering gardens, an outdoor heated swimming pool, and vineyards surrounding the hotel property.

Their spa, Spa Saint-Émilion, is a large facility providing customized treatments using all-natural products for their services. They have a hot tub, two saunas, two Turkish baths, rest areas (both humid and dry), and a fitness gym. The spa is open everyday of the year and is available to non-guests as well.

SAINT-ÉMILION WESTERN SLOPE
Château Hotel, Restaurant & Spa
HÔTEL GRAND BARRAIL

Open: All Year, Everyday
Reservations Available On Their Website
Breakfast: 7:30am-10:30am
Lunch: 12:15pm-2:00pm
Dinner: 7:15pm-9:30pm

A BEAUTIFUL GOURMET RESTAURANT

Whether you are staying at the Grand Barrail or not, this is a restaurant worth your visit. They are open everyday for breakfast, lunch and dinner. It is a Michelin Plate, deserving an even higher rating in my opinion. This place is excellent!

   They have three, four and five course special menus created by the chef. Also à la carte items. Everything is fresh and creative. Into beef tartar? This was the very best tartar I have had in France. So fresh and flavorful, perfect with a glass of Sauvignon Blanc (photo left page). Photos top to bottom: John Dory fillet with a sweet pea, verbena and lemon confit, served with a side of sage gnocchi; Barigoule artichoke in a salad, dried duck breast and Gascony mustard vinaigrette; roasted scallops with a Perigord sauce, roasted vegetables and rosemary.

   The dining room is spectacular (photo above). In good weather, the outside terrace is an enchanting place overlooking the gardens, park and vineyards. There is an elegant lounge with handcrafted cocktails and fine wines. Also a Smokehouse Gentleman's Club with a nice selection of cigars, books, playing cards, board games and flat screen TV.

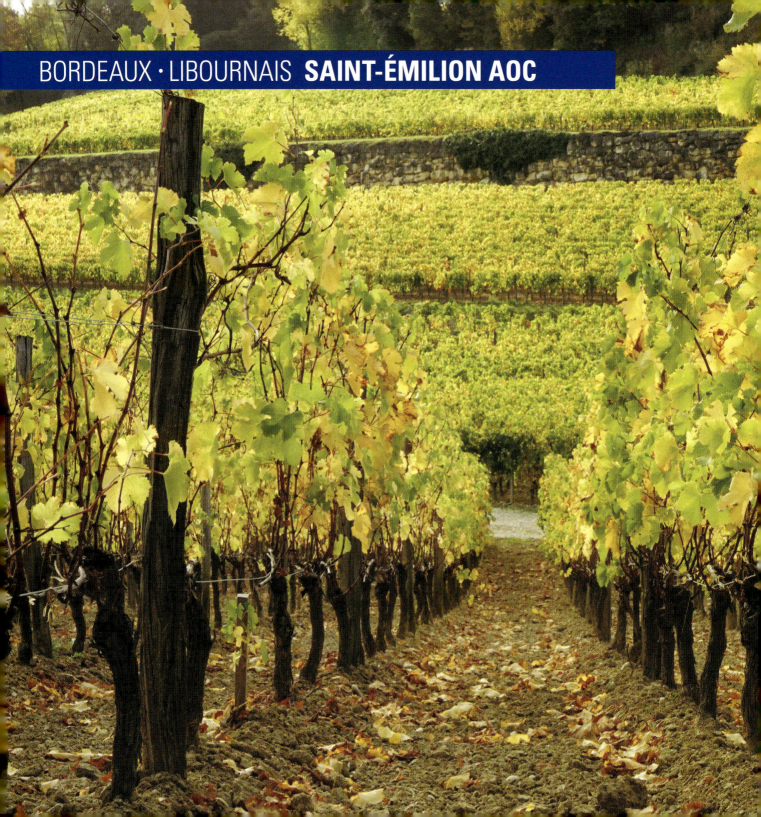

BORDEAUX · LIBOURNAIS **SAINT-ÉMILION AOC**

SOUTHERN SLOPE

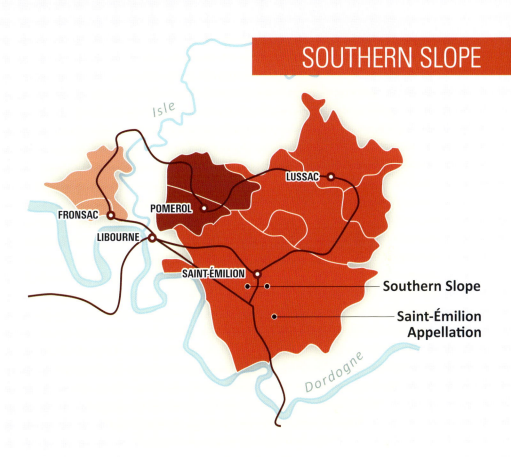

Left page: The sloping terrain and the golden hue of autumn grape leaves turning color in the vineyards of Château Fonplegade

SAINT-ÉMILION SOUTHERN SLOPE

This next quadrant of Saint-Émilion is the Southern Slope. This is the slope just south of the village that drops from the plateau rather dramatically. The châteaux here have most of their vineyards on the slope. Some are also on the edge of the plateau and a few on the foot as well. The other three first-growth châteaux are located here (Premier Grand Cru Classé A).

Here are a few good places to spend the night, including a luxury boutique hotel and a B&B&D (meaning bed & breakfast & dinner). There is also a super good winery restaurant worth visiting.

Here are the châteaux...

Premieur Grand Crus Classés A
- Château Angélus, page 349
- Château Pavie, page 351

Grand Crus Classés
- Château Fonplégade, page 355

Grand Crus
- Union de Producteurs, page 357
- Château La Croizille, page 359
- Château de Candale, page 361

SAINT-ÉMILION SOUTHERN SLOPE
Winery (Château)
CHÂTEAU ANGÉLUS

Saint-Émilion Premier Grand Cru Classé - A

33330 Saint-Émilion, France

+33 (0)5 57 24 71 39
Angelus@Angelus.com

Angelus.com

English, French

Château Angélus is not open to the public; only for industry professionals. Or, you must be recommended by a wine merchant, auction house, importer or a journalist (me). So, if you love Château Angélus wines and would like to go visit them, please write me at: Wineries@ExploringWineRegions.com and I would be happy to make a recommendation for you to visit.

Collection of Wines
Château Angélus
(First Label - Premier Grand Cru Classé)

Carillon d'Angélus
(Second Wine - Saint-Émilion Grand Cru)

No. 3 d'Angélus
(Third Wine - Saint-Émilion Grand Cru)

Since the 18th century, eight generations have been in pursuit of viticulture excellence.

THE BELLS RING

Upon arrival, the bells of Château Angélus (atop the building in the photo above) began playing *The Star-Spangled Banner*, and for a moment I felt at home listening to the United States national anthem. Such a wonderful personal greeting. Thank you.

The bells have rung like this for eight generations. Château Angélus is located in a natural amphitheatre in view of three Saint-Émilion churches and their bells are amplified throughout the valley. The Angelus bells can be heard ringing at 7:00am, noon and 7:00pm identifying the workday and calling people to stop for a few minutes and pray. They really are the angels of Bordeaux.

Their new building was completely reconstructed between 2012 and 2014 with the magnificent bells you see above, which were blessed by the bishop.

Up against the southern slope of the Saint-Émilion plateau, Château Angélus is perfecting the use of this extraordinary terroir, and particularly emphasizes Cabernet Franc (46%) significantly more than other châteaux. It is the distinction in the aromas and flavors of their wine that earned them Premier Grand Cru Classé B in 1996 and elevated them in 2012 to the top first-growth classification of Premier Grand Cru Classé A.

A lot goes into making a wine of this caliber. Although Hubert de Boüard de Laforest grew up at Château Angélus, he left Bordeaux to learn how other wine regions do things differently, then returned with new knowledge and passion for excellence, and has managed the property since 1985.

Walking the vineyards, you can see meticulous care given to the vines. And when he brings in the grapes from his 30 plots, they are kept separate in 30 large wooden vats where they are cared for separately for 22 months in anticipation of a final perfect blend. This is a big bold wine that needs time to evolve, and when it does, the bells ring.

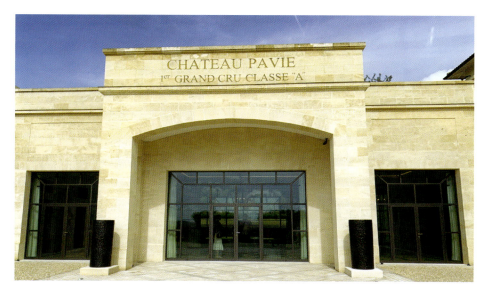

SAINT-ÉMILION SOUTHERN SLOPE
Winery (Château)
CHÂTEAU PAVIE

Saint-Émilion Premier Grand Cru Classé - A

Pimpinelle
33330 Saint-Émilion, France

+33 (0)5 57 55 43 43
Visites@VignoblesPerse.com

VignoblePerse.com

English, French

Open: All Year, Monday-Friday
By Appointment Only
Because demand is high, you must make an appointment weeks in advance during low season and months in advance during high season.

Where the property, winery and cellars are as stunning as the wine.

THE MAKING OF A CRU CLASSÉ A

This place is beautiful. Stunning. Refined. Elegant. Spectacular! Located southeast of the village of Saint-Émilion, the Château Pavie barrel rooms were completely redesigned in 1998 and an entirely new winery was built in 2013 by architect and decorator Alberto Pinto. Magnificent work, as you can see in the photos on these four pages. This will be one of the most beautiful wineries you will ever visit.

The terroir here is just as magnificent, benefiting from the Saint-Émilion limestone plateau, the steep slope and the foothills. All three very different soil compositions here are valuable to the qualities and complexity of their wine. The success in working these terroirs brought them to Premier Grand Cru Classé B status in 1955 and then promoted to first-growth Premier Grand Cru Classé A in 2012.

The terroir here is a combination of the plateau's upper slope of clay-limestone soil, about 85 meters above the Dordogne River. Even during the dry summer months, there is never a lack of water for the Merlot vines planted here. The roots are able to reach down several meters to access the 70% of the water these vines get from flowering to harvest.

There is a completely different terroir here called milieu de côte (which means "middle of the slope"), which is 55 meters above the Dordogne River. This is a thick layer of sand covering very fine brown limestone providing good drainage for the Cabernet Franc that has adapted best to this terroir.

Lastly, they have a large percentage of Cabernet Sauvignon planted, twice the average of Saint-Émilion properties, that are doing well in the sandy clay soils of the foothills. They feel it is a significant ingredient to their success, contributing to the structure necessary in a great wine. The breakdown in percentages are: 60% Merlot, 25% Cabernet Franc and 15% Cabernet Sauvignon.

The average age of the vines that go into the first label is 43 years old and vines under 10 years old go into the second wine.

Château Pavie only offers two tours.
• **The Classic Tour** is 50€ and you get a behind-the-scenes private tour of the property and cellars, plus a tasting of Château Pavie.
• **The Evolution Tour** is 1,200€ for 1 to 12 people and includes three wines, five years apart.

Collection of Wines
Château Pavie
(First Label - Premier Grand Cru Classé)

Arômes de Pavie
(Second Wine - Saint-Émilion Grand Cru)

Next page: Perfectly manicured vineyards of Château Pavie

SAINT-ÉMILION SOUTHERN SLOPE
Winery (Château)
CHÂTEAU FONPLÉGADE

Saint-Émilion Grand Cru Classé

1 Lieu Dit Fonplégade
33330 Saint-Émilion, France

+33 (0)5 57 74 43 11
ChateauFonplegade@Fonplegade.fr

Fonplegade.com

English, French

*Open: All Year, Everyday
Reservations are Strictly Required.
Château Fonplégade is pleased to welcome wine lovers who have a sincere interest in their wines. They would like to hear from you by phone or email of your interest and time in Saint-Émilion so they can prepare for a private appointment.*

A very beautiful property, stunning château and wines that impress.

GRAPE BY GRAPE

When I see two prominent winemaking consultants involved at the same winery, I conclude that the owner must be very serious about producing high-quality wines. And it is true. Denise and Stephen Adams have been perfecting this property for over 15 years and handle each grape with utmost care to orchestrate a perfect wine.

That is their very serious goal. Denise says "At Fonplégade, we farm our vineyard not block by block, not even row by row, but carefully, vine by vine." To me, this is the dedication put forth in order to strive for the highest standards.

Add to this, they are located on the southern edge of the slope sharing the limestone plateau and dramatic slopes of Saint-Émilion's finest vineyards. Château Fonplégade's name translates to "fountain of plenty" and one can be found in the center of the property that dates back to the 13th century when it quenched the thirst of passing pilgrims. Today, it provides much needed water to the vines during the driest summers.

When I first met Denise at a wine event, she was filled with enthusiasm about her property, and insisted I come visit. When in her own element, she was now serious, focused and precise with everything. She designed the most stunning property. Even the vat room is elegant (photo left) with a tile runway leading to beautiful windows with wood and concrete tanks standing proud in their perfection. A beautiful entertaining room with white fabric covered chairs and a grand piano.

They do not do tours here. Instead, they host you and your party and introduce you to their property: its terroir, winery and cellar. The tasting comes with a gorgeous spread of cheese, meats and fruits (photo far right). The château is a stunning complement to their beautiful wines.

Collection of Wines
Château Fonplégade
(First Label - Grand Cru Classé)

Fleur de Fonplégade
(Second Wine - Saint-Émilion Grand Cru)

SAINT-ÉMILION SOUTHERN SLOPE
Winery (Château)
UNION DE PRODUCTEURS

Saint-Émilion Grand Cru
Winner: Best Of Wine Tourism

Lieu-dit Haut, Au Petit Gravet
33330 Saint-Émilion, France

+33 (0)5 57 24 70 71
Contact@UDPSE.com

UDPSE.com

English, French

Open: All Year, Monday-Saturday
Boutique Open Everyday: 9:00am to 7:00pm
Exhibition (Free) Open: During Boutique Hours
Tours: By Appointment Only

State-of-the-art gravity-flow winery with 141 tanks making 10% of Saint-Émilion's wines.

BIG IS BEAUTIFUL

Have you ever been to a wine co-op? This place is massive. They produce 4.5 million bottles annually!

Union de Producteurs (UDP) is comprised of 150 owner/growers who contribute to this success. One-third of them produce their own wine with their own labels. Such a perfect place for the small producer to have access to sophisticated equipment and talent. The other two-thirds contribute their grapes to the co-op for UDP Châteaux and UDP Cuvées wines with sophisticated marketing.

I was skeptical that such a high volume producer from numerous growers could possibly make good wine. I was proven wrong. They sort the very best grapes just like a winery does, and process the better juice with higher quality methods. The results are excellent wines at great prices.

I tasted seven of what they thought were their better wines and which represented a diversity of what they can produce (photo top right). Impressive. At the end of the evening, I kept changing my mind as to which wine was my favorite. A great problem to have.

Imagine this: UDP produces 10% of all of the Saint-Émilion wines and claims that 40% of all wines in France are produced in co-ops facilities. In Bordeaux, UDP is a major player in winemaking and not just by volume. Their big investment in a gravity flow cellar with 141 stainless steel vats is the largest and most sophisticated of its kind in Europe (photo left page).

Can you book a tour here? Yes, indeed. And a tasting too. A UDP tour will take you through this huge state-of-the-art facility, ending in their art gallery for tastings (photo above). In keeping with the UDP motto: "Métier d'Art, Vigneron" (Winemaking as Art), this gallery has paintings and sculptures that rotate every month, reminding us that wine is art.

Their Oenothèque, meaning "wine library" (photo bottom right), is also huge, with the 50 châteaux's wines to taste and buy, plus other excellent wines the co-op produces. I suggest trying the wines that were curated for me (photo top right) and you cannot go wrong.

SAINT-ÉMILION SOUTHERN SLOPE
Winery (Château)
CHÂTEAU LA CROIZILLE
CHÂTEAU TOUR BALADOZ

Saint-Émilion Grand Cru
Global Winner: Best Of Wine Tourism

Lieu-dit Baladoz
33330 Saint-Laurent-des-Combes, France

+33 (0)5 57 74 55 86
Contact@ChateauLaCroizille.com

ChateauLaCroizille.com

English, French

Open: Almost All Year, Closed December
April-October, Everyday
January-March & November, Monday-Friday
By Appointment Only

S ome of the best panoramic views in Saint-Émilion across a valley of stunning vineyards.

THE OLD AND THE NEW

Château La Croizille is a brand new winery built next door across the driveway from Château Tour Balladoz. You get to see two very different châteaux and wines with one stop. Same ownership.

It is nice to see facilities showing how wine has been made for hundreds of years and then walk next door to see new modern architecture and state-of-the-art winemaking.

Between the two wineries is a small vineyard planted with each of the Bordeaux varietals (photo right). It is interesting to see the differences. A grape is not just a grape. They taste different, so they must look different. And they do. See the grape differences as well as their unique leaves.

Where would you like to be? In an underground cave feeling the dark moist air on barrels aging and straining your eyes to see the stained limestone walls, stalagmites and vine roots poking through the ceilings? Or, in a clean modern high-tech facility, overlooking the vineyards through the massive glass windows? Well, here, you don't have to choose. You get to experience both.

When the tour and tasting is complete, the best part begins. Reserve a table on their terrace (photo above) or a spot in their vineyard for a picnic.
• **The Standard Tour** is a tasting of both châteaux.
• **The Picnic Tour** includes a basket full of local savories and your favorite glass of wine.
• **The Privilege Tour** gets you barrel tasting plus a vertical tasting of five vintages of their wines. Either château of your choice.

Collection of Wines
Château La Croizille
(First Label - Saint-Émilion Grand Cru)

Château Tour Baladoz
(First Label - Saint-Émilion Grand Cru)

SAINT-ÉMILION SOUTHERN SLOPE
Winery (Château) & Restaurant
CHÂTEAU DE CANDALE

Saint-Émilion Grand Cru
Winner: Best Of Wine Tourism

1 Grandes Plantes
33330 Saint-Laurent-des-Combes, France

+33 (0)5 57 51 19 91
Visites@MTDecoster.com

MTDecoster.com

English, French

*Open: All Year, Monday-Friday
By Appointment Only*

O fficial tasting center with a gourmet restaurant to experience all four châteaux.

A CENTER OF FOOD AND WINE

As we continue across the Southern Slope to the east, we find Château de Candale and their eight hectares of Merlot and Cabernet Franc on limestone and clay. This was once a property belonging to the Count of Candale, a descendant of King Edward III of England.

Today this is the hub of four châteaux, two Saint Émilion Grand Crus (Château de Candale and Château Roc de Candale) and two Grand Cru Classés (Château La Commanderie and Clos des Jacobins, page 333), a restaurant (next page) and a wine shop where you can taste and buy from all four of these properties. They also start and conclude tours and their tastings here for the other châteaux. This really is a food and wine center where you can spend the day.

The barrel room at Château de Candale has some very interesting things to see in addition to delicious wine aging in oak. The perimeter of the walls has photographs depicting a cooper's numerous steps in manufacturing wine barrels. It is so interesting and educational to follow the process broken down step by step (photo left page).

Notice on the table in the center of the room, between the barrels, are four jars filled with soil. These are the four soils of the four châteaux. Wine is a representation of its terroir and this is a great way to see exactly how the aromas and flavor profiles correlate directly with the soil. They will explain how this works.

All of these wines are unique in their own way. I particularly gravitated to Château La Commanderie. I have tasted multiple vintages (love the 2015 a lot) and enjoyed them with a few different meals. I can only say I wish I had more than the few bottles I purchased and brought home. Time to go back!

They have three tourism options. Each comes with the opportunity to visit one or two wineries. And they all have a three-wine tasting.
• **L'essentielle** is your standard experience touring and tasting, except you can taste two châteaux.
• **L'initée** comes with a Tasting Initiation Workshop along with the L'essentielle above.
• **La Prestige** combines them all. Head to their restaurant on the property for a meal of gastronomic pairings.

Collection of Wines
Château de Candale
(First Label - Saint-Émilion Grand Cru)

Château Roc de Candale
(Second Wine - Saint-Émilion Grand Cru)

Château La Commanderie
(First Label - Grand Cru Classé)

Clos des Jacobins
(First Label - Grand Cru Classé)

SAINT-ÉMILION SOUTHERN SLOPE
Winery (Château) & Restaurant
CHÂTEAU DE CANDALE

BEAUTIFUL RESTAURANT

Where do I begin here? Delicious foods. Attentive service. Beautiful environment. And the full range of wines from all four châteaux of the Château de Candale family. Plus wines from all over Saint-Émilion and beyond. This is the ultimate food and wine experience even more so because the owners, Magali and Thibaut Decoster, make gastronomy the primary focus of their business.

Dine inside with window-lined walls allowing natural light to flow in and for the eyes to take in the views. A private room too. Outside is spectacular, overlooking the vineyards, forest and valley, under a large designer canopy, out of the sun and rain (photo left page).

Staff here is more than happy to assist you with wine pairings. This is their expertise. Foods from top to bottom, counterclockwise...

Slow-Cooked Veal and root vegetables, Basque-style, with my favorite: Chateau La Commanderie.

Layered Seafood Salad with fresh greens and roasted sesame bread sticks.

Pork Chop with marmalade glaze and creamy mashed sweet potatoes.

Chocolate Mousse Cake sprinkled with crushed smoked almonds.

Outside dining or just a glass of wine on the terrace makes for a wonderful afternoon or evening among the vines.

Foie Gras topped with green apple puree served with crispy toast and a slice of caramelized orange and a beautiful glass of Sauvignon Blanc.

L'ATELIER DE CANDALE
Gourmet Dining at Château Candale

Winner: Best Of Wine Tourism

1 Château La Dominique
33330 Saint-Émilion, France

+33 (0)5 57 24 15 45
Atelier@MTDecoster.com

AtelierDeCandale.com

English, French

Open: All Year, 11:00am-10:30pm
(open all afternoon when most places are closed)
Lunch: Everyday • Dinner: Tuesday-Saturday

Reservations Available On Their Website

B&B... &D

Located across the vineyards from Château de Candale in a quiet tucked-away location is in the home of Véronique and Thor Inge. They restored this farmhouse themselves and created five very affordable rooms. Nothing fancy. Very clean and comfortable, filled with personal, home-style family hospitality. The views of the vineyards and forest are spectacular (photo bottom right).

And why the "D" you might ask? This is a B&B, which of course means a bed and breakfast, and a good breakfast at that. Even better though is the "D" as this means dinner too! Thor loves cooking and is known for his impressive dinners. And he prepares delicious home-cooked meals (photo left page and bottom left). And he sources interesting wines (photos below) that you would not normally find in Saint-Émilion.

This sure is a unique experience that I have never come across before. You will dine family-style with Véronique and other guests until Thor eventually joins the table. Their charming son loves to help as well. A beautiful family affair.

SAINT-ÉMILION SOUTHERN SLOPE
Hotel - B&B, &D
LE PETITE MADELEINE

6 Lieu dit Saint-Jean-de-Béard
33330 Saint-Laurent-des-Combes, France
0033667682352
+33 (0)6 67 68 23 52
Le.Petit.Madeleine@Hotmail.com

Le-Petite-Madeleine.com

English, French

Open: All Year, Everyday
Reservations Available On Their Website
Or Major Travel Booking Websites

SAINT-ÉMILION SOUTHERN SLOPE
Château Hotel
CLOS 1906

18TH CENTURY MANOR HOUSE

This extremely nice luxury hotel run by an experienced hotelier is located just south of the Saint-Émilion village and next door to the east of the Château Fonplegade estate. At one time, this was the residence of a winery and vineyard owner. It was updated, you got it, in 1906.

Meticulously restored to perfection, keeping the beauty of this historical home, yet adding luxurious modern conveniences. Take a look at that bathroom for example (photo bottom right). It is spacious and beautiful with its details. The sink is in the center of the room. Separate soaking tub and walk-in shower. Full-length mirror. Wooden stools.

The large king bed is so comfortable. Don't miss the private pool and garden overlooking the vineyards. Such a romantic spot.

The WiFi here is excellent. I am telling you this because I have stayed in many places in and around Saint-Émilion, including very nice accommodations, and the WiFi is either lousy or nonexistent. If WiFi is important to you, this place will make you very happy.

While there are many beautiful antiques throughout the home, there is also an antique gallery on the premises. The collection is very well curated with both vintage and modern items. Most are luxury brands. All for sale.

14 La Gaffelière-Ouest
33330 Saint-Émilion, France

+33 (0)6 76 69 15 11
Info@Clos1906.com

Clos1906.com

English, French

Open: All Year, Everyday
Reservations Available On Their Website
Or Major Travel Booking Websites

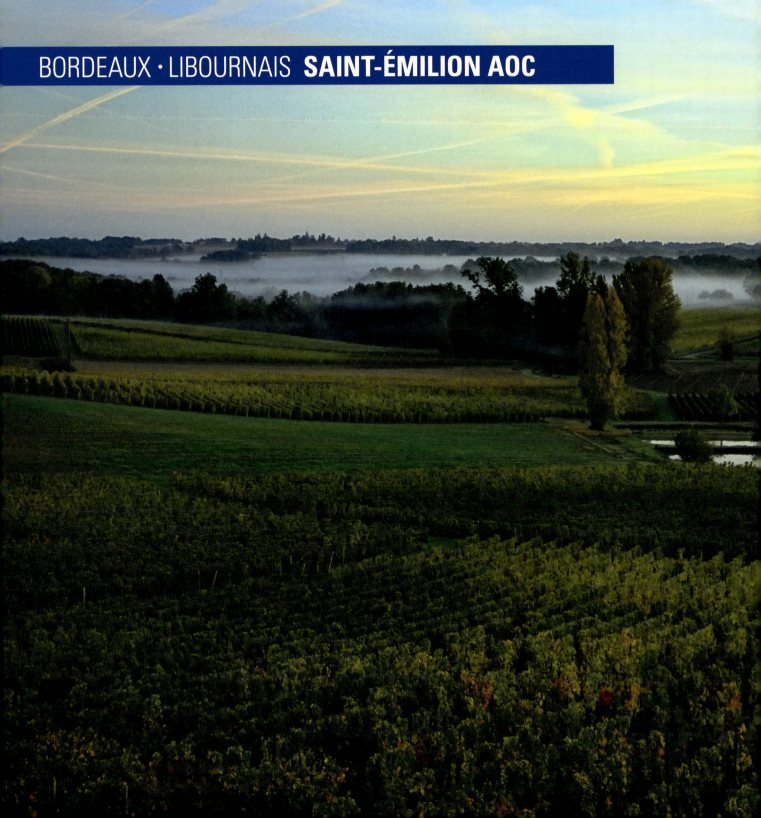
BORDEAUX · LIBOURNAIS SAINT-ÉMILION AOC

EASTERN PLATEAU

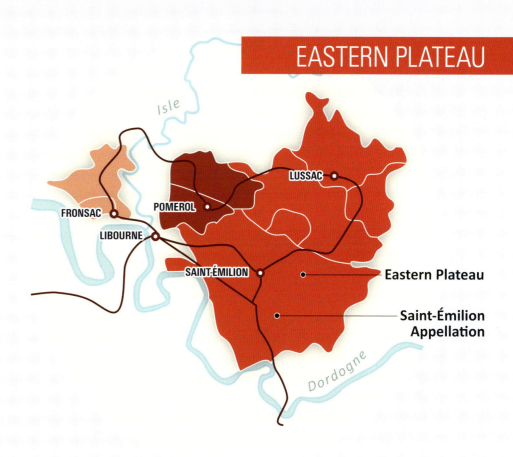

Left page: A peaceful view of early morning fog in the valley of Château Valandraud on the eastern plateau of Saint-Émilion

THE LIMESTONE PLATEAU

Now we are on top of the famous plateau of Saint-Émilion. We will first explore the eastern part of the plateau where we will find some extraordinary châteaux, including a couple of Premier Grand Cru Classés. While located on the top of the plateau, these châteaux also benefit from the terroir found on the slopes, where parts of their properties extend. This is actually significant, as it adds important complexity to their wines.

There are three places here where you can spend the night among the vineyards. They are all very different. **Château Valandraud** has rooms in their winery building. **Château Troplong Mondot** has homes throughout the vineyards, away from the winery. And **Château Fombrauge** is a luxurious castle experience within a château complex. Here are all of the châteaux...

Premieur Grand Cru Classés - B
 - Château Valandraud, page 371
 - Château Troplong Mondot, page 373

Grand Cru Classés
 - Château de Pressac, page 377
 - Château de Ferrand, page 379
 - Château Haut-Sarpe, page 383
 - Château Fombrauge, page 385

Exploring Wine Regions | **Bordeaux** | 369

SAINT-ÉMILION EASTERN PLATEAU
Winery (Château) & B&B
CHÂTEAU VALANDRAUD

Saint-Émilion Premier Grand Cru Classé - B

33330 Saint-Étienne-de-Lisse, France

+33 (0)5 57 55 09 13
Visit@Thunevin.com

Valandraud.fr

English, French

Open: All Year, Monday-Friday
Reservations by Email or On Website

From out of a garage with just .6 hectares, into a Premier Grand Cru Classé in just 20 years.

THE VALLEY OF VALANDRAUD

I love non-conformists, people trailblazing new ideas and succeeding by being innovative with their out-of-the-norm approaches. This is exactly what Jean-Luc Thunevin and Murielle Andraud have done when they created Château Valandraud from scratch. When people or companies buy châteaux, they purchase a deep history and an established name dating back centuries. This is not the case with Valandraud.

They started in 1991 by purchasing a tiny .6 hectare vineyard with all their savings and started making wine in a garage. They had to do basic things, like create a name: Val-Andraud ("Val" means "valley" and Andraud is Murielle's last name). They worked to qualify as a Saint-Émilion Grand Cru right away. They entered the classification process and were awarded Grand Cru Classé in 2002. It gets better! In 2012, they were elevated to Premier status as a Premier Grand Cru Classé B. All this success in just 20 years. And from a garage!

Their garage is much bigger now (left page), and the adjacent house is a B&B where you can stay with a view of their 8.88 hectare valley of vineyards. Ever so beautiful.

Sitting on top of the Saint-Émilion limestone plateau, I call it the Valley of Valandraud (photo above), where very special grapes become extra special wines.

Jean-Luc is often called the bad-boy black-sheep of Bordeaux. To him this is a compliment, so why not turn a compliment into a brand. BadBoy&Co was born. His blending did not comply with regulations (of course), so he had to release the wine under a regular Bordeaux labeling. Next was a Baby Bad Boy (Merlot/Grenache blend).

And what fun could a Bad Boy have without a Bad Girl? So three Bad Girls were born: Bad Girl dry white, Bad Girl rosé, and a Bad Girl crémant (sparkling).

They opened a wine bar, wine shop and boutique in the middle of the Saint-Émilion village. Over the years, they expanded to six caves (wine shops) in the village, plus two more during the summer. They are very much in the wine sales business in this village. They sell wines from many of the châteaux around Bordeaux. Here you can taste and buy all these wonderful wines. I highlight one of them in the Village chapter in the cave section.

Collection of Wines
Château Valandraud
(First Label - Premier Grand Cru Classé)

Valandraud Blanc
(First Label - White Wine - Saint-Émilion Grand Cru)

Virginie de Valandraud
(Second Wine - Red and White - Saint-Émilion Grand Cru)

3 de Valandraud
(Third Wine - Saint-Émilion Grand Cru)

Bad Boy, Petit Bad Boy and Bad Girl
(Two Red Wines, a Dry White, Rosé and a Sparkling)

SAINT-ÉMILION EASTERN PLATEAU
Winery (Château) & Houses
CHÂTEAU TROPLONG MONDOT

Saint-Émilion Premier Grand Cru Classé - B

Château Troplong, Mondot
33330 Saint-Émilion, France

+33 (0)5 57 55 32 05
Hospitality@Troplong-Mondot.com

Troplong-Mondot.com

English, French

Open: All Year, Everyday
By Appointment Only
Call or Email for Reservations

The highest elevation in Saint-Émilion receives a new winery on top of its plateau.

MICHELIN STARS IN A TENT

An entirely new winery has been built here. I was there during this 2.5-year construction project. All I saw was a large crane, so I can't wait to go back.

Funny thing, we accidentally arrived for our appointment two hours early (how embarrassing) and met the CEO of Chateau Troplong Mondot, Aymeric de Gironde, on his way to harvest lunch (how convenient). Of course we accepted his invitation to join him.

Without a building yet, they pitched a tent next to the vineyards (photo above). Harvest lunch is a gracious offering of some châteaux. It is a daily gathering of the entire team, from vineyard picker to winery team to management, during the harvest season. Such camaraderie. Not all châteaux do this. Troplong Mondot does it in an extraordinary way though. With a Michelin star chef! Yes, really.

The old winery had a Michelin star restaurant which was demolished to make room for a new one. The chef is still around while the restaurant is being built, so he prepares the harvest lunches. What a treat that was for everyone. Did I forget to mention a 2006 Chateau Troplong Mondot Premier Grand Cru Classé on the table?

At Troplong Mondot, their newer vintages show their fruit, while the older wines clearly reflect the terroir. I tasted the most beautiful terroir in that '06 bottle! I want more now.

And you can get more too. They do a standard tour called the **Getaway Tour** where you see the property and learn what goes into making a Premier Grand Cru Classé. All visits are private and personal.

The **Immersion Tour** is another story. True to its name, you are fully immersed while roaming the property in a Land Rover. You get to discover the hidden treasures of their terroir. Get your camera ready for unique vantage points as Troplong Mondot has the highest elevation in Saint-Émilion; a full 200 meters above the plateau. This is a completely custom experience just for you. With vintages of your choosing. Verticals. Older vintages. Including foods prepared by their starred chef.

To further feel the unique atmosphere here, I suggest you stay on the property in one of their homes (see next page) and wake up surrounded by this magical environment.

Collection of Wines
Château Troplong Mondot
(First Label - Premier Grand Cru Classé)

Mondot
(Second Wine - Saint-Émilion Grand Cru)

SAINT-ÉMILION EASTERN PLATEAU

Winery (Château) & Houses

TROPLONG MONDOT

HOMES & ROOMS FOR …

Within the vineyards of this pictures…
Château Troplong Mondot has un…
accommodations. Their attention…
hospitality equals that of their win…
with stunning results.

THE VINEYARD HOUSE - Dow…
nestled within their vineyards, is …
home. A cottage. Take one roo…
yours. The view out the back is b…
the vineyards and the Saint-Émi…
tower in the distance (scenic vi…
a 20-minute walk to the villag…

THE MANOR - There ar…
accommodations in this two-…
Art Studio comes with one …
sitting room and private fire…
(photo left) and *The Bell Tow*…
bottom right) are both s…
bedroom suites with spa…
Everyone shares the living…
spaces, with a cozy fireplac…

Wherever you choose t…
be resting blissfully in this…
the true sense this place…
just wine.

Château Troplong, Mondot
33330 Saint-Émilion, France

+33 (0)5 57 55 32 05
…spitality@Troplong-Mondot.com

Troplong-Mondot.com

English, French

Open: All Year, Everyday
Call or Email for Reservations

Exploring Wine Regions | Bordeaux

SAINT-ÉMILION EASTERN PLATEAU
Winery (Château)
CHÂTEAU DE PRESSAC

Saint-Émilion Grand Cru Classé
Winner: Best Of Wine Tourism

Château de Pressac
33330 Saint-Étienne-de-Lisse, France

+33 (0)5 57 40 18 02
Visite@ChateauDePressac.com

ChateauDePressac.com

English, French

Open: All Year, Everyday
By Appointment Only
Reservations Available On Their Website

T**hree distinct terroirs distinguish this estate and define their wines.**

GRAPE VARIETAL OR TERROIR?

I have had the pleasure of chatting with the owner of this château, Jean-François Quenin, on multiple occasions over several years. Each time it has been a profound learning experience.

It all started when Jean-François showed me around his property, beginning with its ancient castle from the Middle Ages surrounded by fortress walls enclosing the grand courtyard. It stands tall on top of the limestone plateau with striking slopes leading into a valley below. He has vineyards on the plateau (of course), as well as the slope and the foot. Three very different terroirs he explained. This was not too difficult to understand when observing such dramatic differences in the landscape.

In the new world of wine, we think of wine in terms of grape variety. We choose a Cabernet Sauvignon or a Pinot Noir. That is our thinking. And it is hard to understand a French wine without the grapes identified. Until the experiment with Jean-François Quenin.

A visitor asks him the same old question, "What grapes are in your bottle?" He replies, "Why does it matter? It is about terroir!" "No," the visitor insists, "it is about the grape." The experiment begins.

Three glasses of wine are presented; the visitor is told two are Merlots and one is a Cabernet Franc. He easily chooses what he thinks is the Cabernet Franc. So he thought. One Merlot and Cabernet Franc were from the plateau (which he said were Merlots because they tasted similar) and said the different tasting wine was the single Cabernet Franc. It was in fact the Merlot. It was the terroir that defined the differences, not the grape variety. This was the most significant lesson for my understanding that learning French wines is about learning the terroir.

The wisdom of Jean-François is found throughout his property. Twelve short years after he bought this historic estate, he was able to elevate his wine to the Grand Cru Classé status in 2012.

This is one of the most interesting estates to visit. Their wines are divine and everything you would expect from an intellectual owner with so much knowledge and expertise. He offers private and group tours, and tours with lunch included.

Interesting fact: The end of the Hundred Year War happened in 1453, with the French winning the Battle of Castillon La Bataille. The victory signing celebration is said to have taken place here at Château de Pressac.

Collection of Wines
Château de Pressac
(First Label - Grand Cru Classé)

Château Tour de Pressac
(Second Wine - Saint-Émilion Grand Cru)

La Rosée du Château de Pressac
(Bordeaux Clairet - Rosé Wine)

SAINT-ÉMILION EASTERN PLATEAU
Winery (Château)
CHÂTEAU DE FERRAND

Saint-Émilion Grand Cru Classé
Winner: Best Of Wine Tourism

Saint-Hippolyte
33330 Saint-Émilion, France

+33 (0)5 57 74 47 11
Oenotourisme@ChateauDeFerrand.com

ChateauDeFerrand.com

English, French

*Open: All Year, Everyday
By Appointment Only
Call, Email or Book on Their Website*

O**n top of their own plateau, surrounded by forests, creating their own ecosystem.**

VISITS, WORKSHOPS, CULINARY

Château de Ferrand is a spectacular place for many reasons. Beautiful architecture. Don't you just love the neutral colors enhancing the craftsmanship of the architecture? You must check out the fully renovated interior filled with high-tech modern elegance. The tasting bar sits on a cool 360-degree rotating platform (photo below). The historic cellar, Grottes de Ferrand, was brought to fame by King Louis XIV who loved to come party at the estate.

With all this said, I feel the outside environment is the most special part of this estate. They sit on their own elevated plateau, on top of the Saint-Émilion limestone, by themselves, surrounded by forests, parks and gardens. It is their own isolated ecosystem with diversified soil characteristic and no herbicides for over a generation.

They work with nature, observing terroir and grape variety compatibility, making no blanket decisions. Rather, choices are based on nature, vine age, weather, and activity from the terroir. When you taste their wine, you will know what I mean about how special this property is and how intuitive the people are who manage it. I predict their quality will bring them Premier status in the near future.

Château de Ferrand has the greatest range of tours, tastings, workshops, activities and culinary opportunities of any château in Bordeaux. I lost count at 22! And they treat every visitor like a professional; tours are sommelier-led, customized to your level of knowledge and interest.

You can do vertical, older vintages, blind, barrel, and magnum tastings. A magnum of the 2009 stellar vintage. Yes. For real. Their sommelier will help you blend your own wine. They will even prepare lunch, dinner or snacks and pairings as simple or elaborate as you wish. Their chef and sommelier can join you and play an active role in the learning experience.

You will not want to leave. The two only families that have owned this estate in the last 300 years feel the same way. Baron Bich, the founder of the Bic Pen Company, purchased this estate from the original family and has passed it down to his descendants. Drawn solely with eight Bic pens, the walls of the tasting room depict the four seasons of the vineyard (photo next page). It took the artist seven months to render this masterpiece.

Collection of Wines
Château de Ferrand
(First Label - Premier Grand Cru Classé)

Le Différent de Château de Ferrand
(Second Wine - Saint-Émilion Grand Cru)

Jean-François Janoueix (photo left), son of founder Joseph Janoueix, is the highly respected patriarch of 16 châteaux. At age 83, I find his mind extremely sharp, has a very big heart and exudes warm hospitality. Here is what others who know him well have to say…

"For as long as I have known Jean-François, I have always found him dynamic, passionate, driven and a great visionary. He lives everyday like it is his last. An enormously charismatic man, warm and generous, he loves meeting people from all walks of life, and treats everyone the same, from the President of France to the gardener in the yard. When you meet him, you are immediately struck by how down to earth the man is despite his family's extraordinary achievements and success. Someone not to be missed when you visit Saint-Émilion!"

– Sophie Cassat, Wine Shop Manager

"If you visit Saint-Émilion, you should visit Château Haut-Sarpe. You will meet an incredible man of 80 years old with 100 keys: Mr. Jean-François Janoueix the owner. This passionate man will tell you about his family story before the wine tasting. He has created the village of Haut-Sarpe with a museum, guest houses, farm, and night club Le Glouglou, open during the harvest for his team."

– Laurent Moujon, Publisher, Bordeaux Wine Editions

SAINT-ÉMILION EASTERN PLATEAU
Winery (Château) & B&B
CHÂTEAU HAUT-SARPE

Saint-Émilion Grand Cru Classé
Winner: Best Of Wine Tourism

33330 Saint-Christophe-des-Bardes, France

+33 (0)5 57 51 41 86
Info@J-Janoueix-Bordeaux.com

Haut-Sarpe.com

English, French

Open: All Year, Monday-Friday
Reservations: +33 (0)6 84 84 73 40
Or Email: Contact.HautSarpe@Orange.fr

THE HAMLET OF SARPE

When arriving at Château Haut-Sarpe, you are actually entering a little village, a real hamlet. A castle, several homes, a winery of course, B&B cottages, meeting rooms, banquet halls, the Glou Glou (an on-site nightclub so the pickers do not have to go into town to party), many farm animals (hundreds of birds), a hostel for pilgrims passing through Saint-Émilion on their way to Saint Jacques de Compostelle, a garage of antique cars, a restored 18th century flour mill museum and windmill, artists' studio buildings, and many spaces for storing wine. The hamlet has it own roads with its own street signs, and feels like a comfortable little village to call home.

There is one tour to taste their wines and see it all. The wines go way beyond Haut-Sarpe. The Joseph Janoueix group consists of 16 châteaux throughout the Libournais region (seven in Saint-Émilion, four in Boredaux Supérior, three in Pomerol, and two in Castillon Côtes de Bordeaux). Over 40 different wines in all.

After meeting Mr. Janoueix and spending three hours with him, neither one of us speaking the same language. I felt his big warm heart, generous soul, kindness, appreciation, humility, and his love for everyone, especially his family. We wandered his property playing charades, giving smiles and using creative gestures… and actually understood each other in each moment we shared.

Collection of Wines
Château Haut-Sarpe
(First Label - Grand Cru Classé)

Château de Sarpe
(Second Wine - Saint-Émilion Grand Cru)

Moulin de Sarpe
(Third Wine - Saint-Émilion Grand Cru)

SAINT-ÉMILION EASTERN PLATEAU
Winery (Château) & Hotel
CHÂTEAU FOMBRAUGE

Saint-Émilion Grand Cru Classé
Winner: Best Of Wine Tourism

Lieu-dit Fombrauge
33330 Saint-Christophe-des-Bardes, France

+33 (0)5 56 73 30 90
Visite@Fombrauge.com

Fombrauge.com

English, French

*Open: All Year, Everyday
By Appointment Only*

The largest estate in Saint-Émilion with an extensive array of tourism experiences.

LUXURY WINE AND TOURISM

Château Fombrauge is part of the Bernard Magrez collection of luxury estates (see page 255). This is one of his four Grand Cru Classés and one of the two largest properties in Saint-Émilion with 81 hectares of vines. This château dates back to the 15th century with the first harvest in 1599.

Many of the Magrez tourism experiences can be found at Château Fombrauge, including his famous helicopter tour of all four estates (this is where I flew from) and his super luxury chauffeur-driven excursions in Magrez's Rolls Royce Phantom.

They have a unique historical tour of their 2,500 years of history, a horse and carriage tour through the vineyards and little town, and a macaron and wine pairing (children participate with grape juice). The B-Winemaker workshop (blend your own wine) can be done with the ultra-premium Margez Fombrauge wine. Bikes are available for free.

They have added interesting technology. An advanced drone photographs the vineyards for vine health and vineyard management, plus giving them precise information for harvest dates. And TED, a robot, cultivates the soil in the vineyards.

The extensive size of their vineyards allow for numerous soil types, starting with the famous plateau limestone, plus a white clay, white molasses rocks, and with multiple sun exposures... all this giving them great complexity for their wines.

In addition to the Grand Cru Classé and the second wine, this property produces two ultra-premium wines in Bernard Magrez's name.

Magrez Fombrauge Rouge - This is a very special blend of 60% Merlot and 40% Cabernet Franc from his Niord Vineyard located on an archaeological site dating back to the 5th century BC. Here, they found a well-preserved skeleton over 2,500 years old and have it on display. The vineyard is only 1.8 hectares and managed by horse and oxen-drawn ploughing. Everything is done by hand through the entire process of making this small quantity exclusive wine.

Magrez Fombrauge Blanc - This is a rare and special white wine coming from 2.2 hectares of vines located in the town of Saint-Christophe-des-Bardes where Château Fombrauge is located. The limestone soil here offers extensive aromatic richness and subtle minerality in this 40% Semillon, 30% Sauvignon Blanc and 30% Sauvignon Gris blend. The Margez white wines tend to be more expensive than his reds, so expect this to be an amazing white wine.

Collection of Wines
Château Fombrauge
(First Label - Premier Grand Cru Classé)

Prélude de Fombrauge
(Second Wine - Saint-Émilion Grand Cru)

Magrez Fombrauge - Rouge
(Premium Selection - Saint-Émilion Grand Cru)

Magrez Fombrauge - Blanc
(Premium Selection - Saint-Émilion Grand Cru)

SAINT-ÉMILION EASTERN PLATEAU
Winery (Château) & Hotel
CHÂTEAU FOMBRAUGE

15TH CENTURY CHARTER HOUSE

This is an exceptional experience in overnight luxury. Just look at the photo of the bedroom (below left), the landscaping of this charter house (below right), and the incredibly delicious meals that you can enjoy at this château. You must have one of their special dinners in the traditional dining room while you are here. The meals are paired with Fombrauge and other Magrez wines from his other Grand Cru Classé estates.

The back patio of the château looks like a beautiful painting. And it is! Although it is actually created by photography. Expect breathtaking beauty and historical charm inside and outside the estate.

Winner: Best Of Wine Tourism

+33 (0)5 57 26 38 34
VisitesChateaux@Bernard-Magrez.com

LuxuryWineExperiences.com

Open: All Year, Everyday
Call, Write or Book On Their Website

BORDEAUX · LIBOURNAIS **SAINT-ÉMILION AOC**

CENTRAL PLATEAU

Left page: View from Château Soutard of balloons rising in the late afternoon over the Saint-Émilion landscape

THE VILLAGE CHÂTEAUX

The Central Plateau, as I have defined it, is the area in and around the Saint-Émilion village. It is very much on top of the limestone plateau. This part of the limestone plateau has been extensively excavated underground to build the structures of the village. Large blocks were cut out from underground for all this construction. The result of this has created massive cave systems underneath many of the châteaux and other buildings.

All four of the châteaux highlighted are walkable from the village. **Château Gaudet** is in the middle of the village and **Château Villemaurine** is adjacent. The other two are a five-minute walk.

Château Soutard has rooms in their castle to stay in so you can be right next to the village, or in the next chapter, I will share with you a very nice place in the village. Here are the châteaux...

Premier Grand Cru Classés - B
 - Château Beau-Séjour Bécot, page 391

Grand Cru Classés
 - Château Soutard, page 393
 - Château Villemaurine, page 397
 - Château Guadet, page 399

Exploring Wine Regions | **Bordeaux** | 389

SAINT-ÉMILION CENTRAL PLATEAU
Winery (Château)
CHÂTEAU BEAU-SÉJOUR BÉCOT

Saint-Émilion Premier Grand Cru Classé - B

1 Lieu dit La Carte
33330 Saint-Émilion, France

+33 (0)5 57 74 46 87
Contact@BeauSejour-Becot.com

BeauSejour-Becot.com

English, French

Open: All Year, Monday-Friday
By Appointment Only

O n top of the Saint-Émilion plateau, a scenic five-minute walk west of the village.

A VERY COOL WALK

A walk from the Saint-Émilion village is a great way to get to Château Beau-Séjour Bécot. Leave from the west side of the village and walk down very narrow roads through vineyards with clos (stone walls on the perimeter of the vineyards) on both sides. A ten-minute walk, maybe longer because you are going to love the views (photo below).

Château Beau-Séjour Bécot is a Premier Grand Cru Classé with caves underground to explore. Standing beautifully on top of the limestone plateau, they have made wine from this extraordinarily great terroir since the Roman period. "Beau-Séjour" means "lovely stay." And that it will be when you go for a visit. Nice hospitality with excellent wine. A great combination.

The Bécot family added their name to the label when they took over this estate in 1969. They also added neighboring vineyards to expand the terroir for greater production and brought the wine to the top tier of the Premier Grand Cru classification.

They are now using the underground caves (seven hectares big) for wine storage holding tens of thousands of bottles. As the vineyards were once cultivated by the monks of the Church of Saint-Martin, a religious sanctuary was added for the sake of tradition. They will take you down below and show you their collection of vintage wines aging in perfect conditions (photo below).

Collection of Wines
Château Beau-Séjour-Bécot
(First Label - Premier Grand Cru Classé)

Petit Becot
(Second Wine - Saint-Émilion Grand Cru)

SAINT-ÉMILION CENTRAL PLATEAU
Winery (Château) & B&B
CHÂTEAU SOUTARD

Saint-Émilion Grand Cru Classé
Winner: Best Of Wine Tourism

Soutard
33330 Saint-Émilion, France

+33 (0)5 57 24 71 41
Contact@Soutard.com

Soutard.com

English, French, German, Spanish

Open: All Year, Everyday
By Appointment Only
The 2:00pm Tour Requires No Prior Reservation

U ltra-modern winery amidst an aristocratic presence of historical beauty.

WONDERFUL VIEWS

Exiting the north entrance of the Saint-Émilion village, Château Soutard is less than a 1,000 feet down the road to the east. The walk down their beautiful driveway lined with linden trees might be longer than the walk getting there. Arrive into a grand courtyard under the backdrop of their castle.

Sitting on top of the Saint-Émilion limestone plateau, Soutard has wonderful views into the valley around them. Take one of their bicycles on a tour around the property, following the signs and explore many interesting features this château has to offer. See the 70% of vines on the limestone clay plateau, 13% on sandy soil and 17% on their rich clay slopes, that gives them much diversity, adding complexity and layers of aromas into their wines.

The large wine shop and boutique off the courtyard caters to many types of tours. The visits here are interesting as you get to see how clearly defined the diverse terroir looks. And enjoy the scenic view. See a bygone era inside the historic castle of an aristocratic past and witness quality winemaking in an ultra-modern winery.

Both simple and advanced tours are available. Plus winemaking workshops, barrel tasting (photo below), food and wine pairings, and picnics on their beautiful grounds – seven different tours in all. The 2:00pm tour requires no reservation.

Collection of Wines
Château Soutard
(First Label - Grand Cru Classé)

Jardins de Soutard
(Second Wine - Saint-Émilion Grand Cru)

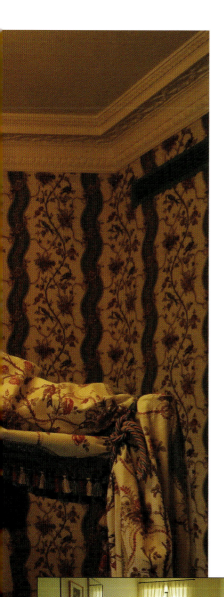

18TH CENTURY MANSION

This three-story castle only has three bedrooms. They are extremely spacious, as you can imagine. And huge modern baths too. You will feel like you have the entire castle (and you can rent the entire castle) as there is no wait staff. You are on your own to relax in your private room, in the shared living room or in the cozy den.

Breakfast is delivered (yogurt, fruits juices, coffee, fresh bread and pastries) to the kitchen, which is available for use. You can cook your own meals or their chef can prepare a formal dinner for you. Or do both.

The guest rooms are magnificently restored to period detail, bringing back the original Soutard aristocratic presence. The furniture and paintings are from this period, purchased in public sales, and all the upholsteries are re-creations of 18th century designs (photos left page and below).

The private garden is nicely set up with everything you need to relax with a glass of wine as you take in the garden and views.

SAINT-ÉMILION CENTRAL PLATEAU

Winery (Château) & Hotel
CHÂTEAU SOUTARD

Winner: Best Of Wine Tourism

+33 (0)5 57 24 71 41
Contact@Soutard.com

Soutard.com

Open: All Year, Everyday
Reservations: Call, Email or Book On Their Website

SAINT-ÉMILION CENTRAL PLATEAU
Winery (Château)
CHÂTEAU VILLEMAURINE

Saint-Émilion Grand Cru Classé
Winner: Best Of Wine Tourism

23 Villemaurine-Sud
33330 Saint-Émilion, France

+33 (0)5 57 74 74 36
Reservations@Villemaurine.com

Villemaurine.com

English, French

*Open: All Year
April-October, Everyday
November-March, Monday-Friday
By Appointment Only
Tours: Book On Their Website*

Adjacent to the Saint-Émilion village with a huge multi-level cave to explore.

MODERN DESIGN RUNS DEEP

Château Villemaurine is located and adjacent to the north entrance of the Saint-Émilion village. It is as old as the ancient village sitting on top of its limestone quarries, dug out to build the village. These quarries go deep, four levels, covering seven hectares (17 acres). Wow, I have never seen anything like this. It is a network of tunnels and rooms on top of each other. It makes me wonder how they know the proper strength of the floor and ceilings.

Their guide will take you deep into these caves and explain how it was all created. There is cool lighting to make this place extra beautiful (photo left page). They keep their wines down here and the aging barrels are in ideal conditions with the natural cool temperature and humidity of these caverns.

Up above, the vineyards are thriving on this clay and limestone plateau. And with a newly constructed modern winery with beautiful colors (photo right), all is happy in the winemaking process of their Grand Cru Classé wine.

Three different guided tours take you through this property where you end up in stunning designer areas like the photo above. Or outside on their beautiful patio.

• **The Vine To Wine Tour**. This takes you through the vineyards, caves, winery and tasting of their wines.
• **The Underground Quarries Tour**. Experience the estate's subterranean heritage in a very unique way. The presentation of a sound and light show is as imaginative as it is educational in discovering the past and present of their massive cave system.
• **The Privilege Tour**. An exclusive tour specifically designed for connoisseurs and enthusiasts wanting to expand their wine knowledge. Learn the philosophy behind the making of the Château Villemaurine wines. Discover their terroir, history, winemaking, barrel and bottle aging, and enjoy a unique tasting in an exclusive setting.

Collection of Wines
Château Villemaurine
(First Label - Grand Cru Classé)

Les Angelots de Villemaurine
(Second Wine - Saint-Émilion Grand Cru)

Clos Larcis
(100% Merlot From A Special Vineyard)

SAINT-ÉMILION CENTRAL PLATEAU
Winery (Château) & B&B
CHÂTEAU GUADET

Saint-Émilion Grand Cru Classé
Winner: Best Of Wine Tourism

4 Rue Guadet
33330 Saint-Émilion, France

+33 (0)5 57 74 40 04
ChateauGuadet@Orange.com

ChateauGuadet.fr

English, French, Spanish, Chinese

*Open: All Year, Everyday
By Appointment Only*

The Lignac family has owned this property since 1844 making Grand Cru Classé wines right in the middle of the village.

KEEPING IT PERSONAL

Château Guadet is located in the heart of the village, on its namesake street, Rue Guadet. This is the home where seven generations have been making wine. When you arrive (you must have reservations), you will be greeted at the front door of their home. The tours are personal, conducted by the family. They will take you into the outside hidden gardens in the middle of their home.

The tour will consist of seeing the old winery where they have been making wine for 150 years. From the courtyard, enter the secret cellar beneath their home, meander the tunnels, see wine aging, and pop up into their tasting room (photo above) on the other side of the courtyard. Here you will enjoy their delicious Grand Cru Classé wines.

The vineyards are managed by owners Guy-Petrus and Vincent Lignac, a father-and-son team. They farm organically and biodynamically. They have extremely healthy vineyards. I have been there, seen it, experienced the harvest (photo left page of Guy-Petrus and team), sampled a few grapes (ok, a lot of grapes!), and tasted the results. Several vintages. Love them all.

They have just one wine. No second label. Their wine is truly a terroir wine, fully representing the property. Their special land is adjacent to the north of the Saint-Émilion village, on the notable limestone clay plateau. Their vineyards are planted with 60% Merlot and 40% Cabernet Franc. The climate makes each vintage unique and distinct. And the people, Guy-Petreus, Vincent and their team, are dedicated to perfecting the results off this special land and then in the cellar.

Since visiting the ancient village of Saint-Émilion is a must, visiting Château Guadet is an easy decision, a must-do experience while you are there.

Collection of Wines
Château Guadet
(First Label - Grand Cru Classé)

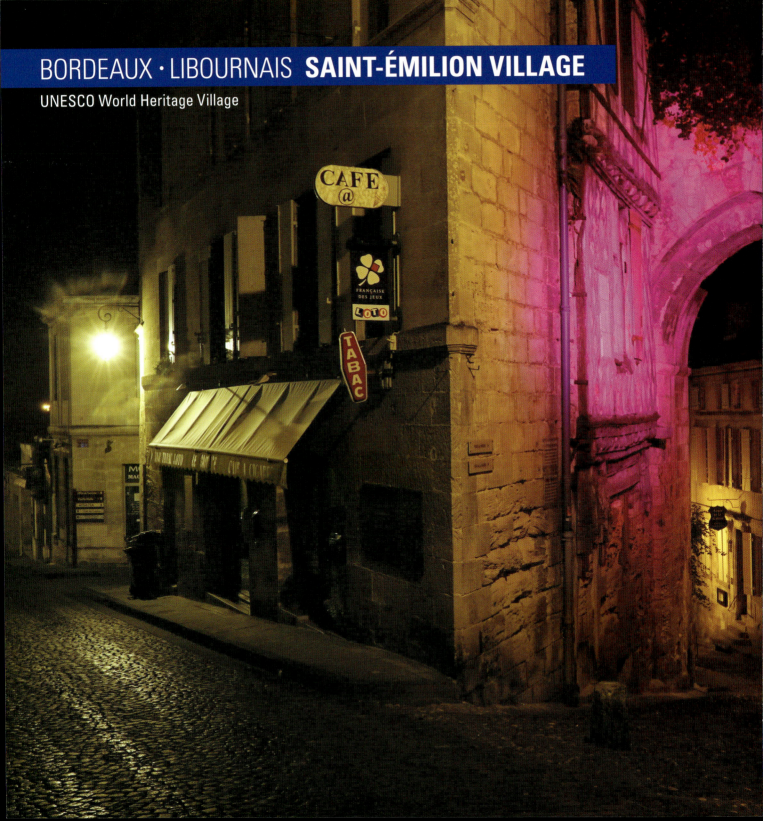

BORDEAUX · LIBOURNAIS SAINT-ÉMILION VILLAGE
UNESCO World Heritage Village

SAINT-ÉMILION VILLAGE

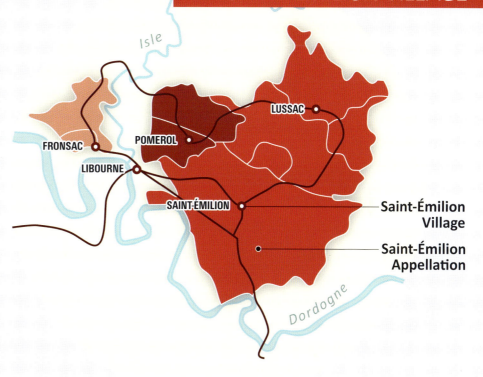

Left page: Before sunrise, the cobblestone streets of Saint-Émilion come alive with colors and character

SAINT-ÉMILION VILLAGE

Saint-Émilion, the village, is 47 km (29 miles) or a 45-minutes drive from the Bordeaux city center, bypassing the city of Libourne. Saint-Émilion is at the center of the Saint-Émilion appellation, on top of the famous limestone plateau. It was from the limestone quarries of the plateau in and around Saint-Émilion that the stone blocks were excavated to build the village.

Under most of the châteaux surrounding the village, and under the village itself, massive cave systems exist from cutting these very large blocks out of the ground and bringing them up to the surface for this construction.

From the 9th to 19th centuries, the number of stone quarries in the Saint-Émilion limestone plateau increased dramatically. Quarriers worked non-stop to extract millions of stone blocks for construction in Saint-Émilion and Bordeaux.

This is an asteriated limestone containing a great number of fossils dating from the Lower Oligocene period 32 million years ago giving rise to many of the monuments seen in Saint-Émilion.

This resulted in a massive cave system of 80 hectares (198 acres) with a maze of tunnels underground stretching 200 km (124 miles). Wow! And we get to explore all this via the many châteaux in and around the village. And in the village itself.

Exploring Wine Regions | **Bordeaux** | 401

SAINT-ÉMILION UNESCO WORLD HERITAGE VILLAGE

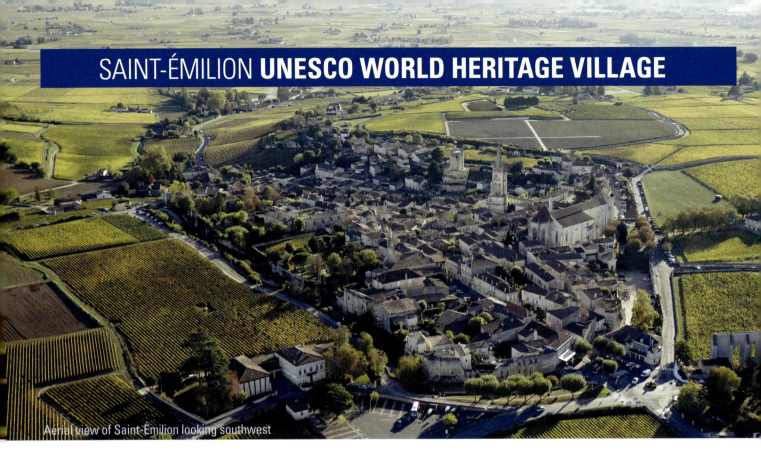

Aerial view of Saint-Émilion looking southwest

In Bordeaux, there are many historic towns, villages and hamlets. Saint-Émilion is one you do not want to miss. The village dates back to prehistoric times with Romanesque architecture and is unique with a very interesting history. The village itself became a UNESCO World Heritage site in 1999.

The village of Saint-Émilion shares its name with both the appellation and the broader appellation of four satellites, plus Saint-Émilion Grand Cru. The village is medieval and the Romans planted grapes here as early as the 2nd century.

In the 4th century, Roman poet Ausonius gave high praise to the grapes here. He eventually retired and started planting grapes and living on the estate that is now owned by renowned Château Ausone, Premier Grand Cru Classé A, which takes its name from him.

In the 8th century, Monk Émilion arrived as a traveling priest known for his miracles. He carved out a cave for himself to live in – his hermitage where he could hide out. Needing fresh water, he caused a river to divert up into his hermitage where it gushed from the ground as a spring. Because of this and other miracles, and his generosity, he attracted many disciples. The monastic complex grew, creating the village that eventually took his name (from Ascumbas to Saint-Émilion). When the Saint died, his companions began to dig the huge monolithic church over the next four centuries.

It was the monks who followed him and started up the commercial wine production. They grew their grapes in the vineyards surrounding the village (super great terroir) and made the wine inside the caves within the village.

In the 12th century, Saint-Émilion was the second largest town of the diocese (after Bordeaux) with nearly 10,000 residents. In contrast today, the Saint-Émilion area has a population of less than 2,000 people in all its 22 villages combined. The village itself has a population of only 200 people. Many more people come to visit Saint-Émilion everyday than the number of people who live there.

As you can see in the aerial photo on the left page, Saint-Émilion is a village nestled in a little valley. The photo is viewed looking south. The north roundabout entrance (at the bottom of the photo) leads directly into the village on Rue Guadet. Or go right and you will find the west entrance, where the large Collegiate Church is located. This is the highest point of the village. As you go north and east, the village drop, sometimes rather dramatically, through its interesting maze of cobblestone streets (photo bottom left). As a UNESCO World Heritage Site, this village is truly an outdoor museum you could easily spend a day or more perusing.

Looking at this aerial photo, the largest building you see (on the right side of the village) is the Collegiate Church and the west entrance to the village. Also in this building is the Tourism Office and Maison du Vins.

The Collegiate Church is 79 meters (260 feet) long making it one of the largest churches in the area. The inside is spectacular. It has the medieval style of both Romanesque and Gothic architecture (photo bottom right). The adjoining cloister has its own open *Garden of Eden* inside, surrounded by a covered walkway of columns leading to the refectory, chapter room, dormitory, and meditation gallery (photo right).

The underground Monolithic Church and its rising Bell Tower took four centuries to build (12th through 15th centuries). The Bell Tower is the highest point in Saint-Émilion, standing tall in its skyline (photos left page). The 196 steps are worth the hike to the top of the tower for an amazing view of the Saint-Émilion village and rolling countryside of vineyards. It's accessible all year for just 2€.

Deep below the Bell Tower is the Monolithic Church, hidden behind two small Gothic doors (photo bottom center). These doors open into the dazzling church, entirely carved out of the limestone rock. Its gigantic proportions make it Europe's widest monolithic church. Its unique size and shape has made it famous worldwide.

SAINT-ÉMILION VILLAGE
Information, Maps & Tours
SAINT-ÉMILION TOURISM OFFICE

Place des Créneaux Le Doyenné
+33 (0)5 57 55 28 28
Saint-Emilion-Tourisme.com

Open: Everyday, 10:00am-5:00pm • Hourly Tours
Night Tours on Tuesday & Thursdays at 9:30pm

Underground Church, Chapel & Tower
MONOLITHIC CHURCH & BELL TOWER
Trinity Chapel & Émilion's Hermitage

Visits are by guided tours through the Tourism Office

Above Ground Church
COLLEGIATE CHURCH

+33 (0)5 57 24 70 81
Paroisse-Saint-Emilion.fr

Open: Everyday, Sunday Mass 10:30am
Saturday Evening Mass 6:00pm

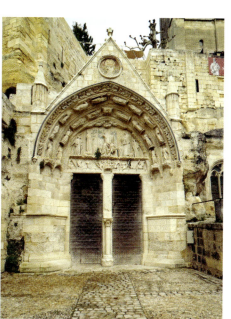

What is most interesting to think about is that this church is made from just one stone. One! In ancient Greek, the word "mono" means "single," and "lithos" means "stone," hence monolithic church. And that it is. The church was truly carved into one great big piece of limestone. In fact, the limestone plateau is one big piece of limestone.

How big is this church? It is 38 meters long by 12 meters high (125 feet long by 40 feet high). All underground. Amazing, isn't it? Think about their intentions with such a large space. It must have been to develop a city around pilgrim activity (and hundreds of them came) with a worship center, to attract a large number of people to their unique congregation. They could easily intrigue visitors with the church's unusual construction.

And there is more. Over the centuries, different religious groups built their own places of worship inside here. This included the Trinity Chapel, decorated with precious polychrome frescoes (photo bottom center), which is alongside other chapels (photo bottom left) inside the walls of this massive underground church.

Also underground are the catacombs of significant priests. Monk Émilion's cave is also connected to the church with its own separate entrance. The original facade (photo right) is hidden around corners, as the monk wanted his secrecy. An obscured door hides the path leading inside and down a slope into his cave. He also carved a special chair into the limestone where he would sit to perform his sacred rituals and miracles (photo bottom right).

The development of the monolithic church over the centuries is interesting. Its excavation started in the 12th century. It was painted in the 14th century, damaged in the 16th century, battered in the 18th during the Revolution, and then restored in the 20th century.

Today, this church is still consecrated and hosts regular religious ceremonies. Concerts are held throughout the year. I can just imagine the acoustics inside, underground, surrounded by stone. The Saint-Émilion Jurade conducts induction ceremonies into the Brotherhood at the church. This Brotherhood consists of 140 Jurats who wear red caps and robes with decorative white trim. They organize induction ceremonies throughout the world with a community of more than 3,000 members who act as ambassadors to the wines of Saint-Émilion.

I hope you are getting the idea that this is a pretty cool place to visit. Nothing like you have ever seen anywhere else in the world. Underground tours are only available with a guide from the Saint-Émilion Tourist Office. Tours are conducted throughout the day and lasts 2.25 hours (90 minutes of a UNESCO tour through the village and 45 minutes underground).

Night tours (Tuesday and Thursday after dark) are offered and led by the night watchman. This is an interesting tour to walk around the village with lanterns – experiencing a very different atmosphere here. Imagine the mysteries you will discover in the shadows of this village.

Photography is not allowed when visiting the underground monuments. Because of this book, I was allowed to take pictures to show you just how amazing and cool this place is to visit.

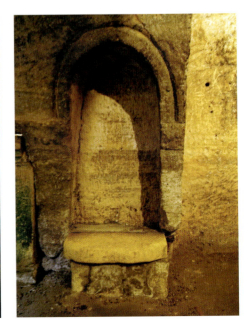

The village is a beautiful place, day or night. It is safe and peaceful. Enchanting actually. There are numerous great restaurants to be found. Two are even Michelin stars. There are excellent places to stay in historic buildings. Wine shops are everywhere. And wine bars, as this is the place to enjoy. There are also a few wine novelty shops and art galleries. And a grocer, a baker and a butcher.

There are three châteaux in the village. I don't mean a retail outlet for their wines. These are actual wineries making their wine in the village. They are…
- **Château Guadet** (Grand Cru Classé),
- **Moulin Galhaud** (Saint-Émilion Grand Cru), and
- **Les Cordeliers** (sparkling wines underground).

All three wineries are open to the public and have underground caves that you can visit.

Have you ever tasted an original macaron? These are not the macarons we know today with pretty colors and different flavors. These are the originals made from the 1620 recipe of the Ursuline nuns who established their convent in the village. Nadia Fermigier is the sole custodian of the real recipe passed down to her. She even hand presses the almonds as they did 400 years ago (photo below).
- **Fabrique des Macarons** is at 9 Rue Guadet.

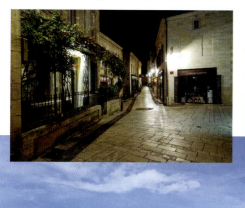

SAINT-ÉMILION VILLAGE
Historic Hotel & Gourmet Restaurant
LOGIS DE LA CADÈNE

LUXURY HOTEL AND MICHELIN STAR RESTAURANT IN THE MIDDLE OF THE VILLAGE

3 Place du Marché au Bois
33330 Saint-Émilion, France

+33 (0)5 57 24 71 40
Contact@LogisDeLaCadene.fr

LogisDeLaCadene.fr

English, French

Open: February-November
Lunch: Tuesday-Saturday, 12:00pm-1:45pm
Dinner: Tuesday-Saturday, 7:30pm-9:30pm

Accommodations
Reception Open: Everyday, 9:00am-6:00pm

Reservations Available On Their Website
Or On Major Travel Booking Websites

Such a nice place to hang out. Cozy-comfortable accommodations with ultra-gourmet cuisine. And perfectly located right in the middle of the Saint-Émilion village.

Logis de la Cadène is located on their own small square, along a steep cobblestone street, with a wisteria arbor entrance. Eat on the arbor-covered patio or in one of the dining rooms. The B&B is on multiple floors, adapting to the interesting 18th century architecture.

This is a very nice luxury property owned by Château Angélus, which was renovated in 2014. They did an excellent job carving out five lavish rooms, along with the restaurant, in such an old charming building. Delicious breakfast included.

Of course you can taste Angélus wines here. Even better, they have a collection of wines from all over the world on the wine list.

The seafood salad you see pictured here is to die for. The dressing is light and savory, poured table-side. I wanted a second! The fish was prepared to perfection. The cod was flaky, delicate, moist, and served atop mouth-watering sauces. Their creativity and atmosphere earned them a well-deserved Michelin star.

VILLAGE RESTAURANTS

You do not need to leave the village to find great restaurants. There are at least a dozen restaurants in the village of Saint-Émilion. And get this: There are two Michelin star restaurants in the village! **Logis de la Candène** has one star (previous spread) and **La Table de Plaisance** has two stars (presented on the next spread).

The following four additional restaurants are all amazing in their own way. One is a bustling French bistro. Another is Italian for a change of pace. The third is underground in a cave. And the fourth is elegant with creative gourmet cuisine.

The underground restaurant of Lard et Bouchon

SAINT-ÉMILION VILLAGE
Bistro Restaurant
L'ENVERS DU DÉCORE

9 Rue du Clocher • 33330 Saint-Émilion, France
+33 (0)5 56 74 48 31 • Reservation@Envers-DuDecor.com
Envers-DuDecore.com • Open: Everyday 12:00-2:00pm & 7:00-9:30pm

A French bistro and wine bar. Established in 1987, it was Saint-Émilion's first wine bar. Now owned by Premier Grand Cru Classé Château Pavie. You can't miss their big red doors. Busy, so make reservations. A spacious covered patio in the back makes it easier to get in. Fresh seasonal foods from the local market. Check out the grilled filet with a creamy seafood sauce. Reservations available on their website.

SAINT-ÉMILION VILLAGE
Casual Italian Restaurant
LA PIZZERIA DU VIEUX LAVOIR

19 Rue de la Grande Fontaine • 33330 Saint-Émilion, France
+33 (0)5 57 24 68 91 • Sarl.pdm@Gmail.com
Open: Everyday, 12:00pm-3:00pm & 6:30pm-10:00pm

Need a change of pace from so much delicious French cuisine? Here is your escape. Italian. Pastas and pizzas. Casual. And Italian wines for another change of taste! Located in the south and lower part of the village under the Kings Tower (tall rectangular monument). Notice the expanded hours and earlier dinner opening time. This may be a nice alternative. And check out the slow-braised and ever so tender lamb over pappardelle pasta.

SAINT-ÉMILION VILLAGE
Underground Cave Restaurant & Wine Bar
LARD ET BOUCHON

22 Rue Guadet • 33330 Saint-Émilion, France
+33 (0)5 57 24 28 53 • Contact@LardEtBouchon.fr
LardEtBouchon.fr • Tuesday-Saturday, 12:00-2:00pm & 7:00-9:00pm

This is a very cool place. Right off the main street and down into a cave for dining. You are in a 14th century cellar, a cave carved into the limestone. A restaurant serving mouth-watering French cuisine. Over 300 bottles of wine behind its cage (photo top left page), 20 wines by the glass! I still remember the scallops, as flavorful as they are colorful. The duck filet tender and juicy! A Michelin mention. Reservations available on their website.

SAINT-ÉMILION VILLAGE
Gourmet Restaurant
LE CLOS DU ROY

12 Rue de la Petite Fontaine • 33330 Saint-Émilion, France
+33 (0)5 24 00 10 37 • Contact@LeClosDuRoy.fr
Wednesday-Sunday, 12:00-1:30pm & 7:30-9:30pm • LeClosDuRoy.fr

Ascend to the second floor and enter this enchanting and elegant restaurant. The young chef here is up to some unique and creative ideas in cuisine. Modern concepts. Rich flavors. And top-level wines from Saint-Émilion. So, a grilled filet with rosemary potatoes seems pretty straight forward? Not when this chef prepares it in the most unpredictable way. Same with the steak. Truth be told, the crunch of the potato will ravage your mouth while the tenderness of the steak and the decadence of the sauce will send you to heaven. A Michelin mention. Reservations available on their website.

TWO MICHELIN STARS

I really wondered... What is the difference between a one-star and two-star Michelin rating? I posed this to their chef, Ronan Kervarrec.

"The difference is style and signature, a personal style found nowhere else."

Chef Ronan's signature is inspired by his childhood and father, who was an innkeeper in Brittany France. With this, he delivers a creative twist to dishes he remembers from his youth. Each course is elegantly presented with a story of its roots and paired with wine by their Sommelier Mylene Gelin. This transportive dining experience earned him two stars from Michelin.

The evening begins in the lounge where you decide on your menu options while enjoying hors d'oeuvres and sipping on a glass of wine (top and bottom inset photos left).

In the dining room the culinary performance begins. Impeccable delivery. Beautiful dishes are served with the sights and smells to get the taste buds going.

Mushroom in Pastry Crust filled with a medley of more mushrooms and walnuts (left page).

Raw Scampi topped with caviar and scampi cream foam (inset left page).

Sausage and Buckwheat Pancake stuffed with potato, served with sour cream and apple cider (bottom right).

Butter Ice Cream in a crispy shell with gold flecks (below).

Tea does not come in a bag here. They bring the garden to your table and you pick the herbs of your choice (photo right).

SAINT-ÉMILION VILLAGE
Two-Star Restaurant
LA TABLE DE PLAISANCE

5 Place du Clocher
33330 Saint-Émilion, France

+33 (0)5 57 55 07 55
Contact@HostellerieDePlaisance.com

HostellerieDePlaisance.com

English, French

Open: February-December, Tuesday-Saturday
Lunch: 12:00pm-1:15pm • Dinner: 7:30pm-9:15pm
Reservations: Call, Email or Book On Their Website
Formal Attire is Required

VILLAGE CAVES

Get this: It is said that there are over 50 caves (wine shops) in this little village of Saint-Émilion. The population is less than 200 people. I heard this several times so I checked with Saint-Émilion Tourism and they confirmed it is true. Wow! That is one wine shop for every four people who live here!

Some wine shops are very fancy. Some have exclusive wines. Some carry the big names and others specialize in unique and small producers. What you can count on is a whole lot of variety. The wine shops are everywhere. I chose a few caves that I know well and are worth visiting. Have fun and fill up your wine luggage.

■ SAINT-ÉMILION VILLAGE
Wine Merchant and Boutique
MAISON DU VIN DE SAINT-ÉMILION

1 Place Pierre Meyrat • 33330 Saint-Émilion, France
+33 (0)5 57 55 50 55 • Open: Everyday, hours by season.

MaisonDuVinSaintEmilion.com

Located along side the grand Collegiate Church, "Maison du Vin" translates to "House of Wine" (of Saint-Émilion). They represent all of Saint-Émilion, including the four outlying Saint-Émilion appellations. This is the official syndicate of wineries of the Saint-Émilion AOC, making their wines available all in one place and at the same price as the wineries.

They carry the wines from 250 different châteaux, 450 different labels, and have a knowledgeable staff to help you find wines to fit your taste. They also have an aroma experience, an interactive video explaining the men and the cycle of the vine, and 35 photos illustrating the production of wine.

■ SAINT-ÉMILION VILLAGE
Underground 14th Century Wine Cave & Boutique
LES CORDELIERS

2 Bis Rue de la Porte Brunet • 33330 Saint-Émilion, France
+33 (0)5 57 24 42 13 • Contact@LesCordeliers.com

LesCordeliers.com • Open: Everyday, 11:00am-5:30pm

This was once a church built in 1383 by Franciscan monks, nicknamed Les Cordeliers. This monastery and underground winery was used for over 400 years. The underground space has been converted into a wine shop (truly a cave) and a winery making sparkling wines. Sparkling tastings too! Upstairs is a super modern shop (photo below) just inside the ancient limestone walls. They also have a wine bar, restaurant and picnics in their garden.

SAINT-ÉMILION VILLAGE
Wine Cave (Wine Merchant)
HM VINS

1 Place du Maréchal Leclerc • 33330 Saint-Émilion, France
+33 (0)5 57 25 29 08 • Sophie.Cassat3@gmail.com, Herve.Marec@gmail.com

HMVins-Shop.com • Open: Everyday, 10:00am-6:00pm

Located at the north main front entrance to the village (Rue Guadet), HM Vins has some great finds from around Saint-Émilion, including many from Château Haut-Sarpe and their sister properties. They also carry old vintages. And old vintages from the Médoc! Not a fancy place, just very nice people and good prices. That's what I like!

SAINT-ÉMILION VILLAGE
Cave (Wine Merchant)
THUNEVIN GIRONDINS

7 Rue des Girondins • 33330 Saint-Émilion, France
+33 (0)5 57 51 32 72 • Admin-Boutique@Thunevin.com
Open: Everyday, 10:00am-7:00pm

This is Château Valandraud's (Premier Grand Cru Classé) cave in the village. Their cave goes beyond just their own wines, as this cave specializes in Grand Crus from all of Bordeaux. Also, enjoy their garden (photo below) with a glass of wine and small bites in a relaxing environment in the village.

Tiny roads through the vineyards bordered by clos leading to the village of Saint-Émilion

BORDEAUX · LIBOURNAIS **FRONSAC AOC**

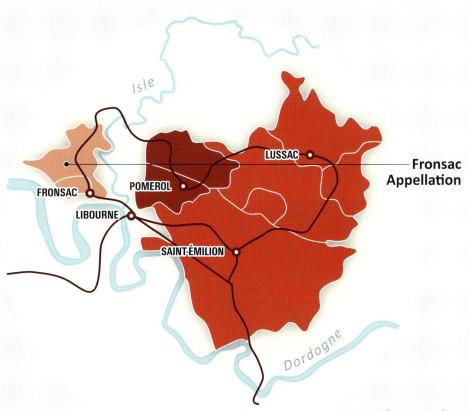

Left page: View from Château Gaby across the countryside to the Dordogne River

FRONSAC AND CANON FRONSAC

The Fronsac AOC is located five minutes northwest of the city of Libourne. It is north of the Dordogne River, and west of the Isle River and Pomerol.

Canon Fronsac AOC is a sub-appellation contained entirely within the Fronsac AOC. It is a small area on the south by the Dordogne River.

The Fronsac AOC only produces red wines. These red wines are primarily Merlot, which is almost 80% of what is planted. The other two grapes are Cabernet Franc (almost 15%) and Cabernet Sauvignon (roughly 5%). There are approximately 123 winemakers here.

The Fronsac terroir is excellent. It has a limestone plateau filled with special clay and chalk soils, ideally suited for growing extraordinary Merlot.

The 18th century was a peak period for Fronsac. The Dutch and the English discovered the quality wines of Fronsac, which created a huge demand and made the region famous. Their wines ended up being the most expensive across all of the Saint-Émilion, Pomerol and Fronsac regions.

At the end of the 19th century, the phylloxera crisis devastated Bordeaux's vineyards. The new fame of the region after recovering from the trauma went to Saint-Émilion and Pomerol. This meant Fronsac was unable to maintain their high price, yet they kept their high quality, resulting in a great value for us today.

Here are six of the Fronsac châteaux...
- Château de La Rivière, page 421
- Château de La Dauphine, page 425
- Château Gaby, page 427
- Château Boutinet, page 433
- Château Dalem, page 435
- Château Fontenil, page 437

THE MEANING **OF FRONSAC AOC**

Fronsac AOC (Appellation d'Origine Contrôlée) does not have any type of classification for their châteaux. Meaning, there are no Grand Crus or Grand Crus Classés as those found in Saint-Émilion, Graves, Sauternes, and the Médoc. The wine labels will simply say Fronsac on them for châteaux here. Some might add Grand Vin de Bordeaux, the marketing term that should indicate their best wine. There are no requirements though, and no rules to follow.

The Canon Fronsac sub-appellation is entirely located within the Fronsac appellation. They used to compete with each other as they both have excellent terroir and each thinks they have the better appellation. The two decided that it would be more fruitful to join forces and take on the other appellations, instead of competing against each other. Today, they work together under the same AOC requirements and criteria.

So, in order to put the Fronsac name on the wine label, there are a few conditions. Some obvious and some meant to maintain a level of quality. As an AOC, Fronsac must adhere to strict government stipulations.

• First, the obvious, is that the château must be physically located in Fronsac. This means specifically within the defined boundaries of delineated Fronsac AOC, which incorporates the municipalities of Fronsac, LaRivière, Saillans, Saint-Aignan, Saint-Germain-de-la-River, Saint-Michel-de-Fronsac and part of the territory of the town of Galgon.
• The vineyards, harvesting of their grapes, any elaboration, vinification, aging, and bottling, must all occur within the Fronsac AOC.
• The vineyards must have a minimum planting density of 5,000 vines per hectare.
• The spacing between vineyard rows cannot exceed two meters.
• The spacing between each vine at its foot on the same row cannot be less than .8 meters.
• The yields for harvests are fixed. For example, 2019 was fixed at 57 hectoliters per hectare.

The Fronsac AOC produces only red wines. Merlot is the primary grape for this Right Bank appellation. Vineyards are planted with 78% Merlot, 13% Cabernet Franc and 7% Cabernet Sauvignon and 2% Malbec. In 2019, there were 123 winemakers in Fronsac producing 5 million bottles per year.

TABLE OF WINES AND TOURISM

CHÂTEAUX **Fronsac AOC**	Classified	Number of Wines	Red Wine	White Wine	Rosé Wine	Sweet Wine	Wine Shop	Boutique	Accommodations	Restaurant	Food Options	Food & Wine Pairings	Tours	Castle Tours	Workshops	Activities	No Reservation Necessary	Tourism Award	Innovations
Chateau Boutinet	N/A	2	✓				✓	✓	✓	✓	✓	✓	2	✓	✓		✓		
Château Dalem	N/A	10	✓	✓	✓		✓	✓	✓		✓		1					✓	
Château de La Dauphine	N/A	2	✓		✓		✓	✓			✓	✓	10	✓	✓	✓	✓		
Château Fontenil	N/A	10	✓										1					✓	
Château Gaby	N/A	3	✓						✓		✓		1					✓	
Château de La Rivière	N/A	5	✓	✓	✓		✓	✓		✓	✓	✓	1	✓			✓		

Below: Barrels of wine aging in the caves of Château de La Rivière
Above left: A 1942 vintage bottle found in the Château de La Rivière caves
Below left: Paintings by Arnaud Roux-Oulié hanging in his cellar of Château Carlmagnus

LIBOURNAIS FRONSAC
Winery (Château) & B&B
CHÂTEAU DE LA RIVIÈRE

Extensive vines, forest, caves, and cellars makes this the largest property in Fronsac.

Winner: Best Of Wine Tourism

Rue de Goffre
33126 La Rivière, Fronsac, France

+33 (0)5 57 55 56 56
Info@Chateau-De-La-Riviere.com

Chateau-De-La-Riviere.com

English, French, Chinese

Open: All Year
May-October, Monday-Saturday
November-April, Monday-Friday
By Appointment Only
Call, Email or Book On Their Website

CASTLE ON THE HILL

Château de La Rivière is an impressive place to visit. Upon arrival, you will be winding through 1.4 km of driveway, flanked with vineyards and forests to the top of the hill. And when you get there, you will be standing in front of a castle that is even more impressive up close.

Being large has many advantages for them. They have diverse terroir: hilltop limestone, slopes of clay (so important to Merlot), and sand and gravel at the foot. We have learned that diversity of soil leads to complex aromas and flavors of great wines. And the wines here are excellent.

Having a forest is also advantageous. Water makes the vines lazy. Here, the forest competes with the vines as it wants to drink lots of water. So the vines struggle, and struggling vines produce better grapes.

Underground is expansive too. Thanks to the limestone blocks carved out for their huge castle, they have 20 hectares of caves and eight hectares of cellars; perfect humidity and temperature for the wine. 100% humidity underground means the oak does not dry and topping off wine is unnecessary.

This cave system is 25km of tunnels and rooms, with a natural spring and two separate sections. This was invaluable during WWII when the Germans took over the castle and thought there was only one cave system. They stayed away from the entrance to the other section of the cave because it looked like a tomb. This allowed the French Resistance to hideout safely.

Being very close to the Dordogne River, the springs and forest all help to deter frost. This was proven in 2017 when the areas were hit hard with frost and many of the châteaux lost most, if not all, of their crops. Château de La Rivière only suffered a 23% impact. And the juice I tasted from the 2017 harvest was extraordinary. Good 2017s are hard to find and this one deserves your attention.

There is a full diversity of grape varieties here. Predominantly Merlot (84%), Cabernet Sauvignon (8%), Cabernet Franc (6%) and even a little Malbec (2%). And now two hectares of Sauvignon Blanc and Sauvignon Gris for a very delicious white wine. They produce a rosé as well.

Xavier Buffo, General Manager and Winemaker, showed me his favorite vineyard, saying these vines are wise and mature. They share his same birth year of 1972.

Collection of Wines
Château de La Rivière
(First Label - AOC Fronsac)

Aria
(AOC Fronsac)

Les Sources de Château de La Rivière
(Second Wine - AOC Fronsac)

Le Blanc de Château de La Rivière
(AOC Bordeaux Blanc)

Le Rosé de Château de La Rivière
(AOC Bordeaux Rosé)

ROMANTIC HISTORIC CASTLE

This massive and impressive 13th century castle can be yours for the night. A room, or the entire castle of five rooms. Includes a hot breakfast in the morning.

This ancient castle was initially two stories. In the 16th century, it was expanded to what you see today, adding the third and fourth floors, and with the Loire Renaissance era tile turrets. All the rooms are beautiful and luxurious (photo left) with period furnishings. Bathrooms are stunning as well (below).

All visitors (and château guests) get to tour the extensive caves and taste their wines. They also offer unique dining options. For example, in the cave is a knights stone table (10 meters long) with 32 stone seats. They do picnics in their vineyards. Lunches and dinners in their Armories room. And poolside cocktails.

LIBOURNAIS **FRONSAC**
Winery (Château) & B&B
CHÂTEAU DE LA RIVIÈRE

Winner: Best Of Wine Tourism

+33 (0)5 57 55 56 51

Chateau-De-La-Riviere.com

Open: All Year, Everyday
Reservations: Call or Book On Their Website

LIBOURNAIS **FRONSAC**

Winery (Château)
CHÂTEAU DE LA DAUPHINE

Global Winner: Best Of Wine Tourism

5 Rue Poitevine
33126 Fronsac, France

+33 (0)5 57 74 06 61
Contact@Chateau-Dauphine.com

Chateau-Dauphine.com

English, French, Spanish

Open: All Year
*Spring-Summer, Monday-Saturday
Fall-Winter, Monday-Friday
By Appointment Only
Reservations Available On Their Website*

The Heritage Tour here won the 2020 Global Award for the Best of Wine Tourism.

TEN INTERESTING TOURS

In 2012, Château de La Dauphine's new owners made two very important hires: Michel Rolland and Marion Merker. This has turned out to be a huge success for them. And us!

We know the world-renowned talents of Michel Rolland. He has elevated the quality of the wines here in many ways. Just to start, I was surprisingly impressed with their rosé. Yes rosé! Not leftover grapes; these are choice grapes deliberately suited for this wine. And if the grapes do not meet their standards, they simply don't make the wine. Pressed immediately. Ever so elegant.

Further, their flagship wine, Château de La Dauphine, is getting the attention of reviewers. I looked at top name reviewers and saw three 91 points, one 90 points and one 93 points for their 2016 vintage. And then I tasted. Wow! It is deep purple, exotic, with ripe fruits, which I love. And the super great price makes me even happier.

Marion Merker was hired as Wine Tourism Manager and created a variety of visitor programs, such as tours, workshops and lunches. So far, her original programs have won four gold medals for the *Best Of Bordeaux Wine Tourism*, making Dauphine the only château in all of Bordeaux to accomplish this success.

Her **Heritage Tour** won the ultimate honor for her innovative efforts: *2020 Global Winner International Award*. This award was chosen out of eight wine regions in the world. The Heritage Tour involves the legendary Citroën 2CV to discover the historical, cultural and gastronomic elements of the estate, including a hilltop tasting with scrumptious foods and a panoramic view. Definitely a winner!

You must come, there is so much more to enjoy...
• **Classic Tour**. Park, vineyard, winery, tasting
• **Luxury Tour**. Classic + tour the 18th century castle
• **Tasting Tour**. Classic + olfactory (aroma)workshop
• **Green Tour**. Biodynamic environmental initiatives
• **Yummy Trilogy Tour**. Classic + 3 wines and 3 foods
• **Tour & Picnic with Panoramic View**. Classic + a picnic basket of foods and wine to enjoy hilltop
• **Tour & Summer Lunch**. Classic + lunch and wine next to the property's beautiful infinity pool
• **Tour & Casual Lunch**. Classic + a three-course barbecue lunch (over vine cuttings) in the château
• **Tour and Gourmet Dining**. Classic + elegant and gourmet 4-course lunch in the château with aperitif and 3 wines

Collection of Wines
Château de La Dauphine
(First Label - AOC Fronsac)

Les Delphis de La Dauphine
(Second Wine - AOC Fronsac)

Château de La Dauphine Rosé
(AOC Bordeaux)

LIBOURNAIS **FRONSAC**

Winery (Château) & B&B
CHÂTEAU GABY

The ultimate view of the countryside from a most engaging château with exquisite wines.

Lieu Dit
33126 Fronsac, France

+33 (0)5 57 51 24 97
Contact@ChateauGaby.com

ChateauGaby.com

English, French

Open: All Year
By Appointment Only
Email for An Appointment
Reservations Available On Their Website

MAGICAL ESTATE

What captured my attention most here? The château for sure. And the inside is very impressive. The view is the most spectacular you could find anywhere. The innovative farming is unlike anything I have seen elsewhere. The 2015 vintage blew me away. Great price too. Where does one begin?

Let's begin with the greeting. The Marketing Director hands me three bottles of wine to taste: 2015, 2010 and 2006. An excellent vertical to get a great feel for the wines. Smart. And smarter than you think. Regularly, wineries fail to give me any wine at all. I am a journalist writing about wine and wineries, and the wine is left out. Kind of silly don't you think? These people at Château Gaby are on-the-ball smart.

I am sure she thought I would open all three bottles and do a tasting there. Nope. I took them across the globe to Fiji where I nestled into a remote part of the island to write this book. We took our time with the wines and paired them with different types of dishes. This was a better environment to think about their wines. And my office view was just as spectacular as their view.

The 2015 rocks my boat. Full of fresh rich fruits. I love a bold wine that holds its fruit. The 2010 is a serious wine from a great vintage. After the third day of the '10, it had opened-up into a beautiful wine. The 2006 was truly ready for the experience. Fourteen years of aging and it was showing very well. Deep black fruits, although I preferred the fruit of the '10. The pairing was perfect with lamb. You know the moment when the food makes you want more wine and the wine makes you want more food? This was that beautiful moment.

I have been reading about the Gaby Cuvée and I was very intrigued. The vertical I tasted was the Château Gaby first wine. The Gaby Cuvée might be even better, being not a second wine. I like that the blend and the grapes are from important choice vineyards on their property.

Let's go to the second greeting. This time from the man who makes it all happen at Chateau Gaby, Damien Landouar. For two decades he has been in charge of creating the great wines here and is always thinking of how to make things better. He moved to organic farming and became certified in 2012. It is much more than organic farming to him though, he calls it "biologic" rather than biodynamic.

Collection of Wines
Château Gaby
(First Label - AOC Fronsac)

Gaby Cuvée
(Second Wine - AOC Fronsac)

Princess Gaby
(Third Wine - AOC Fronsac)

LIBOURNAIS FRONSAC
Winery (Château) & B&B
CHÂTEAU GABY

Biologic. Yes he is a logical guy. He does some very unusual things; however, they are logically based in science. Bio-science! Life sciences for his living vineyards.

Imagine an evening, as I experienced, peacefully drinking a glass of wine (Gaby of course). All of a sudden, there is beautiful music playing, coming from the hills. It's after dinner and it's dark out. Must be Saturday evening church service.

The music is loud and echoes throughout the countryside as though it was a calling for attendance. It goes on for about an hour. Then Sunday morning, the same thing. Very loud music playing to the community for about an hour. An hour's service again I imagined.

So here I was, at Château Gaby, enjoying such a wonderful château (you really must stay there). Thinking, this is quite the church. I had to ask about it. Well, Damian, their innovative oenologist, just looks at me and smiles... and then asks me how do I feel? He goes on to tell me that he is playing the music. Damian is playing the music?!

Loud speakers are placed throughout the vineyards playing very specific music that is designed to increase the immune systems of the vines. Really? It is science, he says. Everything is made up of energy.

True. We are not matter – we are energy. And so are the vines. The vibrations are designed to increase the immune system of the vines during harvest time when the moisture of Bordeaux gets intense and creates fungus, mold and diseases in the vineyards. Just like us, if we have a strong immune system, we can fight off anything. The vines are the same way.

It gets better. During the winter, he plays music to help them sleep during their dormancy. We know about that, the right kind of music helps us sleep as well. In the spring, he plays new music for a new day as the vines blossom. Summer requires different music. All are designed for the optimum health of the vines. Healthy vines produce healthy grapes (photo above). The better the grapes, the better the winemaker can make excellent wine. And that is exactly what Damian does – make excellent wine (winery photo left page).

I could go on and on about Damian's innovative and natural approaches. No herbicides. No pesticides. Simply not needed anymore. He also uses horses to plow the vineyards. Naturally. Could we say that beautiful horses make for happy grapes?

Back to the wine. It's a few days later. The wine has been decanting in the bottles. I have been tasting and pairing with food every day. Pairing with foods. I love the evolution of wine through multiple days. Through just an evening as well. In the end, I score the 2015 as my favorite, followed by the 2010. These were great years of course, and showed me just how excellent Fronsac wines stand strong compared to the other Right Bank wine regions.

And I cannot stop thinking about the music for a healthy immune system and how that will benefit us humans as well. I want some. And I need to do research now. If anyone knows more, please write me. I am intrigued. And ready.

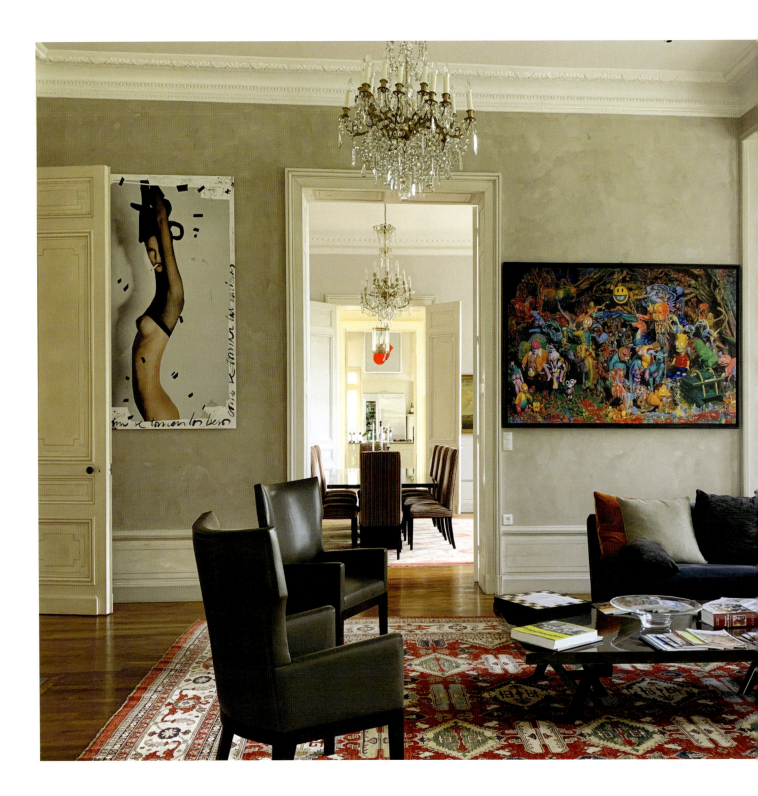

ROMANTIC MANSION

LIBOURNAIS **FRONSAC**
Winery (Château) & B&B
CHÂTEAU GABY

+33 (0)5 57 51 24 97
Contact@ChateauGaby.com

ChateauGaby.com

Open: All Year

Reservations:
Email or Write Them On Their Website

You see the castle photos. It is their beautiful home they share. A seven bedroom mansion, with a grand living room, library, lounge, formal dining room, breakfast room, pool table, terrace, swimming pool, tennis court, and park.

It is the furnishings that does it for me. Super comfortable furniture throughout the house. There is also plenty of entertainment for everyone: videos, books, board games, billiards, and of course there is wine.

I love the modern art mixed with antiques. As a photographer I admired the tastefully seductive large art hanging on the walls.

Comes with breakfast. They can also create meals for you as well, based on request.

LIBOURNAIS FRONSAC
Winery (Château)
CHÂTEAU BOUTINET

Winner: Best Of Wine Tourism

1436 Route des Palombes
33141 Villegouge, France

+33 (0)6 85 79 56 96
ChateauBoutinet@Orange.fr

ChateauBoutinet.fr

English, French, Spanish

*Open: All Year, Sunday-Friday
By Appointment Only
Book On Their Website*

B eautiful people with a beautiful property.

WALK, WINE & DINE

Boutinet means beautiful. Okay, so it doesn't. For me though, it is what I read and think each time I see the name. Maybe because it speaks to the heart of the owners of Château Boutinet, Nathalie and Jérôme Escuredo.

They live there and love the land. They plant legumes, herbs and flowers in their vineyards. They work the land organically. Nathalie deliberately took training in herbal medicine to apply it to the vineyards. It is a healthy place for them and their animals. The vines are stronger without chemicals, and they thrive with the love they receive.

Their 18th century castle has fallen into ruins, so they built a yurt, a round building made from almost 100% natural and recycled materials. Sitting in this calm loving vibe, tasting their wines and eating their foods is a relaxing experience.

They have created a happy place where people, plants and animals live in loving harmony. Just as it should be. And when you arrive, they will bring you into the fold of this happy environment.

Jérôme is an oenologist and a chef, and makes delicious foods to pair with his wines. Isn't that how it is supposed to be? Well, they get the idea and care about the experience of their guests.

A visit here is a fascinating exploration into nature, a walk that takes you through forests and many vineyards. Nathalie is a wonderful conversationalist and educator (instructor at the wine school L'Ecole du Vins de Bordeaux). Before you drink their fresh lively wines and eat some well-paired delights, you will be educated with lots of fun and humor, while witnessing life at a happy, healthy farm.

They are located on a limestone hill planted with 100% Merlot. All three of their wines are 100% Merlot. A first label from their 30-year-old vines. A second wine from the young vines. And a fresh Clairet wine, a nice light aperitif. They are located just outside the Fronsac AOC, a Bordeaux AOC, just a short drive northwest. Definitely worth the visit. You will be happy you visited this engaging couple.

Collection of Wines
Château Boutinet
(First Label - AOC Fronsac)

Thalie de Boutinet
(Second Wine - No New Oak Fruitier Wine)

Clairet de Boutinet
(A Light Clairet Style Wine)

LIBOURNAIS **FRONSAC**
Winery (Château)
CHÂTEAU DALEM

33141 Saillans, Fronsac, France

+33 (0)5 57 84 34 18
Contact@ChateauDalem.com

ChateauDalem.com

English, French

Open: All Year, Monday-Friday
Reservations Required
Call, Email or Book On Their Website

Quality you can count on with a new winery and a smart woman in charge.

EVER SO BEAUTIFUL

I like this place and the woman who runs it. Brigitte Rullier-Loussert has taken over the estate from her father and has made a huge difference in the quality and consistency of the wines here.

She just finished a two-year construction project building a brand new modern winery. I was there when it was finished in August 2019, just in time for harvest. Harvest, as you can see below, goes through an extensive and detailed sorting process to extract only the very best grapes.

Once in the winery, she uses both traditional equipment from the old winery, alongside new modern equipment of the new winery. In the past, you may know their wines to be inconsistent. Not now. Today, Brigitte has developed a reputation for consistency and high quality. The reviewers are scoring her wines with high marks, even 93s.

Her vineyards are on top of the limestone plateau as well as the sloping terrain. She gets both terroirs. She has focused on leaf and soil analysis to better understand what she has in order to optimize very high quality in the grapes.

Château Dalem is in a little village in the north of Fronsac, neighboring Château Fontenil, Dany and Michel Rolland's estate. The elevation is much higher on top of the plateau here.

Dalem's property is beautiful. She has built a gazebo at the end of the plateau that overlooks the dramatic slopes and across the Isle River with a great view of Pomerol. In the distance you can see Saint-Émilion as well. The new winery has a large patio on its roof, so perfect for tasting her wines. The views are amazing. Or grab a glass of wine and enjoy the afternoon sitting in the gazebo.

Collection of Wines
Château Dalem
(First Label - AOC Fronsac)

Tentation de Dalem
(Second Wine - AOC Fronsac)

Château de La Huste
(AOC - AOC Fronsac)

Château La Longua
(Blend of Dalem & Huste)

LIBOURNAIS FRONSAC
Winery (Château)
CHÂTEAU FONTENIL

Cardeneau Nord
33141 Saillans, Fronsac, France

+33 (0)5 57 51 52 43
Contact@RollandCollection.com

RollandCollection.com

English, French

Not Open To The Public; However...
They will receive small groups, well informed
wine connoisseurs, professionals or customers
Write them at the email address above

Through the ups and downs they have created a highly respected winemaking phenomenon.

A SYMPHONY OF WINEMAKING

When I walked in and saw the piano, I couldn't help see the relationship between beautiful music and beautiful wine. The elegance in the decor spoke loudly to me about the Rolland's sensitivity to quality. Wine, as is music, is a work of art.

So it struck me, as I waited for Dany Rolland in her den (above), that each note in the winemaking process was a combination of simultaneous and creative decisions that produce the harmony we love so much in wine – and music. I could not wait to meet the important partner of the world's most esteemed oenologist consultant.

She was in medical school on a specific path until her pharmacist friends studying oenology lured her attention to wine. And Michel. She fell in love with both and decided to follow the same path as Michel. They set out on a journey together; getting married just after receiving their oenology degrees.

It really is a beautiful story about this young couple. Wanting to take a stab at a private viticultural endeavor, they purchased a small seven-hectare vineyard in 1986. Four years later, they acquired and moved into the adjacent home, which was so dilapidated the roof was falling in.

During the same time period, Michel was invited to Napa Valley, which eventually launched his highly-respected, world-renowned, consulting career. This ultimately took him to more than a dozen countries on four continents, consulting with more than 150 client wineries.

While Michel would travel and consult, Dany stayed home and produced their special estate wine, managed their laboratory, their properties and an ever growing number of projects. They are a dynamic team.

Walking around the estate with Dany, I watched how she looked at things. We share a photographic eye, capturing creative angles and framing. I could see her thoughtfulness which transcends into her winemaking.

She is also quite tactile. Always observing and touching. She calls her fermentation room the nursery (photo left page). All of their wines are vinified in wood. She walked softly around her nursery gently touching her babies. You could feel her spirit of love and tenderness towards the wine.

Collection of Wines
Château Fontenil
(First Label - AOC Fronsac)

Filet Rouge
(Second Wine - AOC Fronsac)

Le Défi de Fontenil
(Wine of France)

LIBOURNAIS **FRONSAC**
Winery (Château)
CHÂTEAU FONTENIL

Dany and Michel Rolland in their newly acquired vineyards at Château Fontenil in 1986.

When they rebuilt the winery at Château Fontenil, they used the oak staves from the antique vats as material for making all the windows and doors, and their frames. The results are magnificent works of art (photo left page with Dany Rolland), still looking new and beautiful 30 years later. Plus, the tannins continue to seep out of the oak, reminding them ever so much of the life cycle of wine in their presence.

Then came **THE 1999 EXPERIMENT.**

The story continues with the creativity and inventiveness of Michel and Dany. This was a most fascinating story. I was at the edge of my chair. Absorbed with what Dany was telling me. Enjoying a nice glass of her wine. She wanted to tell me about another wine and its birth.

What do you do when rain comes hard, and comes at the wrong time? This is what happened in 1999 when they had about 150 mm of rain (5.9 inches) arrive 20 days before harvest. This could be disastrous. And the reason vintages vary in Bordeaux, sometime rather dramatically, is because of weather like this.

The Rollands got very clever. They put plastic sheets down in between the rows of vines to keep the water from hitting the ground and absorbing into the soil. Instead, the rainwater ran off the property. That was brilliant. And it worked, too.

They had an excellent harvest that year. While 1999 may not be a good year in Bordeaux for most châteaux, it was a great year for Michel and Dany. They defined this by saying, "The grapes were in perfect sanitary condition and considerably sweeter with a better extractability of the anthocyanins and furthermore had increased maturity of the pips."

This was deserving of a full-on experiment over several years. They chose two specific parcels that had steep slopes (1.6 hectares) for a three-year experiment with strictly Merlot grapes. Everything would depend on weather as to how the plastic would be used. In 2000, the plastic was installed later because they wanted to allow the soil to dry out from July rains. It was August 23rd when they laid out the plastic again, and two days later, they received an official letter from the INAO (The National Institute of Controlled Appellations) ordering them to remove the plastic immediately. They went on to threaten them that if they did not comply, their wine would be declassified to just "table wine."

No official explanation. No technical analysis or study. Not even a visit to the property or a discussion. Just bureaucrats wanting people to follow their rules instead of applying any intelligence or common sence to the situation.

Their professional response was that it would be better to continue the experiment to its end; the technical results needed to be known and exploitable based on scientific methodology.

They took this defiant risk knowing they would not be able to identify their wine as Fonsac AOC or even as a Wine of Bordeaux. They could only say it was a Wine of France. You have to love their tenacity, their obstinance, and their pursuit of greatness in face of extreme adversity and bureaucracy.

They went on to produce 8,000 bottles of table wine that year. They launched a new brand: Le Défi de Fontenil. The results are impressive. You must try it. At least buy a bottle to support the cause. They have produced the wine for several years, and do not even give it a vintage year.

Let's get to the tasting of Château Fontenil. She poured three excellent vintages. 2005, 2010, and 2015. These are stellar years in Bordeaux! How in the world do I evaluate three superior vintages, of already remarkable wines, from two exceptional winemakers? I am not even going to try.

I think you know by now that I am a huge fan of the 2015 vintage here in Fronsac and the rest of the Right Bank. And the Château Fontenil is exactly what makes me love this vintage. Rich nose. Great acidity. Big bold fruit in the mouth. I am happy. Very happy. The other two vintages revealed the great ageability of their wines. I loved them all.

She opened two Le Défi de Fontenil wines, a 2009 and a 2014. So you might ask, how did I know the vintage if these are vintageless wines? Well, she told me. Plus, there is a secret code on the back label in the lot number.

In conclusion, Michel and Dany are the Stradivarius of the wine world. They are creating a fine-tuned symphony of winemaking. I am so happy to know them.

Exploring Wine Regions **Bordeaux** | 439

DOWNTOWN FRONSAC

Fronsac is a very small town with a population of about 1,000 people and just a fraction of that for the village. The village shares the same name and is located in the Fronsac wine region. Canon Fronsac is at the south of the appellation near the river and located in the Fronsac AOC.

Not much in the village, except the **Maison des Vins de Fronsac** and **Château de La Dauphine**, both of which are worth visiting.

What I have learned most about this wine region is that **Fronsac is a Secret Gem**. They have similar terroir as Saint-Émilion, complete with a limestone plateau as well as clay, gravel and slopes for similar diversity. Wines here receive high scores, high praise and are sold at great prices. It is a secret. Go buy their wine and don't tell too many people.

Lake View at Chez Carles

■ LIBOURNAIS FRONSAC DOWNTOWN
Wine Merchant and Tourism Office
MAISON DES VINS DE FRONSAC (AND TOURISM)

2 Rue du Tertre • 33126 Fronsac, France
+33 (0)5 57 51 80 51 • Info@Vins-Fronsac.com

Vins-Fronsac.com

"Maison des Vins" translates to "House of Wines." This is the syndicate of wineries of the Fronsac appellation, making their wines available all in one place. Located in the village, they have 110 vintages for sale from the Fronsac châteaux. No markup, sold at the winery's price.

It is also a Tourism Office for Fronsac where you can get some basic château and restaurant information. Open Monday through Saturday.

■ LIBOURNAIS FRONSAC
AN EVENING OF WINEMAKERS

At the pleasure of Damien Landouar, Château Gaby's Winemaker and General Manager, a small group of winemakers from around Fronsac were invited for an evening of fun, laughter, food, and some serious wine drinking at Château Gaby. Everyone brought at a bottle of their own favorite wine. Some could not decide and brought two bottles!

The group was quite diverse. One was new to winemaking and another was from multiple generations with estates passed down through the family. A husband/wife team. A new arrival to Fronsac. Ages and styles varied. Creativity was as unique as each of them. One thing was common, they were all individuals, not companies, living on their properties, making wine themselves, the way they want to make wine. Fronsac châteaux are primarily family-owned and run, a personal touch to winemaking. We talked about each wine as we tasted. Each special. I loved the unique flavors of each person's techniques. I share the labels below for you to discover.

This evening had an especially magical moment for me because of foie gras. Cheers to Château Gaby's delicious catering. It was fresh and grilled to perfection. The best tasting foie gras I have ever enjoyed. Not easy to find cooked this way. I am always searching.

LIBOURNAIS FRONSAC
LUNCH WITH FRONSAC WINEMAKERS

Four winemakers showed up to lunch at Chez Carles at the invitation of Pierre Rebaud, Château de La Rivière's Marketing & Communication Manager. They all brought a bottle. All were individual château owners living on their properties making their special version of Fronsac wine. We talked about each wine as we tasted the scrumptious foods of Chez Carles.
- 2018 Le Lion de La Rivière. Fresh and fruity, a nice way to begin the afternoon
- 2016 Château Mayne-Vieil. 100% Merlot, young, very fresh, with lots of fruit
- 2010 Château Tessendey. Elegant, soft tannins, good fruit, just enough oak
- 2010 Château Clos de Roy. Lots of fruit, blackberry and spice, very high alcohol
- The "?" mystery bottle. Exposed inside the decanter for all of us to experience. This was an extraordinary bottle of wine. A 2010 Château de la Rivière Aria – they only make this wine in excellent years (2010 was a stellar year) and represents the excellence of Fronsac wines. I went to the winery to buy a bottle the next day.

LIBOURNAIS FRONSAC
Restaurant
CHEZ CARLES MAÎTRE RESTAURATEUR

1 Ave Charles de Gaulle
33240 Saint-Germain de la Rivière, Fronsac, France
+33 (0)5 57 84 44 50 • Contact@Chez-Carles.com
Lunch & Dinner: Tuesday-Friday, 10:00am-3:30pm & 6:45pm-11:30pm
Dinner: Saturday & Sunday, 6:45pm-12:00am

Eat where the winemakers hang out. Notice in the left photo, on the very back wall on the right side... lockers. Wine lockers! This restaurant caters to the Fronsac châteaux. They built wine lockers for local winemakers to keep their wine and to drink with their friends and clients over lunch or dinner. This is the place to mingle with the people who make Fronsac, Fronsac.

Located lakeside in the southern part of Fronsac, very near Château de La Rivière. Outdoor and indoor dining. Long hours here for when you get hungry. Notice the expansive fireplace in the photo. It's the kitchen. Tender steaks grilled over wood embers. The best. Asado! The food here is great. And look at that pineapple dessert. Beautiful, and ever so delicious.

BORDEAUX · LIBOURNAIS **POMEROL AOC**

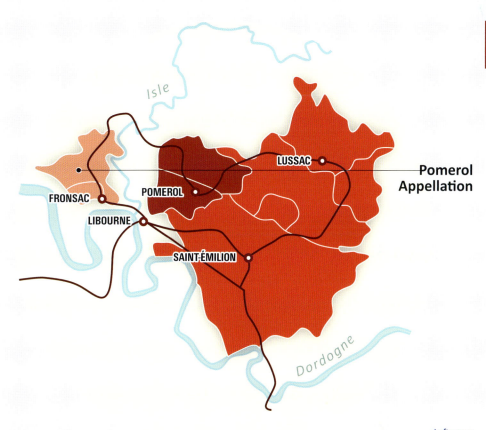

Left page:
The late afternoon sun over the vineyards of Clos René

POMEROL AOC

The Pomerol AOC is located just north of Libourne by a few minutes. It is also north of the Dordogne River; however, it lies between Saint-Émilion and Fronsac. Saint-Émilion is adjacent to the east. Fronsac is to the west and separated by the Isle River.

While Fronsac and Saint-Émilion are known for their limestone plateaus, the terroir of Pomerol is totally different. No limestone at all! This is the land of a very special clay – blue clay. And Merlot loves it!

The way I have organized the châteaux is by beginning at the center of the blue clay mound and working outwards. Château Pétrus is known for being at the top center of this blue clay, and they charge a very pretty penny for it. **Château La Fleur-Pétrus** is also on top of this blue clay mound as their name properly suggests, although their wines are 10% of the cost.

And **Château Gazin** also shares the center of the blue clay and in years past, Pétrus has purchased vineyards from Gazin for their blue clay location. And a little further down the blue clay mound is **Château Beauregard**. Both Gazin and Beauregard wines benefit from the blue clay terroir and deliver excellent wines at even better prices.

All in all, Pomerol AOC produces a Merlot-based wine that I find to be highly attractive to my palate. I hope you explore this region with me.
Here are five Fronsac châteaux...
- Château La Fleur-Pétrus, page 447
- Château Gazin, page 449
- Château Beauregard, page 451
- Château de Sales, page 455
- Château du Tailhas, page 457

AOC POMEROL

Pomerol AOC (Appellation d'Origine Contrôlée) does not have any type of classification or wine ranking for their châteaux. Meaning, there are no Grand Crus or Grand Crus Classés as found in Saint-Émilion, Graves, Sauternes, and the Médoc. The wine labels will simply say Pomerol on them. Some might add Grand Vin de Bordeaux, the marketing term that should indicate their best wine. There are no requirements or rules to this delineation.

The Wine and Agricultural Trade Association of Pomerol was established in 1900. One of their key missions was to prevent the châteaux in the neighboring communes from putting the name Pomerol on their bottles. Pomerol knew they had special terroir and wanted such distinction. One big distinction is their blue clay plateau, which Fronsac and Saint-Émilion do not share. The blue clay is actually blue-green in color (see photo right).

To further establish this distinction, the association defined the boundaries of Pomerol to establish an official AOC, which guarantees the authenticity of the wines in the marketplace. A decree was formalized 1935 by the French Institute of Appellations of Origin (INAO), officially establishing the Pomerol AOC in 1936. And they further updated to stricter rules in 2014.

Now it is easy for Pomerol to protect its name with precise boundaries for its appellation, along with rules and regulations to maintain high-quality wines within, and to further enhance the grand reputation of this unique appellation. To put the Pomerol name on the wine label, these are the requirements:

• First, the obvious, is that the château must be physically located in Pomerol. This means specifically within the defined boundaries of the Pomerol AOC.
• The vineyards, harvesting of their grapes, any elaboration, vinification, aging, and bottling must all occur within the Pomerol AOC.
• The vineyards must have a minimum planting density of 5,500 vines per hectare.
• The spacing between vineyard rows cannot exceed two meters.
• The spacing between each vine at its foot on the same row cannot be less than .8 meters.
• Only three types of pruning are permitted.
• The maximum yield for harvests is 49 hectoliters per hectare.
• Grapes must have sufficient sugar levels prior to harvest, with alcohol exceeding 11.5%.
• Both alcoholic and malolactic fermentations must finish with no residual sugars.
• There are also rules about cellar equipment and quantity of vats.
• Prior to bottling, a blind tasting is conducted by a jury to ensure Pomerol quality standards.
• Only red wine may be produced in the Pomerol AOC, and only from Merlot, Cabernet Franc, Cabernet Sauvignon, Malbec, and Petit Verdot grapes. Merlot accounts for 80% of the vines in Pomerol (Merlot loves the clay here). In the blends, Merlot can reach as high as 95% in content. Cabernet Franc is 15% of the vineyards and usually accounts for the balance of the blends. Only a little bit of Malbec and Cabernet Sauvignon are used here. While Petit Verdot is permitted, it is not planted.

Pomerol estates are small and Pomerol itself is the smallest appellation in Bordeaux. Pomerol is one seventh the size of its neighbor Saint-Émilion. The average estate in Pomerol has only six hectares. And while you think that is tiny, what is super interesting is that 22 of the estates in Pomerol are smaller than one single hectare. Here is the breakdown.

Size of the Estates	Number of Estates
Less than 1 hectare	22
Between 1 and 2 hectares	19
Between 2 and 5 hectares	39
Between 5 and 10 hectares	32
Between 10 and 15 hectares	13
Larger than 15 hectares	11

TABLE OF WINES AND TOURISM

CHÂTEAUX Pomerol AOC	Classified	Number of Wines	Red Wine	White Wine	Rosé Wine	Sweet Wine	Wine Shop	Boutique	Accommodations	Restaurant	Food Options	Food & Wine Pairings	Tours	Castle Tours	Workshops	Activities	No Reservation Necessary	Tourism Award	Innovations
Chateau Beauregard	N/A	3	✓				✓	✓		✓		✓	2				✓		
Château La Fleur-Pétrus	N/A	1	✓										1						
Château Gazin	N/A	2	✓				✓			✓			1						
Château du Sales	N/A	2	✓					✓			✓		1					✓	
Château de Tailhas	N/A	1	✓					✓			✓		1						

CHÂTEAUX Special Additions	Classified	Number of Wines	Red Wine	White Wine	Rosé Wine	Sweet Wine	Wine Shop	Boutique	Accommodations	Restaurant	Food Options	Food & Wine Pairings	Tours	Castle Tours	Workshops	Activities	No Reservation Necessary	Tourism Award	Innovations
Chateau de Bonhoste	N/A	13	✓	✓	✓	✓	✓	✓	✓				1				✓	✓	✓
Château de Reignac	N/A	4	✓	✓			✓	✓		✓			6		✓		✓	✓	
Rémy Martin Cognac	N/A	1					✓	✓		✓	✓		13	✓	✓	✓			

The historic beauty of Château Beauregard's original buildings

LIBOURNAIS POMEROL
Winery (Château)
CHÂTEAU LA FLEUR-PÉTRUS

7 Rue de Tropchaud
33500 Pomerol, France

+33 (0)5 57 51 78 96
Info@JPMoueix.com

Moueix.com

English, French

Open: All Year, Monday-Friday
Email Them To Make An Appointment

Located between Pétrus and Lafleur, Château La Fleur-Pétrus is perched on a stellar location.

TOP OF THE BLUE CLAY MOUND

As location would have it, Château La Fleur-Pétrus is on the perfect terroir between two renowned properties, Lafleur and Pétrus. This is how the combination created their name in the 18th century. They are at the heart of the blue clay.

Jean-Pierre Moueix first started the Moueix company in 1937 as a wine merchant known for selling the top wines of Bordeaux and became the largest wine merchant on the Right Bank. It was not until 1950 that Jean-Pierre began acquiring châteaux. The first being Château La Fleur-Pétrus, followed by Château Pétrus. Now he has 10 estates!

His son Christian Moueix joined the company in 1970 and became directly involved with the management of the vineyards, as he believes that the quality of the wine starts with the quality of the vineyards. And vineyard management is a key component to quality vines. His close relationship with the viticulture team has led him to never miss a harvest lunch with them in 50 years.

Christian is a hands-on guy who works side-by-side with his team. His team is very important to him. He even hired a famous architect to build them a dining hall for his 250 workers. The year-round vine workers prepare the lunches (homestyle and delicious, I might add), and everyone eats, drinks, sings, dances, plays cards, etc. together. Some have been harvesting for Moueix for over 20 years.

The perfection and details in the vineyard are amazing. They don't do each process as a blanket event. They are precise. For example, leaf thinning is done a little at a time as the weather unfolds. Harvest is not by vineyard or plot ripeness. They harvest row by row, handpicking the grapes at optimal ripeness. Sometimes, they harvest multiple times per row to obtain the perfect berries for the winery. Doesn't it remind you of the multiple harvests per row in Sauternes? This is precision quality!

When you taste the wine, you can reflect on this precision quality in your mouth. This wine is that big, bold, with lots of fruit, kind of wine I love. They are methodical in the winery as well, using a maximum of 50% new oak, being ever so careful to keep the beautiful fruits alive in their wine. No spit bucket here – every last sip is savored.

While having lunch with Christian, his wife and son (and enjoying every bite), I came to appreciate their admirable passion and dedication to excellence.

Collection of Wines
Château La Fleur Pétrus
(First Label - AOC Pomerol)

DISTRIBUTORS OF POMEROL BRANDS
Château Certan de May, Croix de Certan,
Château Bourgneuf, L'Hospitalet de Gazin,
Château Plince, Château Moulinet-Lasserre,
Château Chantalouette

DISTRIBUTORS OF LALANDE-DE-POMEROL BRANDS
Château de Bel-Air, Château La Mission,
Château Les Vieux Ormes

LIBOURNAIS **POMEROL**
Winery (Château)
CHÂTEAU GAZIN

1 Chemin de Chantecaille
33500 Pomerol, France

+33 (0)5 57 51 07 05
Contact@Gazin.com

Gazin.com

English, French

Open: All Year, Monday-Friday
Call or Email Them To Make An Appointment

B lue clay plateau for Merlot and gravel topsoil for Cabernet Sauvignon – a remarkable blend.

AT THE HEART OF THE BLUE CLAY

Château Gazin is located on the top of the blue clay hill next to Château Pétrus, sharing this great terroir. Pétrus once purchased some of Gazin's property and continues to make their wines from former Gazin vineyards.

Of historic significance, Château Gazin is the site of the area's original hospital, which they have paid homage by naming their second wine: l'Hospitalet de Gazin. As such, Gazin became a very important resting stop for pilgrims on their way to Santiago de Compostela in Spain. Gazin became a village in and of itself during the 18th century and was the home to many of the vineyard workers.

This property used to belong to the Knights of Saint John of Jerusalem, Knights of Rhodes, and Knights of Malta, until the Baillencourt family, descendents of the Lordes of Landes, purchased the estate in 1918. Today, the sixth generation Baillencourts cherish their heritage and the special terroir on which they sit.

Pomerol was originally divided up in 1711 to 19 different owners. One of them, a barrister, began calling himself Lord of Gazin. Château Gazin was born and quickly began to get the attention of wine merchants with its unbelievable quality. At 24 hectares, Gazin is one of the largest estates (average Pomerol estate is 6 hectares), located on top of the famous blue clay plateau. It is more than twice the size of neighboring Pétrus. Château Gazin began winning medals for their wines in Paris, Barcelona and Brussels. This is a wine you definitely want to experience.

Château Gazin includes a fair amount of Cabernet Sauvignon in their blend, not typical in Pomerol. You can taste this fruit in their blend. It is what we all come to love from this grape. Gazin has excellent gravel topsoil conducive to ripening Cabernet Sauvignon and is further expanding this with new plantings; a huge Cabernet Sauvignon vineyard in front of the château you see in the photo above.

This is a delicious and unique quality of the Château Gazin wine that I particularly like. And stock up, as you can buy three cases of Château Gazin for less than one bottle of Château Pétrus.

Collection of Wines
Château Gazin
(First Label - AOC Pomerol)

l'Hospitalet de Gazin
(Second Wine - AOC Pomerol)

LIBOURNAIS POMEROL
Winery (Château) & B&B
CHÂTEAU BEAUREGARD

Winner: Best Of Wine Tourism

73 Rue de Catusseau
33500 Pomerol, France

+33 (0)5 57 51 13 36
Visite@Chateau-Beauregard.com

Chateau-Beauregard.com

English, French

*Open: All Year, Monday-Friday
They are very tourism-friendly and encourage your visit. Send an email to schedule a time.*

New owners with great vision and passion modernized this historically great property.

IN SEARCH OF EXCELLENCE

As we work our way down the slope of the blue clay soil, we come to Château Beauregard. They sit on the southeast edge of the Pomerol appellation. When you look out their back door, you see across their expansive vineyards (18 hectares) to the border of Saint-Émilion, and into the property of the famous Château Cheval Blanc.

I was expecting exceptional wines here because of the incredible terroir and impressive neighbors, and because I know the philosophy and passion of one of the new owners of this estate. In 2014, Philippe Houzé (Executive Chairman of the Galeries Lafayette) and Daniel and Florence Cathiard (owners of Château Smith Haut Lafitte) purchased Château Beauregard.

I am well acquainted with Daniel and Florence, and their passion for excellence at Smith Haut Lafitte. They turned that château into one of the most respected wine estates in Pessac-Léognan. I have seen them in action, witnessed their drive and commitment to quality, and tasted the magnificent results. I expected the same commitment and passion from them here at Château Beauregard.

It was nice to show up in the middle of batch tastings (photo below) to witness the process, and taste the nuances of fine tuning a vintage. The 2019 vintage is set to be a excellent year. It is exciting to taste the future, seeing the exciting potential today.

Speaking of the future: I also tasted the 2015 and 2016, from the bottle. In a glass, of course. Although these two wines are very enjoyable now, they will be excellent in ten years. As I am a big wine with full fruit kind of guy, the 2015 is my favorite. The 2016 is a serious vintage with great complexity. Big and bold with soft tannins to carry many years. Both are soft and elegant in their differing styles.

Collection of Wines
Château Beauregard
(First Label - AOC Pomerol)

Benjamin de Beauregard
(Second Wine - AOC Pomerol)

Pavillon Beauregard
(AOC Lalande de Pomerol)

LIBOURNAIS POMEROL
Winery (Château) & B&B
CHÂTEAU BEAUREGARD

Winner: Best Of Wine Tourism

+33 (0)5 57 51 13 36
Visite@Chateau-Beauregard.com

Chateau-Beauregard.com

Open: All Year
Room Bookings By Email

A COUNTRY HOME CHÂTEAU

Château Beauregard is an 18th century chartreuse, renovated in 2020 to a luxurious five-bedroom bed and breakfast for you to enjoy Pomerol at its finest.

This two-level country home opens out onto a beautiful historic stone terrace overlooking a moat and beautiful grounds. It is a peaceful and serene environment. You get to feel history in the midst of luxury.

The new owners warmly welcome visitors, so stay awhile. Come for a night, a weekend getaway or stay longer. They can customize lunches or dinners, and pairings with their wines. This is the only place I could find accommodations (and I had the help of locals) in Pomerol. Much less one with such wonderful hospitality.

LIBOURNAIS **POMEROL**

Winery (Château)
CHÂTEAU DE SALES

*I*n the same family for 553 years, Pomerol's largest estate embarks on a new journey.

Winner: Best Of Wine Tourism

11 Chemin de Sales
33500 Pomerol, France

+33 (0)5 57 51 04 92
Visites@ChateauDeSales.fr

Chateau-De-Sales.com

English, French, Spanish, Italian, Portuguese

*Open: All Year, Tuesday-Saturday
By Appointment Only
Reservations By Phone or Email*

TWENTY FIVE GENERATIONS

It is hard to imagine a business in the same family for five centuries, let alone an agricultural winemaking business. This is the case for Château de Sales, which Bertrand de Sauvanelle acquired in 1464. Through descendants and marriages, there have been four families involved. Currently 14 direct cousins own Château de Sales and its 25 generations of success.

It has always been a family member running the estate and making the wines. The last 35 years belong to Bruno de Lambert, who pioneered wine tourism at Château de Sales. He opened up the estate to visitors in order to share their love and passion for the property and its wines.

Bruno went on to be president of the Syndicat Viticole de Pomerol, promoting the Pomeral châteaux to the world and inviting visitors to see and experience Pomerol. Although Bruno decided to retire from both in 2017, it was obvious when I had dinner with him that he will be forever passionate about promoting Pomerol.

The new generation has embarked on a new journey of not managing the estate themselves. Instead, they brought in a industry heavyweight to take them to new levels of success.

In 2017, they hired Vincent Montigaud to take over as the company's CEO. Previously, Vincent spent 23 years with Baron Philippe de Rothschild, which included 16 years as managing director of one of their domains.

Vincent's first full growing season, harvest and vinification was 2018. When we met, he had 10 months of his new baby in barrels. We tasted it. Compared it to four previous vintages. Talked about his style. Marvelous. More concentration, freshness, more ripe fruit, big soft tannins, and juicy black cherries from the greater concentration of Cabernet Sauvignon. I'm in with the cousins' choice for Vincent. I'll be back soon to see you, Vincent.

Château de Sales is expansive with 47.6 hectares (118 acres), the largest vineyard estate in Pomerol. They give a warm welcome to visitors. You will see five centuries of history, much of it unchanged with time, and catch a glimpse of the family's vision.

Two of the 14 cousins can be found at these châteaux...

*Laure de Lambert Compeyrot, proprietor
Château Sigalas Rabaud (page 295)*

*Gonzague de Lambert, Directeur
Château de Ferrand (page 379)*

Collection of Wines
Château de Sales
(First Label - AOC Pomerol)

Château Chantalouette
(Second Wine - AOC Pomerol)

LIBOURNAIS **POMEROL**
Winery (Château)
CHÂTEAU DU TAILHAS

195 Route de Saint-Émilion
33500 Pomerol, France

+33 (0)5 57 51 26 02
Info@Tailhas.com

Tailhas.com

English, French

Open: All Year, Monday-Friday
By Appointment Only
Reservations By Phone or Email
Both Private and Group Tours Available

Queen Elizabeth chose Château du Tailhas for her 50th wedding anniversary.

MINK ELEGANCE

Château Tailhas is located at the most southeast corner of the Pomerol appellation, at the border of Saint-Émilion. Right off the D243 highway from Libourne to Saint-Émilion, this an easy stop. They are next to a little stream, Ruisseau de Tailhas, which separates Pomerol and Saint-Émilion. The terroir is still very much Pomerol, on the southern slope of the blue clay plateau.

Not a fancy environment here. The chateau is simple. Its owner, Luc Nubout (also president of the Pomeral Confrerie), lives in the château and personally gives the tours. He is very smart and holds a doctorate degree in chemistry, which he applies to his wine. Wine is chemistry and Luc can tell you all the little nuances he considers important in creating his great wine. He is also a very sweet man who gladly shares his special place.

Come for a picnic. Luc will make arrangements with his caterer for a scrumptious picnic basket (photo below). You can eat under the trees, in the vineyard, on the lawn, or inside the château as we did. All with a bottle of his delicious wine. What a great way to spend the afternoon.

Queen Elizabeth loves the Tailhas wines! When she married in 1947, she chose legendary Château Pétrus for the wedding. In 1997, she chose Château du Tailhas for her 50th anniversary celebration. Smart lady. I tell you, this is very good wine. Do you want to know the exact vintage? Vintage 1988. And while I was there, I enjoyed a 1990 vintage. Mink Elegance! Need I say more? OK, I will. Chateau du Tailhas is the best value I found in Pomerol, a great price for extraordinarily excellent wine. Get some before they reach Pétrus' prices!

Collection of Wines
Château du Tailhas
(First Label - AOC Pomerol)

VILLAGE POMEROL

Pomerol is a very small area with few homes. The entire Pomerol appellation population is only 700 people. There is a tiny village of Pomerol in the center of the appellation, which I estimate has a population of maybe 10 people. The village is home to the beautiful Pomerol church whose tower can be seen throughout the appellation (photo lower right). Also in the village is the **Maison des Vins** and **Château La Fleur-Pétrus**. Pomerol the village shares its name with the Pomerol AOC.

Of more significance is the Town of Catusseau. In the southern part of the Pomerol appellation, Catusseau has a few businesses, including the notable **Rolland Laboratoire** (photo right) and **Le Table de Catusseau**, a Michelin Gourmand restaurant, the only gourmet restaurant in all of Pomerol.

LIBOURNAIS POMEROL VILLAGE
Wine Merchant
MAISON DES VINS DE POMEROL

8 Rue de Tropchaud • 33500 Pomerol, France
+33 (0)5 57 25 06 88 • Syndicat@Vins-Pomerol.fr

Vins-Pomerol.fr

"Maison des Vins" translates to "House of Wines." This is the syndicate of wineries of the Pomerol Appellation that makes their wines available all in one place. The official name is Syndicat Viticole de Pomerol et Maison des Vins de Pomerol

Located in the Pomerol village across the vineyards from the Pomerol Church, they have 70 wines for sale from the Pomerol châteaux. No markup, sold at the winery's price.

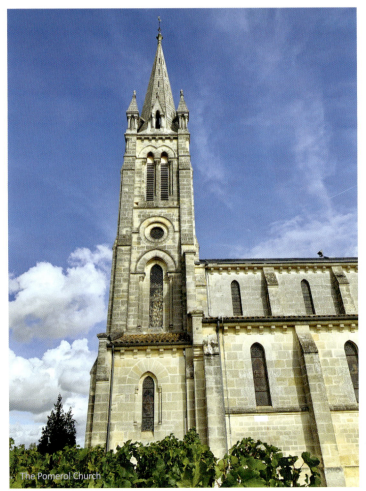

The Pomerol Church

LIBOURNAIS **POMEROL** CATUSSEAU

Restaurant
LA TABLE DE CATUSSEAU

86 Rue de Catusseaue • 33500, Pomerol, France
+33 (0)5 57 84 40 40 • LaTableDeCatusseau@Gmail.com
Reservations: call, email or book on website
Lunch: Tuesday-Friday & Sunday, 12:00pm-2:00pm
Dinner: Thursday-Saturday & Tuesday, 7:30pm-9:00pm

New Caledonian-born Kendji Wongsodikromo moved to France and fell in love with French cuisine and his French wife, Nadège. Together they have created La Table de Catusseau. She brings personality to the front of the house, while Kendji creates some pretty exciting dishes in the kitchen. He calls it "bistronomic cuisine," which is based on fresh seasonal produce. Michelin rates him as a Bib Gourmand. I call him the creative flavor maker. Photos top to bottom counterclockwise:
• Dining Room, a spacious stone room with fireplace and terrace
• Lobster Tartare, seaweed and lemon confit, lobster sauce with coffee flavor
• Seared Scallops, seasonal vegetables, lemon caviar sauce, mustard seed and pimento
• Macaron Saint-Émilion, raspberries, pistachio, praline, and raspberry sorbet

DOWNTOWN LIBOURNE

Libourne is the big city in this area with a population of 25,000. The wine region here carries its name: Libournais. Fronsac AOC is immediately northwest, Pomerol AOC is immediately to the north and Saint-Émilion AOC is northeast by a few miles. Libourne has become the center of business on the Right Bank, with many of the wine merchants' offices here. Big châteaux have offices here too.

Libourne is on the Dordogne River with a port where the wine have been shipping to other countries for centuries. There are restaurants and shops surrounding the town square, and a farmers market every Sunday morning. On the riverfront, there are two restaurants worth checking out. Plus river cruises if you would like to get out on the water.

■ LIBOURNAIS **LIBOURNE** DOWNTOWN
River Cruise down the Dordogne River
DORDOGNE RIVER CRUISE

42 Place Abel Surchamp • 33500 Libourne, France
+33 (0)5 57 51 15 04 • Bienvenue@Tourisme-Libournais.com

Tourisme-Libournais.com

Getting on a small boat for a cruise down the Dordogne River is quite a treat. It is a calm and peaceful ride. They also serve food and wine while you take in the sights. It is a nice half-day trip.

The Libournais Tourism Office can book your cruise. They have several to choose from, which they have already vetted for quality and reputation. Go to their office or write to the email address above.

■ LIBOURNAIS **LIBOURNE** DOWNTOWN
Restaurant
LE ZINC AUTHENTIQUE

42 Rue Fonneuve • 33500 Libourne, France
+33 (0)5 57 25 34 84 • LeZinc-Bar.com
Tuesday-Friday: Lunch, Dinner & Bar, 12:00pm-2:15pm & 5:30pm-2:00am
Saturday: Dinner & Bar, 6:00pm-2:00am • Monday: Lunch, 12:00pm-2:15pm

This is a wine bistro, lively bar and concert venue. Very casual. Menu is on a newspaper. Open until 2:00am Tuesday through Saturday nights. Live music and concerts. Themed nights on a regular basis. They sell wine by the bottle and at good non-restaurant prices. Plus, you can buy bottles to take with you.

Don't be fooled by this being a bar, the food is very good here. Pictured below is a steak and mushrooms dinner that was ever so good. On sunny days, you can dine in a nice interior garden. They are a block from the boardwalk along the Dordogne River.

LIBOURNAIS **LIBOURNE** DOWNTOWN ■
Restaurant
LE BISTROT MARITIME

12 Quai Souchet • 33500 Libourne, France
+33 (0)5 57 51 66 77 • LeBistrotMaritime@Gmail.com
Monday-Friday: Lunch & Dinner, 11:45am-3:00pm & 6:45pm-10:30pm
Saturday & Sunday: Lunch & Dinner All Day, 11:45am-10:30pm

This is a nice casual restaurant on the boardwalk along the Dordogne River in the port of Libourne. They have great views of the river from their outside terrace. Indoor dining as well. The servers are fun, and very attentive to your needs. I wanted an ice cream bar I saw. Come to find out it was only available on the children's menu. The server made it happen.

Great food. Just look at that yummy burger and the salmon tartare. Ever so fresh! And for a change of wine pace, they have several nice micro-brews on tap. Open everyday and very popular, so be sure to make a reservation or show up early as we did.

Left page:
The Dordogne River

BORDEAUX SUPÉRIEUR

While the Entre-Deux-Mers (between the two rivers) wine region may be known as a place for volume wines, there are two standout châteaux that you must explore in this region.

In the hierarchy of Bordeaux wines, the Bordeaux AOC represents the entire Bordeaux area without specificity to location or classification. The next level up is Bordeaux Supérieur, which promises a greater quality wine because winemakers must meet higher standards to attain this designation.

They are required to use older vines of densely planted vineyards, lower harvest yields, ripe fruit with natural sugar levels upon harvest, and at least 12 months of barrel aging. Plus, only the six Bordeaux grape varietals are acceptable for use.

Putting Bordeaux Supérieur on the label carries an implied promise of "superior" quality. However, quality definitely varies. The two châteaux on these pages are going above and beyond these standards and producing high quality wines that would be rated much higher if they were geographically located elsewhere.

Also, both of these two châteaux have excellent tourism reasons to visit. They both have won Best Of Tourism Awards. Here are the two châteaux...
- Château de Bonhoste, page 465
- Château de Reignac, page 467

How about an interesting side trip to Cognac to visit a large cooperage and see how wine barrels are made? And visit a historic Cognac distiller while you are there. Here they are...
- Cooperage Seguin Moreau, page 469
- Rémy Martin Cognac, page 471

SPECIAL ADDITIONS **BORDEAUX SUPÉRIEUR**

Winery (Château)
CHÂTEAU DE BONHOSTE
COUP 2 FOUDRES

Winner: Best Of Wine Tourism

Chateau de Bonhoste
33420 Saint-Jean-de-Blaignac, France

+33 (0)5 57 84 12 18

ChateauDeBonhoste.com
Coup2Foudres.com

English, French

*Open: All Year, Everyday, 9:00am-7:00pm
Reservations Not Needed*

Across the river from Saint-Émilion with the same limestone plateau and caves.

LOVE AT FIRST SIGHT

A foudre is the name of the oak barrel we commonly see used in cellars to either ferment or age the wine. Foudres are made in many sizes, including a super grand size that is large enough to sleep in. Complete with a full-size bed, bathroom and sitting area with kitchenette. The foudres you see to the left were custom made for Château de Bonhoste and are available for stay in their vineyards.

The name is a play on words and an interesting French saying. Yes, "2 Foudres" means they have two wine barrels for overnight guests. Foudres also means electricity, sparks or lightening. Combined, "coup 2 foudres" is a saying in French that means "love at first sight" or "the sparks of two people." This is a perfect place for two lovers to enjoy a night together. Picnic box included.

They are located ten minutes drive across the river south of Saint-Émilion and situated on the limestone plateau, with just the Dordogne River crossing in between. Caves (photo above) were also dug here for the limestone blocks to build the beautiful historic buildings. Here they call their wines Bordeaux Supérior, with much lower pricing.

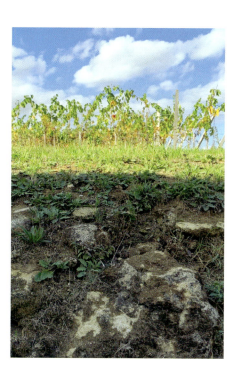

Collection of Wines
Château de Bonhoste
(First Label - AOC Bordeaux Supérieur)

Château de Bonhoste
(Bordeaux Red, Bordeaux Rosé, Bordeaux White Dry, Bordeaux White Dry Cuvée Prestige, Bordeaux Superior Cuvée Prestige, Crémant of Bordeaux White, Crémant of Bordeaux Rosé)

Château de Bergerac
(Bergerac Red, Bergerac Red Cuvée Prestige, Côtes de Bergerac White Medium Sweet)

SO^2 Libre
(Red Wine Without Sulphites)

Coup de Foudres
(Celebration Red Wine of The Foudres)

SPECIAL ADDITIONS **BORDEAUX SUPÉRIEUR**

Winery (Château)
CHÂTEAU DE REIGNAC

Global Winner: Best Of Wine Tourism

38 Chemin de Reignac
33450 Saint-Loubès, France

+33 (0)5 56 20 41 05
Visites@Reignac.com

Reignac.com

English, French

*Open: All Year, Monday-Friday
Call or Email To Make An Appointment
There are a lot of experiences here, as they were named Best Tourism Winery in Bordeaux for 2018*

Buy Château de Reignac Wines Direct
By Writing To: Info@Reignac.com

Collection of Wines
Grand Vin de Reignac
(First Label - AOC Bordeaux Supérieur)

Château de Reignac
(Second Wine - AOC Bordeaux Supérieur)

BALTHVS
(100% Merlot, using a special patented method)

The White of Reignac
(Sauvignon Blanc, Semillon, Sauvignon Gris)

O n terroir of extraordinary quality, without a famous appellation, achieving top accolades.

A BLIND TASTING SURPRISE

What does Yves Vatelot do after inventing the first electric epilator and selling the Silk-épil patented brand to Gillette for huge amounts of money? He fulfills his childhood dream of owning a vineyard and château in Bordeaux, of course.

The dilemma though is how do you select a château when there are many prestigious appellations in Bordeaux? So, Yves calls his good friend Michel Rolland. Michel tells him of one in Entre-Deux-Mers (not a prestigious address) although it has remarkable terroir. He goes on to tell him that he could make excellent wine here, yet it will never get the esteemed recognition of the well-known appellations that consumers admire.

Yves was up for the challenge and purchased Château Reignac in 1999, a 135-hectare estate with 77 hectares of vines, 35 hectares of valuable forest and an important 7 hectares lake. He hired Michel Rolland as his consultant and Nicolas Lesaint as Technical Director, who also happens to be a very talented illustrator, making fun wine-inspired drawings as part of the tourism experiences, which has won them top awards. Furthermore, Yves has been developing various patents on specialized techniques for winemaking in barrels. BALTHVS is one of those amazing wines.

Speaking of results, let's talk about the wine they are making. While enjoying lunch with Yves, his wife Stéphanie, and Nicolas, Yves hands me two glasses of wine, with the numbers 2 and 3 engraved on the glass. He said, "let's do a blind tasting."

Looking at the glasses, many things run through my mind. Two different vintages of his wine? Different Reignac wines to compare? A comparison with another château's wine? He says, "let's start with vintage. They are the same, what do you think?" I looked, smelled and tasted. Older, not too old. I believed it to be 15 to 18 years. The vintage was 2001, 16 years old at the time. Off to a good start. He said we were comparing his wine to another château. I had no idea who! I'm not *that* good.

He wanted to know what I thought of the wines. My response: One wine was at its prime, with old flavors, and had the orange-edge color of an aged wine. The other wine was quite different. It was fresh, more powerful in its nose, richer in flavors in the mouth, and the color was lively with at least another ten years to age.

He commented that this was an '01 blind tasting with a first-growth. So now he tells me. He brings out the bottles (photo right), and reveals I picked the Reignac. Whew! Yet, the truth really was that his wine beat the first-growth fair and square. It was significantly better. Then he says, "I can deliver my wine to your door in California for $35." And you know how much that first-growth will set you back!

Exploring Wine Regions | **Bordeaux** | **467**

SPECIAL ADDITIONS **COGNAC**
Cooper (Barrel Maker)
COOPERAGE SEGUIN MOREAU

Avenue de Gimeux, 10225 Merpins
16111 Cognac, France

+33 (0)5 45 82 62 22
Info@Seguin-Moreau.fr

Seguin-Moreau.fr

English, French

*Open: All Year, Monday-Friday
Call or Email To Make An Appointment*

Visiting a cooper brings greater appreciation for the oak barrels that impact our wines.

THE MAKING OF A WINE BARREL

Seguin Moreau is a very large and sophisticated cooperage headquartered in Cognac France, which is a one-hour drive northeast of Bordeaux. Coopers are the woodworking craftsmen who make the barrels used for aging wine in cellars and the vinification of finer wines. Seguin Moreau made the gigantic wine barrels that you can sleep in at Coup 2 Foudres (see review on page 465).

As far back as 1838, the Seguin and Moreau companies separately made barrels only for aging Cognac. Remy Martin eventually purchased the companies to optimize control of their barrels (next page). It wasn't until the 1980s that Seguin Moreau chose to make barrels for wine, and created a partnership with the oenology department at the University of Bordeaux. This enabled both organizations to better understand the interaction between wine and wood on a sophisticated level.

Seguin Moreau hired Andrei Prida PhD, whose dissertation was on "The Chemical Characterization of Oak Wood and its Role in Ageing Wines and Spirits," as R&D Manager. Andrei has made a career here working with winemakers to fine tune the wood's qualities needed for the style of wine intended. There are no other cooperages with this type of department and expertise. Every barrel is lab tested for quality and aroma standards.

It would be easy to believe that to make a barrel, you would cut down an oak tree, cut long planks, and then put them together with metal rings to create a barrel. It is neither quick nor simple at all. Being a wine lover, visiting a cooperage was a very interesting experience, especially when witnessing the sophistication of Seguin Moreau in action.

It starts with waiting 150 to 200 years for a quality oak tree to mature. After harvest, the selected tree must be cut into appropriated lengths and allowed to rest for a month. Rough cuts are then made of the planks and stacked on pallets to mature in open air for two years. The planks are watered to slowly pace the curing.

After the curing, they are brought inside to a very sophisticated milling machine. This machine can cut each individual piece of a barrel and knows how many planks are needed and groups them per barrel. Each plank is unique with varying widths. Mathematical algorithms are used to cut each angle and joint. It is amazing to watch this in action.

As the barrels are being assembled, rings are added and removed many times to create its shape. Heat is used to make the wood more pliable, and ultimately fire is used to toast the wood inside. Barrels are filled with water to check that it is sealed and a chemical analysis is conducted at every step along the way. Each barrel is custom made to order based on the winemakers exact specifications.

SPECIAL ADDITIONS COGNAC
Cognac (Distilled Wine)
RÉMY MARTIN COGNAC

20 Rue de La Société Vinicole
16100 Cognac, France

+33 (0)5 45 35 76 66
Visites.RemyMartin@Remy-Cointreau.com

VisitesRemyMartin.com

English, French

*Open: All Year, Monday-Saturday
Call or Email To Make An Appointment*

Cognac is made from wine grapes off Cognac vineyards and distilled into its tastiness.

MAKING HIGH QUALITY COGNAC

The original facilities of Rémy Martin dates back to 1724 and is now a historical landmark in downtown Cognac. The facilities are still being used for aging their Cognacs and there is a museum for visitors.

Rémy Martin has always been focused on producing top-quality Cognac. They even bought the cooperage (Seguin Moreau, previous pages) who was making their oak aging barrels in 1958, so they could oversee and control the quality to the ultimate degree.

They make all levels of Cognac: VS, VSOP, XO and their top of the line Louis XIII. This is a tribute to King Louis XIII, the first monarch to recognize Cognac as a unique drink category from the terroir of the Cognac Grande Champagne region near Bordeaux.

Louis XIII de Rémy Martin is as special as it gets. It takes a century to make. It is truly the life achievement of generations of cellar masters, 50 to 100-year-old vineyards, and crystal from glass cutters and engravers. A staggering 1,200 individual batches go into the final blend. At $3,000 a bottle, it suddenly does not seem that expensive.

Rémy Martin XO is the signature of the Cellar Master who artfully blends up to 400 different batches to express its full aromatic complexity. It is rich, opulent and velvety. I could sit and sip this for hours. It was floral, fruity and spicy all in one mellow sensation that lingers long in the mouth.

Rémy Martin wants you to visit and has created 13 unique tours ranging in price from 20€ to 1,200€, and everything in between. The pricier tours include Louis XIII tastings, pairings and other special experiences. All 13 tours are listed on their website.

Cognac is made from grapes grown in vineyards just the same as wine. The difference is Cognac is distilled wine. And the higher quality Cognacs are aged longer in barrels. Cognac is the Grande Champagne region near Bordeaux and only Cognac is made in the Cognac AOC.

Cognacs Produced
Louis XIII de Rémy Martin
(A Tribute - A Century In The Making)

Remy Martin XO
(Extra Old - Aged for 10+ years)

Remy Martin VSOP
(Very Superior Old Pale - Aged for 4 years)

MY BORDEAUX DISCOVERIES

Imagine... three years, six trips, encompassing 21 weeks on the ground in Bordeaux, plus all the research in between. It took this kind of immersion to truly understand Bordeaux. I went to each of their wine regions on multiple occasions. It is what it takes! I connected with brilliant people at the forefront of producing great wines and others who are creating compelling new tourism opportunities. People who have lived in Bordeaux all their lives are even learning things from me. They say, "Wow, that is interesting. I didn't know that." It makes me realize that I have really come to know Bordeaux.

Bordeaux is no longer complicated for me. The most important thing I learned from this quest was that Bordeaux wines are all about the terroir. Winemakers make wine from the grapes of their land. They blend their wines just as a gourmet chef uses different ingredients to create a meal. If they want a different grape, or grape percentage, they plant it. And they study their terroir in order to plant the best varietal for each individual plot. This is essential. Just consider the broad stroke of Cabernet Sauvignon being dominant in the Left Bank and Merlot being dominant in the Right Bank. This is not by simple desire for wanting a particular grape variety. This is a function of terroir; the soil and climate dictate what type of grape will flourish in each plot of each vineyard. Once I understood this concept, I could then choose wines I enjoy most based on the terroir. This is a key point in figuring out where to find the wines you love.

The perfect example of this is the experiment that was conducted at Château de Pressac (page 377). During a blind tasting, a visitor insisted he could identify the grape variety of different wines based on its similarity in taste, when in fact the wines with similar taste shared terroir (of different grapes). Without knowing, he was distinguishing terroir.

In the beginning of this book, we discussed the challenge of French wines not identifying the grape variety in the bottle. You no longer have to be hindered by this concept of grape variety. French wines are all about the terroir. This is why traveling to Bordeaux will make all the difference in your discovery and enjoyment of wine. You will be wiser with the skills to choose the wines you love.

Read my book and choose your favorite châteaux to explore. Discover the terroir you like best. I know today that if you took me to a wine bar where I did not recognize the Bordeaux wines, I would still be able to pick out a wine I would love to drink. You can do the same. This book helps you figure it out even if you don't travel to Bordeaux. But still, you should go! This is the world's mecca of wine.

Go! I promise you the landscapes are breathtakingly beautiful, the castles are magnificent, the food is delectable, and the people are ever so nice and welcoming.

Happy Tasting,

Michael C. Higgins, PhD

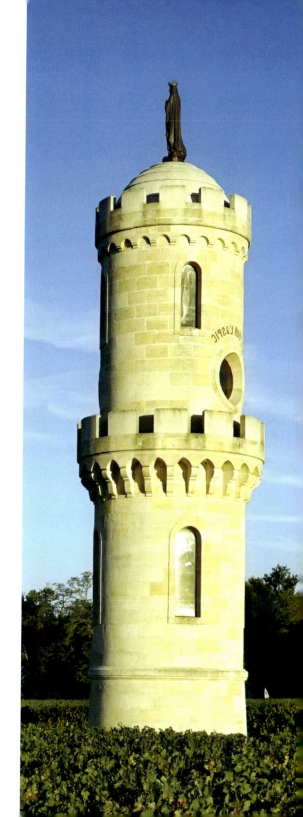

THE INDEX
Finding Your Way Around Easily

WINERIES	PAGES
Ch d'Agassac (Haut-Médoc, Médoc)	69
Ch Ambe Tour Pourret (Saint-Émilion, Libournais)	337
Ch Angélus (Saint-Émilion, Libournais)	349
Ch Batailley (Pauillac, Médoc)	179
Ch Baudan (Listrac-Médoc, Médoc)	123
Ch Beau-Séjour Bécot (Saint-Émilion, Libournais)	391
Ch Beauregard (Pomerol, Libournais)	451
Ch Bellevue-Cardon (Pauillac, Médoc)	173
Ch Beychevelle (Saint-Julien, Médoc)	151
Ch de Bonhoste (Bordeaux Supérieur, Entre-Deux-Mers)	465
Ch Boutinet (Fronsac, Libournais)	433
Ch Brillette (Moulis-en-Médoc, Médoc)	119
Ch de Candale (Saint-Émilion, Libournais)	361
Ch Cantenac (Saint-Émilion, Libournais)	341
Ch Cap Léon Veyrin (Listrac-Médoc, Médoc)	127
Ch Castera (Médoc, Médoc)	213
Ch Cheval Blanc (Saint-Émilion, Libournais)	321
Ch Climens (Barsac, Graves)	305
Ch Coutet (Barsac, Graves)	301
Ch Le Crock (Saint-Estèphe, Médoc)	201
Ch La Croizille (Saint-Émilion, Libournais)	359
Ch Dalem (Fronsac, Libournais)	435
Ch de La Dauphine (Fronsac, Libournais)	425
Ch Deyrem Valentin (Margaux, Médoc)	111
Ch La Dominique (Saint-Émilion, Libournais)	323
Ch de Ferrand (Saint-Émilion, Libournais)	379
Ch La Fleur-Pétrus (Pomerol, Libournais)	447
Ch Fombrauge (Saint-Émilion, Libournais)	385
Ch Fonplégade (Saint-Émilion, Libournais)	355
Ch Fonroque (Saint-Émilion, Libournais)	335
Ch Fontenil (Fronsac, Libournais)	437
Ch Franc Mayne (Saint-Émilion, Libournais)	329
Ch Gaby (Fronsac, Libournais)	427
Ch Gazin (Pomerol, Libournais)	449
Ch Giscours (Margaux, Médoc)	93
Ch La Grace Dieu des Prieurs (Saint-Émilion, Libournais)	339
Ch Gravas (Barsac, Graves)	307
Ch Gruaud Larose (Saint-Julien, Médoc)	143
Ch Guadet (Saint-Émilion, Libournais)	399
Ch Guiraud (Sauternes, Graves)	285
Ch Haut-Sarpe (Saint-Émilion, Libournais)	383
Ch Haut-Bailly (Pessac-Léognan, Graves)	259
Ch La Haye (Saint-Estèphe, Médoc)	203
Ch Lafon-Rochet (Saint-Estèphe, Médoc)	197
Ch Lagrange (Saint-Julien, Médoc)	147
Ch Lamothe Bergeron (Haut-Médoc, Médoc)	135
Ch Larose Trintaudon (Haut-Médoc, Médoc)	133
Ch Lascombes (Margaux, Médoc)	87
Ch Léoville Poyferré (Saint-Julien, Médoc)	145
Ch Loudenne (Médoc, Médoc)	217
Ch Lynch-Bages (Pauillac, Médoc)	185
Ch Lynch-Moussas (Pauillac, Médoc)	181
Ch Margaux (Margaux, Médoc)	81
Ch Marquis d'Alesme (Margaux, Médoc)	89
Ch Marquis de Terme (Margaux, Médoc)	99
Ch Moulin-à-Vent (Moulis-en-Médoc, Médoc)	121
Ch Mouton Rothschild (Pauillac, Médoc)	163
Ch Ormes de Pez (Saint-Estèphe, Médoc)	205
Ch Paloumey (Haut-Médoc, Médoc)	73
Ch Le Pape (Pessac-Léognan, Graves)	261
Ch Pape Clément (Pessac-Léognan, Graves)	251
Ch Paveil de Luze (Margaux, Médoc)	107
Ch Pavie (Saint-Émilion, Libournais)	351
Ch Pédesclaux (Pauillac, Médoc)	175
Ch Pichon Baron (Pauillac, Médoc)	169
Ch de Portets (Graves, Graves)	269
Ch de Pressac (Saint-Émilion, Libournais)	377
Ch Prieuré-Lichine (Margaux, Médoc)	95
Ch de Rayne Vigneau (Sauternes, Graves)	289
Ch de Reignac (Bordeaux Supérieur, Entre-Deux-Mers)	467
Ch Reverdi (Listrac-Médoc, Médoc)	125
Ch de La Rivière (Fronsac, Libournais)	421
Ch Roquetaillade (Graves, Graves)	273
Ch de Rouillac (Pessac-Léognan, Graves)	257
Ch Saint Ahon (Haut-Médoc, Médoc)	77
Ch Saint-Christoly (Médoc, Médoc)	221
Ch de Sales (Pomerol, Libournais)	455
Ch Sigalas Rabaud (Sauternes, Graves)	293
Ch Smith Haut Lafitte (Pessac-Léognan, Graves)	263
Ch Soutard (Saint-Émilion, Libournais)	393
Ch Suduiraut (Sauternes, Graves)	291
Ch du Tailhas (Pomerol, Libournais)	457
Ch du Taillan (Haut-Médoc, Médoc)	75
Ch du Tertre (Margaux, Médoc)	101
Ch Tour Castillon (Médoc, Médoc)	219
Ch Troplong Mondot (Saint-Émilion, Libournais)	373
Ch Valandraud (Saint-Émilion, Libournais)	371
Ch Venus (Graves, Graves)	271
Ch Villemaurine (Saint-Émilion, Libournais)	397
Ch d'Yquem (Sauternes, Graves)	279
Clos des Jacobins (Saint-Émilion, Libournais)	333
Rémy Martin (Cognac, Cognac)	471
Union de Producteurs (Saint-Émilion, Libournais)	357

THE INDEX
Finding Your Way Around Easily

RESTAURANTS	PAGES
Le 1925 (Downtown, Bordeaux)	37
Le 7 (Downtown, Bordeaux)	52
L'Atelier de Candale (Saint-Émilion, Libournais)	363
Auberge Les Vignes (Sauternes, Graves)	297
Bar du Boucher (Downtown, Bordeaux)	40
Le Belem (Port-Médoc, Médoc)	227
Big Fernand (Downtown, Bordeaux)	40
Bistrot Chez Mémé (Saint-Julien, Médoc)	159
Le Bistrot Maritime (Libourne, Libournais)	461
La Boca Foodcourt (Downtown, Bordeaux)	49
Le Bontemps (Haut-Médoc, Médoc)	139
La Brasserie Bordelaise (Downtown, Bordeaux)	39
Le Café Français (Downtown, Bordeaux)	39
Le Café Lavinal (Pauillac, Médoc)	183
Chapelle de Guiraud (Sauternes, Graves)	287
Le Chapon Fin (Downtown, Bordeaux)	41
Château Cordeillan-Bages (Pauillac, Médoc)	191
Chez Carles Maître Restaurateur (Fronsac, Libournais)	441
Claude Darroze (Langon, Graves)	309
Le Clos du Roy (Saint-Émilion, Libournais)	409
Le Cochon Volant (Langon, Graves)	309
Comptoir Cuisine (Downtown, Bordeaux)	36
Le Don Camillo (Langon, Graves)	309
L'Envers du Décore (Saint-Émilion, Libournais)	408
Fufu Ramen (Downtown, Bordeaux)	39
Les Halles de Bacalan (Downtown, Bordeaux)	51
Hôtel de La Plage (Cap-Ferret, Médoc)	239
Hôtel Grand Barrail (Saint-Émilion, Libournais)	345
Hôtel Restaurant de France (Pauillac, Médoc)	193
Lard et Bouchon (Saint-Émilion, Libournais)	409
LB Restaurant Crêperie (Médoc Atlantique, Médoc)	229
Le Lion d'Or (Haut-Médoc, Médoc)	138
Logis de la Cadène (Saint-Émilion, Libournais)	407
Maison Ballet (Pauillac, Médoc)	192
La Maison Du Douanier (Médoc, Médoc)	222
El Nacional (Downtown, Bordeaux)	51
Restaurant Nomade (Margaux, Médoc)	115
Osteria da Luigi (Downtown, Bordeaux)	40
La Pizzeria du Vieux Lavoir (Saint-Émilion, Libournais)	408
Le Quatrième Mur (Downtown, Bordeaux)	37
Le Saint-Julien (Saint-Julien, Médoc)	157
Le Salamandre (Pauillac, Médoc)	193

RESTAURANTS	PAGES
Le Saprien (Sauternes, Graves)	297
Restaurant Le Savoie (Margaux, Médoc)	114
Sister (Downtown, Bordeaux)	51
La Table d'Agassac (Haut-Médoc, Médoc)	71
La Table de Catusseau (Pomerol, Libournais)	459
La Table de Plaisance (Saint-Émilion, Libournais)	411
La Terrasse Rouge (Saint-Émilion, Libournais)	325
VitalParc Hôtel Restaurant (Lacanau Océan, Médoc Atlantique)	237
Le Zinc Authentique (Libourne, Libournais)	461

ACCOMMODATIONS	PAGES
Château Beauregard (Pomerol, Libournais)	453
Château Beychevelle (Saint-Julien, Médoc) -CASTLE-	155
Château Cap Léon Veyrin (Listrac-Médoc, Médoc)	129
Château Cordeillan-Bages (Pauillac, Médoc)	189
Château Du Tertre (Margaux, Médoc)	105
Château Franc Mayne (Saint-Émilion, Libournais)	331
Château Frombrauge (Saint-Émilion, Libournais) -CASTLE-	387
Château Gaby (Fronsac, Libournais) -CASTLE-	431
Château Lagrange (Saint-Julien, Médoc)	149
Château Le Pape (Léognan, Graves) -CASTLE-	261
Château Ormes de Pez (Saint-Estèphe, Médoc)	207
Château Pape Clément (Pessac, Graves) -CASTLE-	253
Château Paveil de Luze (Margaux, Médoc) -CASTLE-	109
Château de La Rivière (Fronsac, Libournais)	423
Château Sigalas Rabaud (Sauternes, Graves)	295
Château Soutard (Saint-Émilion, Libournais) -CASTLE-	395
Château Troplong Mondot (Saint-Émilion, Libournais)	375
Clos 1906 (Saint-Émilion, Libournais)	367
Coup 2 Foudres (Bordeaux Supérieur, Entre-Deux-Mers)	465
Hôtel L'Écume des Jours (Médoc Atlantique, Médoc)	229
Euronat (Montalivet, Médoc Atlantique)	231
Grand Hôtel de Bordeaux (Downtown, Bordeaux)	35
Hilton Garden Inn (Downtown, Bordeaux)	49
Hôtel Grand Barrail (Saint-Émilion, Libournais) -CASTLE-	343
La Grande Maison (Downtown, Bordeaux)	54
La Maison Du Douanier (Médoc, Médoc)	223
Le Petite Madeleine (Saint-Émilion, Libournais)	365
Lodging Le Lac (Médoc Atlantique, Médoc)	235
Logis De La Cadène (Saint-Émilion, Libournais)	407
Seeko'o Hôtel Design (Downtown, Bordeaux)	50
VitalParc Hôtel & Spa (Lacanau Océan, Médoc Atlantique)	237

WINE REGIONS	PAGES
LEFT BANK (North of Bordeaux City)	56
■ Médoc Wine Regions	64
◆ Haut-Médoc (South)	66
◆ Margaux	78
◆ Moulis and Listrac	116
◆ Haut-Médoc (Central)	130
◆ Saint-Julien	140
◆ Pauillac	160
◆ Saint-Estèphe	194
◆ Médoc	210
LEFT BANK (South of Bordeaux City)	240
■ Graves Wine Regions	244
◆ Pessac-Léognan	246
◆ Graves	266
◆ Sauternes	274
◆ Barsac	298
RIGHT BANK (East of Bordeaux City)	310
■ Saint-Émilion Wine Regions	316
■ Fronsac Wine Regions	416
■ Pomerol Wine Regions	442
OTHER (Northeast of Bordeaux Region)	462
■ Entre-Deux-Mers Wine Regions	463
■ Cognac Wine Regions	469

Left page: Concrete fermentation tank at Château Cheval Blanc in Saint-Émilion

Above: Concrete fermentation tanks at Château Beauregard in Pomerol

Both concrete tanks are proprietary designs customized and patented by these châteaux

Exploring Wine Regions
USA California

Written & Photographed by
Michael C. Higgins, PhD

SUNNY CALIFORNIA RIPENS THE WORLD'S FAVORITE WINE GRAPES

COLLECT OUR BOOKS
The Exploring Wine Regions Book Series

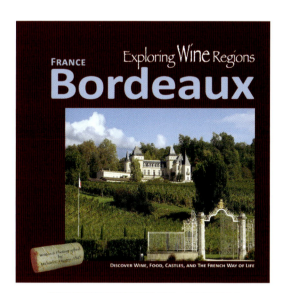

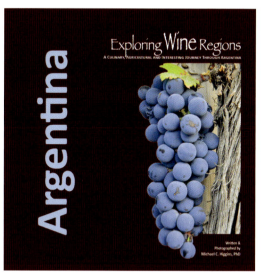

EXPLORING WINE REGIONS – BORDEAUX
Discover Wine, Food, Castles, and The French Way of Life

Exploring Wine Regions – Bordeaux France is the second book in its series that takes you on a journey to explore the region's long and fascinating history of wine, gastronomy, castles and *joie de vivre*, the French way of living life.

Bordeaux wines are presented by each region separately to better understand their nuances. We help you navigate your own way through this historic wine region with detailed maps and insider tips. We highlight the châteaux worth visiting, including the ones where you can stay in their castles, as well as excellent restaurants and unique tourism experiences.

Everyone can learn how to develop a palate to appreciate the finest wine and food the French have to offer. A must-have book for expanding your knowledge of Bordeaux and its wines.

COMING SOON - EXPLORING WINE REGIONS – CALIFORNIA
Sunny California Ripens the World's Favorite Wine Grapes

The next book in the series will reveal California's best terroirs within the quality wine producing regions of Napa Valley, Sonoma County, Paso Robles, Monterey, and Santa Barbara. We will even venture further south into Valle de Guadalupe in Baja California.

EXPLORING WINE REGIONS – ARGENTINA
A Culinary, Agricultural and Interesting Journey Through Argentina

Exploring Wine Regions – Argentina is our debut book that has won "Best Travel & Wine Book 2016" and "Best Travel Book 2017". This first book of the series sprung from my personal quest. What is Argentina's secret to producing the best Malbec? And will I ever meet a Malbec I don't like?

Argentina offers so much more than just Malbec. Our journey unveiled the Bonarda, the Tempranillo and the Torrontés just to name a few. And the tango. Wow! A most beautiful dance to go with the beauty of their people and landscape. There is so much to see and do here. Jump into all the adventures Argentina has to offer.

Follow us to this magnificent country's top three wine regions: Mendoza, Salta and Patagonia. Mendoza produces extraordinarily great Malbec that put Argentina on the map as the fifth largest wine country in the world, Salta boasts the world's highest elevation vineyards, and Patagonia makes delicious Pinot Noirs thanks to its cool climate.

A must-have book for those wanting to explore one of the world's top wine regions. And learn the answer to my question.

SPECTACULAR WINE CELLARS
We take you into the most amazing wine cellars.

INSIDER WINE TASTINGS
We introduce you to notable winemakers and special wine tastings.

TRAVEL WITH US

ACTIVITIES

COME JOIN US... on extraordinary trips exploring wine regions all over the world!

We put together over-the-top trips that are unforgettable! Our groups are small and intimate, carefully selected, to ensure the best possible experience for everyone. Our events are exclusive and unlike anything available to the general public. These are special activities we curate specifically for our trips. Meet the who's who of the wine industry. Experience one-of-a-kind excursions.

Join us! Uncover the best wines. Take part in unique activities. Meet some of the most interesting wine industry experts: winemakers, sommeliers, chefs, proprietors and more. Enjoy mouth-watering cuisines, paired with wine of course! And your accommodations are included and will be just as special. We take out the guesswork and take you in through the back door.

Our trips are special. We have been putting together quality trips since 2005, ranging from spectacular to luxurious.

Write us at **JoinUs@ExploringWineRegions.com**. Tell us where you are from, why you want to join us and what kind of experiences you would like. We will then put you on our private invite list.

If you unable to join us and would like us to put together an itinerary for you, let us know!

TESTIMONIALS

"The best part about Michael organizing our tour: all the hard work was already accomplished, the best locations were chosen. There was nothing left to do but enjoy. Being on a tour with other wine lovers was extra enjoyable because we already had something in common with everyone else and could share stories of other trips and wine experiences."
– Lee and Carolyn Jones

"Dr. Higgins does everything 1st class or not at all!"
– Mike Goering

For many more testimonials, go to our website:
ExploringWineRegions.com/testimonials

MAISON LASCOMBES
Eight Extraordinary Restaurants

THE MAISON LASCOMBES RESTAURANTS

Encouraged to set out on a journey to discover all Nicolas Lascombes' restaurants, I made it to five of his eight restaurants. Each unique and extraordinary in their cuisine, atmosphere and experience. All have his trademark touch of quality: good food, good service and a nice atmosphere.

BRASSERIE BORDELAISE   page 39
Steakhouse in Downtown Bordeaux

LE PUY PAULIN
French Bistro in Downtown Bordeaux

FAMILIA (Les Halles de Bacalan)   page 51
Brasserie across from La Cité de Vin

LE 7 RESTAURANT   page 52
7th Floor of La Cité de Vin

LE PETIT VESTIAIRE
Bistrot near Bordeaux Airport in Mérignac

HÔTEL DE LA PLAGE   page 239
In Cap-Ferret along Bordeaux's Atlantic Ocean

LA CHAPELLE   page 287
At Château Guiraud in Sauternes

LA TERRASSE ROUGE   page 325
Rooftop Terrace of Château La Dominique

A RESTAURANT EMPIRE OF UNIQUENESS AND QUALITY

I knew a restaurant was coming. At Château Guiraud in Sauternes. Restaurant La Chapelle. It was supposed to be extraordinary. My introduction was over lunch with Guiraud's owner Xavier Planty, tasting so many of his favorites off the menu. And drinking wines, his and others, so perfect for our dishes.

I was about to discover that this was actually an introduction to a series of restaurants. Nicolas Lascombes (Maison Lascombes) joined us at the table. Nicolas is the inspiration, creativity and brains behind this establishment, his eighth unique restaurant in Bordeaux. Nicolas had the vision to create gourmet dishes from local resources to fit into the natural organic ecosystem of Château Guirard. He pulled it off flawlessly! I was hooked, especially when I found out he cellars all of the Grand Cru Classé wines.

In a world of restaurants that come and go, Nicolas Lascombes (photo left) is in a league of his own. With eight restaurants, all in the Bordeaux area, Maison Lascombes shows no signs of slowing down. I had to find out why? How does he do it?

Talking with Nicolas, I discovered that he started off at a young age in the restaurant industry. He cultivated close relationships with many winemakers in Bordeaux to offer an impressive wine list in all of his restaurants. Makes sense since wine pairs so well with food and he is located in this great wine region. Bordeaux wines often makes up 90% of his wine lists. Typically his restaurants have 500+ bottles.

In 2008, Nicolas purchased Brasserie Bordelaise, a steakhouse in the heart of downtown Bordeaux. His first customers were these winemakers that made deliveries in the city and stayed with him for a great meal. Lascombes found his calling. He continued opening more restaurants, some being amongst the most unique and original. He is the first to have a restaurant in a Premier Grand Cru château (La Chapelle) and he created Le 7 (photo above) on the seventh floor above La Cité du Vin, the one-of-a-kind wine museum. He tells me each location starts with an idea, a passion, an opportunity, and then evolves organically.

Is that his secret to success in such a competitive business? Wine? Well, wine does help. However, it can't be that simple, yet the answer is pretty simple. Nicolas asked the question: What is it we all look for when we go to a restaurant? First and foremost, quality. Good food, good service and a nice atmosphere. Nicolas learned this early on and has been able to implement this concept in all of his restaurants. Successfully. Perhaps it's because he takes it seriously and is authentic and passionate about his business. Perhaps it is his calm and cool and confident approach. And surrounding himself with a team whose main goal is to satisfy their customers. Perhaps, it's all of that.

BEST OF WINE TOURISM AWARDS
Great Wine Capitals is Inspiring Wine Tourism All Over the World

Great Wine Capitals is a global network of ten wine capitals around the world. These are wine regions of significance in ten different countries: **Adelaïde** (Australia), **Bilbao/Rioja** (Spain), **Bordeaux** (France), **Lausanne** (Switzerland), **Mainz/Rheinhessen** (Germany), **Mendoza** (Argentina), **Porto** (Portugal), **San Francisco/Napa Valley** (USA), **Valparaiso/Casablanca Valley** (Chile), and **Verona** (Italy).

Established in 1999 and headquartered in Bordeaux France, Great Wine Capitals is a cooperative platform to create worldwide relationships between these countries in order to share best practices in tourism, economics and innovation. They develop common projects, engage in co-op marketing, and promote sustainable farming and winemaking.

The **Best Of Wine Tourism** awards were established in 2003, and has become a huge success in recognizing those who go above and beyond in wine tourism. There are seven different categories: Accommodations, Architecture & Landscapes, Art & Culture, Innovative Wine Tourism Experiences, Sustainable Wine Tourism Practices, Wine Tourism Restaurants, and Wine Tourism Services.

Think about it. This is exactly what we are looking for when we are traveling and exploring the wine regions. This organization is inspiring greater quantity and higher quality wine tourism activities, which helps improve our tourism experiences when visiting wine regions.

In Bordeaux, more than 1,400 applicants have competed over the years for these seven winning categories. Great Wine Capitals sends out a "secret shopper" so to speak to each château entry. A mystery couple, who is unfamiliar with Bordeaux and unknown to the participants, arrives to engage in the wine tourism experiences as if they were just regular visitors. This is how they determine who really delivers quality tourism experiences.

I have included 50 of these winners throughout this book and have listed them here under the award(s) they won. Some have won multiple awards. All winners from around the world compete to be awarded the ultimate Global Winner. Plus Bordeaux also has a Jury's Favorite award.

GLOBAL WINNER - INTERNATIONAL AWARD
Ch La Croizille	(Saint-Émilion, Libournais) -2015-	359
Ch de La Dauphine	(Fronsac, Libournais) -2020-	425
Ch Lynch-Bages	(Pauillac, Médoc) -2016-	185
Ch Marquis de Terme	(Margaux, Médoc) -2017-	99
Ch de Reignac	(Bordeaux Supérieur, Entre-Deux-Mers) -2018-	467
Ch de Rouillac	(Pessac-Léognan, Graves) -2014-	257
Ch Smith Haut Lafitte	(Pessac-Léognan, Graves) -2019-	263

ACCOMMODATIONS
Ch de Bonhoste	(Bordeaux Supérieur, Entre-Deux-Mers)	465
Ch Franc Mayne	(Saint-Émilion, Libournais)	329
Ch Giscours	(Margaux, Médoc)	93
Ch Le Pape	(Pessac-Léognan, Graves)	261
Ch Pape Clément	(Pessac-Léognan, Graves)	251
Ch du Tertre	(Margaux, Médoc)	101

ARCHECTURE & LANDSCAPES
Ch d'Agassac	(Haut-Médoc, Médoc)	69
Ch Beauregard	(Pomerol, Libournais)	451
Ch Castera	(Médoc, Médoc)	213
Ch La Croizille	(Saint-Émilion, Libournais)	359
Ch de La Dauphine	(Fronsac, Libournais)	425
Ch de Ferrand	(Saint-Émilion, Libournais)	379
Ch Fombrauge	(Saint-Émilion, Libournais)	385
Ch Gruaud Larose	(Saint-Julien, Médoc)	143
Ch Lafon-Rochet	(Saint-Estèphe, Médoc)	197
Ch Lagrange	(Saint-Julien, Médoc)	147
Ch Lascombes	(Margaux, Médoc)	87
Ch Pape Clément	(Pessac-Léognan, Graves)	251
Ch Paveil de Luze	(Margaux, Médoc)	107
Ch Pédesclaux	(Pauillac, Médoc)	175
Ch Pichon Baron	(Pauillac, Médoc)	169
Ch de Portets	(Graves, Graves)	269
Ch de Pressac	(Saint-Émilion, Libournais)	377
Ch de Reignac	(Bordeaux Supérieur, Entre-Deux-Mers)	467
Ch de La Rivière	(Fronsac, Libournais)	421
Ch de Sales	(Pomerol, Libournais)	455
Ch Soutard	(Saint-Émilion, Libournais)	393
Ch du Taillan	(Haut-Médoc, Médoc)	75

ART & CULTURE
Ch Castera	(Médoc, Médoc)	213
Ch La Dominique	(Saint-Émilion, Libournais)	323
Ch de Ferrand	(Saint-Émilion, Libournais)	379
Ch Gravas	(Barsac, Graves)	307
Ch Guadet	(Saint-Émilion, Libournais)	399
Ch Haut-Sarpe	(Saint-Émilion, Libournais)	383
Ch Smith Haut Lafitte	(Pessac-Léognan, Graves)	263
Union de Producteurs	(Saint-Émilion, Libournais)	357

INNOVATIVE WINE TOURISM EXPERIENCES
Ch Boutinet	(Fronsac, Libournais)	433
Ch de La Dauphine	(Fronsac, Libournais)	425
Ch Lamothe Bergeron	(Haut-Médoc, Médoc)	135
Ch de Ferrand	(Saint-Émilion, Libournais)	379
Ch Marquis de Terme	(Margaux, Médoc)	99
Ch de Rayne Vigneau	(Sauternes, Graves)	289
Ch de Reignac	(Bordeaux Supérieur, Entre-Deux-Mers)	467
Ch Venus	(Graves, Graves)	271
Ch Villemaurine	(Saint-Émilion, Libournais)	397

SUSTAINABLE WINE TOURISM PRACTICES
Ch Boutinet	(Fronsac, Libournais)	433
Ch Climens	(Barsac, Graves)	305
Ch de La Dauphine	(Fronsac, Libournais)	425
Ch Guiraud	(Sauternes, Graves)	285
Ch Larose Trintaudon	(Haut-Médoc, Médoc)	133
Ch Paloumey	(Haut-Médoc, Médoc)	73
Ch Saint Ahon	(Haut-Médoc, Médoc)	77
Ch du Tertre	(Margaux, Médoc)	101

WINE TOURISM RESTAURANTS
Ch d'Agassac	(Haut-Médoc, Médoc)	69
Ch de Candale	(Saint-Émilion, Libournais)	361
Ch de La Dauphine	(Fronsac, Libournais)	425
Ch La Dominique	(Saint-Émilion, Libournais)	323
Ch Guiraud	(Sauternes, Graves)	285
Ch Haut-Bailly	(Pessac-Léognan, Graves)	259
Ch Lynch-Bages	(Pauillac, Médoc)	185

WINE TOURISM SERVICES
Ch d'Agassac	(Haut-Médoc, Médoc)	69
Ch de Candale	(Saint-Émilion, Libournais)	361
Ch La Croizille	(Saint-Émilion, Libournais)	359
Ch de La Dauphine	(Fronsac, Libournais)	425
Ch Fombrauge	(Saint-Émilion, Libournais)	385
Ch Lynch-Bages	(Pauillac, Médoc)	185
Ch Pape Clément	(Pessac-Léognan, Graves)	251
Ch Prieuré-Lichine	(Margaux, Médoc)	95
Ch de Rouillac	(Pessac-Léognan, Graves)	257
Ch Soutard	(Saint-Émilion, Libournais)	393

JURY'S FAVORITE
Ch Cantenac	(Saint-Émilion, Libournais)	341

One of many sculptures at Château Smith Haut Lafitte

DISCOVER OUR WEBSITE
ExploringWineRegions.com

Read our Blogs & Posts

Book Discounted Travel

Join Behind-The-Scenes Trips to Wine Regions

Purchase our Photography and Calendars

Find Cool Wine Goodies

FOLLOW US ON SOCIAL MEDIA
FACEBOOK: Exploring Wine Regions
INSTAGRAM: @ExploringWineRegions

Bring Wine Home Safely with Wine Luggage

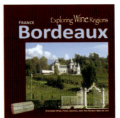

The Only Website To Get Autographed Copies of the Books
$10.00 off, use code: 10$OFF

OUR EXTRA CHAPTERS – FREE
There is more and more to share with you!

As of the printing of this book, I have already written more chapters to share with you. There are so many more things to tell you about. I have discovered additional interesting places to stay in the vineyards that I did not get to review in time for the book. I have organized my favorite hot spots and romantic places. I share some of my valuable travel tips. And so much more! I will send them to you digitally at no extra charge. Just ask, as I am happy to share. Here are a few of the chapters...

Receive Extra Chapters (for free)

Send us your full name, email, zip code, and where you purchased this book to:

Extra@ExploringWineRegions.com

SHIP WINE HOME... FOR FREE

This is not a list of wineries who will ship for free when you buy their wines. Some wineries will do that though, if you buy enough of their wine. I am referring to how to ship multiple bottles from many different wineries, all for free.

International shipping can be very expensive, especially for wine because it weighs a lot. Discover my little secret in how to ship dozens of bottles for free. I will also give you important packing tips to protect your precious wines.

HOW TO PACK A CARRY-ON LUGGAGE FOR LONG TRIPS

YES! It really is possible to travel for a month or more with only carry-on luggage. I do it. All the time! It works so well that this is now the only way I travel.

A carry-on is so much easier at the airport. Less lines. Less cumbersome. Less advanced arrival time. You move through with ease and grace.

I know you do not believe me, as I was initially doubtful I could do it. And ladies, I promise you can do it too. I have seen it first-hand.

This includes casual clothes, business clothes and nice evening wear, as well. At first, I did it for three weeks. Then for five weeks, a couple of times. Last year, I did it for two months. Twice! That's right, just one carry-on luggage.

There are numerous techniques to make this all possible. I detail everything in this extra chapter.

TOP TEN ROMANTIC PLACES

Would you like to know the most magical places to share a kiss? How about the most romantic places to dine? Inside, outside, or underground in caves? How about the best places to cuddle up with your sweetheart?

This chapter is for the lovers of the heart, those with passion and desire. I am insatiable and never miss discovering those magical romantic settings.

I was there. Took pictures. Indulged. And now I am sharing them with you.

BEST BATHROOMS IN BORDEAUX

ROMANTIC HOT SPOTS

SECRET BEDROOMS

ACCOMMODATIONS IN THE VINEYARDS

HOW TO GET INTO THE PREMIER GRAND CRU CHÂTEAUX

OTHER SUB-APPELLATIONS

DEFINITIONS
Glossary of Wine Terminology

WORDS
1er – 1st, premier, first
Accueil – Home
Actualités – News
Bistrot – Small home-style French restaurant
Boulangerie – Bakery
Brasserie – Casual restaurant
Cave – Wine shop
Château – Castle, wine estate
Chais – Cellars
Clos – Short walls surrounding vineyards
Cotes – Hillside or slope of a contiguous hill region.
Crémant – Sparkling wine
Cuvier – Vat
Degrees – Percent of alcohol
Entrée – Appetizer
Plate – Main courses
First Label – Best and primary blend
Second Wine – Leftover wine not used in first label
Fermentation – Turning grape juice into wine
Foudre (Foeder) – Large wooden vat
Gare – Train
Maison – Home
Millésime – Vintage
Noble Rot – Botrytis-inflicted grapes
Orangeraie – A house for orange trees in the winter
Patisserie – Pastry
Pigeage – Punch down
Pips – Grape seeds
Remontage – Pump over
Rive Droit – Right Bank (clay and limestone)
Rive Gauche – Left Bank (sand and gravel)
Technical Director – Chief Winemaker
Terroir – Soil, grape variety, climate, people
Terre – Soil
Toast – Burnt wood inside the wine barrel
Toilettes – Toilets
Vat – Tank (stainless steel, concrete and wood)
Vinification – Fermenting grape juice
Vintage – Year of harvest

CONCEPTS
Alcoholic Fermentation – Biochemical process in which sugar is converted into alcohol.

Malolactic Fermentation – The process in winemaking in which tart-tasting malic acid, naturally present in "grape must," is converted to softer tasting lactic acid.

AOC – Appellation d'Origine Contrôlée, French certification granted to certain French geographical indications for wine, cheese, butter, and other agricultural products.

Appellation – A legally defined and protected geographical area used to identify where grapes for wine are grown.

Cuvée – Not regulated, it is generally a wine that is a special blend of the house.

Floors in Buildings – The first floor is actually floor two. Ground floor is floor one. Confusing. When someone says they are on the first floor, they do not mean the ground level, they are actually on the second floor.

Green Harvest – Removing some of the green clusters of grapes so the other clusters get more nutrition and energy from the plant.

Leaf Removal – Removing leaves so more air flows into the vines and more sun shines on the grapes.

Meniscus – Edge of the wine in the glass, the color determines the vintage, age of the wine.

Tipping – Removing the new growth at the top so the energy can flow to the grape clusters.

Veraison – Onset of the grapes ripening, as grapes turn from green to red, as grapes change from growing to ripening.

ACTIVITIES IN THE VINEYARD
January – Pruning
February – Till soil and remove vine shoots
March – Staking and tying (to training wires)
April – Bud break and till soil (at vine base)
May – Bud pruning
June – Flowering and tipping (removing tops)
July – Fruit sets and leaf thinning
August – Veraison, green harvest and leaf thinning
September – Monitor ripeness and harvest
October – Harvest and fermentation
November – Plowing vineyards
December – Pruning

BORDEAUX GRAPES
Bordeaux Red Grapes – Cabernet Sauvignon, Cabernet Franc, Merlot, Petit Verdot, Malbec, and Carménère.

Bordeaux White Grapes – Sauvignon Blanc, Sémillon and Muscadelle

LEFT BANK & RIGHT BANK
Left Bank – West of the Garonne River and Gironde Estuary, including the appellations of Médoc and Graves (Pessac-Léognan). Primary grapes are Cabernet Sauvignon, plus Merlot and Petit Verdot.

Right Bank – East of Garonne River and along the Dordogne River, including the appellations of Saint-Émilion, Pomerol and Fronsac. Primary grapes are Merlot, plus Cabernet Franc.

BEST AND WORST VINTAGES
Best Vintages – 2000, 2005, 2009, 2010, 2015, 2016, 2018, 2019 (considered similar to 2010).

Best Sauternes Vintages – 2005, 2009 2014. The 2009 is considered one of the best years ever.

Lesser Vintages – 2007 (considered the worst), 2013 (a weak vintage), 2017 (frost year).

TRAVEL EASIER
WITH OUR
E-BOOK TRAVEL EDITIONS
On Apple Books and Amazon Kindle

THE BENEFITS

I get it. The books are too nice and you do not want to get them damaged while traveling. Plus, they are big, take up space, and weigh down your bag. I understand, as I have carried the books with me when I travel. I have created a great solution... **eBOOK TRAVEL EDITIONS**. They go onto your smart phone and tablets. And they are more convenient than the printed book for traveling. It has all the exact same content, AND MORE...

In these digital Travel Editions, I have made all the websites, phone numbers, email addresses, and physical addresses *live links* so you can easily click and go directly to the page of the winery, restaurant, resort, attraction, etc.

• Time to navigate? Click on the *address link.*
• Want to call them? Click on the *phone number link.*
• Need more information? Just click on their *website link.*
• Want to email with questions or book a stay? Click on the *email link.*

For me, the eBook Travel Editions are indispensable. Easy. Handy. Everything is at my fingertips.

Available on
Amazon Kindle
and **Apple Books**

ACKNOWLEDGEMENTS

The Exploring Wine Regions Team

Michael C. Higgins, PhD
Author, Photojournalist & Publisher

Janey Shay
Executive Vice President

Dany Rolland
The Foreword

Stephanie Corral
Editor

Arlind Rexhmataj
Web Development & Administration

Gregory Franco
Map Design & Production

Baker & Taylor Publisher Services
Worldwide Distribution

Reach us through our website at:
ExploringWineRegions.com/Contact
Or call us at: +1 (626) 618-4000

International Exploration Society
Box 93613 • Pasadena, CA 91109 USA

It Takes A Team...

This book is the culmination of numerous people's efforts. Each and every contribution has a meaningful mark on the quality of this book. I am endlessly appreciative and I thank you all. There are three people who have been on this journey with me all the way and I would like to give them extra acknowledgement here.

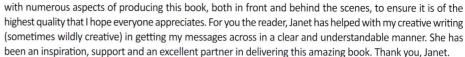

The most important thank you I have to give is to **Janet Shay**. Janet has been infinitely helpful as my right hand, (and as my left hand, and probably some fingers thrown in too). In all seriousness, Janet has helped with numerous aspects of producing this book, both in front and behind the scenes, to ensure it is of the highest quality that I hope everyone appreciates. For you the reader, Janet has helped with my creative writing (sometimes wildly creative) in getting my messages across in a clear and understandable manner. She has been an inspiration, support and an excellent partner in delivering this amazing book. Thank you, Janet.

Another important thank you is to **Brinda Bourhis**. Brinda has been with me on this project from before it even began. She has been instrumental in guiding me from the very start when I was not sure where to venture. Brinda introduced me to many key people that you find in my acknowledgements below. Many of the châteaux you read about in this book stem from Brinda and her personal introductions or through her contacts. Whenever I needed anything, Brinda was always there, and always came through. I appreciate you very much, Brinda.

Another important thank you is to **Laurent Moujon**. I met Laurent on my first day in Bordeaux. He is a very successful publisher of French publications, so we connected on many levels. Laurent has been the perfect sounding board with great feedback and ideas. He took me to see many of his wine industry friends throughout Bordeaux. I am convinced Laurent knows everyone. And this has made a huge difference to the development of this book and its content. Besides, driving through the wine regions with Laurent and hanging out with his friends was a real treat. Laurent, your friendship is forever treasured.

My appreciation and gratitude go out to many people who made this book a reality. I thank you very much!

- **Brinda Bourhis** - President, Winevox • **Laurent Moujon** - Publisher, Bordeaux Tourisme Editions • **Dany Rolland** - Rolland wineries & estates and Rolland Laboratories
- **Catherine Leparmentier Dayot** - Managing Director, Great Wine Capitals and Best Of Wine Tourism • **Jean-Marc Quarin** - Bordeaux Wine Critic
- **Sylvain Boivert** - Directeur, Conseil des Grands Crus Classés en 1855 • **Philippe Castéja** - President, Conseil des Grands Crus Classés en 1855
- **Jennifer Mathieu** - Director, Alliance des Crus Bourgeois du Médoc • **Jérémy Broutin** - Communications Manager, Alliance des Cru Bourgeois du Médoc
- **Stephan Delaux** - Deputy Mayor of Bordeaux and President of the Bordeaux Tourism Office • **Lloyd Lippons** - Gérant, Château La Haye
- **Virginie Ramond** - Press Relations, Conseil des Vins de Saint-Emilion • **Jean-François Galhaud** - President, Conseil des Vins de Saint-Emilion and Owner, Maison Galhaud
- **Emilie Renard**, Communication Manager, Conseil des Vins de Saint-Emilion • **Laure de Lambert Compeyrot** - Owner, Château Sigalas Rabaud
- **Nicolas Jabaudon** - Directeur Général, Médoc Atlantique • **Sophie Dabudyk** - Manager, Conseil des Vins de Fronsac
- **Guy-Petrus Lignac** - President, Saint-Émilion Tourism and Owner, Château Gaudet • **Bruno de Lambert** - Past-President, Conseil des Vins de Pomerol and Château de Sales

NEED A PROFESSIONAL SPEAKER
Fun and Entertaining Education

EXPERIENCES WITH MICHAEL
Michael is a natural storyteller... engaging, charismatic and full of personality! With his immense knowledge of wine and many wine regions around the world, Michael is the perfect speaker for your event, no matter its size. Whether it is a corporate function or fun social gatherings for connoisseurs or novices, he is guaranteed to entertain and educate your group! Pick from one of the options below or we can come up with something perfectly suited for your group.

An Evening Exploring Wine Regions
Choose Argentina, Bordeaux or California! Michael offers a fun, entertaining and educational evening with an amazing food and wine pairing from the subject country. Learn about what makes the particular wine region special and how to choose their wines. Enjoy authentic cuisine, excellent wines and engage in fascinating conversations.

How to Find Your Wine
Michael will show you how to find wines you like in a fun and approachable way. It's very common for people to not understand their preferences. They are intimidated by the restaurant wine list and end up simply ordering the house wine. They walk into a wine shop and are completely overwhelmed. Michael can help! He will teach you easy ways to sift through the long lists and unfamiliar options to uncover the wines you love! Let Michael help you taste your way to success.

Send us an email (Booking@ExploringWineRegions.com) or call us (626-618-4001) for more ideas and to book your event.

MEDIA RESOURCE
Television, Newspapers, Magazines, Radio, Podcasts and Blogs

Need a good story? Need information for the development of your story? Need a good interview? On or off camera, Michael makes for a very interesting interview. With his vast knowledge of travel, wine and wine regions, he is the perfect resource for everything you may need to know.